Christine June Wunderli

Elie Wiesel, the Shtetl, and Post-Auschwitz Memory

Forum Christen und Juden
Forum Christians and Jews

Band / Volume 22

LIT

Christine June Wunderli

Elie Wiesel, the Shtetl, and Post-Auschwitz Memory

LIT

Copyright cover picture: Rebecca Jeffery

Das vorliegende Buch basiert auf einer Dissertation, für welche im Jahr 2019 der Doktortitel an der Kultur- und Sozialwissenschaftlichen Fakultät der Universität Luzern vergeben wurde.

This book is based on a dissertation for which a doctoral degree was awarded in the year 2019 by the Faculty of Humanities and Social Sciences of the University of Lucerne.

Gutachter/Supervisors:

Prof. Dr. theol. Verena Lenzen

Judaistik und Theologie/Christlich-jüdisches Gespräch/Jewish Studies and Theology/Christian-Jewish Dialogue Institut für Jüdisch-Christliche Forschung/Institute of Jewish-Christian Research Universität Luzern/University of Lucerne

Prof. Dr. Reinhold Boschki

Abteilung Religionspädagogik, Forschungsstelle Elie Wiesel/Department of Religious Education, Elie Wiesel Research Center Universität Tübingen/Tübingen University

This book is printed on acid-free paper.

Bibliographic information published by the Deutsche Nationalbibliothek

The Deutsche Nationalbibliothek lists this publication in the Deutsche Nationalbibliografie; detailed bibliographic data are available on the Internet at http://dnb.dnb.de.

ISBN 978-3-643-91217-6 (pb)
ISBN 978-3-643-96217-1 (PDF)
Zugl.: Luzern, Univ., Diss., 2019

A catalogue record for this book is available from the British Library.

Flössergasse 10
CH-8001 Zürich
Tel. +41 (0) 76-632 84 35
E-Mail: zuerich@lit-verlag.ch https://www.lit-verlag.ch

Distribution:

In the UK: Global Book Marketing, e-mail: mo@centralbooks.com
In North America: Independent Publishers Group, e-mail: orders@ipgbook.com
In Germany: LIT Verlag Fresnostr. 2, D-48159 Münster
Tel. +49 (0) 2 51-620 32 22, Fax +49 (0) 2 51-922 60 99, e-mail: vertrieb@lit-verlag.de

Legend tells us that one day man spoke to God in this wise:

"Let us change about.
You be man, and I will be God. For only one second."
God smiled gently and asked him:
"Aren't you afraid?"
"No. And you?"
"Yes, I am," God said.

Nevertheless he granted man's desire.
He became a man, and the man took his place
and immediately availed himself of his omnipotence:
he refused to revert to his previous state.
So neither God nor man was ever again what he seemed to be.

Years passed, centuries, perhaps eternities.
And suddenly the drama quickened.
The past for one, and the present for the other,
were too heavy to be borne.

As the liberation of the one
was bound to the liberation of the other,
they renewed the ancient dialogue
whose echoes come to us in the night,
charged with hatred, with remorse,
and most of all, with infinite yearning.

— Elie Wiesel, *The Town Behind the Wall*

Acknowledgments

There are a number of individuals who have offered me guidance and support during my research and writing. I wish to acknowledge them here. My doctoral supervisor, Professor Verena Lenzen, director of the Institute of Jewish-Christian Research at the University of Lucerne, has supported this project from its inception, and has been invaluable in guiding me to its completion. Her knowledge, acuity, perspicacity, wisdom, and personal encouragement throughout various stages of this project, have all borne their fruit in me as an academic and as a human being. I am indebted to her for the kindness she has shown during the course of my studies in Lucerne—and beyond.

My second supervisor, Professor Reinhold Boschki of the University of Tübingen and director of the Elie Wiesel Research Center in Tübingen, has likewise offered guidance and counsel. His passion to keep Elie Wiesel's vision for a better world alive has encouraged me to no end. It was he who so graciously approached LIT Verlag regarding the publication of my manuscript. For his involvement in and commitment to this project, I am thankful.

Others who have supported me, in various capacities both professional and personal, include: Christine Cavedon, managing director of the Graduate School of Humanities and Social Sciences, University of Lucerne; Martin Steiner, academic assistant to Professor Lenzen; Timna Holzer of LIT Verlag; Katherine Pippy; Mike Wood Daly; Jan Wood Daly; Rebecca Jeffery; Mary Pippy; my parents, John H. C. (died 2019) and B. Jane Pippy; Mark Pippy and Esther Pippy; Douglas Pippy; Jörg Schlichting; Elizabeth Nef; Andreas Marti; Nicole Butt; Richard and Maya Blättel; Daphne Cross; Paul and Diane Butt; Kathleen Hynes; and other colleagues, family members, and friends. To all of these individuals, near and far, I express my gratitude now.

I would also like to thank LIT Verlag for their generosity in publishing my manuscript within their series, "Forum Christen und Juden."

Finally, I would like to thank my brother, John D. Pippy, and my dear friend, Silvia Schenkel, for their support and friendship over the course of many years. This book is dedicated to both of them.

"Weder Weg noch Ziel, sondern Begegnung."

Table of Contents

Table of Figures

Preface

Many years ago, a friend slipped a German copy of Elie Wiesel's *Night* into my hand with the cautionary words, "Be careful with this book, it tends to upset people." Not yet able to read much German, and with no other edition immediately available, I was forced to tackle the text with a small German-English dictionary that was hardly adequate to decipher so many terrible words. I studiously penciled English translations into the margins of the pages, hoping to understand the story by linking them all together.

I recall now how that first reading affected me. Slowly, as I translated each page, Wiesel's chronicle leaped out from the text like fire. His words burned, his images seared, his voice was scorching hot. I was bereft, shattered. Yes, it was the fire of testimony.

I still find *Night* difficult to read. It continues to devastate in relaying events not one of us can understand. It reveals and conceals; it draws near, and then pushes away. We ourselves draw near it, and then we withdraw. We circle around it from a distance, we peruse it from afar as would a night-bird in strange, new territory. We watch, we observe, we inquire. But we cannot *know*.

This study makes no absolute, definitive claims. It is but one more attempt at understanding within the difficult process of drawing-near. It is an attempt, not an accomplishment. It has entailed thinking through themes and confronting realities I wish could have been avoided. It has been an intense journey, and not one that I would take again lightly.

Since the onset of writing this book, and since its completion, much has transpired. The Rohingya in Myanmar have been ravaged by genocide; thousands of Uyghur in China remain interned, subjected to beatings, forced labor, rape, and unspeakable humiliations; the United States has seen power change hands twice, deepening divides and inflicting wounds that will take long to heal; migrants have flooded Europe from war-torn and poverty-stricken regions, and their presence there has incited hate, violence, and profound social and economic upheaval;tensions in the Middle East have not greatly abated; and in Israel, peace is still far away. The arrival of the COVID-19 pandemic two years ago granted some hope that humanity might confront its evils and unite against them, but that hope has been muted, tinged with cynicism and despair as nations have struggled to bury their dead. Most recently, Europe has again become familiar with war. As images of the Russian invasion of Ukraine, begun in February 2022, flood our living rooms, we struggle all over again to find any sense in atrocity.

Holocaust survivors have died too, many of them of old age, having spent lifetimes trying to remember and not-forget. Notable Holocaust authors left us aswell: Marcel Reich-Ranicki (2013), Miriam Winter (2014), Ben Abraham

(2015), David Faber (2015), Imre Kertész (2016), Max Mannheimer (2016), Fanya Heller (2017), Schoschana Rabinovici (2019), Magda Herzberger (2021)-—to name a few. Elie Wiesel himself died in 2016, a watershed moment for our collective memory. With each one of these deaths, a voice has been silenced whose message still needs to be heard; with each silenced voice, the dangers of forgetting gain momentum. The passing of time brings with it its own evils, some of them less conspicuous than others, but all of them rooted in humanity's proclivity to bracket the past in meeting the present. As we do, we stumble and fall, and inevitably, new atrocities are committed. Indeed, the eclipsing of past evils can never bear fruit, but only bring about new destruction and new genocide.

The nebulous dimension of hope, and the ambiguity of hope, are always rooted in existential disorientation. As modern psychology has taught us, and as both historians and philosophers have confirmed, it is only through understanding the past that the future can be truly open. Without understanding, past traumas will always resurface, both on individual and collective levels, and infiltrate the present in ways that incite them all over again. In the end, if left untreated, collective pathologies will cement our future, even as we deem it open. Hope that is blinded by ignorance of the past is destined for self-destruction. Hope born in illusion is delusion, and it will always mislead us, and will always keep all genuine moral progress at bay. Without a strong moral compass, without a common vision for a world without genocide and atrocity, humanity will continue to run aground in the deep mire of its own undoing—until it is no more.

So where does this leave us? Is there no true hope? Holocaust testimony such as Wiesel's indicates to us that there is hope, although it be a cautious, tenuous, fragile hope. The fact that Holocaust survivors have testified at all, the fact that they have continued to admonish and warn, reveals that we have not yet reached critical mass. Hope remains a viable category in moving forward, even in its wounded state. However, it must relinquish its illusions if it is to be effective at all.

For this reason, testimony must continue, and we must listen. Testimony, as we have learned, is more than simple remembering, something different than merely recalling past events, regardless of how horrible these might have been. Testimony is memory infused—implicitly or explicitly—with message; it is a non-forgetting that rebukes, reproaches, reprimands, and, most of all, *warns*. Testimony pushes outwards from the past, into the present and then through it, and touches, however furtively, the future. It is a difficult process; it dissects and very often divides. But just as human anatomy can only be understood by way of dissection, so too can humanity know itself only by naming explicitly the historical components of its own inherent evil.

The hope to be found in admonishment forfeits all propensity to sentimentalism and illusion. It is directly connected to historical events that we take into account and from which we must learn. This kind of hope is not a peaceful force, but a dire and unsettling one. It is replete with reality. It pulls us forward, entreating us to escape the vortex of human evil before it engulfs us entirely. We hope to escape because it is not unchartered territory. We hope to endure because we know something of the past. We are not lost, at least not yet, and that knowledge grants enough courage and tenacity to continue on.

Wiesel has taught the world about hope. For him, hope is possible. It is hope that grants courage to continue, indeed, to live at all. His incessant "and yet, and yet" is indicative of his hope, and serves as the hallmark of his vision for a better world. However, hope is paradoxical in the wake of Auschwitz, and in order for it to be viable at all, it *must* coincide with a radical ethic, one that is committed to overcoming human evil at every juncture in our story's unfolding, and at all costs. Indeed, hope is only possible if we never relinquish our individual and collective struggle for peace, and a world free of atrocity.

This study embraces, at its heart, a search for collective moral renewal. In tracing Wiesel's "search for the lost shtetl", my own sense of searching has intensified. It has become clear to me that each new generation must grapple with the past in its own distinct way. However, as we move forward and review the past, and as we listen to the testimonies of people such as Wiesel who survived its horrors, we can never do so in a vacuum. As heirs of collective human experience; as the sum of all we have ever encountered and undertaken; and as members of a human continuum of past, present, and a projected future; we encounter testimony both idiosyncratically *and* commensurately. We do this individually, and we do it collectively, as a generation; we do it consciously, and we do it intuitively. Indeed, we cannot read, hear, and listen to the stories of the past without being in the historical present, and without some sense, however inadequate, of who we are, how we arrived here, and why we are here. In a strong sense, this is a good thing, for it compels us to re-evaluate, re-orient, and regroup as time unfolds.

The present moment, however, can also deceive. We easily succumb to the fallacy that the present is all we have. It is not. We have the past, and the future is in our hands. For this reason, we must listen to the past, and translate its message to meet current and future demands. Should we fail to do this, and fail as well to act upon what we have learned, the vortex of human evil will certainly engulf us in the end.

Can we ever know the depth of another's suffering or passion? How can we understand? We cannot. Are there spaces that must not be entered at all because their ground is too sacred to bear the profane feet of the ignorant? Of course, there are. Testimony such as Wiesel's has shown us that. But testimony has shown us, too, that there can be no hope without attending to the past, and without heeding it, and that the past concerns us all. It has stories to tell and messages to convey, and the only path to understanding them is first to listen, and then to try to understand.

Elie Wiesel longed for the shtetl, and by way of telling and re-telling stories, he sought his way back home to it. I believe he found it in the end, for while seeking it, he discovered its vision for a better and more just world. This study wishes to honor that search, and to listen to its call forward. We cannot know

Wiesel's shtetl, just as we cannot know the horrors it endured, but we can begin to distill its message for the present as we look to the future.

May we listen, and may we heed.

Christine June Wunderli
St. John's, Canada
April 2022

Introduction

Elie Wiesel and the Search for the Lost Shtetl

Preamble

In January of 1945, as some 60,000 inmates death-marched their way out of Auschwitz-Birkenau, Elie Wiesel walked with them. Wiesel survived the march to Gleiwitz, and was then transferred on to Buchenwald. Many others, though, had been murdered or had died on route.[1] Wiesel's account of that ill-fated event is well known. Not yet seventeen, he had witnessed atrocities that had taken from him not only most of his family members and friends, but also his profound innocence and young religious faith. Beginning with the deportation of the Jewish population of Sighet to Auschwitz some eight months earlier, the small but utopic world Wiesel had known had been annihilated.

Sighet, however, never left Wiesel. Haunted by the memory of Auschwitz, the author set out on a journey to recover Sighet as a touchstone of sanity and hope. Beginning with the publications of *Night* ten years after the end of the war, Wiesel developed "Sighet" into one of his most vital literary motifs. It consistently reappears in both his fiction and nonfiction writing, posing as a poignant presence juxtaposed with Auschwitz.

Wiesel's frequent inclusion of Sighet in his writing could be considered a clever literary technique meant to accentuate more dramatically the horrors of Auschwitz. My suggestion, however, is that the lost shtetl of Sighet can better be understood as the point of departure for *all* of Wiesel's writing. His literary reconstruction of the shtetl is indicative of his existential search to retrieve, through memory, something of the life he once knew. As this search proceeds, the shtetl becomes more and more an internalized place that grants him a sense of orientation by which to gauge his experience of darkness.

In the works that follow *Night*, Wiesel sketches more fully his pre-Auschwitz faith, life, and social context in countless essays and speeches, as well as in his two-volume autobiography *All Rivers Run to the Sea* and *And the Sea is Never Full*.[2] In each of his works, his portrayal of Sighet as an astonishingly naïve faith community is telling. Saturated with religious fervor, driven by the love of God,

---

[1] See "Death March from Auschwitz," United States Holocaust Memorial Museum website, accessed February 23, 2022, https://www.ushmm.org/learn/timeline-of-events/1942-1945/death-march-from-auschwitz.

[2] Elie Wiesel, *All Rivers Run to the Sea: Memoirs, Volume One, 1928-1969*, (London: Harper Collins Publishers, 1997); and *And the Sea is Never Full, Memoirs, 1969-*, trans. Marion Wiesel (New York: Alfred A. Knopf, 1999).

and led by a pristine ethic, the shtetl emerges as an entity left largely unmoved by the evils that mounted around it on all sides. The result is a striking literary image that carries with it a sense of mystery and myth.

The literary development of Sighet as a world unto itself is central to this study. In addition to begging questions of historical accuracy, it hints at salient dynamics involved in Wiesel's narration process. I contend that such a process draws from both the author's experience of trauma and his pre-Auschwitz experience of the shtetl. Sighet precedes Auschwitz and so serves to frame and direct Wiesel's experience of Auschwitz. Post-Auschwitz, the author comes to remember and, ultimately, write about Auschwitz in terms of how he experienced it at the time, that is, by way of the specific, faith-oriented worldview of the shtetl. At the same time, the memory of the shtetl is altered by its stark juxtaposition with Auschwitz.

In this context, narration arises as a complex interpretive process. To remember events is itself an interpretive act, impacted by the whole of experience. As such, telling the story of past events can never be objective or purely factual; it is always selective and indicative of the sources from which it draws.

At the meta-level, these suggestions relate to issues of language and literary representation. Language use always reflects one's social context, past and present experiences, and, most importantly, one's way of being-in-the-world. Literary representation is also dependent on these factors in its attempt to convey ideas and experiences.

With respect to language post-Auschwitz, concerns of literary representation are profoundly problematic. How language remains capable of expressing anything meaningful becomes pivotal. In spite of the controversy surrounding the issue of metaphor, I contend that the capacity of language to convey anything at all hinges on its practical metaphorical use. In the wake of Auschwitz, what is conveyed is not direct knowledge of the Holocaust per se, but rather a sense of its grave horrors and the need to respond with a responsible ethic to these atrocities.

An alternate reading of Wiesel's texts lends an eye to these issues. The experience of trauma, memory, the narration process, language, and literary representation—all of these issues converge in such a reading. My aim is to explore Wiesel's storytelling in light of them.

Within this broader theoretical context, the image of the shtetl can be understood as central to Wiesel's overall literary agenda. In as much as this agenda is simultaneously a literary and a humanitarian one, the image is bound to the ethical message he intends to convey.

Theses

The theses that guide this study hinge on all of the above. With the establishment of relevant theoretical parameters, I set out to investigate how the shtetl's legacy impacts Wiesel's writing and overall discourse. In so doing, I have selected four works for critical review: *Night*, *Dawn*, *Four Hasidic Masters and Their Struggle Against Melancholy*, and *The Forgotten*. Very generally, I approach each of these texts by inquiring how traces of the author's earliest *Sitz-im-Leben* are evidenced there. Specifically, I explore the given texts in relation to the Hasidic tradition of the shtetl, a tradition with which Wiesel himself so keenly identified. My thesis maintains that his narratives are replete with Hasidic elements that reveal Hasidic influences.

Concomitantly, and drawing from this first thesis, I maintain that Wiesel has (re)constructed the shtetl (referred to in this study interchangeably by the term "Sighet") literarily as a powerful *antipole* to Auschwitz. This provides for a significant counterpoint in his fugal writing and thought, which bears its marks upon, however furtively, the entire oeuvre. Here, an enduring power play between Sighet and Auschwitz is evident as both entities vie to obtain the upper hand in memory.

I suggest this power dynamic can be understood by visualizing an ellipse. With Sighet and Auschwitz as the ellipse's focal points, memory draws from both in its construction of testimony. I develop this model by implementing elements of Pierre Bourdieu's theory of literary field and aspects of James E. Young's narrative theory.

This two-fold thesis assists in developing a more differentiated evaluation of Wiesel's discourse on memory. Sighet, though not able to obliterate the impact of Auschwitz on memory, opposes the latter's vehement craving for hate, death, and barbarism. In so doing, it emerges as indispensable in guiding the author's post-Auschwitz assessment of the human condition and his vision for humanity. In functioning as a kind of inner landscape—at times a place of retreat—within his otherwise anguished memory, the shtetl offers him a degree of orientation and hope.

Research Relevance

The discussion surrounding the literary representation of the Holocaust has proven complex and, at times, convoluted. Elements of this discussion will be touched upon in greater detail in chapters three and four of this study. For the moment, however, what can be stressed is that opinions concerning representation have diverged greatly. Theodor W. Adorno's provocative adage, proclaiming the impossibility of poetry following Auschwitz, is still fresh. In its time, the pronouncement served as a springboard to a prolonged and difficult debate. This has, in my opinion, proven helpful in fanning out the plethora of issues at hand.

Indeed, the debate has borne fruit. Language surrounding the Holocaust—which is to say, the narration of events and themes in its myriad forms—must be held to account. Even more so, the absurd expansion of Holocaust "literature" has necessitated the ever-evolving review of the possibilities, capacities, and efficacy of both language and literature to portray, relay, and transmit events of trauma. Drawing from the arguments put forward by memory theory, trauma theory, literary critics, historians, and even Holocaust deniers, the matter of the representability of Holocaust events remains poignant.

Critics of the efficacy of language following the Holocaust (beyond Adorno) such as George Steiner, Paul Celan, Jean Améry, Imre Kertész, Saul Friedländer, Klaus Briegleb, Alvin H. Rosenfeld, and Elie Wiesel have each voiced their concerns regarding representation, with varying degrees of adamance. More moderate critics, such as James E. Young, Lawrence Langer, Sidra Dekoven Ezrahi, and S. Lillian Kremer, have acknowledged the limits of language, but also recognized the efficacy and possibilities of language to express traces of the inexpressible. Significantly, however, all of these critics have written about the Holocaust. Whether in poetry or prose, in fiction or nonfiction, in memoirs and testimonials or historical writing and critical analysis—all have something to say about the cataclysmic events of the Holocaust, and whether or not one can speak of or write about them at all. This fundamental paradox is striking but understandable. Language remains the means by which we are able to reflect upon language, and so it is, as many have suggested, all we have.

This study hinges, at least in part, on this acknowledgment. It presupposes the ability of language to transmit something urgent to the modern human being whose own propensity to forget is often met with ignorance or indifference. However, it precludes the possibility of language to convey, or reify, the objective reality or knowledge of events themselves. In this context, my exploration walks a thin line between granting and denying language a vital role in the continued, strained efforts of not-forgetting. While this position potentially exposes itself to innumerable pitfalls, it is meaningful in its attempt not to merely make sense of Holocaust literature but, ultimately, to underscore its most noble calling—remembrance.

The formation and function of the literary image of the lost shtetl of Eastern Europe within collective memory is an important theme in this study. Modern research has highlighted how this image has gradually come of age as a striking symbol for a pure, unadulterated, but irretrievably lost Judaism, as chapter five indicates. The literary reality of the shtetl engendered by this image has been instrumental in forming post-Holocaust Jewish identity, despite the historical inaccuracies that the image often embraces.

Wiesel's autobiographical and fictional accounts of the shtetl have contributed to this composite image of the lost shtetl as well. However, unlike many writers, his desire to portray the shtetl is driven by his role as a Holocaust survivor. It is here that several vital issues converge. Although language—and literature—exhibit a decisive powerlessness in the wake of Auschwitz, it can yet yield images, including that of the shtetl, whose metaphorical power has been able to profoundly impact collective memory. This impact will be examined in this study.

Unlike other author's images of the shtetl, however, Wiesel's shtetl has come to play a vital, determinative role in his overall attempt at remembering Auschwitz. Accordingly, his testimony bears the marks not merely of his experience of trauma, but also of a life and a faith that extend beyond Auschwitz. This is important to this study.

In Wiesel's literary world, Hasidism remains omnipresent. As Wiesel's prewar *Sitz-im-Leben*, Hasidism emerges as a dynamic entity that flows within and infiltrates all of his writing. The Hasidic elements evident in his narratives lend them not only their distinct form and style, but also their persuasive urgency and thrust. The Hasidic message, clothed in modern language, is one that grants hope; however, it is also one that admonishes and warns against the enduring power of human evil.

These claims are not entirely new. However, by relating them to issues of language, literary representation, the narration process, and, importantly, to Hasidism as representative of a unique literary field, my exploration of Wiesel's writing is granted its own particular lens and, with it, new relevance.

Wiesel never ceased to identify himself as a Hasidic Jew. He writes:

> When I am asked about my Jewish affiliation, I define myself as a *Hasid. Hasid* I was, and *Hasid* I remain . . . Hasidism for me brings back the world of my childhood. In that time the Jewish heart was broken. Its song was raised and raised me as a rampart against the melancholy and the anguish that, in exile, seeks to hold it back, if not to put it into chains. What would I be without it?[3]

The confession is striking. Although it does not serve as the basis of this study, it does provide further incentive to investigate the sense in which this may be true.

References to the Hasidic dimension of Wiesel's thought have trickled down through critical reviews since the 1970s. Some of this work merits mention here. Alvin H. Rosenfeld and Irving Greenberg's anthology *Confronting the Holocaust: The Impact of Elie Wiesel* represents one of the first more comprehensive appraisals of Wiesel's works.[4] In it, Michael Berenbaum proposes that Wiesel's "struggle with the covenantal framework of traditional Judaism, . . . was intensified by his exposure to two of the doctrines of the Jewish mystical tradition, the

---

[3] In Elie Wiesel, *Souls on Fire: Portraits and Legends of Hasidic Masters*, trans. Marion Wiesel (Northvale: Jason Aronson, 1993), vii-viii. Cited in Gershon Greenberg, "The Hasidic Spark and the Holocaust," in *Elie Wiesel: Jewish, Literary, and Moral Perspectives*, ed. Steven T. Katz and Alan Rosen (Bloomington: Indiana University Press, 2013), 83.

[4] Alvin H. Rosenfeld and Irving Greenberg, eds., *Confronting the Holocaust: The Impact of Elie Wiesel* (Bloomington, IN: Indiana University Press, 1978).

doctrine of the *Tikkun* and the doctrine of chosenness."[5] Berenbaum identifies these doctrines as rooted in the Kabbalah and in Hasidism, respectively. Wiesel's proposals of the "rupture with the Jewish past" [6] in the wake of the Holocaust, and therewith of the existence of an "additional covenant" between God and humanity, are suggestive of Hasidic influences.

More recently, and more explicitly, Reinhold Boschki has underscored Hasidic influences in Wiesel's works and how they are informative of the broad scope of his writing. He writes: "As is the case with Kafka . . . Wiesel's writings are full of allusions to and the integration of Jewish motifs originating in Hasidism, the Kabbalah, the Talmud, the Torah, Jewish tales, and customs. They are the background, the stage upon which the plot unfolds."[7] Boschki highlights Wiesel's integration of mystical content into his novels in particular. He observes how Wiesel has woven the Jewish past into the present, granting both past and present a strong sense of continuity. With this, the stories pose as a force capable of combating communal despair. He writes:

> What do all [Wiesel's] writings hold in common, what is the red thread running through all of them? It is the attempt to listen to and read stories again and to tell them anew within the horizon of the experience of suffering. With this, the inherited stories become "stories against melancholy" in the here and now, stories against grief and death. It is the attempt to return to the centuries-old sources of the Jewish people in order to spite the experience of death in our time.[8]

He extends this thought:

> In all of Wiesel's genres . . . Hasidic stories, tales of Hasidic masters [are treated] with a fine stroke of the pen, a pointed sense of joy and humor, a joy pitted against despair, a humor to spite suffering.[9]

---

[5] Michael Berenbaum, "The Additional Covenant," in *Confronting the Holocaust*, ed. Rosenfeld and Greenberg, 170. Wiesel later takes issue with the claims made by Richard L. Rubenstein in *After Auschwitz: History, Theology and Contemporary Judaism*, (Indianapolis, IN: Bobbs Merrill, 1966), who announced the post-Auschwitz dissolution of the covenant and therewith the death of God.

[6] Berenbaum, "The Additional Covenant," 171.

[7] Reinhold Boschki, "Heimweh nach Sighet. Einführung in die literarische Welt Wiesels," in *Das Gegenteil von Gleichgültigkeit ist Erinnerung. Versuche zu Elie Wiesel*, ed. Dagmar Mensink and Reinhold Boschki (Mainz: Matthias Grünewald Verlag, 1995), 54-55. Translation mine.

[8] Boschki, "Heimweh nach Sighet," 58. Translation mine.

[9] Boschki, "Heimweh nach Sighet," 59. Translation mine.

Boschki continues his exploration of Wiesel by stressing the need to read Wiesel "in the mirror of his autobiography."[10] Particularly important for this project is Boschki's proposal of the presence of a conceptual ellipse in Wiesel's thought, in which Sighet and Auschwitz function as dynamic focal points:

> Wiesel has hardly written more than about the town of his childhood, at times openly and unequivocally, at times literarily distanced in the stories of his [literary] characters. His childhood and early adolescence represent one focal point of the ellipse of his entire work; the other is provided by his experience of Auschwitz. Both, the landscape of Sighet as being impacted by Hasidism, and the ravaged desert of the annihilation camps leave their imprint on his every line, on his every thought.[11]

It is in this proposal that my own model of an ellipse finds its origin and orientation.

More broadly, Boschki suggests that Wiesel's incorporation of the Jewish faith tradition into his writing has aided him in formulating his renowned "and yet, and yet":

> Wiesel does not tire of using [his] "and yet" in expressing his attitude of "in spite of God and the world." This is just as characteristic as his integration and working-through of, however changed, the Jewish tradition in his literature, a tradition which, by the way, has always dwelt within his spiteful "and yet." At the end of his latest autobiography, he arrives at this spiritual attitude. This is one that protects him from final despair and serves to save the humane.[12]

In a similar fashion, Rosemary Horowitz stresses the impact of Wiesel's Hasidic upbringing and, in particular, the influence that his Hasidic grandfather had on his writing. She presents Wiesel as first and foremost a storyteller whose earliest Hasidic influences are palpably present in his tales. She writes:

> The hasidic style of storytelling and the hasidic value of storytelling play a large role in Wiesel's style. He publishes interpretations of tales told by and about hasidic masters and gives

---

[10] Reinhold Boschki, "Zum Autor: Elie Wiesel im Spiegel seiner Autobiographien," in *Kultur allein ist nicht genug. Das Werk von Elie Wiesel—Herausforderung für Religion und Gesellschaft,* ed. Reinhold Boschki and Dagmar Mensink, with Britta Frede (Münster: Lit Verlag, 1998), 22-37. Translation mine.
[11] Boschki, "Zum Autor," 33-34. Translation mine.
[12] Boschki, "Zum Autor," 37. Translation mine.

> lectures on hasidic masters. In his speeches, he draws on their oral traditions. He repeats the tales because he believes that their messages are still relevant. For Wiesel, the lives of the hasidic masters contain lessons about hope, despair, joy, madness, friendship, and other human feelings and actions.[13]

Similarly, David Patterson identifies, among other aspects, Hasidism—in particular, its stories and storytelling tradition—as providing one central frame of reference or context for Wiesel's own storytelling.[14] He summarizes his findings by identifying Wiesel as the quintessential Maggid, referencing the Hasidic itinerant storyteller whose tales communicated lessons to learn and messages to heed.[15]

Steven T. Katz and Alan Rosen's important collection of essays, *Elie Wiesel: Jewish, Literary, and Moral Perspectives*, offers suggestions that coincide with the theses of this study. Arthur Green, in understanding Wiesel as continuing within the "context of neo-Hasidism,"[16] presents him as Hasidism's "*eynekl* (grandchild), moving back over one generation in search of a piety that belonged to the grandparents' generation."[17] Green maintains that Wiesel has "recreated" Hasidim in light of the Holocaust. In this context, he writes:

> The Holocaust is always there. Sometimes it is like the background of a chosen tale, like that of the Hasid who ate and ate, making himself fatter so that he would take longer to burn. Elsewhere it comes back in italicized passages, comments and counterpoints to the narrative that the author interjects.[18]

What is more, he observes, Wiesel pays attention "to the human situation in its broadest and most profound sense, as refracted through the tales as a prism."[19]

Green argues that Hasidism is Wiesel's tutor as he grapples with the most urgent questions confronting humanity. It is here that Wiesel takes the lead in "the universalizing of the Holocaust survivors' message."[20] In so doing, it becomes a message applicable to all the current crises humanity inflicts upon itself. With this, Wiesel has "helped to allow for, and even taken a lead in, the healing

---

[13] Rosemary Horowitz, "Introduction," in *Elie Wiesel and the Art of Storytelling*, ed. Rosemary Horowitz (Jefferson, NC: McFarland and Company, 2006), 7.
[14] See David Patterson, "The *Maggid* of Sighet: Jewish Contexts for Wiesel's Storytelling," in *Elie Wiesel and the Art of Storytelling*, ed. Horowitz, 102-22.
[15] Patterson, "The *Maggid* of Sighet", 116-17.
[16] See Arthur Green, "Wiesel in the Context of Neo-Hasidim," in *Elie Wiesel: Jewish, Literary, and Moral Perspectives*, ed. Katz and Rosen, (Bloomington: Indiana University Press, 2013), 51-58.
[17] Green, "Wiesel in the Context of Neo-Hasidism," 54.
[18] Green, "Wiesel in the Context of Neo-Hasidism," 54.
[19] Green, "Wiesel in the Context of Neo-Hasidism," 55.
[20] Green, "Wiesel in the Context of Neo-Hasidism," 56.

of the Holocaust wound that has inevitably been taking place over the past several decades."[21] In reference to the Hasidic song recorded at the end of Wiesel's novel *The Gates of the Forest*, Green writes:

> Wiesel learned that lesson, the lesson that one can sing rather than scream, in part surely by writing that book. In a certain sense he let himself become that rebbe, singing instead of screaming, but without betraying memory. That act, surely faithful to the spirit of the Baal Shem Tov, is Elie Wiesel's most important neo-hasidic legacy, one we could not do without.[22]

From an alternate perspective, Katz explores the authenticity of Wiesel's version of Hasidism as evidenced by his transliteration of Hasidic tales.[23] He links this authenticity to Wiesel's earliest Hasidic influences, which is to say, to his biography.[24] Specifically, Katz bases the authenticity of the tales on their consistency with vital aspects of the Halacha; the Kabbalah; the teachings, miracles, and wonders associated with the Hasidic teacher and leader, the Tzaddik; as well as Jewish messianic theology.[25] In this light, Wiesel's Hasidic tales are deemed authentic, acting as "a permanent legacy of the world of Eastern European Jewry from which they come. And a testimony to the way in which Elie Wiesel has kept faith with this world."[26]

Gershon Greenberg extends Katz's claims by suggesting that Wiesel's particular rendition of Hasidism remains unique in as much as it reflects his existential struggle to understand Auschwitz.[27] Wiesel's observations regarding Hasidism's proclivity to paradox, contradiction, and silence, for example, are reflective of his response to the Holocaust. [28] Wiesel follows a "hasidic [p]ath *through* the Holocaust."[29] Along this path, and with an eye to Auschwitz, Wiesel expands Hasidism by integrating Hasidic elements into his post-Auschwitz evaluation of contradiction and protest, God's "absolute absence," God's "alienation" of humanity, and silence and prayer.[30] Despite his anguished findings, Wiesel has continued to stress—again, by way of a Hasidic image—that the "inner spark" of the

---

[21] Green, "Wiesel in the Context of Neo-Hasidism," 57.
[22] Green, "Wiesel in the Context of Neo-Hasidism," 57.
[23] Steven T. Katz, "Reflections on Wiesel's Hasidic Tales," in *Elie Wiesel: Jewish, Literary, and Moral Perspectives*, ed. Katz and Rosen, 59-68.
[24] Katz, "Reflections," 60.
[25] Katz, "Reflections," 60-67.
[26] Katz, "Reflections," 67.
[27] See Gershon Greenberg, "The Hasidic Spark and the Holocaust," in *Elie Wiesel: Jewish, Literary, and Moral Perspectives*, ed. Katz and Rosen, 83-99.
[28] Greenberg, "The Hasidic Spark," 83-85.
[29] Greenberg, "The Hasidic Spark," 86. Emphasis mine.
[30] Greenberg, "The Hasidic Spark," 88-96.

divine in humanity has not been extinguished, even in the wake of Auschwitz.[31] Greenberg concludes: "Deeply knowledgeable of the sources, drawing from the classical texts of Hasidism and his own memories, infusing all with literary imagination, [Wiesel] created his own universe of hasidic life and thought."[32]

This study emphasizes the presence of Hasidic elements in Wiesel's thought and examines Wiesel's re-creation of Hasidism. I extend these emphases to explore Wiesel's identification with Hasidism in the context of his ongoing search for Sighet. This search acts as a driving force behind his literary and, concomitantly, his humanitarian agenda.

This suggestion has also been addressed in both older and more recent research. Robert McAfee Brown's 1983 study, *Elie Wiesel: Messenger to all Humanity*, remains among those who have addressed Wiesel's allegiance to Hasidism most directly.[33] McAfee Brown isolates Wiesel's overall mission as constitutive of *tikkun*, the Kabbalistic and later Hasidic notion of the restoration of the world.[34] Within the context of this mission, Wiesel sets out to recover his identity in terms of the past.[35] This identity is first and foremost that of storyteller: the one who serves as a vital link between events past and present. Wiesel is a storyteller entangled in the events he narrates. This idea of entanglement is "characteristically Hasidic;"[36] as such, Hasidism remains Wiesel's anchor and guide throughout his exploration of memory. McAfee Brown continues by stressing that Wiesel's memory of Auschwitz is preceded by his memory of Sighet.[37] The discrepancy between these two is striking. He writes:

> The immediate past, in Elie Wiesel's case, is irredeemable. It is the world of Auschwitz, a world of nihilistic proportions, capable only of destroying the ability to believe, even the will to live.
>
> But behind the memories of an eternity in Auschwitz are the memories of a boyhood in Sighet, a little town "somewhere in the Carpathian mountains of Transylvania," that had earlier provided a fulcrum of meaning. Sighet is now a lost reality, shattered by Auschwitz, but a reality Wiesel constantly seeks to piece back together and reclaim. Sighet may well loom larger in Wiesel's future writing; it haunts him, not so much as a dream from which he was irretrievably awakened, but more as

---

[31] Greenberg, "The Hasidic Spark," 85-86, 96.
[32] Greenberg, "The Hasidic Spark," 83.
[33] Robert McAfee Brown, *Elie Wiesel: Messenger to All Humanity* (Notre Dame, IN: University of Notre Dame Press, 1983).
[34] McAfee Brown, *Elie Wiesel: Messenger to All Humanity*, 111.
[35] McAfee Brown, *Elie Wiesel: Messenger to All Humanity*, 111.
[36] McAfee Brown, *Elie Wiesel: Messenger to All Humanity*, 111.
[37] McAfee Brown, *Elie Wiesel: Messenger to All Humanity*, 113.

> a reality from which he was irretrievably snatched—elusive because never fully recoverable, always to be sought.[38]

The juxtaposition of Sighet with Auschwitz is devastating, but still elicits hope:

> Auschwitz . . . Sighet. Irreconcilable realities. Incapable of existing in the same world. At first the destructive flames of hatred and dispassion in Auschwitz extinguished the creative flames of love and ardor in Sighet. But they could not fully do so. For although the flames of Sighet are searing, seeking to revive a people destroyed by other flames, they also contain foretastes of healing, as Wiesel recreates the world of his childhood for us—glancing references here, allusions there, stories *of* Sighet on one page, stories *from* Sighet on another, this character reanimated, that character redrawn. The rest of us are beneficiaries of his anguished creativity.[39]

In his inability to return to the Sighet of the past in reality, Wiesel decides to return there by way of memory. Indeed, McAfee Brown notes that it is through memory and narrative that Wiesel seeks Sighet:

> Today Sighet represents "a world that no longer exists," and it represents a world being sought. In 1981 Wiesel writes, "I am seeking my childhood. I will always be seeking it. I need it. It is necessary to me as point of reference, as a refuge."
>
> There is pathos here. Let us pause before it . . .
>
> But there is also dynamic. The search for the unattainable continues. And if Elie Wiesel cannot go *to* Sighet, he will go *through* it, every day, to what lies beyond it—the Hasidic world he first encountered there, the world of stories old Dodye Feig shared with a young grandson sitting enthralled on his knee, the world where celebration is not a hollow word, the world where stories draw generations together across the bands of time, across the bonds of death.[40]

Wiesel's journey into Hasidism impacts him profoundly. It not only aids him in re-establishing his identity following Auschwitz but also enables him to "recover a perspective on the world that empowers celebration, community, humor, an

---

[38] McAfee Brown, *Elie Wiesel: Messenger to All Humanity*, 113.

[39] McAfee Brown, *Elie Wiesel: Messenger to All Humanity*, 113.

[40] McAfee Brown, *Elie Wiesel: Messenger to All Humanity*, 116. The Wiesel quotation included in this passage was originally published in Elie Wiesel, "Recalling Swallowed-Up Worlds," *The Christian Century*, May 27th, 1981: 609.

ongoing struggle with God, and a recognition that events are never closed to the emergence of new possibilities."[41] It is the author's Hasidism that enables him to say, "And yet."[42] Finally, it "provide[s] Wiesel with his vehicle of communication—the tale."[43]

Akin to McAfee's Brown's observations, Nehemia Polen highlights Wiesel's longing for the shtetl. [44] He writes:

> We now come to the matter of lost childhood and [Wiesel's] endless, futile quest for a destroyed home. . . . The memory of [his] loved ones has been a constant theme in his writing, but so has the memory of his town. Indeed, he has returned, or attempted to return, to his birthplace time and again, but each attempt is painful, inconclusive, unfulfilled, because the Jewish town he seeks (as opposed to the geographical location) has been not just destroyed but erased.[45]

He elaborates this analysis further, writing:

> The longing to return to the town of his youth motivates many passages in Wiesel's writing, and remains present in his life. The very last page of the second volume of memoirs, *And the Sea is Never Full*, published in 1999, contains the sentence, "And yet I want to go back to Sighet one last time."
>
> There is a deep connection between the futile search for a hometown erased from history, on the one hand, and the recognition of the role of the zaddikim in Hasidism's postwar rebirth, on the other hand. Childhood memories are intimately intertwined with the sense of self, one's feeling of place in the world.[46]

Finally, Sandu Frunză takes up the themes of seeking and longing in Wiesel's discourse.[47] Behind the author's passion to remember and to testify, Frunză suggests, lies his profound melancholy in having lost Sighet. [48] This melancholy is

---

[41] McAfee Brown, *Elie Wiesel: Messenger to All Humanity*, 121.
[42] McAfee Brown, *Elie Wiesel: Messenger to All Humanity*, 121.
[43] McAfee Brown, *Elie Wiesel: Messenger to All Humanity*, 121.
[44] Nehemia Polen, "Yearning for Sacred Space: Wiesel's Hasidic Tales and Postwar Hasidism," in *Elie Wiesel: Jewish, Literary, and Moral Perspectives*, ed. Katz and Rosen, 69-82.
[45] Polen, "Yearning for Sacred Space," 76.
[46] Polen, "Yearning for Sacred Space," 76.
[47] Sandu Frunză, "Elie Wiesel and Nostalgia for a Lost Paradise," *Transylvanian Review* XVIII, no. 2 (Summer 2009): 101-5.
[48] Frunză, "Elie Wiesel and Nostalgia for a Lost Paradise," 101.

indispensable in driving his "symbolic construction" of the "universe of his childhood," which is, indispensable to his literary reconstruction of the shtetl.[49] Within this context, Sighet functions as his "Paradise Lost," the "Happy Isles"[50] that stand in stark contrast to the death camps.

Frunză identifies Sighet and Jerusalem as indispensable, inextricable, and interchangeable metaphors within Wiesel's writing.[51] As metaphors, they not only lend expression to Wiesel's sense of the past, but also grant him a way of communicating with those he has lost.[52] Both are associated with deep longing, with the pain of Jewish exile, and with the hope of ending that exile. Still, Frunză stresses:

> [Wiesel] is constantly on the road to Sighet. More precisely, we always see him as a wanderer on the road between Sighet and Jerusalem, at the same time a resident of both.[53]

Walker similarly writes:

> The memory of Sighet and those lost in the Holocaust creates an almost unbearable tension in Wiesel's writing as it does in his own life. For this reason, Wiesel is isolated on the island of his memory where he is perpetually searching for a passage that will link the past and the present together. Wiesel's search for passage leads us over the depths of his experience which we cannot possibly fathom.[54]

Important to this study in the aforementioned research are the indications of how Wiesel's early Hasidic influences remain discernable in his writing and thought. Equally important is the sense in which Sighet emerges as a striking, central metaphor for longing and loss. The search for the lost shtetl emerges too as a metaphor in its own right, one that lends form to Wiesel's yearning to remember, bear witness, and honor the dead.

The isolation of the Hasidic dimensions of Wiesel's unrelenting search for the shtetl is central to this study. It helps us to explore how Sighet and Auschwitz may constitute two disparate poles in his thought, and, by way of their inherent juxtaposition, lend his narratives their persuasive dynamism and power.

---

[49] Frunză, "Elie Wiesel and Nostalgia for a Lost Paradise," 101.
[50] Frunză, "Elie Wiesel and Nostalgia for a Lost Paradise," 101.
[51] Frunză, "Elie Wiesel and Nostalgia for a Lost Paradise," 102.
[52] Frunză, "Elie Wiesel and Nostalgia for a Lost Paradise," 102.
[53] Frunză, "Elie Wiesel and Nostalgia for a Lost Paradise," 104.
[54] Graham B. Walker, Jr., *Elie Wiesel: A Challenge to Theology* (Jefferson, NC: McFarland and Company, 1988), 5. Quoted in Frunză, "Elie Wiesel and Nostalgia for a Lost Paradise," 104.

Ultimately, the tension inherent in the ongoing struggle between Sighet and Auschwitz torments Wiesel as it calls forth the memory of the dead. In bearing witness, he honors them. He writes:

> I owe the dead my memory. I am duty-bound to serve as their emissary, transmitting the history of their disappearance, even if it disturbs, even if it brings pain. Not to do so would be to betray them, and thus myself. I simply look at them. I see them and I write.[55]

Wiesel's task is daunting. It reignites past anguish and incites new pain. However, his sense of obligation to memory remains. It is exactly this extraordinary attempt at not-forgetting that makes Wiesel so unique.

Project Outline

Following this introduction, chapter two addresses methodology. I begin by introducing sociology of literature as supporting best the theses of this study. Within this broader domain, I isolate aspects of Pierre Bourdieu's theory of literary field which provides a constructive, practical framework within which to develop these theses. I suggest that an application of the theory lends itself to the Hasidic tradition and, with this, to a consideration of the Hasidic shtetl as its microcosm, its field. In contrast, I argue against Auschwitz as a field in a technical sense, positing it instead as an anti-field, a *univers concentrationnaire*, or "universe unto itself." [56] Finally, I conclude the chapter with a short reflection on how the theory of literary field is commensurate with upholding the integrity of Holocaust literature.

Chapter three sketches out the discourse, discussion, and debate surrounding Holocaust literature. This chapter seeks to introduce the reader to the problems of language and literary representation following the Holocaust. Tracing the rise of Holocaust awareness in America, Germany and, though peripherally, in Israel, I underscore the problem of Holocaust representation in all art forms and in all discourse. The problem reaches into the very naming of the Holocaust in as much as each name reflects some particular theological position or bias.

I continue by examining the themes of language and literary representation more extensively. While exploring the views of Theodor W. Adorno, George Steiner, Paul Celan, Primo Levi, and Jean Améry, I identify core issues of the debate. From here, I outline Young's theories of Holocaust representation and the

---

[55] Elie Wiesel, "Why I Write," in *From the Kingdom of Memory: Reminiscences* (New York: Schocken Books, 1990), 16.
[56] See David Rousset, *L'univers concentrationnaire* (Paris: Édition du Pavois, 1946).

metaphorical use of language that, in conjunction with aspects of the theory of literary field, will assist in my review of Wiesel's texts.

Chapter four addresses Wiesel's own perspectives on memory, testimony, the powerlessness and power of language, the possibilities of literary representation, and the crucial role of the storyteller.

Chapter five introduces the reader to Eastern European Hasidism. Outlining salient features of its history, theology, spirituality, and forms of folklore not only provides a backdrop to examining Wiesel's writing, but also seeks to establish Hasidism—and therewith the shtetl—as *field*. This claim is vital to this study. With the rise of Hasidism, the shtetl emerges as a dynamic social entity that, with time, assumes tremendous symbolic power throughout the Jewish world. I trace here the development of the image of the shtetl, as well as the formative influence that this image has had on modern Jewish identity. I conclude this chapter with a view to the history of the Jewish shtetl of Sighet.

Chapter six represents the crux of this study as it sets out to explore four texts by Wiesel: *Night*, *Dawn*, *Four Hasidic Masters and Their Struggle Against Melancholy*, and *The Forgotten*. Each evaluation functions as a stepping stone in establishing my theses.

With *Night*, I begin by examining the shtetl and its social architecture as constitutive of the young Wiesel's field. The work emerges as the core of the oeuvre in its provision of this vital foundation. I highlight elements of Wiesel's testimony in terms of the theory of field and investigate how Wiesel's faith construct provides him with the interpretive parameters of his camp experience. I expose therewith varying layers of the narrative.

On the one hand, this discussion serves to demythologize Wiesel's text. On the other hand, it reveals the complex process of narration involved there. In applying Young's theory of representation, I outline this process with a clear and concise diagram. From there, the aforementioned ellipse emerges, with Sighet and Auschwitz serving as its focal points. In concluding this section, I state that *Night* is the first extension of Wiesel's literary field.

In my review of Wiesel's second book, *Dawn*, I build upon my findings in *Night*. Presupposing the shtetl as literary field, I trace Hasidic elements in the volume: its literary style as well as Hasidic themes, legends, tales, legendary figures, and motifs. I contend that all of these contribute to *Dawn*'s functioning as a vital extension of *Night*. In so doing, it evidences a development in Wiesel's thought—and with this, a new variation of the ellipse—in terms of memory's subtle movement towards the shtetl. A provisional hope is present in the text, even in the context of its darkness.

In my examination of Wiesel's *Four Hasidic Masters and Their Struggle Against Melancholy*, I set out, above all, to explore Wiesel's unique relation to Hasidism. In retelling the tales of the masters, I consider how he reinterprets them in light of Auschwitz. I observe how Wiesel furtively weaves the memory of Auschwitz into his reinterpretations of the tales, evidencing a particular bias and, once again, his interpretive framework. Be that as it may, the masters remain figures of hope and instruction, even in the face of past and present despair. In their presence, sadness, rage, doubt, and anguish are tempered by laughter, faith, and even celebration and joy.

Wiesel's relationship to Hasidism can be considered unique in as much as it cannot be separated from his relationship to Auschwitz. In his exploration of Hasidism and its masters, he seeks the shtetl as a place of rest and refuge in the wake of Auschwitz. In this context, both the shtetl and the search for the shtetl emerge as vital literary motifs that guide his memory. In his search for and reconstruction of the shtetl, an image emerges that reveals his narrative process; the ellipse revises its form once again as memory draws nearer the shtetl. In this close proximity, the shtetl's call to not-forget becomes clearer and more urgent.

The fourth and final work that I examine is *The Forgotten*. I approach the novel with a view to its Hasidic themes and motifs and, in drawing from these, its arresting message. In this work, Wiesel resumes his search for the shtetl through characters whose trauma ultimately drives them to make peace with the past. Ultimately, the shtetl is found, though deeply wounded by atrocity. Here we learn that healing—if only a remnant of healing—cannot happen by chance; it always requires the conscious, painful journey of remembering, testifying, and ultimately, ethical response.

The Forgotten represents one of Wiesel's most complex novels. Unraveling its Hasidic themes and motifs assists in understanding better this complexity. Once again, the ellipse's constellation changes as Wiesel's memory is torn between the shtetl and Auschwitz. And although the conclusion of the novel renders it open-ended and enigmatic, its "categorical imperative" is clear: hate and revenge must be replaced by love, reconciliation, and the courage to begin again.

Finally, chapter seven provides a summary and concluding reflections on Wiesel's literary representation of the Holocaust and his metaphorical use of language. I conclude by offering a trajectory meaningful for our understandings of good, evil, and human responsibility.

Chapter One

Methodological Considerations

Literary Theory, Critical Theory, and Sociology of Literature

Literary theory represents a vast portion of research and debate. Defined as the theoretical basis for the study of texts, literary theory distinguishes itself from literary criticism (also referred to as critical theory).[57] Literary theory aims to establish the meaning of literature itself and its plethora of manifestations, and to support these findings with theoretical reasoning from diverse schools of thought. The application of literary theory to texts guides readers toward original and innovative approaches to literature and the critical textual analysis of its forms. On the other hand, literary criticism focuses on the study and analysis of literary texts[58] and has often been considered subservient to and integrated into literary theory.

Literary theory endeavors to illuminate the central elements of production, distribution, and reception of texts that are often misunderstood, overlooked, or bracketed by literary criticism. In turn, alternative readings are proposed that can shed new light on the analysis and interpretation of a text. Within this context, a modified version of the hermeneutical circle emerges; views to texts and their contexts impact their exegesis, resulting in the critic moving forward to more differentiated levels of understanding. These then allow for new readings and new analyses, and so on. Subsequently, texts can then be placed in wider and more complex nexuses of meaning both intra- and intertextually.

This evaluation of texts, however important, does not represent literary theory's sole focus. Its concomitant concern is to look to, but also beyond, texts to offer significant critique of exactly those social structures and contexts in which literary works have emerged and developed. Such critique has proven scathing and provocative at times, replete with literary, historical, and political implications. Exposing texts, their forms, goals, and biases as impacted by social influences and structures has been vital in this critical task.

---

[57] Here, "critical theory" distinguishes itself from the Critical Theory of the Frankfurt School. In German, critical theory is known as *Literaturwissenschaft*. For an overview of Critical Theory see Rainer Baasner and Maria Zens, *Methoden und Modelle der Literaturwissenschaft. Eine Einführung*, 3rd ed. (Berlin: Erich Schmidt Verlag, 2005), 191-206.

[58] See Mario Klarer, *Einführung in die Grundlagen der Literaturwissenschaft. Theorien, Gattungen, Arbeitstechniken* (Darmstadt: Wissenschaftliche Buchgesellschaft, 2011), 15ff.

Sociology of literature is an important area of literary theory in the post-modern era. It is posited as a wide-reaching and diverse array of theories applicable to literature and, indeed, to many forms of representation. As is the case with literary theory in general, sociology of literature is concerned with how literature might be investigated before any textual analysis is to begin at all; with how texts can and should be read; as well as with the kinds of outcomes and meanings engendered within these pre-set interpretive parameters. More specifically, and as a whole, sociology of literature is actively engaged with questions and assumptions of culture, history, and context and how these impact narrative development, both generally and specifically.

As such, the sociology of literature strives to extract clusters of meanings within texts, drawing largely from examining their specific historical origins and frameworks. Views to the social conditions, contexts, and settings in which a work has been produced (by the author); to how it has been distributed (with regard to its production and publication for a particular audience, group, or society); as well as to how it has been received (reader reception) have all been important in forming the sociology of literature as a novel and dynamic offshoot of both sociology and literary theory.

Sociology of literature, as method, tends to procure results that diverge—at times diametrically—from more traditional approaches in as much as it subjects texts to wider, more far-reaching scrutiny. In this sense, it diverges from those schools of theory seeking the 'plain and simple' intratextual sense or meaning of texts alone; from those attending to internal textual structure alone (as with the Russian Formalist school); and from those concerned with reader reception alone (reader-response or reception theory).

Structuralism and Poststructuralism

This study takes structuralist and poststructuralist approaches to literature into consideration. Both philosophical movements are concerned with the study of texts as reflections of modern culture. In their embrace of linguistic analysis, structuralists stress intertextuality and focus on the analysis of literary structures or forms. As such, textual comprehension is facilitated by a form of code-breaking in which individual elements or units of texts—such as words or symbols—are evaluated in terms of their interrelatedness and how they refer to or signify larger structures of meaning. Generally speaking, structural theorists have been concerned with turning literary theory into a rational, objective science that is able to isolate overarching meaning through logical investigation.[59]

---

[59] See Baasner and Zens, *Methoden und Modelle der Literaturwissenschaft,* 3rd ed. (Berlin: Erich Schmidt Verlag, 2005), 115-36. For a more thorough review of structuralism, see François Dosse, *Geschichte des Strukturalismus*, unabridged ed. 2 vols. (Frankfurt am Main: Fischer-Taschenbuch-Verlag, 1999).

Poststructuralists, likewise a heterogeneous assemblage of theorists, are preoccupied with textual analysis as well, but with very different emphases. Poststructuralists reject structuralist claims to certainty and universal truths in keeping with their broader philosophical agenda. They emphasize instead the dynamic, forceful, and unstable nature of history, stressing that no fixed, static meaning can be attached to texts. Meaning and knowledge are in a constant state of flux, as is the reader, influenced by a continuous flow of social, cultural, and psychological influences. Accordingly, poststructuralists are resolute to understand the reader's historical context, and to distill meanings linked to reader self-perception and therefore to culture and its preferences and biases. Justifiably, poststructuralism has been seen at times to have destabilized or decentered the author insofar as they have shifted out of the philosophical spotlight and been placed by the reader.[60]

According to Michel Foucault, knowledge is determined by analyzing discourse that is encountered within texts.[61] These are examined by exposing discourses that illuminate those operations of power that have unconsciously shaped society and have thus instigated the domination of some groups over others. This step forward in the timeline of literary theory is important as it directly impacted both Foucault's contemporaries and the theorists who followed them.

Structuralism and poststructuralism are diverse schools of thought whose theorists repeatedly denied allegiance to either school. Accordingly, theorists emerged whose works, in blurring the lines between both schools, have often been interpreted as overlapping and occupying both camps. Since both structuralists and poststructuralists were concerned with social structures and historical contexts in their interpretation of culture and society, this overlap is perhaps not surprising.

---

[60] Emmanuel Levinas writes: "Language refers to the position of the listener and the speaker, that is, to the contingency of their story. To seize by inventory all the contexts of language and possible positions of interlocutors is a senseless task. Every verbal signification lies at the confluence of countless semantic rivers. Experience, like language, no longer seems to be made of isolated elements lodged somehow in a Euclidean space . . . [Words] signify from the world and from the position of one who is looking." See Emmanuel Levinas, "Signification and Sense," in *Humanism of the Other*, trans. Nidra Poller (Chicago: University of Illinois Press, 2003), 11-12, quoted in *The New World Encyclopedia Online*, s.v. "Post-structuralism," last modified May 26, 2015, http://www.newworldencyclopedia.org/entry/Post -structuralism. These are also central concerns of reader reception theory. See Baasner and Zens, *Methoden und Modelle der Literaturwissenschaft,* 179-90. For an earlier but still helpful synopsis of the impact of poststructuralism on literary theory see Terry Eagleton, *Literary Theory: An Introduction* (Minneapolis: University of Minnesota Press, 1983), 127-50.

[61] See Baasner and Zens, *Methoden und Modelle der Literaturwissenschaft*, 138-39; and Michel Foucault, *Archeology of Knowledge and the Discourse on Language*, trans. A. M. Sheridan Smith (New York: Pantheon Books, 1972).

Many such theorists would come to impact literary theory and the sociology of literature. The methodology of this project centers on the theories of one such author, Pierre Bourdieu.

Pierre Bourdieu and Literary Field

Pierre Bourdieu, a French pioneer in modern sociology, has often been considered a *Grenzgänger* between structuralism and poststructuralism.[62] He began developing his theories in the 1960s. These reached their pinnacle of importance and popular approval in the 1990s and have continued to impact modern literary theory.

Bourdieu's sociological model hinges on an innovative analysis of the structures of both society and the human being. His paradigm contains four central, interrelated concepts or building blocks: *field, habitus, disposition*, and *capital*. Taken together, these comprise the most essential elements of his analytic method. Inextricably intertwined and interdependent, they constitute a complex and very differentiated theory of understanding history, society, culture, and cultural production.

A brief summary of the major tenets of his theoretical model and their general application to this project is intended to clarify my approach to Wiesel's texts.

Field

Beginning with the idea of field, Bourdieu dismisses the notion of society as a closed and static totality, as a "homogenous container with one single structure."[63] Instead, he identifies society as a historically—emerging, social space of organized fields whose rules, particular to each field, allow for the relative amount of autonomy of the field.[64] These fields can be seen as areas of play in which the rules order internal, self-directing structures. Given that rules have been, over time, well-rehearsed and then integrated into the structured fields, the

---

[62] *Grenzgänger*, from the German, meaning: one who commutes between two neighboring countries or regions or between one or more bodies of thought. With time, Pierre Bourdieu's structuralist tendencies would weaken, evidencing instead "an ethnology of modern (French) society that encompasses studies of knowledge and education and a theory of social inequality." Baasner and Zens, *Methoden und Modelle der Literaturwissenschaft,* 229. Translation mine.

[63] Gerhard Fröhlich and Boike Rehbein, eds., *Bourdieu Handbuch. Leben–Werk–Wirkung* (Stuttgart: J.B. Metzler Verlag, 2009), 100. Translation mine.

[64] Derek Robbins, ed. *Pierre Bourdieu*, vol. 2 (London: SAGE Publications, 2000), 120. This notion stands in contradiction to Marx's theory of fixed classes. Bourdieu considers these "illusions."

actors of fields have developed, through repetitive play, an unquestioning belief in the rules' legitimacy and thus in—what they consider to be—the unrestricted freedom their fields afford.[65] This belief, Bourdieu contends, is illusory.[66] In reality, these fields impact actors in ways that unknowingly affect their singular interests, strategies, and goals. The goals of all actors evidence commonality and cohesion in their being bound to a common field and therefore to one another in configurations of rule-regulated play. This fact is important in considering the consistencies in cultural production; all actors within a given field are inextricably linked to that field, even in the face of the competition and the conflicts between them. In essence, they stand together, interrelated and interdependent, despite their apparent individuality and divergences. As a result, the cultural production within a given field shows elements of consistency, at times even harmony, even though individuals when acting as cultural producers may stray and deviate from one another.[67]

When fields are compared, it becomes evident that they have the same rules-structure. They are based on rules of play, illusion, competition, and varying degrees of the exercise of power.[68] In spite of this, there is a certain amount of freedom of movement within fields that allows for a degree of modification of its rules as actors strive towards change and betterment—albeit only within the context of their own set of resources and their social position within the field. This being the case, the actor's possibilities and prospects for the future are not limitless.[69]

Habitus

Habitus, according to Bourdieu, is a constitutive element of field and is directly impacted by the rules of field. Habitus entails unconsciously embodied habits or patterned behaviors that are acquired through habit-forming learning and play within fields.[70] It can also be understood as "the principles of acting,

[65] Fröhlich and Rehbein, *Bourdieu Handbuch*, 100.

[66] Fröhlich and Rehbein, *Bourdieu Handbuch*, 100. Bourdieu, however, rejects a psychoanalytic understanding of the actor's relationship to all aspects of their field: "unconsciousness" relates instead to the historical origins and emergence of field and habitus. See Markus Schwingel, *Pierre Bourdieu. Zur Einführung*, 6th ed. (Hamburg: Junius Verlag, 2009), 63.

[67] See Pierre Bourdieu, *The Rules of Art: Genesis and Structure of the Literary Field*, trans. Susan Emanuel (Cambridge: Polity Press, 1996), 215ff.

[68] Bourdieu's notion of "the game" which embraces all these elements is central here. See, for example, Bourdieu, *Rules of Art*, 13, 33-34, 172-73, 227-28, 248.

[69] See Bourdieu, *Rules of Art*, 223ff.

[70] Bourdieu uses the word "embodiment" in a literal sense: bodily, as opposed to mere mentally/psychologically. Fröhlich and Rehbein, *Bourdieu Handbuch*, 111. Translation mine. See also pages 81ff.

perceiving, and thinking of social individualities,"[71] as the *lex insitia*, or the inherent laws, of behavior that an actor embraces.[72] As such, habitus is intrinsic to the foundation of fields out of which actors' lives emerge and within which they advance.

An actor's social origin impacts their habitus directly, playing an indispensable role in the unfolding of their life. The kind of parenting and education an actor receives allows for positions of greater or lesser importance within the field. Accordingly, children of those overseeing the field (who are persons of power) adapt best and, in accordance with their socialization, possess greater advantages for success and advancement later in life. They can therefore be viewed as mirroring patterns of behavior of their parental role models, opening up the possibility for future positions within the field not dissimilar to those of their parents or other family members. In this way, children are factors in a field that allow for social and cultural continuity between generations.[73]

However, habitus does not always function unconsciously. Indeed, actors' behaviors are not always unconscious; in fact, many behavioral patterns are conscious reflections of observed behavior. Social behaviors thus contain aspects of both automatism and awareness, of being both conditioned and consciously self-engendered. In light of these realities, social contexts within given fields are never identical; actors, conditioned by way of class and education, can exhibit non-predictable deviations of patterned behaviors. This important factor allows for variations between, and divergences within, fields.[74]

Dispositions

According to Bourdieu, habitus also forms the foundation of *dispositions*. Dispositions are defined as those "*predispositions*, *tendencies* [or] *attitudes*"[75] that have developed through complex multi-faceted and dialectical processes within habitus and are systematically unified there.[76] Dispositions are also understood as those schemata of perception, thinking, and acting that comprise an actor's practical sense (*le sens practique)* of society, which is to say, one's ability to orient themself within society.[77] These schemata are, of course, socially and culturally determined.[78] With this, and in light of the limitations and freedoms

---

[71] Fröhlich and Rehbein, *Bourdieu Handbuch*, 111. Translation mine.
[72] Fröhlich and Rehbein, *Bourdieu Handbuch*, 111.
[73] Fröhlich and Rehbein, *Bourdieu Handbuch*, 112ff.
[74] Fröhlich and Rehbein, *Bourdieu Handbuch*, 115.
[75] Fröhlich and Rehbein, *Bourdieu Handbuch*, 73. Translation mine.
[76] Fröhlich and Rehbein, *Bourdieu Handbuch*, 73.
[77] Schwingel, *Pierre Bourdieu*, 63.
[78] Schwingel, *Pierre Bourdieu*, 61. Schwingel states that, viewed anthropologically, it is the inner "systematically structured predispositions" of the human being that allow for dispositions. Translation mine.

granted to actors by a field, it is the dispositions of actors that allow for both the consistencies *and* the variations and irregularities of social expression found there.

Bourdieu describes dispositions as the actor's perpetual "internalization of [the] outwardness"[79] of one's field. Accordingly, these dispositions hold the potential to be expressed outwardly in terms of both lifestyle (which accounts for "a certain readiness in the actor to give themselves to their specific situation"[80]) and the actor's overall acceptance of the field.

Dispositions also allow actors to develop a respective style or talent that characterizes their general behavior.[81] This results in patterns of behavior that can be transferred to other situations or even, rarely, to other fields. Importantly, however, this transferability does not ensure the practicality or meaningfulness of their implementation within other fields.[82] It is for this reason that actors seldom move beyond their field and that fields tend to retain a degree of autonomy and internal homogeneity.

Bourdieu proposes that dispositions are bound to the unique relationship between field and habitus since the latter two remain in constant conversation with one another. In essence, field and habitus collide, interact, and compete with one another as actors within the field do the same. This dialectic accounts for the "externalizing" of the individual dispositions that comprise the human actor; as actors struggle for greater positions of wealth, influence, and power, their inner predispositions to act in particular ways come to full expression. These externalizations can be understood as those practices or forms of acting by which social structures are both reproduced and propelled forward.[83] With this, Bourdieu developed his so-called "theory of practice"[84] which went on to profoundly impact modern social theory.

Capital

The fourth—but no less important and constitutive—aspect of Bourdieu's theoretical construct is the notion of *capital*. Capital is posited as those resources made available to each actor that enable them to act individually within the field. More specifically, capital possesses a kind of staying power within the field as its forms directly impact an actor's possibilities of being, living, and acting within

---

[79] Pierre Bourdieu, *Sozialer Sinn. Kritik der theoretischen Vernunft*, trans. Günter Seib (Frankfurt am Main: Suhrkamp, 1987), 102. Translation mine. Cf. Fröhlich and Rehbein, *Bourdieu Handbuch*, 74.
[80] Fröhlich and Rehbein, *Bourdieu Handbuch*, 74. Translation mine.
[81] Fröhlich and Rehbein, *Bourdieu Handbuch*, 112.
[82] See Fröhlich and Rehbein, *Bourdieu Handbuch*, 111ff.
[83] Schwingel, *Pierre Bourdieu*, 76-77.
[84] See Pierre Bourdieu, *Outline of a Theory of Practice*, trans. Richard Nice (Cambridge: Cambridge University Press, 1977).

one's respective field. The forms of capital an actor possesses are highly influential with respect to their existence in the field in as much as an individual increases or decreases the chances of gaining profit and of succeeding and advancing in their field.[85] Bourdieu distinguishes four sub-types of capital: *economic*, *cultural*, *social*, and *symbolic*.

These four sub-types of capital are briefly defined as follows. *Economic capital* refers to socially-determined material (often financial) resources that are made available to an actor by way of their social background, social position, and work or practice. *Cultural capital* denotes those material objects of cultural significance (books, art, technical instruments, etc.) that reflect an actor's economic capital. It also denotes those abilities made accessible to an actor through education (both social and academic education) in general and group membership in particular.[86]

Social capital diverges from economic and cultural capital as it refers to resources that draw from an actor's social connections and largely institutionalized relationships upon which they can depend for various forms of support. These groups can constitute families or academically or politically-oriented bodies. The stronger an actor's relationship is with their groups, the better chances they have of both obtaining profit and advancing within their field.[87]

Symbolic capital is of another nature altogether. It denotes the forms of perceived and legitimate social, field-bound recognition, appreciation, and prestige that an actor receives within their field. Put differently, symbolic capital consists of status, influence, and power symbols that allow for greater privileges within a given field. Accordingly, symbolic capital is intrinsically related to and derived from all other forms of capital. The latter, taken individually and as a whole, contribute to and are constitutive of symbolic capital.[88] Indeed, in as much as the economic, cultural, and social forms of capital can open doors to privilege and social advancement, symbolic capital can be seen as, in an unequivocal sense, dependent on them. Still, symbolic capital is a phenomenon unique within the field: its only adequate explanation is sociological and not economic.[89] It has much to do with those unique social structures of the field in which the legitimation and recognition of actors is central.

All forms of capital are crucial in the dialectical interplay of field and habitus. The struggles inherent between actors for recognition and the preservation or further accumulation of forms of capital serve to structure the habitus and the field with its plethora of rules. In turn, the rules of the field impact the ways in which these struggles ensue—and so the circle continues. The circular nature

---

[85] Schwingel, *Pierre Bourdieu*, 85-86.
[86] Schwingel, *Pierre Bourdieu*, 88ff.
[87] Schwingel, *Pierre Bourdieu*, 92.
[88] Schwingel, *Pierre Bourdieu*, 92.
[89] Schwingel, *Pierre Bourdieu*, 93-94.

of this dialectic lends capital a vital and dynamic role in Bourdieu's social theory.[90]

Literary Field

Given that Bourdieu's findings are rooted in empirical research in specific cultural settings,[91] he believed his model to be legitimate and, as such, able to establish a practical, applicable theory of human society and social development. Indeed, the implications of Bourdieu's theory allow for several possible applications. Our concern for this project, however, is its significance for literary theory and its impact on sociology of literature.

In 1992, Bourdieu released his *Les Règles de l'art. Genèse es structure du champ littéraire*.[92] It took sociologists and literary theorists by storm. With this publication, Bourdieu demonstrated the ways in which his larger theoretical model was directly applicable to cultural production, which is to say, to the production of all forms of art. However, what he put forward was a much clearer presentation of his previously posited model of literary field.[93] Bourdieu had, over time, increasingly understood the literary field to be a constitutive part of social reality. The notions of field and literary field became conflated, one and the same; in turn, literary production became Bourdieu's primary focus. As such, the notion of literary field emerged not simply as an application of his earliest theory of field, but rather as essential to understanding social structures and the myriad ways in which these impact society's functioning and unfolding.[94]

Bourdieu's discourse surrounding these matters is, as is his theory of field in general, not entirely straightforward. Still, *Les règles de l'art* sets out to outline, in complex, seminal fashion, the ways in which artists—as actors—function within their fields. Accordingly, Bourdieu sought to trace the specifics of literary production and output, the possibilities for both authors and literature to develop, the reasons for variations both within the field and between literary works, the intrinsic relatedness of these works in spite of their divergences, as well as the place and significance of the reader and the literary theorist in society.

Bourdieu abandoned traditional forms of sociology of literature with their supposedly reductionist claims that the significance and meaning of works of literature lie only in their description of social contexts, production, and

---

[90] This circularity mirrors the hermeneutical circle: field affects capital, capital goes on to affect field—and the circle continues.

[91] Bourdieu's research of the Berber culture in Algeria was seminal and set the foundation for *The Rules of Art,* which would come much later. See Bourdieu's *Outline of a Theory of Practice*.

[92] Pierre Bourdieu, *Les règles de l'art. Genèse et structure du champ littéraire* (Paris: Éditions du Seuil, 1992).

[93] See Fröhlich and Rehbein, *Bourdieu Handbuch*, 369-70.

[94] Fröhlich and Rehbein, *Bourdieu Handbuch*, 361.

intentions. Simultaneously, he rejected those literary theories that emphasized the interpretation of literary works as enclosed entities of isolated meaning. Instead, Bourdieu posited the centrality of the "social meaning of their aesthetic position and method,"[95] underscoring the significance of their aesthetic value. In this way, Bourdieu attempted to take very seriously and to consolidate both the aesthetic significance and the social contexts and meanings of literary works.

The field represented, for Bourdieu, not a mere milieu or social context but an autonomous energy field in which specific but very dynamic rules for acting were at play. Bourdieu sought to address the field with respect to its structures of power (*champ de pouvoir*[96]), the relations of its individuals and groups within the context of its relative autonomy, its systems of dispositions, as well as those institutions that assign legitimation to cultural production itself.[97]

Bourdieu contended, in equally complex fashion, that society has no real direct or determinative causal effect on the field as such. Instead, the field is formed and determined by way of the dynamism of the internal struggles and interactions between members and groups within it. These are in constant competition for positions of greater influence and recognition. This tension opens up a sphere of possibilities in which these members and groups, in conjunction with their interests in competing forms of literary discourse, develop and advance within the field.[98]

The field also mediates artistic-aesthetic values and norms that guide and direct its artistic production. The ways in which artists struggle within the sphere of possibilities, however, are determined by their social positions and by the capital made available to them. This is what Bourdieu refers to as the "space of positions."[99] The specific forms of capital (in particular its economic and cultural forms) that actors possess in drawing from their social positions allows for significant differences between artists, as well as differences within their overall literary output. Be this as it may, this output is, in general, commensurate with that larger, homogenous structure of literary norms that the field has afforded.

Important to this project, and implicit above, is Bourdieu's claim that the aesthetic dimension and quality of any work of art is indicative of its source, more specifically, of the particular social origin of its production at the hands of the artist, who is free to move, create within, and even extend (though rarely) their cultural sphere and field.

The sphere of works can be understood as that broadest possible range of literary works produced by artists as influenced by their social position and

---

[95] Baasner and Zens, *Methoden und Modelle der Literaturwissenschaft*, 233. Translation mine.

[96] See Pierre Bourdieu, "Champ de pouvoir, champ intellectuel et habitus de classe," Scolies, no. 1 (1971), 7-26.

[97] Baasner and Zens, *Methoden und Modelle der Literaturwissenschaft*, 233-35.

[98] See Bourdieu, *Rules of Art*, 231-39, 256ff.

[99] See Bourdieu, *Rules of Art*, 234-39, 256ff.

individual capital.[100] With this, the interdependent nature of all spheres is established; in as much as social position and capital open up the sphere of possibilities, the latter mediates the sphere of works with all possible variations—naturally, given the individual structure of the field.

The intense, highly differentiated structure of artistic production is, at its core, dynamic and alive. In essence, it is the artistic struggle that provides for great divergences within the field in as much as artists, though conditioned by their social context, are capable of moving forwards in creative production with a much greater degree of autonomy and freedom than a cursory glance at Bourdieu's theory might lead one to think. It is this very dynamism that allows for the vibrancy of history's unfolding, as well as the colorful, extremely diversified plethora of literary forms, themes, and styles. As such, the field is in a state of constant transformation, producing a sphere of works that is ever-growing and changing.

In its time, Bourdieu's model of the literary field represented a significant breakthrough in social theory. In offering analyses not only of society but of history and of being human, Bourdieu's theories have incited interest in other academic areas, including sociology, history, anthropology, political science, and economics.

Elie Wiesel and Pierre Bourdieu

Approaching the "Kingdom of Memory"

Throughout his works, Elie Wiesel refers to his "kingdom of memory."[101] For Wiesel, this sphere constitutes a large, yet intimate, inner domain where the past not only remains alive but is a living, forceful, and dynamic entity that comes to infiltrate the present. In drawing from his vast "kingdom," and as one who bears witness, Wiesel seeks to offer memorial to the dead, sending, at the same time, a universal warning to humanity. Within the context of this unique testimony, his narratives are born.

Delineating how Wiesel's texts, as Holocaust literature, might be approached critically is crucial here. To address this, I have chosen an adaptation of Bourdieu's theory and practical model of literary field to address my critical

---

[100] Bourdieu always refers to the *relative* autonomy of fields. Joseph Jurt writes: "The autonomy of field is never reached once and for all; there are different degrees here. The process of becoming autonomous does not unfold linearly." Joseph Jurt, "Die Theorie des literarischen Feldes von Pierre Bourdieu," *LiTheS, Zeitschrift für Literatur- und Theatersoziologie* (Universität Graz), no.1 (December 2008), 11. Translation mine. See also Bourdieu, *Rules of Art*, 220-221, 248; Fröhlich and Rehbein, *Bourdieu Handbuch*, 100ff.

[101] As indicated by the title of Wiesel's work, *From the Kingdom of Memory: Reminiscences.*

interrogation of Wiesel's post-Holocaust discourse. Specifically, in as much as Bourdieu is concerned with an author's literary output (in terms of its composition, forms, content, themes, and style) and its relation to their historical and social context, position, cultural influences, as well as individual resources (capital), his model proves helpful in examining Wiesel as an author whose texts beg the very question of their origin and influences.

I intend to use Bourdieu's theory of field as a lens through which specific texts of Wiesel's might be read. Coupled with aspects of the narrative theory of James E. Young, as we shall see, and without giving continual reference to Bourdieu's theory of field as such, the model lends this assessment direction and focus.

The Shtetl-as-Field

Central to the thesis of this study is an examination of the Hasidic world of the shtetl as constituting a unique field.[102] This theoretical basis sets the parameters that guide my textual analysis. Positing the shtetl as field assists in examining how Wiesel's earliest religious context has come to impact his post-Holocaust discourse. In as much as the Hasidic world of the shtetl emerges as that distinct field in which Wiesel's story begins, the sociological considerations of this study are well supported.

Understanding the shtetl as field provides a novel focus in considering Wiesel's texts. Questions surrounding the impact of the Hasidism of the shtetl on Wiesel's works remain important. These questions frame the textual work here. This approach links Wiesel's biography to his narrative production, that is, to the stories he tells. In this way, both sociological and literary concerns are given ample room to address the nature and significance of Wiesel's texts. This methodology corresponds well with Bourdieu's focus on taking the historical, sociological, *and* literary dimensions of texts seriously, granting them equal weight in considering texts' purposes and meaningfulness.

A review of the historical background to both Hasidism and the shtetl will be offered in chapter five, supporting my proposal of the shtetl as field.

Auschwitz as Anti-Field

An important word must be offered here with respect to Auschwitz and field. In proposing the shtetl to be field and in considering this field as setting the

---

[102] As evidenced in *The Rules of Art*, Bourdieu came to increasingly conflate field and literary field. There, in his exploration of Gustave Flaubert's *Sentimental Education*, he uses the notion of field as the starting point of his literary inquiry. Importantly, his analysis concludes with a review of how this work is most reflective of Flaubert himself. See Bourdieu, *Rules of Art*, 3-43. Cf. Fröhlich and Rehbein, *Bourdieu Handbuch*, 369-70.

parameters of Wiesel's literary work, it could be suggested that Auschwitz too represents field, one adjacent to that of the shtetl. This is a suggestion I reject.

Fields constitute those social contexts of human life that have become well-established in terms of culture, language, traditions, and cultural production. Auschwitz represents none of these. Instead, as a universe unto itself, as a *univers concentrationnaire*, Auschwitz contradicts anything that might resemble any humane social context, reducing persons from subjects of freedom, worth, and dignity to objects of hate and destruction. Auschwitz can thus be considered anti-field, an inhuman domain that seeks to destroy human life, rather than a sphere wherein human beings might continue to exist, thrive, and develop. As a sphere contrary to all humanity, Auschwitz is indeed a parallel universe, and one without parallel.

The Shtetl, Auschwitz, and the Sociology of Holocaust Literature

The theory of field offers an original approach to the discussion surrounding the historicity of Holocaust texts. In taking the historical contexts seriously out of which such texts arise, Bourdieu's model, employed wisely, serves to uphold the inherent historical basis of Holocaust testimony. At the same time, it underscores the literary significance ("literariness") of texts rooted in given historical contexts, upholding the testimonial nature of Holocaust texts, and honoring those dimensions that embrace, but also lie beyond historicity. In this sense, in its refusal to bracket the literary significance, purpose, and meaningfulness of texts, Bourdieu's theory can do justice to the truth-seeking nature of Holocaust texts as testimony.

Bourdieu's notion of field emerges as a working theory adequate to the task of examining the ways in which Wiesel's earliest influences have impacted his post-Holocaust memory and discourse. Understood as that autonomous, dynamic sphere embraced by a given social context and embracing a wide range of artists whose possibilities for cultural production are contingent upon the intricate structure of that context, the notion of field guides my approach to Wiesel's biography on the one hand, and to his literary output on the other. To reiterate: "The aesthetic dimension and quality of any work of art is indicative of its source . . . of the particular social origin of its production at the hands of the artist, who is free to move, create within and even extend (though rarely) their cultural sphere."[103] This study explores how particular texts by Wiesel reflect this axiom, which is to say, how his texts are indicative of his earliest field and how he has continued, however furtively, to work within that field.

Ultimately, by investigating how influences of the shtetl as field become evident in Wiesel's texts, something of the nature and origin of Wiesel's humanitarian message is revealed.

---

[103] See section 2.3.6. "Literary Field."

Chapter Two

Holocaust Literature: Discourse, Discussion, and Debate

The Rise of Holocaust Consciousness

In her publication *Der Holocaust in der literarischen Erinnerung: Autobiographische Aufzeichnungen von Udo Dietmar und Elie Wiesel*, Antonia Barboric outlines the emergence of Holocaust literature in four separate phases of development: the first from 1933 to 1945, the second from 1945 to 1950, the third from 1950 to 1980, and the fourth from 1980 to the present day.[104] Our immediate focus is on phases two to four.

Critical responses to the literary testimony emerging soon after the war were staggered by some fifteen years, reaching well into the 1970s and not peaking until the 1990s. Significantly, these responses were largely reactionary in America, answering to trends in popular culture where the demand for depictions of the Holocaust in text and film was growing. Such developments proved to be dismaying for the many survivors whose experiences of the Holocaust were incommensurate with those presentations seeking to make the Holocaust more easily "accessible" to the public. Accordingly, survivors began to feel an increased sense of alienation from the growing public fascination with their fate. Intellectual circles, too, were beginning to cast a critical eye on the egregious flaunting of profound human suffering. As a whole, the development was beginning to cast shadows across America—for Jews and non-Jews alike.

This movement in America stood in need of correction. Survivors, authors, and filmmakers set out to provide necessary amendments. Beginning in the late 1970s, these attempts unleashed discussion and heated debate, raising at times the ire of those seeking the more accommodating approaches and simplified guidelines demanded by popular culture.

These historical developments are highlighted briefly in the present chapter. This leads to an examination of the questions that surround literary representations of the Holocaust. Because this complex cluster of questions is central to the theses that guide this study, and given that America remains the veritable hub of Holocaust discourse, tracing both the ascendency of this discussion and the salient tenets of the debate there is meaningful. A cursory view to developments in Germany is also provided.

The discussion continues by centering on the thought of five prominent Holocaust intellectuals (including Elie Wiesel in chapter four) who have

[104]Antonia Barboric, *Der Holocaust in der literarischen Erinnerung. Autobiographische Aufzeichnungen von Udo Dietmar und Elie Wiesel* (Vienna: Böhlau Verlag, 2014), 45.

profoundly impacted Holocaust discourse well beyond popular trends. Their understanding of language, and Holocaust representation in particular, are highlighted. This intends to illustrate the extent to which perspectives on language and Holocaust discourse have diverged dramatically from those of popular culture.

The study then moves towards a meaningful theory of literary representation. As this theory illuminates important relationships between sociological concerns, human experience, and the use of language, it assists in buttressing, developing, and deepening the theses of this project.

Early Attempts at Testimony

The earliest forms of Holocaust literature that appeared in the phase directly following the war (1945-1950) were largely overlooked on both sides of the Atlantic. Survivors' efforts to have their stories published and heard were strained by the self-absorption of a world recoiling from war.[105] Post-war Germany, traumatized and broken, would have little space for exhaustive critical reflection on the Jewish genocide for some years to come.[106] America, deeply mired in its own complex process of reorientation, was confronted with its commitment to help rebuild a tattered Germany while, at the same time, was struggling to come to terms with the implications of Hiroshima and Nagasaki. It, too, had little capacity to listen to tales of atrocity. Accordingly, survivors (then considered refugees) could not reckon with an immediate outpouring of compassion from the world. They would struggle to have their stories told.

Still, efforts were being made. Thomas Geve's *Youth in Chains*,[107] an account of the author's wartime experiences, including his incarceration in KZ Buchenwald, represents one such effort. In 1949, the first version of *Youth in Chains* was rejected for publication. An editor explained to Geve, "The time is not yet ripe for this book."[108] Although a longer version of the book was published

---

[105] For more concerning the difficulties inherent in these struggles see Andrea Reiter, "*Auf dass sie entsteigen der Dunkelheit." Die literarische Bewältigung von KZ-Erfahrung,* (Vienna: Löcker Verlag, 1995).

[106] Indeed, the politics of the whole of Europe were to be impacted by Germany's post-war attempts, however strong and however weak, in coming to terms with its recent past. For a more thorough analysis see Jan-Werner Müller, ed. *Memory and Power in Post-War Europe: Studies in the Presence of the Past* (Cambridge: Cambridge University Press, 2002).

[107] Thomas Geve, *Youth in Chains* (Jerusalem: Rubin Mass, 1958).

[108] Doris Gehring, *Die Holocaust Autobiographien als Speicher der Erinnerung im Wandel der Erinnerungskultur. Eine Analyse des Erinnerungsdiskurses anhand autobiographischer Texte von Thomas Geve, Elie Wiesel, Inge Deutschkron, Ruth Klüger, Binjamin Wilkomirski und als Vergleichsfall Wolfgang Koeppen mit der Bearbeitung von Jakob Littners: "Mein Weg durch die Nacht"* (master's thesis, University of Bern, 2010), 40. Translation mine.

under its original title in 1958, it did not achieve international recognition until it appeared in its third edition as *Guns & Barbed Wire: A Child Survives the Holocaust* by a publisher in Chicago in 1987.[109]

Such struggles were hardly encouraging for survivors who were not yet ready to tell their stories. The impetus to speak out was weak. Some survivors spoke of their experiences of the Holocaust;[110] however, many survivors decided to remain silent. Robert Schindel asserts, "after the catastrophe the silence was notorious" on all sides. Neither Jewish survivors nor non-Jews wished to speak of the darkness of the atrocities;[111] the events were yet too close. Worse still, Phil C. Langer writes, "no one wanted to hear the testimony."[112] Constanze Jaiser supports this claim:

> At that time time there existed quite a number of concentration camp reports—except that they were often given no attention and were then forgotten. The [actual] circulation of texts by Holocaust survivors, however, was small, although in the German-speaking world between 1945 and 1949 the first wave of publications was taking place.[113]

These early narrative attempts were characterized first by the pressing need of survivors to tell their stories,[114] and secondly, by the literary representations of

---

[109] Gehring, *Die Holocaust,* 40. See also Thomas Geve, *Guns & Barbed Wire: A Child Survives the Holocaust* (Chicago: Academy Chicago Publishers, 1987).

[110] Reiter, "*Auf dass sie steigen in der Dunkelheit,"* 222.

[111] Robert Schindel, "Schweigend ins Gespräch vertieft. Anmerkungen zu Geschichte und Gegenwart des jüdischnichtjüdischen Verhältnisses in den Täterländern," in *Literatur und Holocaust,* ed. Heinz Ludwig Arnold, *Text & Kritik*, Heft 144 (Munich: Edition Text & Kritik, 1999), 6. Translation mine.

[112] Phil C. Langer, *Schreiben gegen die Erinnerung? Autobiographien von Überlebenden der Shoah* (Hamburg: Krämer, 2002), 46. Quoted in Barboric, *Der Holocaust in der literarischen Erinnerung*, 53.

[113] Constanze Jaiser, "Die Zeugnisliteratur von Überlebenden der deutschen Konzentrationslager seit 1945," in *Die Shoah in der Literatur,* ed. Norbert Otto Eke and Hartmut Steinecke (Berlin: Erich Schmidt Verlag, 2006), 109. Quoted in Barboric, *Der Holocaust in der literarischen Erinnerung*, 53. Translation mine.

[114] Barboric argues that the survivor's need to relate their story was often a clandestine attempt to work through their traumatic experiences psychologically. Whether this need stood in the foreground has been debated. For more on the survivor's "imperative to tell" see Dori Laub, "Bearing Witness *or* the Vicissitudes of Listening," in Shoshana Felman and Dori Laub, *Testimony: Crises of Witnessing in Literature, Psychoanalysis, and History* (New York: Routledge, 1992), 57-74. Importantly, Wiesel admits to his own sense of crisis: "If someone else could have written my stories . . . I would not have written them. I have written them in order to testify. And this is the origin of the loneliness that can be glimpsed in each of my sentences, in each of my silences." From Elie Wiesel, "The Loneliness of God," published in *Dvar Hashavu'a*, magazine of the newspaper

experience this need produced. Often with little personal analysis, these texts were structured as reports whose intentions were to relay, in as objective and factual a manner as possible, what had been experienced.[115] Many of the testimonies, however, proved to be highly subjective and steeped in emotion.[116] These narratives would later fall prey to cynics and Holocaust deniers who, in isolating inaccuracies in a number of these accounts, would call into question the worth and reliability of such testimony in general.[117] This devastating trend would serve to intensify the debate about the purpose, meaning, and intention of testimony.

Given the incapacity of the western world to absorb the events of the Holocaust, it would take time for Holocaust testimony to find its true footing on both sides of the Atlantic. It was not until the third phase of testimony development, beginning in the 1950s with the publication of certain landmark titles, that more general interest in the Holocaust was generated. One of these titles was Anne Frank's *Diary of a Young Girl*, first published in English in 1952.[118] A second, Elie Wiesel's *La Nuit*, appeared in French in 1958,[119] followed by the English translation *Night* in 1960. Both of these texts had a significant impact on the rise of Holocaust consciousness, although their characters and content differed greatly. As such, the impact of each of these diverged significantly.

In the opening to her 1999 publication *The Americanization of the Holocaust*, Hilene Flanzbaum highlights the enormous ongoing impact that *The Diary* has had on popular culture since the publication of the first English edition. She remarks that it had been named (at least up until 1996) the "predominant source of Holocaust education" in America.[120]

Flanzbaum observes that although the reasons for the continuing popularity of Frank's diary are many,[121] how this single text has continued to impact popular perspectives on the Holocaust is significant. Its content, at times "unfailingly optimistic,"[122] presents itself as far removed from the dark atrocities taking

---

Dava, Tel-Aviv, 1984. Quoted in *Testimony: Crises of Witnessing*, 3. Translated by Felman.

[115] Barboric, *Der Holocaust in der literarischen Erinnerung*, 54-55.

[116] Barboric, *Der Holocaust in der literarischen Erinnerung*, 66-68.

[117] For a detailed overview of Holocaust denial see Stephen E. Atkins, *Holocaust Denial as an International Movement* (Westport, CT: Praeger, 2009).

[118] Anne Frank, *Diary of a Young Girl*, trans. B. M. Mooyaart-Doubleday (Garden City, NY: Doubleday, 1952).

[119] Elie Wiesel, *La Nuit*, with a preface by François Mauriac. Paris; Les Editions de Minuit, 1958.

[120] Hilene Flanzbaum, ed. *The Americanization of the Holocaust* (Baltimore, MD: The Johns Hopkins University Press, 1999), 1.

[121] For a more detailed analysis of the impact of Frank's diaries see David Barnouw, *Das Phänomen Anne Frank*, trans. Simone Schroth (Essen: Klartext Verlag, 2015).

[122] Flanzbaum, "Introduction: The Americanization of the Holocaust," in *The Americanization of the Holocaust*, 2. Flanzbaum's expression paraphrases Lawrence Graver's statements in *An Obsession with Anne Frank: Meyer Levin and the Diary* (Berkeley:

place across Europe when Frank was writing. For some, the text inspires more than it informs, a reality that continues to inflame ongoing discussion concerning its efficacy and place in Holocaust education.[123]

Wiesel's *Nuit*, on the other hand, was a text whose dark content would, with time, raise Holocaust consciousness to a new level, inciting very different kinds of discussions. There, the naivety of the young Frank was replaced by the image of a tender youth shattered by his encounter with the darkness of humanity. With time, Wiesel would emerge as one who would be perceived as the quintessential "Auschwitz survivor."

Holocaust Consciousness in America and Germany

Several other events inflamed Holocaust consciousness and discussion; a few prominent ones will be highlighted here. The Eichmann trial in Jerusalem in 1961 was certainly one of these. The testimony that emerged from the trials shocked the world; the word "Auschwitz" began to take on newer, darker undertones. Hannah Arendt's investigations of what she called "the banality of evil" are by now well known, and the heated debate surrounding her theses is well-worn.[124] However one might regard her analyses, both the trial and Arendt generated international attention to matters of the Holocaust.

This development was not entirely positive. In America in particular, while playing on the growing public fascination with the plight of the Jews, authors and filmmakers alike would take turns addressing the Holocaust. From dramatic fictional accounts by non-survivors to the nation-wide broadcast of *Holocaust* in 1978,[125] a turn was taken that, for many, undermined the cause that these

---

University of California Press, 1995). See Flanzbaum, "Introduction: The Americanization of the Holocaust," 2n, 225.

[123] See Flanzbaum, "Introduction: The Americanization of the Holocaust," 1-3.

[124] See Hannah Arendt, *Eichmann in Jerusalem. Ein Bericht von der Banalität des Bösen* (Munich: Piper Verlag, 2013). With her claim to the "banality of evil," Arendt rejected the Kantian notion of "radical evil." Discussion and debate— philosophical, theological, and ethical—were quick to follow. Habermas has offered both positive and critical reviews. See Jürgen Habermas, *Philosophisch-politische Profile*, expanded edition (Frankfurt: Suhrkamp, 1987), 10, 236, 405. In his analysis of Arendt's proposal, Zimmermann attempts to expose Arendt's misunderstanding of Kant in particular. He argues for the occurrence of a break in the philosophical notion of evil, laying claim to a concomitant break in the genus of ethics. See Rolf Zimmermann, *Philosophie nach Auschwitz. Eine Neubestimmung von Moral in Politik und Gesellschaft* (Reinbek bei Hamburg: Rowohlt Taschenbuch Verlag, 2005), 9-11, 25ff, 29.

[125] See Hilene Flanzbaum, "The Imaginary Jew and the American Poet," in *The Americanization of the Holocaust*, 18-32; Jeffrey Shandler, "Aliens in the Wasteland: American Encounters with the Holocaust on 1960s Science Fiction Television," in *The Americanization of the Holocaust*, 33-34; and Henry Greenspan, "Imagining Survivors:

productions claimed to support.[126] Very quickly, the terms "Holocaust" and "Auschwitz" fell prey to a vernacular use that was derogatory for survivors and their families.[127]

In particular, the television series *Holocaust* constituted a watershed in the rise of Holocaust awareness; with this production, a definitive turn had been taken. However, many critics and survivors, including Wiesel, condemned the images that the series depicted. They contended that *Holocaust* dangerously misrepresented the events that had taken place, and that the production was created more to feed the curiosity of the masses than to honor the memory of the dead.[128]

Flanzbaum contends that in America, due to a growing array of narratives and films such as *Schindler's List* (1993), Holocaust awareness soon slipped into a disturbingly popular form.[129] She argues that Holocaust interpretation had taken on a decidedly American gestalt and that much of the American public had begun to feel that they "knew" what had "happened" in Auschwitz. What is more, she states, feelings and passions surrounding the Holocaust among the Jewish American population were intensifying to the extent that a growing number of Jews were beginning to define their identity through the Holocaust, and this with an increased sense of victimization.[130]

Flanzbaum based her scathing analysis on the ideas of Alvin H. Rosenfeld, who, in 1995, had first coined the notion "the Americanization of the Holocaust."[131] At that time, Rosenfeld had taken issue with authors who openly supported distinctly American interpretations of the Holocaust.[132] His dismay centered on what he perceived to be the widespread undermining of the "uniqueness" of the Holocaust through the backdoor of American cultural concepts, norms, and social and political demands. Prefiguring Flanzbaum then, Rosenfeld was critical of the ways in which America had come to embrace the Holocaust as a universal, rather than singular, event. He claimed that the Holocaust had all too quickly been transformed into a metaphor for countless situations of human victimization. This was a trend he vehemently rejected:

Testimony and the Rise of Holocaust Consciousness,"in *The Americanization of the Holocaust*, 45-47.

[126] Flanzbaum, "Introduction: The Americanization of the Holocaust," 4-5.

[127] Flanzbaum, "Introduction: The Americanization of the Holocaust," 7-8.

[128] Wiesel considered the series an insult. See Peter Reichel, *Erfundene Erinnerung. Weltkrieg und Judenmord in Film und Theater* (Frankfurt am Main: Fischer Taschenbuch Verlag, 2007), 253.

[129] Flanzbaum, "Introduction: The Americanization of the Holocaust," 5.

[130] Flanzbaum, "Introduction: The Americanization of the Holocaust," 11-14.

[131] See Alvin H. Rosenfeld, "The Americanization of the Holocaust," *Commentary* 99, no. 6 (June 1995): 35-40.

[132] Berenbaum argued that portrayals of the Holocaust needed to be more "accessible" to the public, a position diametrically opposed to Rosenfeld's. See Rosenfeld, "The Americanization of the Holocaust," 35.

> This tendency has, in fact, been prominent right from the start in American understandings of the Holocaust. But today it is growing exponentially, especially within those segments of American culture intent on developing a politics of identity based on victim status and the grievances that come with it. The rhetoric of "oppression" has become a commonplace of contemporary American political, academic, and artistic discourse, and its exponents frequently take recourse to the signs and symbols of the Nazi Holocaust to describe what they see as their own "victimization" within American society.[133]

Rosenfeld's critical review of the 1993 *Holocaust Project*,[134] a multi-media undertaking by Judy Chicago depicting the Holocaust and related themes, reinforced his concerns. He focused on the artist's universalizing of the Holocaust, contending that she had relativized the suffering of the Jews to such an extent so as to portray it as representative, and even symbolic, of all kinds of human suffering. Reflective of a deeply-embedded and growing narcissism in American culture, Chicago's work, Rosenfeld claimed, did little else than promote the themes of personal and group victimization, while, at the same time, diminish, dilute, and downplay the "dark and brutal sides of life," and placing a "preponderant emphasis on the saving power of individual moral conduct and collective deeds of redemption."[135]

For Rosenfeld, Steven Spielberg's 1993 film *Schindler's List*,[136] although widely acclaimed, was also problematic. He contended that it served more to glorify stories of rescuers and redemption, rather than recognize and honor survivors and their stories of trauma.[137] Rosenfeld and like-minded critics contended that the production mitigated the profound suffering of the Jews during the Holocaust through the secondary role that Jewish victims and survivors played in the film.[138]

---

[133] Rosenfeld, "The Americanization of the Holocaust," 36.

[134] See Judy Chicago and Donald Woodman, *The Holocaust Project: From Darkness into Light* (New York: Penguin Paperbacks, 1993).

[135] Rosenfeld, "The Americanization of the Holocaust," 37.

[136] See Alvin H. Rosenfeld, *The End of the Holocaust* (Bloomington: Indiana University Press, 2011), 81-82; 90-91.

[137] Rosenfeld quotes Lanzmann, the creator of *Shoah*, as saying: "To tell the story of the Holocaust through a German who saved Jews can only lead to a distortion of the truth, because for the overwhelming majority of Jews things like this did not happen." See Claude Lanzmann, "The Twisted Truth of Schindler's List," in *London Evening Standard*, February 10, 1994. Quoted in Rosenfeld, *The End of the Holocaust*, 83.

[138] For Rosenfeld's analysis of the film and its critics see *The End of the Holocaust*, 83-85.

Again, the result was a decidedly Americanized version of the Holocaust, replete with the kind of happy ending American audiences found satisfying.[139]

Be that as it may, Rosenfeld did grant the production some merit, for the film had aided in crystalizing further the increasingly prominent role of the Holocaust survivor in American society.[140] Indeed, since the 1960s, the Holocaust survivor's role had been transforming. Here again, Rosenfeld provides insightful analysis:

> [B]eginning in the mid-to-late 1960s and carrying up to the present day, a radical change of attitude has taken place, so much so that the "survivor" has become a much honored figure and, in some instances, enjoys something close to celebrity status. Elie Wiesel has played an important role in this regard, as have others. The result is that those who formerly had been regarded as "war refugees" have given up that unenviable status and taken on a new symbolic importance as "Holocaust survivors."[141]

The release of *Holocaust* in 1978 and *Schindler's List* in 1993 on television and movie screens marked decisive turning points in the unfolding of popular Holocaust awareness in America. Holocaust survivors took on ever more important roles in relaying Holocaust atrocities to the world. This development was both positive and negative, and there are a number of reasons for this. What is important here, however, is that this new status began to encourage many survivors to tell their stories, and that, when they did tell them, these stories were finally being heard.

As the spotlight on survivors intensified, so did the discourse on Holocaust stories in America. The paradigm shift in Holocaust consciousness generated by the increase in survivor testimony, literature, and film productions in the 1970s and 1980s had now become definitive.[142] With this shift, critical reflection and debate skyrocketed in the 1990s, as new dimensions of discourse emerged within what was now becoming known as the "culture of memory."

As America arose as the center of Holocaust discussion, developments in Europe, though lagging chronologically behind those of its American counterparts, were significant and necessary. The delay in Holocaust discussion in Europe was tied to several factors. Most important was the relatively long post-war

---

[139] Rosenfeld writes: "What version of the Holocaust, then, does *Schindler's List* present? A recognizably American one, by which I do not mean a historically 'false' one but rather one that interprets history along lines that Americans seem to require or at least instinctively prefer." Rosenfeld, *The End of the Holocaust*, 85.

[140] Rosenfeld, *The End of the Holocaust*, 78-79.

[141] Rosenfeld, *The End of the Holocaust*, 77-78.

[142] See Greenspan, "Imagining Survivors," 45-67, in particular 56ff.

silence of most Germans with regard to the crimes that their nation had committed during the Holocaust.[143] Although many intellectuals had made earnest attempts to examine Germany's recent past, the shame felt by many after 1945 was widespread. Most Germans were resolute in focusing solely on the restoration of their nation. Even the Nürnberger trials of 1945 to 1949, which held a number of Nazi war criminals accountable for the crimes they committed, and which contributed substantially to a growing worldwide awareness of the Holocaust, proved unable to provide the impetus necessary to accelerate a collective, nationwide, and more comprehensive *Vergangenheitsbewältigung* than had been achieved up to that point in time.[144]

By the late 1960s, in conjunction with acute social and political upheaval in Germany, a new epoch had arrived, and *Vergangenheitsbewältigung* was finally placed higher on the German national agenda. The fall of the Berlin wall in 1989 served to further the discussion as a now-united Germany attempted anew to make sense of what had led to the country's divide in 1949. The nation's efforts in cultivating its own "culture of memory," or *Erinnerungskultur*, have since been recognized.[145] The movement, however, was never left undisputed; even during its first phases, many Germans had demanded that a *Schlusspunkt* be drawn. The reasons for this, too, are numerous and complex and lie beyond the immediate concerns of this study. As time progressed, however, *Erinnerungskultur* forced Germany to consider the nature of its new and growing national cultural identity, providing necessary caution with regard to its status as an emergent economic and political superpower.[146]

---

[143] See Gottfried Wagner and Abraham J. Peck, *Unsere Stunde Null. Deutsche und Juden nach 1945. Familiengeschichte, Holocaust und Neubeginn. Historische Memoiren* (Vienna: Böhlau Verlag, 2006), 308 ff.

[144] The term *Vergangenheitsbewältigung* may be translated as "overcoming the past." For a more thorough discussion, see Aleida Assmann and Ute Frevert, *Geschichtsvergessenheit—Geschichtsversessenheit. Vom Umgang mit deutschen Vergangenheiten nach 1945* (Stuttgart: Deutsche Verlags-Anstalt, 1999); and Norbert Frei, *Vergangenheitspolitik. Die Anfänge der Bundesrepublik und die NS-Vergangenheit* (Munich: C. H. Beck, 1996).

[145] Aleida Assmann argues for a "crescendo" in the culture of memory in Germany with respect to the Holocaust. For an introduction to themes surrounding the German *Erinnerungskultur* see Aleida Assmann, *Das neue Unbehagen an der Erinnerungskultur. Eine Intervention* (Munich: C. H. Beck, 2013). See in particular pages 33-56. The work of Aleida and Jan Assmann has been central to the ongoing work in the fields of social, collective, and cultural memory. See Aleida Assmann, *Erinnerungsräume. Formen und Wandlungen des kulturellen Gedächtnisses* (Munich: C.H. Beck, 1999); Jan Assmann, *Das kulturelle Gedächtnis. Schrift, Erinnerung und politische Identität in frühen Hochkulturen* (Munich: C. H. Beck, 1992); and Aleida Assmann, *Der lange Schatten der Vergangenheit. Erinnerungskultur und Geschichtspolitik* (Munich: C.H. Beck, 2014).

[146] For an overview and analysis of Germany's struggles in the context of its *Vergangenheitsbewältigung* see Reinhard Rürup, *Der lange Schatten des Nationalsozialismus. Geschichte, Geschichtspolitik und Erinnerungskultur* (Göttingen: Wallstein Verlag, 2014).

Germany's attempts to confront and work through its conflicted past did contribute to deepening and expanding the Holocaust awareness that was growing abroad. In general, though, the country's emerging culture of memory did not mirror the popular cultural trends in America. The voices of Holocaust survivors that had remained in Europe—survivors such as Theodor W. Adorno, Primo Levi, Ruth Klüger, Imre Kertész, Jean Améry, and Paul Celan—reverberated worldwide, providing a very much-needed ballast to the trends that characterized American cultural representations of the Holocaust in particular. European survivors contributed significantly to critical discussion surrounding the use of language with regard to the Holocaust—a discussion important to this study. A closer look at the contributions of a number of these thinkers is provided later in this chapter.

Naming the Holocaust: The Deepening of Discourse

The ways in which the Holocaust can be addressed and represented literarily is a theme central to this project. The very naming of the Holocaust arises as strikingly relevant to this larger discussion. Given this, a brief overview of the most familiar names and designations for the Holocaust is meaningful.

In general, the varying terms used to reference the Holocaust are reflective of diverse understandings of the Jewish genocide. These terms reflect diverging understandings of the nature of the event, namely, as being either unprecedented, unique, and unrepeatable, or as but one event in a larger historical continuum. These distinctions prove important for understanding the myriad ways in which the Holocaust has been represented in art and literature. For this reason, some clarification of the "names" for the Holocaust is merited.

The debate surrounding the designation "Holocaust" for the Jewish genocide continues today. The word stems from the Greek *holocaustos*, meaning "a sacrifice wholly consumed by fire."[147] While there is evidence that the expression did surface during the course of World War II,[148] it was arguably Elie Wiesel who, in the 1950s, first applied it in a definitive way, positing it as the primary reference to the Jewish genocide of World War II.[149]

---

[147] *The Oxford Encyclopedic English Dictionary*, ed. Joyce M. Hawkins and Robert Allen (Oxford: Clarendon Press, 1991), s.v. "holocaust," 680.

[148] Wolfgang Benz, ed. *Lexikon des Holocaust* (Munich: C. H. Beck, 2002), 100ff.

[149] See Gunnar Heinsohn, *Lexikon der Völkermorde* (Reinbek bei Hamburg: Rowohlt Verlag, 1998), 175n6. Quoted in Barboric, *Der Holocaust in der literarischen Erinnerung*, 14; and Sascha Feuchert, ed. *Holocaust-Literatur. Auschwitz.* Arbeitstexte für den Unterricht. Für die Sekundarstufe 1 (Stuttgart: P. Reclam jun., 2000), 9. That Wiesel was the first to apply "Holocaust"to the Jewish genocide continues to generate debate. Although the word appears as early as 1957 in the *Yad Vashem Bulletin*, Wiesel insisted to have implemented it earlier.

Wiesel vehemently defended this specificity, often dismayed at the ensuing generalizing usage that served both to dilute and undermine its intended application. As it developed into a more universal term, the word "holocaust" slipped into the vernacular. "Holocaust" began to be implemented freely and frequently in referencing the murder of both Jews and non-Jews alike in the Holocaust. As well, it was being applied to genocide in general and to events such as the Armenian and Rwandan genocides in particular.[150] Worse yet, the word entered colloquial vocabulary: "holocaust" became commonplace jargon, applied at times to situations far removed from those to which it had originally referred. As a result, in contending that the expression had been misused and even abused, some circles began to abandon it entirely, in particular those groups who defended the uniqueness of the Jewish genocide so vehemently.

Accordingly, many felt compelled to implement a term that would reference the specifically Jewish nature of the genocide.[151] This was intended to serve as a clear and differentiating alternative and to counteract the increasing equivocality of the term "Holocaust." Certainly, the best known of these is "Shoah," which stems from the Hebrew *shoah*, meaning "devastation," "ruin," "storm," or "waste."[152] With "Shoah," the ambiguity of the word "Holocaust" was ostensibly overcome. "Shoah" is largely understood to be a specifically Jewish designation to an exclusively Jewish event.[153] In connection with this exclusivity, "Shoah" has also sought to reflect the extent of the "devastation" as being unparalleled.[154]

---

[150] The discussion has been at times acute. See Barboric, *Der Holocaust in der literarischen Erinnerung*, 14-20.

[151] Yitzchok Hutner associates the beginning of the use of the expression "Shoah" for the Jewish genocide with the founding of Yad Vaschem in Jerusalem. See Yitzchok Hutner, "Bürde der Erwählung" in *Wolkensäule und Feuerschein. Jüdische Theologie des Holocaust*, ed. Michael Brocke and Herbert Jochum, trans. Gaetano Hassdenteufel and Michael Brocke (Munich: Kaiser Taschenbücher, 1993), 28-29. Barboric marks the diverging of the meaning of "Shoah" from "Holocaust"in Walter Reich's address at the inauguration of the Holocaust Memorial in Washington in 1999. See Barboric, *Der Holocaust in der literarischen Erinnerung*, 21. In actual fact, the 1948 Israeli Declaration of Independence included the words, "The catastrophe (sho'ah) which recently befell the Jewish people— the massacre of millions of Jews in Europe." See the Israeli government website, accessed 30 January 2019: http://www.mfa.gov.il.

[152] William Gesenius, *Hebrew and English Lexicon of the Old Testament with an Appendix Containing the Biblical Aramaic*, trans. Edward Robinson (Oxford: Clarendon Press, 1906; repr. Oxford: Oxford University press, 1951), 996.

[153] Habermas's delineation of "Shoah" as the "Kern des Holocaust" ("the core of the Holocaust"), however, only serves to underscore the extent to which "Holocaust" has become equivocal in its reference. For many like Habermas, "Shoah" differentiates the Jewish genocide from within the larger event "Holocaust," which included the murder of many non-Jews. See Barboric, *Der Holocaust in der literarischen Erinnerung*, 21-24.

[154] See Hutner, "Bürde der Erwählung," 28-29. Hutner also notes that the word *shoah* in Hebrew—as does the word "Holocaust" in English—refers to a single catastrophe that evidences no connection with anything that transpired either before or after it. See

The third word, *churban*, derived from the Hebrew *kurban,* meaning "sacrifice" or "offering,"[155] seeks to isolate the Jewish genocide as a distinctly Jewish event. Significant here, however, are the theological implications inherent in the term. In referencing the Holocaust as an occurrence neither unprecedented nor unique in Jewish history, *churban* deviates significantly from both "Holocaust" and "Shoah." According to its advocates, the Jewish genocide remains but one event among several which can be understood as *churban.* By definition, *churban* references those divine interventions in history through which God has attempted, by way of a painful act of rebuke and punishment, to beckon a wayward people to repentance, renewal, and a return to the fundamentals of obedience and faith.[156] In this sense, *churban*, as an expression long used by the Jewish faith tradition, references an understanding of the Jewish genocide, as a part of Jewish history, as a faith-oriented event with grave theological and spiritual implications and repercussions.

In particular, the term *churban* underscores the extent of the debate between diverging theological, philosophical, and historical groups in naming the Jewish genocide. Those who employ *churban* understand the genocide as a recognizable event in the history of a people whose story is replete with disobedience towards God. Individuals in both religious and non-religious camps who employ the expressions "Holocaust" and "Shoah" insist on the unparalleled nature of the Jewish genocide. They emphasize it as a break in both history and in civilization (*Zivilisationsbruch*). These discrepancies have been the source of deep rifts between Jewish communities and factions, and between Jews and non-Jews alike.

Hutner, 40-41. The expression *haShoah* has been established at the national level in Israel, with the intention of offsetting the worldwide equivocal use of "Holocaust." The inauguration of Holocaust Remembrance Day, *Yom haShoah*, in 1953 is indicative of this use. See Tom Segev, *Die siebte Million. Der Holocaust und Israels Politik der Erinnerung,* trans. Jürgen Peter Krause and Maja Ueberle-Pfaff (Reinbek b. Hamburg: Rowohlt, 1995), 573–78.

[155] The English translation of Gesenius defines *churban* as "offering" or "oblation." See Gesenius, *Hebrew and English Lexicon,* 898.

[156] Ignaz Maybaum relates *churban* to the destruction of the temple at the times of both Solomon and Herod, events in which God had called his people back to himself. In this context, Maybaum contends, the *churban* is to be understood as a messianic event. God has acted as a surgeon who cuts out past elements of humanity in order for it to begin again. See Ignaz Maybaum, "Der dritte *Churban*" in *Wolkensäule und Feuerschein*, ed. Brocke und Jochum, 9. Paraphrase mine.

Holocaust Literature and the Discourse of Survival

Approaching Holocaust Literature

The heated nature of this debate is significant because it reflects the extent to which language concerns have come to permeate Holocaust discourse. Notably, the discussion surrounding the naming of the Holocaust has proven to be indispensable in distilling, clarifying, and elucidating very important issues at stake—not the least of these are the ways in which the Holocaust can be referenced in literature, art, or in critical discourse.

The questions of appropriate reference are multifaceted, digressing, at times, into the purely theoretical. Still, these issues have arisen from the existential realities confronted by survivors lying at the heart of atrocity and thus well beyond all theory. Given the struggle felt by survivors in deciding whether to speak about their experiences or to remain silent, the question of how language might be used has actually been predicated by *whether* it can be used at all. This dimension of the discussion is important because it emphasizes the authority of the survivor.

And yet the testimonies of survivors made available to the world have—as have all forms of literature and testimony—fallen into the hands of both historians and critics alike. Their focus has been to make sense of testimonies, to assess their purposes and concerns, and to identify their status as historical representations, or as something beyond them. The debate surrounding the validity and place of literary representation has become yet more impassioned as the influx of Holocaust literature written by non-survivors (and even non-Jews) has increased.

The purpose of the second half of this chapter is to examine more closely the issues of language and the literary representation of the Holocaust. First, I trace the contributions of five Holocaust survivors as they relate to the theme of language after Auschwitz. In drawing from these considerations, I move the discussion to Young's theory of literary representation. This theory proves commensurate with particular tenets of sociology of literature, particularly those of Bourdieu presented here.

T. W. Adorno and the Barbarism of Poetry

In 1949, in an essay first published in a *Festschrift* for sociologist Leopold von Wiese in 1951, Theodor W. Adorno, himself a philosopher, sociologist and Holocaust survivor, wrote the following:

> Cultural criticism finds itself faced with the final state of the dialectic of culture and barbarism. To write poetry after

> Auschwitz is barbaric. And this corrodes even the knowledge of why it has become impossible to write poetry today.[157]

The scathing contention had rippling effects on both sides of the Atlantic, provoking at once both harmony and discord among intellectuals, poets, and artists of every field. All were concerned about the interpretation of Adorno's dictum. Whether Adorno was referring to poetry only or to all art forms in general was debated intensely. Unfortunately, confusion was most often incited by placing Adorno's dictum out of its original context. This proceeded to draw yet more individuals into the discussion and served only to convolute it further.[158]

At the core of the dictum lies a caustic critique of post-Enlightenment industrialized society.[159] According to Adorno, human beings had been robbed of all true subjectivity over time. Instead, they had been transformed into mere objects (*Verdinglichung*). As a result, the totalitarianism and barbarism of Nazi Germany was inevitable. What remained in the wake of the atrocities of the Nazis was the rubble of society and culture. Devastatingly, art in all forms had fallen victim as well. The questions emerging from the dictum were poignant: Was it not an *affront* to Holocaust victims and survivors to continue employing conventional art forms once used to advance a culture that proceeded to commit unthinkable, unprecedented offenses? Was not the continuation of these forms little else than a tool, distracting humanity from brutality? Did not this brutality completely discredit modern culture? And finally: Must not humanity be demanded to abdicate (and prohibit) all those conventions that comply with a culture that produces murder?

The contentious questions that ensued from the Adorno debate were disconcerting to many. The corollary to Adorno's dictum, the implication that after Auschwitz, silence alone was in order, polarized as well. Upon hearing an echo

---

[157] Theodor W. Adorno, *Prisms*, trans. Samuel and Shierry Weber (London: Neville Spearman, 1967), 34. The German: "Kulturkritik findet sich in der letzten Stufe von Kultur und Barbarei gegenüber: nach Auschwitz ein Gedicht zu schreiben ist barbarisch, und frisst auch die Erkenntnis an, die ausspricht, warum es unmöglich ward, heute ein Gedicht zu schreiben." See Theodor W. Adorno, "Kulturkritik und Gesellschaft," in *Gesammelte Schriften*, Band 10.1: *Kulturkritik und Gesellschaft I. Prismen. Ohne Leitbild* (Frankfurt am Main: Suhrkamp, 1977), 30.

[158] Literature addressing the Adorno debate directly and indirectly is plenteous. For example, see Petra Kiedaisch, ed. *Lyrik nach Auschwitz? Adorno und die Dichter* (Stuttgart: Reclam, 1995); Marc Kleine, *Ob es überhaupt noch möglich ist. Literatur nach Auschwitz in Adornos ästhetischer Theorie* (Bielefeld: Aisthesis, 2012); and Elaine Martin, *Nelly Sachs: The Poetics of Silence and the Limits of Representation* (Berlin: De Gruyter, 2011).

[159] Adorno adapted this thesis from the earlier one addressed in Max Horkheimer and Theodor W. Adorno, "Dialektik von Kultur und Barbarei," in *Dialektik der Aufklärung. Philosophische Fragmente* (Frankfurt am Main: Fischer, 1969).

of Ludwig Wittgenstein's "whereof one cannot speak, thereof one must be silent,"[160] opinions diverged further.

With time, Adorno clarified and modified his dictum.[161] There are several reasons for these adjustments, although they lie outside the scope of this discussion. Important here is that Adorno, although certainly concerned about art and literature, was most deeply concerned with ethics and human (cultural) responsibility in the face of a culture that had had the capacity to generate an Auschwitz. Clearly, though, Adorno was not left unmoved by a number of artistic attempts to address Holocaust atrocities; indeed, he came to re-evaluate the presence of powerful lyric such as Paul Celan's "Todesfuge"[162]— undoubtedly the work that moved him to reconsider and temper his statements.[163] These divergences, a relief to many, were significant and, in some respects, helped to promote new reflections on and approaches to post-Holocaust art and literary forms.[164]

Adorno's dictum remains one the strongest stimuli in the debate involving the use of language surrounding the Holocaust; indeed, no such discussion can

---

[160] Ludwig Wittgenstein, *Tractatus Logico-Philosophicus*, trans. C. K. Ogden, with an introduction by Bertrand Russell (Mineola, NY: Dover Publications, 1998), proposition 7.

[161] Adorno's milder tone with regard to poesy was qualified with a dictum no less scathing: "Perennial suffering has as much right to expression as a tortured man has to scream; hence it may have been wrong to say that after Auschwitz you could no longer write poems. But it is not wrong to raise the less cultural question whether after Auschwitz you can go on living—especially whether one who escaped by accident, one who by rights should have been killed, may go on living." Theodor W. Adorno, *Negative Dialectics*, trans. E. B. Ashton (New York: Continuum, 1973), 362-63. The German: "Das perennierende Leiden hat soviel Recht auf Ausdruck wie der Gemarterte zu brüllen; darum mag falsch gewesen sein, nach Auschwitz ließe sich kein Gedicht mehr schreiben. Nicht falsch aber ist die minder kulturelle Frage, ob nach Auschwitz noch sich leben lasse, ob vollends es dürfe, wer zufällig entrann und rechtens hätte umgebracht werden müssen." Theodor W. Adorno, *Negative Dialektik: Jargon der Eigentlichkeit*, ed. Rolf Tiedemann (Frankfurt: Suhrkamp, 1973), 355.

[162] Paul Celan, *Die Gedichte. Kommentierte Gesamtausgabe in einem Band*, ed. Barbara Wiedemann (Frankfurt am Main: Suhrkamp Taschenbuch, 2012), 40-41.

[163] Adorno: "His poetry is permeated by a sense of shame stemming from the fact that art is unable either to experience or to sublimate suffering. Celan's poems articulate unspeakable horror by being silent, thus turning their truth content into a negative quality." Theodor W. Adorno, *Aesthetic Theory*, ed. Gretel Adorno and Rolf Tiedemann, trans. C. Lenhardt (London: Routledge and Kegan Paul, 1984), 444. The German: "Diese Lyrik ist durchdrungen von der Scham der Kunst angesichts des wie der Erfahrung so der Sublimierung sich entziehenden Leids. Celans Gedichte wollen das äußerste Entsetzen durch Verschweigen sagen. Ihr Wahrheitsgehalt selbst wird ein Negatives." See Theodor W. Adorno, *Ästhetische Theorie* (Frankfurt am Main: Suhrkamp, 1973), 477.

[164] The Adorno debate is ongoing and remains relevant. For example, see Giorgio Agamben, *Was von Auschwitz bleibt: Das Archiv und der Zeuge,* trans. Stefan Monhardt (Frankfurt am Main: Suhrkamp, 2003); and Dieter Lamping, "Nachwort"in *Dein aschenes Haar Sulamith. Dichtung über den Holocaust* (Munich: Piper 1992), 271-89.

circumvent it. However, relevant to this analysis is the sense in which the dictum, in its trajectory, points to further considerations. Not only has it been instrumental in helping to flesh out issues surrounding the literary representation of the Holocaust, it also obliquely directs us to the matter of responding ethically to literary representations of the Holocaust.

George Steiner and the Retreat of the Word

Adorno was not alone in his concerns about the use of language following the Holocaust. Philosopher and literary critic George Steiner, himself having narrowly escaped extermination by the Nazi regime at the onset of World War II, has endeavored in the context of his life's work, to address the meaning of language, literature, and human existence in a world after Auschwitz. Significantly, in his earliest work, Steiner scathingly insists—as does Adorno—that all language following Auschwitz is, of necessity, distorted in its legitimacy, meaning, and meaningfulness. In his 1967 groundbreaking work *Language and Silence: Essays on Language, Literature, and the Inhuman,*[165] Steiner provokes his readership by posing questions and drawing conclusions not dissimilar to Adorno's own. He insists on a direct link between earlier cultural developments and the atrocities committed by the Nazi regime during the war. For Steiner, high culture is not, and will never be, a substitute for a humane humanity. In his preface, he writes:

> My own consciousness is possessed by the eruption of barbarism in modern Europe; by the mass murder of the Jews and by the destruction under Nazism and Stalinism of what I try to define in some of these essays as the particular genius of "Central European Humanism." . . .
>
> The blackness of it did not spring up in the Gobi Desert or the rain forests of the Amazon. It rose from within, and from the core of European civilization. The cry of the murdered sounded in earshot of the universities; the sadism went on a street away from the theaters and museums . . . In our own day the high places of literary, of philosophy, of artistic expression, became the setting for Belsen.[166]

In the preface to the 1969 German edition, Steiner also reflects on the use, misuse, and abuse of language in the context of modern civilization and in the face of the Holocaust:

---

[165] George Steiner, *Language and Silence: Essays on Language, Literature, and the Inhuman* (New York: Atheneum: 1967).
[166] George Steiner, *Language and Silence: Essays on Language, Literature, and the Inhuman,* viii-ix.

> To the extent that language is the true element of human behavior, traces of the extreme crisis of humanity come to expression in it.[167]

Steiner avows the disintegration and demise of language as he traces the "retreat from the word" through the history of literary representation. He concludes that the fall of the meaning and meaningfulness of the spoken and written word found its beginnings in the seventeenth-century—and then moved beyond it.[168] In the three centuries that followed, language's retreat intensified. Finally, under national socialism, the disintegration of language was completed. With this, the Holocaust had not only become possible, but inevitable. Steiner's praise of the contributions of Wittgenstein, Weber and Cage, each of whom had a proclivity for silence, was consistent with his apprehensions concerning both language and society itself.[169] For Steiner, language after Auschwitz had lost all credibility, mutilated by modernity. In accordance with this, Steiner declares Auschwitz itself unspeakable. He writes:

> The world of Auschwitz lies outside speech as it lies outside reason. To speak of the *unspeakable* is to risk the survivance of language as creator and bearer of humane, rational truth. Words that are saturated with lies or atrocity do not easily resume life.[170]

In confronting the claim that the Holocaust lies beyond all description, a post-Auschwitz world must face the piercing question, once again, as to the meaningfulness of attempting to represent a *univers concentrationnaire.*[171]

---

[167] George Steiner, *Sprache und Schweigen. Essays über Sprache, Literatur und das Unmenschliche*, trans. Axel Kaun (Berlin: Suhrkamp Taschenbuch, 2014), 10. I have paraphrased here Kaun's translation.

[168] Steiner, *Sprache und Schweigen*, 56-57.

[169] Verena Lenzen, "'Reden ist schwer, Schweigen unmöglich.'"(Elie Wiesel) Sprache und Schweigen im Schatten der Schoah,"in *Kultur allein ist nicht genug*, ed. Boschki and Mensink, 59.

[170] George Steiner, *Language and Silence: Essays 1958-1966*, 2nd ed. (London: Faber and Faber, 1985; repr., London: Faber and Faber, 1990), 146.

[171] Steiner, as did Adorno, came to soften his position after publishing his first edition of *Language and Silence* in 1967. In his preface to the 1985 edition, he writes: "Poets such as Bobrowski and Celan, writers of prose fiction such as Grass, Ingeborg Bachmann or Thomas Bernhard have restored to German a vital genius of innovation and of truth. They have done so precisely by confronting, either directly or by allegorical implication, the world of the unspeakable. The compulsions of resilience inside a language are stronger that I had realized." See Steiner, *Language and Silence: Essays 1958-1966,* 2nd ed., 15. In 2012, in an interview given to Swiss national television, his tenor was indicative of evolving perspectives on the power and possibilities of language. See SRF

Language and Silence in the Lyric of Paul Celan

As is the case with all forms of Holocaust representation, questions surrounding poetry's potential to convey atrocity differently than other genres are debated. Specifically, critics query as to whether or not verse can grant the reader alternative "access" to the realities of atrocity. At the heart of the debate lies the issue of whether or not Holocaust poetry is able to retrieve language from the depth of its collapse and redeem it from barbarism.

Here, too, opinions vary. In his study of post-Holocaust lyric, Hermann Korte contends that "Holocaust poems" do not exist at all. Poems about the Holocaust are:

> Not like poems of nature, of great cities, of love and of everyday things that exist. And there are no Auschwitz poems, not like there are poems about Rome, Paris, and Berlin. Poems about Rome, Paris, and Berlin are possible because they are, for the most part, based on perspective and experience, subjective impressions and individual experiences. In such literary topography, the standpoint of the subject at least can be more nearly determined. In contrast, the places of the Holocaust withdraw from the poem in a principal way. The lyrical subject reconstructs spaces of experiences and produces pictures and images of the topography of cruelty and death. However, [the subject] is excluded from the experiences themselves.[172]

For Korte, poetry stands diametrically opposed to conveying the realities of Auschwitz. Given that lyric generally makes no claims to historical proof or accuracy, it belongs to a very different genre than, for example, historical accounts, diaries, and memoirs. Poetry cannot be evaluated in the same way as historical chronicling or testimony. Lyric, by nature, retracts from history and transforms all subject matter into the non-historical.[173] Lyrical representation of the Holocaust must of necessity exemplify this reality at an infinitely dark level; it encloses and hides rather than divulges and discloses historical details and

---

Kultur, Sternstunde Philosophie, "George Steiner: Die Schule des Lesens," interview aired on August 19, 2012, posted on the internet on January 3, 2014, video, 56:31, https://youtu.be/ ZByK3cXCAv4. Steiner, however, has never been without his critics. Even those expounding his theses have remained at times skeptical about their far-reaching implications. For example, see Lawrence L. Langer's subtle critique in *The Holocaust and the Literary Imagination* (New Haven, CT: Yale University Press, 1975), 14-19.

172 Hermann Korte, "'Es ist in aller Trauer der Hang zur Sprachlosigkeit.' Der Holocaust in der Lyrik nach 1945," in *Literatur und Holocaust,* ed. Arnold, 25. Translation mine.

173 Korte, "Es ist in aller Trauer der Hang zur Sprachlosigkeit," 25.

ontological realities. These elements are withdrawn into a domain where the reader is given no point of entry, putting them at the mercy of the lyric—not vice versa.

Perhaps no other poetry reflects this tendency more than that of Paul Celan. At the time of his suicide in 1970, Celan was not yet 50 years old. Both the murder of his parents in the Holocaust and the ambiguity of his own survival left the poet incapable of bearing the paradox of existence; all meaning in remaining sane was eclipsed. His death shocked the world, and the silencing of his voice reminded the world that the story of Auschwitz was far from closed.

Celan's verses echo his story of profound human vulnerability. His lyric shatters, moving its readers to depths unfamiliar and full of fear. His voice, prophetic and yet fragmented, dares to expose readers to a world that has been utterly defiled. Because of these dimensions, his work has escaped critics' efforts to dissect and understand; indeed, it flees analysis just as it flees all meaning, keeping both at bay.

It is important for this study to locate Celan in the line of discourse that postulates the gross ambiguity that exists between language and silence. Whereas Adorno and Steiner adopted the critical study of culture and art in voicing their views on the link between the corruption of language and the demise of human civilization, Celan articulated his judgments through verse. His estimation of the collapse of language was made most evident by the ways silence permeated his lyric. Indeed, he established silence as the topography of all his works, and it is exactly this phenomenon that is telling and of interest here.

The reception of Celan's "Todesfuge" in 1952 was marked by both positive critique as well as ridicule and disdain.[174] This divide reflected the inaccessibility and grotesqueness of the images and tropes that Celan implemented in his texts. His "black milk at daybreak" did not resonate with audiences in the ways the poet had intended. Even the most well-meaning critics overlooked the dark history of the work and focused more on its unusual lyrical quality and compelling power. Author and poet Heinz Piontek writes of Celan: "'His lyric is *poésie pure*, magical collage, comparable to Marc Chagall's paintings.'"[175] Such response lay well beyond the poet's intentions. As "Todesfuge" came to embrace iconic status within the growing culture of memory, it eventually led to Celan's dismay.[176]

Although space does not permit a thorough examination of "Todesfuge" and its impact on Holocaust discourse, the stimulus that the poem continues to provide to the debate surrounding language and silence is significant. With a lyric

[174] The reactions to *Todesfuge* by *Die Gruppe 47* in 1952 devastated Celan. Cf. Celan, *Die Gedichte. Kommentierte Gesamtausgabe,* 40-41; and Heinz Ludwig Arnold, *Die Gruppe 47* (Reinbek: Rowohlt, 2004).

[175] Quoted in John Felstiner, *Paul Celan: Poet, Survivor, Jew* (New Haven, CT: Yale University Press, 1995), 71.

[176] Korte, "'Es ist in aller Trauer der Hang zur Sprachlosigkeit,'" 27-28.

that defies all classification, whose starkly fragmented structure, sounds, rhythms, and imagery both devastate and elude, and whose vast and endless grief extends beyond the reaches of human imagination, the poem relays *l'univers concentrationnaire* in such a way as to put to task the meaning of all language following the Holocaust. As such, the work continues to ignite debate about the power and efficacy of language versus silence.

As a whole, Celan's silent landscape of atrocity assists in exposing the complete collapse of language after Auschwitz. This is made most clear by the ways in which he keeps his subjects impermeable to the reader. As he references the lethal realities of the Holocaust, he barricades them, blocking the reader's access to them. His language never does reveal or release the Holocaust to the reader. Instead, it removes it, once again and for all time, from the present moment. In Celan's world, language must be understood as having lost all familiar function, logic, and usefulness, as well as all power to disclose and make known that which is unknown and unknowable. All that is left in the wake of atrocity, then, is the silence that screams its way into the collective memory of humanity.

Tellingly, however, it is in the guise of language that Celan declares just how deeply language has fallen. For Celan, language remains the only medium of expression available. It is a reality that haunts him:

> [Language], in spite of everything, remained available. But it had to find sustenance in its own ability to explain, to go on living through a dreadful imposed silence, survive through a thousand nights of death-dealing speech. It went on living and gave birth to no words to describe what had happened; but it survived these events.[177]

These realizations only served to exacerbate Celan's anguish.

Of interest to this study is the strong dichotomy between the futility of language and the inherent usefulness of language (as a tool) as indicated in Celan's writings. The emotional nexus of questions surrounding literary representation of the Holocaust is intensified. In what sense can language both reveal and hide that which it is trying to convey? Can poetry bring us closer to Holocaust realities in ways that other genres do not? Can the transmission of that "other universe" be made possible, if only in part? Or is the notion of poetry of the Holocaust not barbaric after all? The figure of Paul Celan embodies these questions more than perhaps any other Holocaust poet.

[177] Quoted in Langer, *The Holocaust and the Literary Imagination*, 9. No reference provided.

Primo Levi and the Fragility of Objectivity

As was the case with Paul Celan, Primo Levi's tragic death in 1987 shocked the world. The circumstances surrounding his death remain unclear. Decisive proof of suicide is absent, although there are indications that Levi did take his own life.[178] In the years leading up to his death, Levi suffered repeated bouts of profound depression. Whether his struggle to retain his usual poised equanimity extended back into his story of surviving Auschwitz is a question that remains open.[179]

Levi's best-known work, *If This is a Man*,[180] written in 1946—just a year after he was liberated from Auschwitz—is testament to a journey of determination, survival, and, in spite of the humiliations he had suffered at the hands of the Nazis, dignity. Written with astonishing intellectual objectivity and at times almost scientific detachment, the work offers a detailed account of life in the camps. Levi's efforts to provide analysis of events and situations presented as textual excursions within his exhaustive chronology disclose the author's brilliant propensity for scientific inquiry and an enduring but bitter quest for truth.

Primo Levi spent his life, both during his career as a chemist and then as a full-time writer, attempting to impart the realities of the Holocaust to the world. His relentless drive to chronicle, reflect, and understand, impregnates his work with a tacit sense of longing. Whether expressed through fiction or nonfiction, in verse, lectures, or interviews, Levi's struggle to grasp how the Holocaust happened has remained a significant part of his legacy.

As has been the case with Adorno, Steiner, and Celan, our interest here focuses on the ways in which Levi represents the Holocaust in his writings. For Levi in particular, his factual literary style and systematic approach in relaying "the story" are significant and telling. His attempts to analyze the efficacy of language in portraying atrocity are evidenced in his writing. Convinced that the clearly written and spoken word were in fact necessary in such portrayal, Levi was critical of writers such as Celan, whose cryptic and fragmented style, Levi felt, only served to distort rather than grant clarification. In his essay, "On Obscure Writing," he concludes that, "it is not true that disorder is necessary to depict disorder; it is not true that the chaos of the written page is the best symbol of

---

[178] Rosenfeld, *The End of the Holocaust*, 185ff.

[179] Indications for this can be elicited from correspondence. On March 29th, 1987, Levi wrote to Alvin H. Rosenfeld: "I am suffering now from an episode of depression (not my first one; I suppose they are a heritage from the Lager). I hope you have never experienced such an alteration of the soul . . . Naturally I am under medical care, but I cannot tell how long it will last." Levi killed himself on April 11th, 1987. See Rosenfeld, *The End of the Holocaust*, 208.

[180] Primo Levi, *If This is a Man* and *The Truce*, trans. Stuart Woolf (London: Abacus, 1987).

the ultimate chaos to which we are fated."[181] More elaborately, in "Ex-Chemist," he contends:

> Writing is a way of "producing", indeed a process of transformation: the writer transforms his experiences into a form that is accessible and attractive to the "customer" who will be the reader. . . . Now, the things I have seen, experienced, and done during my preceding incarnation (as a chemist) are today for me as writer a precious source of raw materials, of events to narrate and not only events: also of those fundamental emotions which are one's way of measuring oneself against matter.[182]

Still, Levi struggled in knowing that words themselves remained insufficient to tell tales that are never believed. In *If This is a* Man, he writes:

> Just as our hunger is not that feeling of missing a meal, so our way of being cold has need of a new word. We say 'hunger,' we say 'tiredness,' 'fear,' 'pain,' we say 'winter' and they are different things. They are free words, created and used by free men who lived in comfort and suffering in their own homes. If the Lagers had lasted longer a new, harsh language would have been born; and only this language could express what it means to toil the whole day in the wind, with temperatures below freezing, wearing only a shirt, underpants, cloth jacket and trousers, and in one's body nothing but weakness, hunger and knowledge of the end drawing nearer.[183]

Finally, in his last work, *The Drowned and the Saved*, Levi cites the words of an SS officer from Simon Wiesenthal's novel *Murder Among Us:*

> However this war may end, we have won the war against you; none of you will be left to bear witness, but even if someone were to survive, the world will not believe him. There will be perhaps suspicions, discussions, research by historians, but there will be no certainties, because we will destroy the evidence together with you. And even if some proof should remain and some of you survive, people will say that the events you describe are too monstrous to be believed: they will say

[181] Quoted in Ruth Franklin, *A Thousand Darknesses: Lies and Truth in Holocaust Fiction* (Oxford: Oxford University Press, 2011), 47. No reference provided.
[182] Quoted in Franklin, *A Thousand Darknesses,* 49. No reference provided.
[183] Levi, *If This is a Man* and *The Truce*, 129.

> that they are the exaggerations of Allied propaganda and will believe us, who will deny everything, and not you. We will be the ones to dictate the history of the Lagers.[184]

Levi's inclusion of this passage in his own volume is telling. He revealingly responds: "[B]oth parties, victims and oppressors, had a keen awareness of the enormity and therefore the non-credibility of what took place in the Lagers."[185] Wiesenthal's words ring true.

For Levi, the futility of speaking to a world that would never really comprehend was something that dismayed him, particularly in his later years. Levi's observations of ambivalence among the Germans in their post-war efforts to come to terms with their crimes only intensified his sense of resignation, just as the attempts made by revisionist historians to rewrite the Holocaust distressed him.[186] With time, Levi began to doubt even his own efforts at giving testimony: "Have we—we who have returned—been able to understand and make others understand our experience?"[187] No, in spite of the power of language, language would never prove to be enough.

These observations demonstrate a clandestine but real dichotomy in Levi's life and work. This dichotomy is most apparent in Levi's realization that Auschwitz would always remain beyond the grasp of non-survivors, even if he were to strain, his entire life, to convey what had happened there. Levi came to realize that language, even in the context of its strength to communicate, scrutinize, and analyze events past, ultimately cowers, revealing instead its utter incapacity to make comprehensible the realities of the Holocaust to the world.

This partition between giving testimony and the sense of personal powerlessness indicates the profound paradox Levi experienced in survival. His writings express this paradox as they relate, in no uncertain terms, the absurdity of living a life of relative normalcy after having survived atrocity. Rosenfeld suggests that, in the end, Levi's eloquence and virtuosity, his mastery of the word, did not give him the objective stance on survival that he had hoped for, but instead only served to exacerbate his despair.[188] In one of his most poignant texts, Levi describes the lethal power of memory to dominate and dictate the survivor's life. His words echo the reality of many survivors:

> I am sitting at a table with my family, or with friends, or at work, or in the green countryside; in short, in a peaceful and relaxed environment, apparently without tension or affliction;

---

[184] Levi, *The Drowned and the Saved*, trans. Raymond Rosenthal (New York: Summit Books, 1988), 11-12.
[185] Levi, *The Drowned and the Saved*, 12.
[186] Rosenfeld, *The End of the Holocaust*, 198-99.
[187] Levi, *The Drowned and the Saved*, 36.
[188] Cf. Rosenfeld, *The End of the Holocaust*, 203.

> yet I feel a deep and subtle anguish, the definite sensation of an impending threat. And in fact, as the dream proceeds, slowly or brutally, each time in a different way, everything collapses and disintegrates around me, the scenery, the walls, the people, while the anguish becomes more intense and more precise. Now everything has changed to chaos; I am alone in the center of a grey and turbid nothing, and now, I *know* what this thing means, and I also know that I have always known it; I am in the Lager once more, and nothing is true outside the Lager. All the rest was a brief pause, a deception of the senses, a dream; my family, nature in flower, my home. Now this inner dream, this dream of peace, is over, and in the outer dream, which continues, gelid, a well-known voice resounds: a single word, not imperious, but brief and subdued. It is the dawn command of Auschwitz, a foreign word, feared and expected: get up, '*Wstawàch*'.[189]

Jean Améry: Language, Rage, and the Limits of Mind

In the wake of the Holocaust, human wisdom has at times taken on unfamiliar, even shocking, forms. Wisdom, we have learned, need not be the product of placid equanimity, but can consist instead of courage, anger, resistance, rebellion, and revolt; in other words, of absolute clarity. Acceptable and conventional forms of wisdom are replaced by provocative words that strongly reflect the events and experiences from which they are drawn. Here, ensuing from the trauma of atrocity, wisdom finds expression in the language of distress and anguish. Such unconventional wisdom, hardly sympathetic to all, constitutes the radical testimony that the Holocaust survivor and intellectual Jean Améry has left us.

The writings of Améry bring our consideration of language and Holocaust representation to an entirely different level; indeed, the constellations of what one might call Améry's "wisdom of rage," imbued with the psychological residue of torture, compel us to consider literary forms that can be painful to read. In contrast to Adorno and Steiner, both (among other things) literary critics, Améry, with his central work *At the Mind's Limits: Contemplations by a Survivor on Auschwitz and its Realities*,[190] removes all purely abstract reference to and analysis of atrocity. Instead, he remains obsessed with one concrete, corporeal

---

[189] Levi, *If this is a Man* and *The Truce*, 379-80.

[190] Originally published in German as Jean Améry, *Jenseits von Schuld und Sühne. Bewältigungsversuche eines Überwältigten* (Munich: Szczesny Klett-Cotta, 1966); the volume appeared in English translation in 1980 as Jean Améry, *At the Mind's Limits: Contemplations by a Survivor on Auschwitz and its Realities,* trans. Sidney Rosenfeld and Stella P. Rosenfeld (Bloomington: Indiana University Press, 1980).

theme: victimization. Améry's shocking treatment of this theme is the focus of this next section.

Améry's essay "Torture," which provides an account of the author's detainment and torture at the hands of the Gestapo in July of 1943, builds the epicenter of this slim volume.[191] His account refuses to spare the reader any injury of mind; it renders explicitly the trauma that constituted for him a fundamental breach of trust not only with humanity, but also with life itself. The grief incurred by this loss, clothed in the language of rage, revolt, and scathing admonition to the German people, infiltrates his text, allowing for its vigilance, urgency, and prophetic clarity.

The five essays that form *At the Mind's Limits* are organized thematically, with each chapter building upon the theme of victimization. Each merges seamlessly into the chapters that follow. Améry's conclusions are severe; there is no "banality" in the evil he and millions of others had experienced, and certainly no evil in a universal sense—only evil in the purest, most concrete, and radical forms. No amount of abstract speculation in "working through" the past, no *Vergangenheitsbewältigung*, can be effective; indeed, there will be no forgiveness and reparation for such crimes, no "laying aside" of Auschwitz. No one is exonerated; the entire nation of Germany, in both its active and passive cooperation with national socialism, carries a collective guilt.[192] For Améry, the only possibility remaining for Germany and all Germans, is, under the supervision of the Jewish people, to remorsefully embrace their guilt, and to ensure that such atrocity not be repeated.[193]

A critical approach to Améry's text must seriously consider the work's dark content. Despite the evocative quality of his explicit, confrontational literary style, Améry insists, akin to Adorno, Steiner, Celan, and Levi, that it is impossible for language to convey the actual pain of torture. He states this openly in the context of the torture scene itself:

> It would be totally senseless to try and describe here the pain that was inflicted on me. Was it "like a red-hot iron in my shoulders," and was another "like a dull wooden stake that had been driven into the back of my head"? One comparison would only stand for another, and in the end we would be hoaxed by turning on the hopeless merry-go-round of figurative speech. The pain was what it was. Beyond that there is nothing to say. Qualities of feelings are as incomparable as they are indescribable. They mark the limit of the capacity of language to

[191] See Améry, "Torture," in *At the Mind's Limits*, 21-40.

[192] Améry, *At the Mind's Limits*, 65, 72-73.

[193] Améry's insistence on this necessity, however, was met with his own extreme pessimism; he doubted whether the scenario would ever become reality. See Améry, *At the Mind's Limits*, 78ff.

> communicate. If someone wanted to impart his physical pain, he would be forced to inflict it and thereby become a torturer himself.[194]

With this assertion of the incommunicability of pain, Améry underscores that the "limits of mind" (and with them, the limits of the body, which is to say, the actual physical experience of torture and atrocity) lie well beyond the limits of language. In this sense, the pain, by remaining "what it was," dwells on within the survivor and is limited to the survivor. The isolation ensuing from his conclusions was something that, with time, became intolerable for Améry.[195]

In a way similar to that of Primo Levi, Améry, though laying claim to the incapacity of language to mediate or even describe Holocaust events, chooses the medium of language in his attempt to convey to the world what took place. Strikingly, the book's overall purpose and radical admonitions render his language an unquestionable ethical dimension.

Most critics concur in their analysis of Améry's use of language as being radical. Sylvia Weiler argues that Améry's language is an inextricable part of his ethic, intending to both "touch the reader" and to "mediate [their] perception."[196] It exudes an "almost bodily presence" indicative of both the depth of his trauma and his convictions.[197] Therefore, the body can be considered a *Denkbild* (thought-picture) within Améry's text, one that serves to mediate his story.[198] Sven Kramer extends this claim by suggesting an interdependence of feelings and language in Améry's writing so strong that it renders the words capable of actually mediating the feelings. These words, Kramer explains, function as "translations" of feelings that are capable of evoking similar feelings within the reader. According to Kramer, the contention that such expression of pain is only metaphorical has gone too far, as has Amery's own insistence on the incommunicability of his experiences.[199]

Kramer's claims are extreme. However, Améry's explicit and unfiltered use of graphic language, together with the images this provides, does afford us a form of literary representation that demands attention. Améry's text, although unable to mediate the actual pain of the torture (i.e., it is unable to replicate it), is able to provoke feelings of horror in the reader. Here, one might argue that this kind of communication holds metaphorical power, meaning that images are

---

[194] Améry, *At the Mind's Limits,* 33.

[195] Cf. Amery's essay, "How Much Home Does a Person Need?" in *At the Mind's Limits*, 41-61.

[196] Sylvia Weiler, *Jean Amérys Ethik der Erinnerung. Der Körper als Medium in die Welt nach Auschwitz* (Göttingen: Wallstein Verlag, 2012), 315.

[197] Weiler, *Jean Amérys,* 315.

[198] Weiler, *Jean Amérys,* 316.

[199] Sven Kramer, *Die Folter in der Literatur. Ihre Darstellung in der deutschsprachigen Erzählprosa von 1740 bis 'nach Auschwitz'* (Munich: Wilhelm Fink Verlag, 2004), 453ff.

provided that remind the reader of other, albeit very different, types of pain. It is in this context only that one might assert that these images, in *pointing to* the author's pain, are evocative, and that language, although incapable of mediating and reproducing actual pain, *does retain some form of emotionally evocative power as it reminds the reader of their own pain*. However, what must be excluded here is the possibility that the reader is rendered capable of actually *understanding* the author's pain. Améry's insistence that the abyss that exists between his experiences and the perceptions of the reader is one that cannot be crossed is, in my opinion, accurate; indeed, no empathy—and certainly no pain—is capable of being evoked through Améry's words, for there are no words commensurate with the experiences he describes.

It was Améry's sense of the powerlessness of language that left him and survivors like him in states of profound loneliness. Ironically, Améry's strength of expression, his open rebellion, and his prophetic clarity continue to leave his readers not only shaken but also disturbed. This phenomenon is telling.

In the decade that followed the publication of *At the Mind's Limits*, Améry came to sense, for complex reasons, that his admonitions were no longer being heard.[200] Disillusioned by the Germans' growing desire to put the past behind them and mark the end of *Vergangenheitsbewältigung*, Améry committed suicide in 1978, just one year after the reissue of *At the Mind's Limits*. With his death, the world lost one who had dared to walk the dangerous tightrope between wisdom and despair.

The Literary Representation of the Holocaust

Literary Representation and the Agency of Metaphor

The parameters of the larger debate surrounding the possibility of a "genre" of Holocaust literature are, in some sense, peripheral to this discussion.[201]

[200] Rosenfeld, *The End of the Holocaust*, 180ff.

[201] Wiesel too joined this debate. In an early text, he writes: "One generation later, it can still be said and must now be affirmed: There is no such thing as Holocaust literature, nor can there be. The very expression is a contradiction in terms. Auschwitz negates any form of literature, as it defies all systems, all doctrines. . . . A novel about Auschwitz is not a novel, or else it is not about Auschwitz. The very attempt to write such a novel is blasphemous." See Elie Wiesel, "For Some Measure of Humanity," *Sh'ma* 5/100 (October 31, 1975), 314. Rosenfeld also addresses these questions. He maintains that literature of the Holocaust is more than topical, more than mere fiction and more than a reflection of the zeitgeist of one particular culture and epoch. Instead, it engenders a break with literature as we know it, and inhabits its own universe. It embraces dimensions diametrically opposed to those of all literary forms with which we are familiar. As such, literary testimony draws from experiences that lie beyond any human grasp of them. Rosenfeld writes: "[H]olocaust literature is a striving to express a new order of

Significant, however, is how a mounting body of literature, in forcing the debate of testimony and witness upon us, serves to clarify the central role and function of Holocaust testimony. In their proximity to events, the writings of both victims and survivors are vital to our understanding of the extent of the collapse of language and— most of all—of the *Zivilisationsbruch* that has taken place. It is within this context that testimony takes on strong ethical dimensions.

Understanding the nature of testimony is pivotal to this study. In positing testimonial literature as both the indispensable core of, and reference point for, that larger literary body that has, rightly or wrongly, become known as Holocaust literature, we are at liberty to explore the ways in which testimonial literature embraces language in its attempt to communicate the incommunicable.

This study embraces an understanding of the nature of testimony as a kind of truth-telling that extends beyond historical chronicling. Importantly here, the nature and the purpose of testimony are linked. Testimony moves beyond providing raw historical data as historical "proof" of events, constituting instead a search for truths that lie within and beyond history. Because of this, testimony can be understood as an attempt to mediate both truth and meaning.

Of interest to this study are the ways in which the nature and purpose of literary testimony are related to the narration process. An exploration of this process is the focus of the following sections.

Memory, Imagination, and Language

James E. Young's 1988 publication, *Writing and Rewriting the Holocaust: Narrative and the Consequences of Interpretation*,[202] broke new ground in Holocaust theory. The volume serves as a poststructuralist study of the nature and function of literary testimony (referred to by Young as testimonial narrative). It focuses on the process of narrative formation in particular. Young, relying on concepts developed in Hayden White's *Metahistory*,[203] presents an articulate,

---

consciousness, a recognizable shift in being. The human imagination after Auschwitz is simply not the same as it was before. Put another way, the addition to our vocabulary of the very word Auschwitz means that today we *know* things that before could not even be imagined. . . . Stunned by the awesomeness and pressure of event, the imagination comes to one of its periodic endings; undoubtedly, it also stands at the threshold of new and more difficult beginnings. Holocaust literature, situated at this point of the threshold, is a chronicle of the human spirit's most turbulent strivings with an immense historical and metaphysical weight." See Alvin H. Rosenfeld, "The Problematics of Holocaust Literature" in *Confronting the Holocaust: The Impact of Elie Wiesel*, ed. Rosenfeld and Greenberg, 2.

[202] James E. Young, *Writing and Rewriting the Holocaust: Narrative and the Consequences of Interpretation* (Bloomington: Indiana University Press, 1988).

[203] Hayden White, *Metahistory: The Historical Imagination in Nineteenth Century* Europe, 40th ann. ed. (Baltimore, MD, MA: Johns Hopkins University Press, 2014).

exhaustive, and, in my opinion, a reasonable understanding of narrative and the narration process that subsequent theorists have found difficult to circumvent. This study applies Young's theory of literary representation to testimonial narratives.[204] The following sections and subsections outline the relevant features of this theory.

Young contends that no given narrative can ever function as an objective, uninterpreted account of past events. Narration is a process that always entails interpretation. In the same way that memory, in its embrace of language, is constantly impacted by a plethora of determining factors, so too does the narration of memory constitute an interpretive act. Young claims that narration always entails an interpretation of events; indeed, is itself an interpretive event.[205] Young's theory hinges entirely upon this central claim.

The theory is underscored by specific pre-understandings of the nature of testimonial narrative, and of memory and language. For Young, testimonial narrative provides very different kinds of knowledge than those offered by historical chronicling.[206] Notably, the knowledge supplied by testimony is linked to the very process by which it is generated, one where both memory and language play prominent roles. It is in this larger context that narrative is understood as possessing an interpretive dimension. Without undermining the historical dimension present in testimonial literature,[207] Young seeks to establish the ways in which testimonial narratives represent events through language.[208]

The theory merits closer evaluation. For Young, memory, in seeking to convey events of atrocity, is continually being determined by influences

[204] Young does offer applications of his theory to other forms of Holocaust literature such as the controversial contributions of Sylvia Plath or the memoirs of WWI soldiers. See Young, *Writing and Rewriting the Holocaust*, 117-133, 134-146.
[205] See Young, *Writing and Rewriting the Holocaust*, 5.
[206] Young compares the "truth" of Holocaust narratives with that of other religious texts. He writes of them: "The 'truth of everything' here includes something more than previously authoritative facts that happen to contradict one another." Young, *Writing and Rewriting the Holocaust*, 2. With relation to Holocaust narratives, he emphasizes their interpretive nature and ethical implications: "For the significance and meaning of events created in [Holocaust] texts often reflect the kind of understanding of events by victims at the time; and as these 'mere' interpretations led to their responses, the interpreted versions of the Holocaust now lead us to our actions in the world in light of the Holocaust. That is, by sustaining the notion of these interpretations' agency in events, the contemporary critic can assert both the historicity of events and the crucial role interpretation played in the events themselves." Young, *Writing and Rewriting the Holocaust*, 3.
[207] To reiterate: "[T]he contemporary critic can assert both the historicity of events and the crucial role of interpretation played in the events themselves." Young, *Writing and Rewriting the Holocaust*, 3:
[208] Young writes that "only in their narrative and cultural reconstructions, the interrelated problems of literary and historical interpretation might now be seen as conjoining in the study of '*literary historiography*.'" Young, *Writing and Rewriting the Holocaust*, 1. Emphasis mine.

extending beyond the experience of those events alone. As such, memory can be understood as a reconstruction of past events within a larger sphere of cultural, ideological, philosophical, and religious influences. Taken as a whole, these influences provide an interpretational framework for memory. The process of remembering thereby functions as an interpretive act, constitutive of a complex intersection of events, narration, and interpretation.

Memory, in reconstructing events of atrocity, is also impacted by the trauma of atrocity. Although Young circumvents any detailed discussion of trauma theory, he implies that trauma can have a debilitating effect on memory. In this sense, both the trauma experienced and pre-existing determinants can be understood as the most important factors at work in memory's representation of events.[209]

Young also considers the role of the *imagination* as constitutive of the interpretive functioning of memory. Imagination plays the important role of facilitating the narration process in as much as it, under the impact of both events and past influences, directs and guides memory. In essence, the events that have impacted memory have also impacted the imaginative capacity to refigure, recast, and reconstruct events. As such, imagination assists in both the act of remembering and in the narration of memory.[210]

For Young, language, too, is bound to memory. As such, it proves indispensable to the process of remembering, selecting, and understanding past events. It is here that the process of narration becomes clearer.

Event, Narration, and Interpretation

According to Young, the narration of past events constitutes a complex interplay of memory, imagination, and language. By lending expression to memory, narration is impacted by those pre-existing (or "pre-event") influences that guide the imaginative process. This process never takes place in a vacuum, as it reconstructs remembered events through language, interprets them, and places them within the context of their interpretive framework. Put differently; narration can be understood as an act of interpretation in which events are

---

[209] In stressing the impact of trauma on memory, however, Young also maintains that experiences of the Holocaust can then proceed to figure other experiences. The function of memory thus expresses itself as complex and multifaceted. See Young, *Writing and Rewriting the Holocaust*, 126. In general, Young's overall avoidance of the word "trauma"—he appears to replace it with the word "event"—is undoubtedly intentional: his central concern surrounds literary testimony and narration and its interpretive dimension. However, in taking to task the writings of the controversial Sylvia Plath, he does address the theme of pain, referencing the therapeutic work of Doris Laub and the crises of Holocaust survivors such as Levi and Celan. See Young, "The Holocaust Confessions of Sylvia Plath," chap. 7 in *Writing and Rewriting the Holocaust*.

[210] See Young, *Writing and Rewriting the Holocaust*, 5-11.

represented through language, forms, and concepts drawn from that interpretive framework. Within this context, we discover *that there are no representations of past events that are not already an interpretation.*

With the passing of time, past events will come to be known only in terms of the ways in which they have been represented.[211]

The interplay of events, narration, and interpretation can be thus understood as a process in which narration, itself an interpretive act of memory, figures past events, and thus figures the ways in which they will be both remembered and interpreted. Very succinctly, one might sketch the process in the following way (see figure 1):

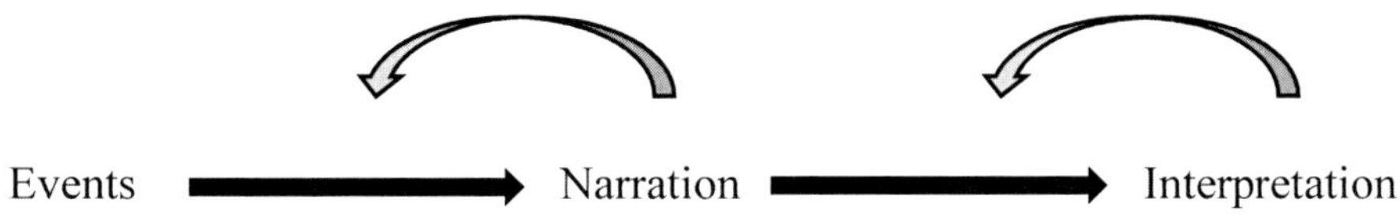

Figure 1 — Narration Dynamic

Here, narration as an interpretive act stands between events and their final interpretation by determining how events are represented. Historical events will always be interpreted by continually referring back to the ways in which events are represented or figured in narrative. Accordingly, narration can be understood as mediating between the memory of events and their later, external interpretations, impacting both as an unfolding act of interpreting and representing.[212]

Implicit in this process is how the interpreted event has already been interpreted *once* in the actual experience of the event itself. Indeed, nothing can be experienced without being understood in the context of past experiences that exist

---

[211] "What is remembered of the Holocaust depends on how it is remembered, and how events are remembered depends in turn on the texts now giving them form." See Young, *Writing and Rewriting the Holocaust*, 1.

[212] Young writes: "For both events and their representations are ultimately beholden to the forms, language, and critical methodology through which they are grasped. Religious meaning and significance, historical causes and effects, are simultaneously reflected and generated in Holocaust narratives. . . . What is remembered of the Holocaust depends on how it is remembered, and how events are remembered depends in turn on the texts now giving them form." See Young, See Young, *Writing and Rewriting the Holocaust*, 1. Indeed, this statement constitutes the entire thrust of Young's investigation. In concluding his study, Young also suggests that knowledge gained by texts assists posterity in guiding its future: "This is to suggest that by remaining aware of both the ideational character of interpretation and the potential in this knowledge for its utility as agency in the world, writers and critics of Holocaust texts remain able to produce further knowledge of the Holocaust, even as they regulate the practical consequences of this knowledge." Young, *Writing and Rewriting the Holocaust*, 191.

within the larger interpretive framework of abiding influences of culture, tradition, language, religion, etc. As such, later interpretations of events are also made in terms of how they were interpreted at the time they were experienced.[213] In the case of those Holocaust survivors whose stories are narrated years after events have transpired, experiences made in the time that has lapsed will also affect the language, content, and shape of testimony. With this, we can observe how the sum total of experiences comes to impact the process of narration. Ultimately, this will have an impact on the form that collective memory assumes.[214]
One can now extend the sketch in the following way (see figure 2):

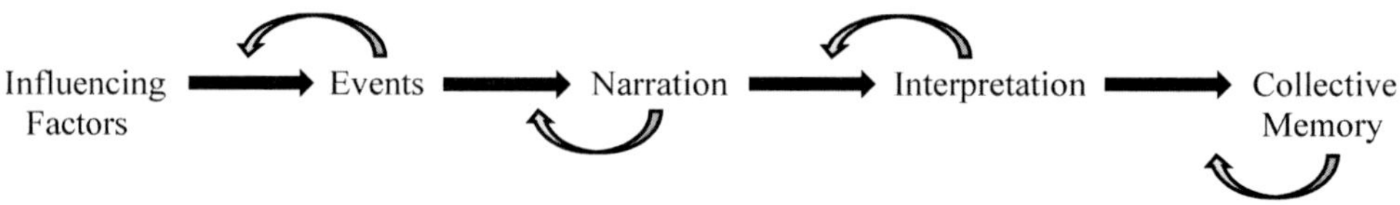

Figure 2 — Extension of Narration Dynamic

[213] Young: "This is to suggest that the events of the Holocaust are not only shaped *post factum* in their narration, but that they were initially determined as they unfolded by the schematic ways in which they were apprehended, expressed, and then acted upon." Young, *Writing and Rewriting the Holocaust*, 5.

[214] The theme of collective memory, although implicit throughout his text, is not more thoroughly addressed by Young. Instead, in this one volume at least, he appears to employ the notion of "knowledge of the Holocaust." This knowledge has, for him, practical implications. See his conclusion, pages 190-192. My extension of Young's theory is that "knowledge of the Holocaust" must always and only be ethical knowledge and/or awareness. The notion of "collective memory"was first formulated by French sociologist Maurice Halbwachs in the 1920s and 1930s, in particular with his *Les cadres sociaux de la mémoire* (1925) and his *La mémoire collective*, first published posthumously in 1950. See Maurice Halbwachs, *La mémoire collective* (Paris: Presses universitaires de France, 1950); and *On Collective Memory*, trans. Lewis A. Coser (Chicago: University of Chicago Press, 1992). In general, Halbwachs was concerned about the memory of groups (a kind of "social remembering") beyond those of individuals per se. With this, he moved beyond theories offered by Bergman, Nietzsche, and Freud (among others), drawing from perceived connections between the areas of historiography, political theory, sociology, art theory and history. In this sense, collective memory was a "social and collective phenomenon." See Nicolas Pethes, *Kulturwissentschaftliche Gedächtnistheorien. Zur Einführung*, 2nd ed. (Hamburg: Junius Verlag, 2013), 51. Translation mine. As stated, Aleida Assmann's and Jan Assmann's theories of cultural, collective, and communicative memory are among those most referenced in memory studies; their list of publications is long. However, the notion of collective memory has often been implemented quite generally in referencing the memory of humanity as a whole. It is this broader sense of the notion that I employ in this study.

Past influences can thus be understood to impact both the experience of the event and the narration of the events in question. The process of narration then impacts the ways in which events are interpreted and, subsequently, remembered at the level of collective memory. Here, we begin to sense how factors other than the events themselves can lend form to the ways in which events are remembered by those far distant from them.

With this, Young concludes that the literary representation of the historical events of the Holocaust will always have a direct impact on the ways in which posterity remembers those events.[215] One could also say that the story comes to be understood in terms of the way it has been told. In Young's own words: "[To] know what happened in how it is represented."[216] Importantly, Post-Holocaust generations have come to know, understand, and thus interpret Holocaust events under the guidance of their myriad representations. The knowledge elicited by these representations will come to demand dynamic response.[217]

Metaphor and Archetype

Central to Young's study is a pragmatic understanding of how language employs metaphors, that is, of how language functions in terms of employing metaphor at the most basic, everyday level. Metaphors, he emphasizes, are embraced by the whole of language in so far as they form the very basis of human communication; as such, they are necessary for anything to be communicated at all.[218]

Young links language's basic use of metaphor in general to narrative testimony in particular. While affirming that metaphors will, "never be able to present the tremendum, the caesura, the traumatic breach we infer in the events of the Holocaust,"[219] he contends that no narration of Holocaust events is ever undertaken without the use of metaphor. In being constitutive of the basic unfolding of narrative, metaphors are involved in relating events of the Holocaust even in

---

[215] Young describes the nature of all historical writing as interpretive. In the process of narrating history, the basic principles guiding narration in general are also at play. With this, Young continues to draw from the not uncontroversial theses of Hayden White in his *Metahistory*.

[216] Young, *Writing and Rewriting the Holocaust*, 5.

[217] Young does explore the differentiated nature of the response elicited by Holocaust representations. However, he maintains that responses made to the Holocaust, while being impacted by testimony and other forms of Holocaust literature, are also made in the context of a plethora of other factors at work in society and culture. For this reason, as well, responses to the Holocaust diverge, ranging from ones embracing moral and civil responsibility, to those that have furthered Holocaust denial and antisemitism.

[218] Cf. Young, *Writing and Rewriting the Holocaust*, 84. Young appears to be puzzled by the refusal of particular scholars to accept an "everyday use"of metaphors in understanding Holocaust testimony. See 89–92.

[219] Young, *Writing and Rewriting the Holocaust*, 97.

their inability to reify, replicate, or mediate Holocaust events. Indeed, they still play a central role in a survivor's narration of them.

A specific pre-understanding of metaphor, its formation, and its role in literary representation underlies Young's claims. He understands metaphors as drawing from and relying intrinsically upon the cultural factors that impact the process of narrative formation. In essence, metaphors are formed in the depths of human experience and in the context of past events and influences. These same events and influences will later come to impact future interpretations of past events. In the context of this study, they can thus be understood as a constitutive part of the process of narration involved in producing testimonial literature.

In general, metaphors always reflect the images, themes, tropes, myths, legends, and overarching archetypes that a culture has produced over time. The meanings and associations linked to metaphors will become crucial in terms of how new events are interpreted and understood in the future. Metaphors assist in relating us to the events and objects they reference as we recall—consciously or unconsciously—those meanings and associations linked to them, both past and present.

In the process of interpretation, metaphors thus play a significant role. First of all, they directly impact the way an event is experienced and interpreted at the time of its unfolding. Secondly, and drawing from those first interpretations, metaphors come to impact the ways in which events are remembered and interpreted during the actual process of narration. Finally, as we have seen, the literary representations that accrue during the narration process come to impact collective memory.[220]

Young implies here that memory, narration, and interpretation are not impacted by past influences and their metaphors alone, but also by particular events as they unfold—with respect to this discussion then, the events of the Holocaust. As such, the tropes, myths, archetypes, and other cultural narratives embodied in metaphors are not left unaffected by events; events, too, impact the metaphors that then give shape to memory, narration, and interpretation. We can understand this in the following diagram that serves to complement and extend the other two (see figure 3):

[220] Young writes: "Indeed, to leave Auschwitz outside of metaphor would be to leave it outside of language altogether: it was known, understood, and responded to metaphorically at the time by its victims; it has been organized, expressed, and interpreted metaphorically by its writers; and it is now being remembered, commented upon, and given historical meaning by scholars and poets of the next generation." Young, *Writing and Rewriting the Holocaust*, 91.

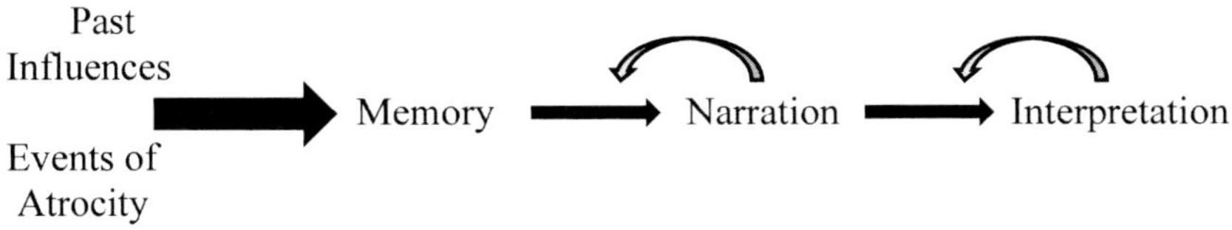

Figure 3 — The Impact of Past Influences and Atrocity on Narration

As an example of the function of metaphor in Holocaust representation and interpretation, Young references perhaps the most poignant example of all, the naming of the Holocaust. He isolates here the notion of *churban*.[221] *Churban* references the Holocaust not as an unprecedented event, but as one in a continuum of events where God has intercepted history in punitive acts that seek to draw his people back from sin to himself. In this respect, Young argues that *churban* functions as a metaphor, and in so doing has come to function as a paradigmatic framework for understanding the Holocaust. By embracing a deeply religious story, it has shaped how particular communities have responded to the Holocaust.[222]

The notion of archetype is also central to Young's theses. Here, "archetype" refers to those conscious and unconscious paradigms that act as the foundation of the cultural images, myths, and tropes involved in the formation of metaphors—metaphors that will later direct how events are remembered and interpreted.[223] Interestingly, Young is concerned not only with the ways in which such paradigms have come to impact interpretations of Holocaust events, but also with how the Holocaust, through the influence of archetypes, has *itself* become an archetype. Here, Young cites the example of the "Holocaust Jew." The expression has come to represent "the embattled victim, the sufferer and martyr" in general.[224] With this reapplication, the expression has been interpreted in ways that extend the original archetype. Here, we see how archetypes, in the context of atrocity in particular, can eventually facilitate in positing new interpretations and, ultimately, new applications and responses. Young concludes that this trend towards metaphor:

> is inevitable, for as new experiences are necessarily grasped and represented in the frame of remembered past experiences,

[221] Young, *Writing and Rewriting the Holocaust*, 85-86.
[222] See Young, *Writing and Rewriting the Holocaust*, 85ff.
[223] See Young, *Writing and Rewriting the Holocaust*, 95ff.
[224] Young, 99. Young points to the ways in which the Holocaust has become an at times universal archetype for human suffering in general. In this context, he writes, "the Holocaust might be said to have become 'its own archetype.'" Young, *Writing and Rewriting the Holocaust*, 100.

> "incomparable" experiences like the Holocaust will always be made—at least rhetorically—comparable. . . . [I]t is also a reflexive literary operation for knowing or representing anything at all . . .[225]

Undoubtedly, the inevitability of the extension and reapplication of Holocaust interpretations to contexts beyond the Holocaust have made testimony all the more vulnerable to the many misunderstandings which it has met.

The Strengths and Limits of Metaphor

As we have seen, metaphors—though innately powerful—remain incapable of replicating, mediating, or reifying both Holocaust events and survivors' experiences of those events. As such, metaphors do break with the past. It is exactly here, that language has collapsed. It follows that, in having no ontological access to the Holocaust, we can now have no "true knowledge" of it.[226] This fact impresses upon us the inherent limits of metaphor. The powerlessness felt by survivors such as Adorno, Steiner, Celan, Levi, Améry, and Wiesel, is certainly indicative of language's grave deficiencies, however descriptive language might be.

Evident here is the potential for literary testimonies to actually misrepresent events by eclipsing the events they attempt to convey. Worse still, testimony can actually serve to displace the Holocaust in ways that can prove detrimental to collective memory.[227] Wiesel maintains that words, "destroy what they aim to describe, they alter what they try to emphasize. By enveloping the truth, they end up taking its place."[228] Young reinforces this sentiment when he states, "[survivors] suspect that if events are perceived after the fact as coming to exist only in their literary testimony, then their experiences might also be perceived as having never existed outside of their narrative."[229] Concerning, indeed, are how the limits of metaphor endanger the life of testimony by holding the potential to give inadequate and even detrimental shape to future understandings of events. In this context, it is striking that stories of the Holocaust have been told and continue to be told at all.

---

[225] Young, *Writing and Rewriting the Holocaust*, 99.

[226] Young's observations regarding the criticisms of metaphor indirectly underscore his own theory of the efficacy of metaphor. He writes: "The dilemma implicit in these objections to metaphor stems from the writers' dual recognition of their unavoidable dependence on the metaphorical qualities of language to transmit facts to the reader and of the qualities in metaphor by which readers are transported away from these facts to something else." Young, *Writing and Rewriting the Holocaust*, 91.

[227] Young, *Writing and Rewriting the Holocaust*, 22-25.

[228] Elie Wiesel, *A Beggar in Jerusalem* (New York: Random House, 1970), 135. Quoted in Young, *Writing and Rewriting the Holocaust*, 22.

[229] Young, *Writing and Rewriting the Holocaust*, 23.

What remains clear in any case is that "knowledge of the Holocaust" must be something very different than often assumed, and that metaphors, although limiting, play a necessary role in the formation of this "knowledge." As stated in connection with Améry, metaphors in Holocaust testimony present us with images that affect us, and that can remind us of experiences we ourselves have made, or of others with which we can identify. In this sense, metaphors ensure that we can relate to Holocaust literature at all; indeed, they ensure that literary representations of the Holocaust are not void of meaning for us altogether.

Thus, the claim can be made that the highly-criticized metaphor has assisted in the Holocaust being spoken about at all. One might even go on to say that it has aided in preventing the Holocaust from becoming so "mystified" that nothing can be said about it at all. Although our knowledge of the Holocaust may be conceived of as being trapped in the metaphors employed in its portrayal, we have still gleaned some kind of knowledge. Amery writes:

> For as the "end" of history, tradition, or archetypes, the Holocaust falls outside all paradigms of knowledge: it becomes unknowable. But as long as we name the events of this period, remember them, or figure them in any form, we also know them—however poorly, inappropriately, or dangerously . . . After such a breach, we may stand humbled in our repertoire of archetypes and figures and the tentative understanding they bring to the Holocaust—but we continue to know the Holocaust by these figures nevertheless.[230]

Young contends that it is only within the context of representation that any understanding of the Holocaust can take shape and that any kind of knowledge of it can be obtained. "Knowledge of the Holocaust" thus tends to reflect directly its representations. Young states that, "[w]hat is remembered of the Holocaust depends on how it is remembered, and how events are remembered depends in turn on the text now giving them form." [231] In other words, we come to interpret events commensurate with the ways in which they have been represented and with the power of the language employed. Young continues:

> Instead of isolating events from their representations, this approach recognizes that literary and historical truth of the Holocaust may not be entirely separable. That is, the truths of the Holocaust—both the factual and the interpretive—can no longer be said to lie beyond our understanding, but must now

---

[230] Young, *Writing and Rewriting the Holocaust*, 98.
[231] Young, *Writing and Rewriting the Holocaust*, 1.

> be seen to inhere in the ways we understand, interpret, and write its history.[232]

Whether one consents to the vigor of this statement or not, it must be emphasized that Young's primary concern remains a hermeneutical one. In as much as our interaction with and grasp of literary representations depends upon the metaphors embraced by them, we remain concerned not only about knowledge of the Holocaust as such, but also about the ways in which the language of testimony impact both the interpretation of testimony and the "knowledge of the Holocaust" that ensues.

Here, Young's interest in the cultural influences on survivors becomes pivotal. The conclusion he draws is decisive for this study. Literary testimony, in seeking truths that lie beyond mere historical facts, functions as a kind of historical exegesis in as much as its metaphors are reflective of those deep structures of culture, tradition, and language that have guided its shape and purposes.[233]

Literary testimonies, because they are impacted by the cultural paradigms of their writers as well as the events of the Holocaust itself, tend to demonstrate both continuity and discontinuity with the primary cultural influences that form their basis.[234] This, too, indicates both the strengths and limits of metaphor. Due to the vital role that culture, tradition, and language play in how a writer remembers, interprets, and narrates Holocaust events, traces of these influences can be found in their testimonies, lending them, however furtively, some degree of continuity with the past. Conversely, due to the dramatic shift many survivors experience over the course of their lifetimes, new paradigms of interpretative experience infiltrate their writings. These divergences are at times distinguishable by the ways that traditional metaphors are devised anew in the language that survivors employ in their narratives. This is also true of Elie Wiesel. As a next step, we shall investigate his understanding of memory, language and literary representation.

---

[232] Young, *Writing and Rewriting the Holocaust*, 1.

[233] Young writes: "In the alternative hermeneutics of Holocaust testimony that follows, I attempt to shift critical emphasis away from the diaries' and memoirs' claim to documentary evidence, to their more tenable function as historical exegesis." Young, *Writing and Rewriting the Holocaust*, 11.

[234] As is demonstrated by the extended use of the term "Holocaust" in general. Young further illustrates this tendency in referencing Wiesel's "retranslation" of ancient figures of the Torah by reading back into them themes and issues of the Holocaust, highlighting therewith both the continuity and discontinuity that Wiesel's texts possess. See Young, *Writing and Rewriting the Holocaust*, 106-109.

Chapter Three

Elie Wiesel, Post-Auschwitz Memory, and the Word

The Duty of Memory

On December 11th, 1986, upon receiving the Nobel Peace Prize, Elie Wiesel opened his acceptance speech with the following story:

> A Hasidic legend tells us that the great Rabbi Baal-Shem-Tov, Master of the Good Name, also known as the Besht, undertook an urgent and perilous mission. He wanted to hasten the coming of the Messiah. The Jewish people, all humanity, were suffering too much, beset by too many evils. They had to be saved, and swiftly. For having tried to meddle with history, the Besht was punished. He was banished along with his faithful servant to a distant island. In despair the servant implored his master to exercise his mysterious powers in order to bring them both home. "Impossible," the Besht replied. "My powers have been taken from me."
>
> "Then, please, say a prayer, recite a litany, work a miracle."
>
> "Impossible," the Master replied, "I have forgotten everything." And so they fell to weeping.
>
> Suddenly the Master turned to his servant and asked: "My friend, remind me of a prayer, any prayer."
>
> "If only I could," said the servant. "I too have forgotten everything."
>
> "Everything, absolutely everything?"
>
> "Everything," said the servant, "except . . ."
>
> "Except what?"
>
> "Except the alphabet!"
>
> At that the Besht cried out joyfully, "Then what are you waiting for? Begin reciting the alphabet, and I shall repeat after you." And together the two exiled men began to recite, at first in whispers, then more loudly, the Hebrew equivalent to the ABC's: "*Aleph beth gimmel,*" and over again, *"Aleph beth gimmel*," and each time more vigorously, more fervently, until

> the Besht ultimately regained his memory and thus his powers.[235]

Wiesel's inclusion of this story is indicative of the sense of urgency that saturates his life's work. It is more, however; the story also serves as an allegory for his understanding of memory and language, and of the duty inherent in both. Although these understandings also embrace Jewish ones, they have changed in the wake of Auschwitz. A brief examination of these is relevant to this study. It expands and deepens the discussion surrounding Holocaust literature in general and helps position Wiesel in relation to other Holocaust authors in particular.

The legend recounted here serves as a valuable starting point. For Wiesel, who considers himself "first a Jew and only then a writer,"[236] memory's central function is to connect past and present; it embraces the very heart of Judaism. In recalling the Jewish story that reaches back some four thousand years, the Jewish people have sought to ensure its continuation. Wiesel states:

> If you remove the Jew today from his past, if you remove him from his people and place him in the present alone, he cannot survive. He cannot survive either as Jew or as a human being. A Jew without a past is worse than a man without a future. It is the past that is his treasure.[237]

Indeed, without memory, Jewish identity would have long been extinguished by outside influences of culture, language, ethnicity, and religion. Memory has thus stood as the key to Jewish survival and embraces the very heart of Judaism. To remember has been to ensure that each generation of Jews learns the stories that have shaped and defined them as a people.[238]

---

[235] Wiesel, *From the Kingdom of Memory*, 237-238.

[236] Elie Wiesel, quoted in Irving Abrahamson, ed. *Against Silence: The Voice and Vision of Elie Wiesel* (New York: Holocaust Library, 1985), 1:10, and 1: 288, previously published as "First Louis L. Kaplan Lecture", from his lecture, Baltimore Hebrew College, Baltimore, MD, October 23, 1973. With his introduction to this three-volume compendium of Wiesel texts, Abrahamson offers a helpful synopsis of Wiesel's religious influences, working philosophy, and overall goals. This synopsis, buttressed by excerpts from Wiesel's writing, has assisted me in fleshing out salient features of Wiesel's thought in this chapter. See Abrahamson, ed. *Against Silence*, pages 7-74.

[237] Elie Wiesel, quoted in Abrahamson, ed. *Against Silence*, 1:53, and 3:302, from a lecture in Great Neck, NY, 21 October, 1975.

[238] Wiesel understands his role as assisting in keeping the memory of his people alive, a memory of suffering that extends back several thousand years. Transmission of memory is central for Wiesel: "If we cannot transmit, we are dead," he maintains. Elie Wiesel, in Abrahamson, ed. *Against Silence*, 2:77, previously published as "Interview with Lily Edelman," in *National Jewish Monthly* (Nov 1973).

For the Jewish people, the stories remembered portray their arduous journey with God. Beginning with the Torah and extended by the Talmud in particular, these stories have given the Jewish people a focal point, a frame of reference, and a continuing sense of unity in spite of exile, tragedy, persecution, and, ultimately, of near-annihilation during the Holocaust. These stories reflect a common destiny that unites all Jews. Wiesel writes:

> We [as Jews] all embody the intense destiny of our people—a destiny which resists being divided into sections and selected periods. Each Jew represents all Jews and is Jewish history. He who remains faithful reflects the secret which makes of us a living community, obstinate and different from others. Each of us is therefore responsible for the past and the future of Israel.[239]

To remember is no end in itself: its focus is a life with God maintained through faith in God. As such, the Jewish commitment is to life, and not to despair.[240] Life, therefore, assumes deeply moral dimensions. For Wiesel, the gift of the law at Sinai represents the most significant event of Jewish history—outside of the Holocaust.[241] The law remains inscribed in the collective memory of the Jewish people and defines their relationship with God in a fundamental way. In this context, their overarching narrative is one of drawing near, drawing away, and drawing near again to God through faith in him and his law.

Although its function and purpose are specific, Jewish memory has taken on a moral dimension that moves beyond its own particular faith context. For Wiesel, the law given to his people at Sinai embraces a universal dimension that reveals a moral message for the world. At the same time, however, it remains first

---

239 Elie Wiesel, quoted in Abrahamson, ed. *Against Silence*, 1:24, and 1:246, previously published as "On Being a Jew," *Jewish Heritage* (Summer 1967): 51-55.

240 Jewish communities often reference the call to "choose life" found in Deuteronomy 30:19: "I summon heaven and earth to witness against you this day: I offer you the choice of life or death, blessing or curse. Choose life and you and your descendants will live." See *The Revised English Bible with the Apocrypha* (Oxford and Cambridge: Oxford University Press and Cambridge University Press, 1989), 175.

241 Wiesel writes: "[The Holocaust is] the most important event in Jewish history and in human history, with the possible exception of the Revelation at Sinai." Elie Wiesel, quoted in Abrahamson, ed. *Against Silence*, 1:28, and 1:211, from "The Holocaust and the Future," lecture, National Conference of Christians and Jews, St. Louis, MO, November 3, 1976. As well: "[In the Holocaust we] were all there, standing alongside all of them, at Sinai as well as in the dark kingdom which, to me, represented the other side of Sinai, the dark side of Sinai." Elie Wiesel, quoted in Abrahamson, ed. *Against Silence*, 1:28, and 1:239-40, from "Herbert R. Abeles Memorial Address," lecture given at the 39th General Assembly of the Jewish Council of Jewish Federations and Welfare Funds, Kansas City, MO, Nov 14, 1970.

and foremost a Jewish message. Wiesel writes: "[There is] no contradiction between the Jewish and the human: the Jewish vision can be universal only when it is thoroughly Jewish."[242] Here we find that the story of the Jewish people is a universal, human story. As such, the Jewish people stand as a microcosm of humanity.

The legend that tells of the Besht left devoid of memory and power is, for Wiesel, a parable and a paradigm whose message must be revived for a post-Holocaust world. The memory of the Jewish people, universal and relevant, must be kept alive at a new level, with new urgency, and in a manner that the world might understand.

The Function and Form of Memory

For Wiesel, memory is to be fostered through the study of ancient texts, specifically, the Torah, the Talmud, and the Midrash. The yet-unfolding story of the Jewish people can be understood in relation to these sources; they discover their sense of orientation and meaning there. These texts thus serve as a touchstone by impacting and forming, ever anew, their identity as a diverse but linked community.[243]

As is the case for many Jews, Wiesel understands memory as being inextricably linked to language. The legend of the Besht serves as a parable for the ancient teaching; the words, even the letters of language form the basis of memory; the two cannot be separated. The preservation of language is thus the prerequisite for keeping memory alive, and is understood as playing a key role in redemption, both of themselves and the world.

---

242 Elie Wiesel, quoted in Abrahamson, ed. *Against Silence*, 1:26, and 2:51, previously published as "Conversation with Nelly Sachs," trans. Hillel Halkin, in *Jewish Heritage* (Spring 1968): 30-33.

243 Wiesel stresses the impact of his childhood biblical learning on his present-day understanding of the importance of its stories. See Wiesel's "Vorwort"in Elie Wiesel, *Adam oder das Geheimnis des Anfangs. Legenden und Porträts*, trans. Hanns Bücker (Freiburg i. B.: Herder, 1980), 7-10. See also Abrahamson, *Against Silence*, 1:23-28. Maurice Friedman identifies in Wiesel a passion for biblical tales that has shaped his own Jewish identity. Wiesel maintains that a Jew is "someone who feels every blow felt by his ancestors," someone who "is crushed by their mourning and buoyed by their triumphs, someone for whom they were living men and women, not symbols, someone involved in all the legends and stories retold by the Bible and commented on by the Midrash. To be a Jew is to remember what Abraham and Isaac lived and endured and to tell their tale, not with tears but with laughter." See Elie Wiesel, *Messengers of God: Biblical Portraits and Legends*, trans. Marion Wiesel (New York: Random House, 1976), xii, quoted in Maurice Friedman, *Abraham Joshua Heschel and Elie Wiesel: You Are My Witnesses* (New York: Farrar, Straus, Giroux, 1987), 201.

The attention that Wiesel gives to the legend of the Besht also lends insight into Wiesel's self-awareness as a writer, his sense of obligation to memory and his understanding of the role and power of literature.

For Wiesel, although the Torah may form the basis of Jewish memory, the diverse contexts that have otherwise nurtured Jewish memory are vital. Central for Wiesel, of course, has been the Hasidic context. He writes:

> I myself love Hasidism because I grew up in a Hasidic milieu. Whenever I want to write something good, I go back to my childhood. The soul of every writer is his childhood, and mine was a Hasidic one. I love Hasidism because of its tales, because of the intrinsic fervor that makes them Hasidic tales. I love Hasidism for something else too: it contains all the themes that haunt my work.[244]

As we shall see, these themes are not left unchanged in the context of Wiesel's experience of the Holocaust. Be that as it may, the Hasidic world out of which they were born lends form, momentum, and continuation to the questions he has known both during and after Auschwitz.

Wiesel remains obsessed with questions. Within the context of his religious upbringing, he was encouraged to pursue questions of God and his world. This pursuit never left him: "To be a Jew, therefore, is to ask a question—a thousand questions, yet always the same—of society, of others of oneself, of death and of God."[245] The question is the core, and thus most important: "There are no answers to true questions. There are only good questions, sometimes painful, sometimes exuberant. All I have learned in my life is questions, and whatever I have tried to share with friends is questions."[246]

In light of Auschwitz, in the wake of the devastation engendered by the catastrophe, the questions of Wiesel's childhood have radically changed in depth and scope. The answers that he finds remain provisional at best, for, in transcending all other historical events, the Holocaust has itself become transcendental: "[The Holocaust] transcends all dimensions of consciousness. We still cannot grasp how it all happened and why. The mystery remains intact."[247] As "the mystery of all mysteries,"[248] it is, "the question of questions. It is both man's way of

---

[244] Elie Wiesel, quoted in Abrahamson, ed. *Against Silence*, 1:23, and 2:255, previously published in *Jewish Heritage* (Fall/Winter 1972).

[245] Elie Wiesel, *One Generation After*, trans. Lily Edelman and Elie Wiesel (New York: Schocken Books, 2011), 176; also quoted in Abrahamson, 1:27.

[246] Elie Wiesel, quoted in Abrahamson, ed. *Against Silence*, 2:151, from "Commencement Address", given at Manhattanville College, Purchase, NY, May 27, 1972.

[247] Elie Wiesel, quoted in Abrahamson, ed. *Against Silence*, 1:41, and 2:293, from a review of *Auschwitz*, by Bern Naumann, *Hadassah Magazine* (January 1967).

[248] Elie Wiesel, quoted in Abrahamson, ed. *Against Silence*, 1:41, and 2:133, from lecture, Olin-Sang Institute, Oconomowoc, WI, Summer, 1966.

questioning God and God's way of questioning man. And there is no answer coming from either side. There cannot be."[249]

Tradition grants Wiesel orientation in the face of the silence that has followed Auschwitz. As a constitutive part of Jewish memory, however, silence has always been understood to precede the spoken or written word. For Wiesel, silence is fundamental to speech and writing, lying even between the words.[250] In this silence, the author finds the solace and solitude he has needed for all of the questions inherent in a broken faith. Strikingly, Wiesel indicates the validity of a faith that has been profoundly violated:

> "No heart is as whole as a broken heart," said Rebbe Nachman of Bratzlav. I would like to rephrase his words and say, "No faith is as pure as a broken faith." He who says today that he is at peace with himself and with God is estranged from both. Today the protestor, the angry believer, and perhaps the angry non-believer may be called the true believers. [251]

As such, for Wiesel, memory—with all its questions, its link to both language and silence, and in its embrace by the Jewish people and their faith—is revealed as a deeply human quest that is, in the wake of the Holocaust, both mystical and relentless. Ridden with struggle, doubt, anxiety, and often despair, it reflects that long tradition in which answers have proven to be less important than the questions themselves.

Holocaust Not-Forgetting

As was the case with the Besht's despair in having forgotten everything, Wiesel's concern for memory is founded in the threats posed to humanity's continuation as a race. The Holocaust elicits the call to remember, and with this the call, to save humanity from self-destruction. The urgency of this call cannot be understated; as was the case in the legend of the Besht, it concerns the very survival of humanity. That being said, humanity's all-pervasive and infectious impulse to forget the Holocaust poses the most serious, fundamental, and existential threat to memory.

---

[249] Elie Wiesel, in Abrahamson, ed. *Against Silence*, 1:41, and 1:144, from Leo Beck Memorial Lecture, Westchester Reform Temple, Scarsdale, NY, Dec 4, 1975.
[250] Wiesel: "If you want to bring back at least a certain fragment of truth, you must be responsible for the words but also for the white space between the words." Elie Wiesel, quoted in Abrahamson, ed. *Against Silence*, 1:56, "Are We Worthy of the Story?" statement in unrevised transcript.
[251] Elie Wiesel, quoted in Abrahamson, ed. *Against Silence*, 1:32, and 1:144-5, from Leo Beck Memorial Lecture, Westchester Reform Temple, Scarsdale, NY, Dec 4, 1975.

For Wiesel, the Holocaust stands as an "anti-Sinai" out of which the stories of the suffering of the Jewish people can be chronicled anew to form a new Torah:

> [When] the Messiah will come, as we are told, Elijah will give him his chronicles, his book of Jewish suffering, and that book will become the new *Sefer Torah*. That book will become the new Torah, the New Law, the Messiah's Law. Thus the Messiah will remember our suffering.
>
> I know few legends as beautiful and as poignant.
>
> Not one tear should be wasted. Not one sigh should go astray. Nothing should be lost.[252]

This new chronicle has given birth to a new philosophy, a new order of knowledge within the Jewish tradition. Wiesel maintains that redemption from Jewish suffering, including the sufferings endured during the Holocaust, can only be attained through memory. The message embodied in memory is that of a people whose "history is the heart of History."[253] Ironically, the implications of the Holocaust for humanity are based in the uniqueness of the Holocaust as a specifically Jewish event.[254] It is "a unique event," Wiesel writes: "There was nothing like it before and there will be nothing like it after. To know that it was unique is to know that it will remain unique."[255] Wiesel's insistence on the uniqueness of the Holocaust is one expressed directly and indirectly throughout his oeuvre.

Wiesel insists that the Holocaust is the result of concrete, human evil. In its universality and uniqueness, however, the Holocaust is an ontological event that transcends every aspect of human existence: "It goes beyond history because it includes history and perhaps denies history. . . . Something was said, something was given, something was revealed or taken back that we must face now in order to go on living as human beings."[256]

---

[252] Elie Wiesel, quoted in Abrahamson, ed. *Against Silence*, 1:46, and 3:47, adapted from lecture, Schara Tzedek Synagogue, Vancouver, B.C., May 6, 1978.

[253] Elie Wiesel, quoted in Abrahamson, ed. *Against Silence*, 1:25, from *City College Alumnus* (Oct 1973), 7.

[254] Wiesel writes: "Whatever happened one generation ago happened first of all to my people, the Jewish people, but through it to mankind. Whatever happened then has affected the destiny of man and the human condition." Elie Wiesel, quoted in Abrahamson, ed. *Against Silence*, 1:41, and 2:106, adapted from lecture, Colloquium of Scholars, California Lutheran College, Thousand Oaks, CA, April 27, 1977.

[255] Martin Panzer, previously published in "No, It Cannot Happen Again," in *Indianapolis Jewish Post and Opinion*, June 12, 1981, 12; also Abrahamson, ed. *Against Silence*, 1:40,

[256] Elie Wiesel, quoted in Abrahamson, ed. *Against Silence*, 1:28, and 1:21, from "The Holocaust and the Future," lecture, National Conference of Christians and Jews, St. Louis, MO, November 3, 1976

It is this "something" of the Holocaust that stands in need of being remembered. It encompasses the murder of six million Jews, the magnitude and depth of which is and will remain incomprehensible. Story by story, the dead are to be remembered, their names inscribed in the annals of Jewish and human history. This process of remembering is agonizing, but, for Wiesel, is and will always be the only way.

Jewish memory of the Holocaust touches the collective memory of the world. The world's duty is to hear and bear the tension of the message of memory, and in so doing, translate it into action and prevention. The legend of the crisis of the Besht in exile emerges here as paradigmatic in relating memory as the only means available for redeeming the world.

The Word

The Powerlessness of the Word

As we have seen, Elie Wiesel's understanding of language is inextricably linked to his understanding of memory. As was the case with the Besht, Wiesel recognizes that, without memory, humanity would be bereft. There would be no access to the past, no access to anything that was once meaningful to humanity, and thus nothing with which to define itself. The very survival of humanity hinges on memory and thus on language; indeed, both are crucial for humanity's continuation.

For Wiesel, however, Auschwitz has generated a fundamental crisis of language. As both a unique and universal, transcendental event that has no parallel, the Holocaust has rendered language powerless to adequately relate the tale of Jewish suffering. Powerless, too, to seek any meaning at all in the suffering. Akin to Steiner, Wiesel declares language to be in exile.[257] "What does exiled language mean?" he asks. "It refers to the distance between words and what they mask. It signifies the tension between language and its subject."[258] It is exactly the impotence of language that has become the greatest dilemma for those survivors who wish to tell their tales. Their attempts have been constantly thwarted by language itself, which has been rendered incapable of relating even the most basic facts and feelings of their experiences. Wiesel concludes it is for this reason that so many survivors have remained silent until now:

> [T]hey feared being inadequate to the task, betraying a unique experience by burying it in worn-out phrases and images. They were afraid of saying what must not be said, of

[257] See Wiesel, *From the Kingdom of Memory*, 14, 31.
[258] Wiesel, *From the Kingdom of Memory*, 31.

> attempting to communicate with language what eludes language, of falling into the trap of easy half-truths.[259]

Again, to this theme, Wiesel includes his own experience:

> We all knew that we could never say what had to be said, that we could never express in words—coherent, intelligible words—our experience of madness on an absolute scale. . . . All words seemed inadequate, worn, foolish, lifeless, whereas I wanted them to sear.
>
> Where was I to discover a fresh vocabulary, a primeval language?[260]

Thus, in light of language's present status, Auschwitz has remained inaccessible for all who were not there. Wiesel emphasizes:

> For what happened goes beyond words, beyond imagination. To make words of it would be blasphemous. Rebbe Mendel of Kotzk said that truth can sometimes be communicated by words, though there is a level of truth so deep that it can be conveyed only by silence. And then, lastly, there is somewhere in man a truth so profound and so disturbing that it cannot be transmitted at all. The Holocaust must then be placed in this last category.[261]

It is a universal dilemma, this inability to "transmit" that which needs to be transmitted most of all. The ensuing silence is thus a self-enforced one. In the context of the Jewish call to memory, to be accountable to its story as one standing in a long continuum, survivors may wish not to remember; they may in fact, wish for a fresh start without memory or even long for death. And should a survivor decide to embrace the call to remember and thus keep the Jewish story alive, the difficulties inherent in testimony remain. How might one speak when one feels that nothing at all can be conveyed? And when there is no one at all who will understand?

As an ontological event that transcends history and language, the Holocaust remains for Wiesel a sacred event, a kind of "secret" closed to humanity forever. Ultimately, this secret remains with the dead. Wiesel writes: "Auschwitz cannot be explained nor can it be visualized. . . . Everything about it inspires fear

---

[259] Elie Wiesel, *One Generation After*, 8.

[260] Wiesel, *From the Kingdom of Memory*, 14-15.

[261] Elie Wiesel, quoted in Abrahamson, ed. *Against Silence*, 1:239, from "Herbert R. Abeles Memorial Address", lecture, 39th General Assembly of the Council of Jewish Federation and Welfare Funds, Kansas City, MO, Nov 14, 1970.

and leads to despair. The dead are in possession of a secret that we, the living, are neither worthy of nor capable of recovering."[262] In spite of this, Wiesel views the Holocaust mystery as a story that has to be told:

> The magnitude of the catastrophe, the absurdity of the tragedy, the silence of the world, the responsibility of the accomplices, the very fact that it could have happened, and the very fact that it could have been avoided—all these elements make it into a mystery, almost a religious mystery, with theological implications. This is really the story that we try to tell.[263]

It is striking that Wiesel, even in the face of these great challenges, attempts to tell the story at all. His decision to write—framed by his now familiar "and yet"—is the focus of the next section. However, Wiesel's struggle to come to terms with language in the face of the powerlessness of the Word is one that persists and permeates all of his writing.

The Power of the Word

If the powerlessness of the word (that is, of language) builds one strong theme in Wiesel's works, then it might well be said that the power of the word builds another. This dichotomy reveals a poignant paradox, and reflects the tension with which the author himself lived. It is to this paradox we shall turn next.

For Wiesel, the act of remembering through the spoken and written word represents an attempt to combat the silence embodied by and embedded in memory. Silence has several faces. First of all, there is the silence born by the whole of memory, the mystical silence of the spiritual quest for answers to questions that have none. Secondly, there is the silence of survivors, traumatized and either seeking to forget or fearful of remembering. Thirdly, there is the silence found in the memories themselves, in the vast domain of the "Kingdom of Night." The silence of the indifferent masses follows suit, of those who will not and cannot know, that silence that helped foster Hitler's violent response to the so-called "Jewish Question." And there is the silence of our post-Holocaust world, a world so quick to speak of forgiving and forgetting that it has already bypassed the story. And finally, there is the silence found within speaking itself, rooted in the futility and powerlessness of language. It is this particular kind of silence out of which testimony emerges. In this context, testimony constitutes nothing less than a

[262] Elie Wiesel, quoted in Abrahamson, ed. *Against Silence*, 1:158, previously published in "Holocaust," in *The New York Times,* April 16, 1978.

[263] Harry James Cargas, *Harry James Cargas in Conversation with Elie Wiesel* (New York: Paulist Press, 1976), 85-86.

powerful "gesture . . . against indifference."[264] Strikingly, silences emerge as the foundation for memory, for remembering, for telling the tale. It is this particular understanding of silence that concerns us next.

The reality, necessity, and inevitability of silence post-Auschwitz are constitutive of the difficulties of communicating the very message that needs to be told. Be that as it may, Wiesel admits, language is all we have:

> Nevertheless we write. We do so because survival—the key work in our life and in our experience—carries certain privileges as well as certain duties. All are combined in one word: "transmission." Whatever we have seen we must transmit. Whatever we have endured we must convey. Whatever tales we have heard must be passed on. One single obsession makes the entire history of the Jewish people: transmission.[265]

Wiesel's paradoxical embrace of language, in spite of both the power of silence and the powerlessness of the word following the Holocaust, is one he undertakes with anxiety. He confesses that he is fearful of words: "I am obsessed with silence because I am afraid of language," he admits. "I am afraid of the spoken word, and even afraid of the written word."[266] Still, "[w]e must give truth a name, force man to look."[267] The word continues to be the source of life for the Jews, and so it must become that source for the world in its fight against evil.

And so it is that Wiesel, in the face of grave misgivings, chooses language as that medium that contains a remnant of power to transmit, if only to transmit the urgency of the message. Just as the Besht learned to reconstruct memory in the simplest of ways—by repeating the alphabet—Wiesel reconstructs, simply, and in an embrace of all the silences that live within and between words, his experience of the Holocaust by writing stories of the Holocaust. It is exactly this decision to give form to memory that is crucial here.

Wiesel understands the act of reading literature as possessing an element of mystical power. The power exists in the active interplay between writer, reader, and words themselves:

---

[264] Elie Wiesel, quoted in Abrahamson, ed. *Against Silence*, 2:82, from Lily Edelman, "The Use of Words and the Weight of Silence," previously published as "Interview with Lily Edelman," *National Jewish Monthly* (Nov 1973).

[265] Elie Wiesel, quoted in Abrahamson, ed. *Against Silence*, 1:13, from lecture, Cornell University, 5 Dec, 1971.

[266] Elie Wiesel, quoted in Abrahamson, ed. *Against Silence*, 2:111, from interview by Ira Nadel, in *Audience*, Canadian Broadcasting Corporation, September 29, 1979.

[267] Elie Wiesel, quoted in Abrahamson, ed. *Against Silence*, 2:117, from interview, adapted by Heidi Anne Walker, *Journal of Education* (Boston University), 162 (Spring, 1980): 57-63.

> If the Torah is so beautiful, and it is; if the prophets were so great, and they are; it is not only because they were great but also because we keep them alive. The fact that we repeat today a prayer composed 3,000 years ago gives that prayer another dimension . . . If you go to the Louvre in Paris or the Prado in Spain or the Hermitage in Leningrad, certain pictures, certain Rembrandts or Goyas, are not only great because Rembrandt and Goya painted them but also because all of the thousands of people who saw these paintings left something of their eyes in the paintings. That is true of literature as well. That is the mystical quality of art, of literature, and of history.[268]

It is this bond between writer and reader that lends literary forms what might be considered a residue of power. In the act of reading, writer and reader converge; as such, literature is a dialogue in which the silence and solitude of both meet and embrace one another. In this sense, it is akin to the solitude that human beings encounter when they face God. Wiesel writes:

> The creative process is a strange one: it comes from solitude, it goes to solitude and yet it's a meeting between two solitudes. It is just like man's solitude faced with God's solitude. Once you have this confrontation, you have art and religion and more. You have certain communion in the best and purest sense of the word. Exactly the same thing happens when you write and someone reads you; your solitude is faced with the reader's and you join with that solitude. When both are sincere, God is there. Whenever one man speaks to another, ultimately he involves God.[269]

Within the act of telling, the author must appeal to the reader's imagination to make space for this meeting. Indeed, literature itself is an act of the imagination:

> A poet takes everyday words like *bread* or *wine* or *air* or *life* or *childhood* and somehow, by putting them one after the other and by introducing silence into them, he produces a certain electric current. Suddenly routine words burn and burst in

---

[268] Elie Wiesel, quoted in Abrahamson, ed. *Against Silence*, 3:247, "Questions and Answers: At Brandeis-Bardin, 1978," adapted from Q&A, Brandeis-Bardin Institute, Simi Valley, CA, Jan 22, 1978.
[269] Cargas, *Harry James Cargas in Conversation with Elie Wiesel*, 6.

> your heart, in your mind, and in receiving these words you become poetically receptive.[270]

Wiesel's grasp of the power of language is linked to his understanding of literature's power to effect moral change in the reader. This link is rooted in the long tradition within Judaism that understands words as having the capacity to recreate the past. In his embrace of the Jewish anthropology that grants a receptive, moral capacity in the human being, Wiesel possesses a remnant of hope that humanity might listen to the warnings of the Holocaust. "The only thing for me to do is to have faith in man and faith in God. If not, then we are all lost. So I have faith *in spite of* everything."[271] In the context of "giving truth a name," that is, of testimony, the author hopes to break the spell of humanity's indifference. His goal of employing literature is to guard against this indifference. "The danger is apathy. Indifference means death,"[272] he contends. It is a warning to humanity of the danger of its self-destruction.

Testimony and Literary Representation

The Storyteller

Wiesel considers himself a storyteller at work within a specific storytelling tradition. His self-understanding is one of a witness-writer who bears witness through storytelling. Tellingly, he identifies his Eastern-European Hasidic heritage as formative for his writing and refers to himself as a kind of sage:

> I try to be a storyteller who goes from city to city, while remaining in the same place. I use the words and am afraid of them, but I use them nevertheless. I try to make them into something much bigger than I am, to cling to some secret which I carry within me but which is much larger than I am.[273]

The moral dimension of his role as storyteller is underscored here. This is reminiscent of Walter Benjamin's understanding of storytelling as "counsel." Benjamin suggests that, in offering counsel, storytelling is involved in the transmission

---

[270] Elie Wiesel, quoted in Abrahamson, ed. *Against Silence*, 1:18, and 3:290, from "What is a Poet?" transcript, *The Eternal Light*, Chapter 1437, May 24, 1981.
[271] Elie Wiesel, quoted in Abrahamson, ed. *Against Silence*, 1:60, 3:261-62, adapted from Frank Reynold, *Directions*, ABC-TV, June 18, 1978.
[272] Elie Wiesel, quoted in *Against Silence*, Abrahamson, ed. 1:19, from Kathleen Hirsch, "On Silence, Words, and Salvation," in *World* (Boston University) October 15, 1980.
[273] Elie Wiesel, quoted in *Against Silence*, Abrahamson, ed. 1:11, and 2:7, from address, World Federation of Bergen-Belsen Associations, Jerusalem, July 9, 1970.

of the wisdom, meaning, and truth gleaned from the experiences of one's life. In this transmission, the very life of the storyteller comes, however subtly, to expression as well. As such, storytelling is also an act of self-discovery. Benjamin writes:

> [The storyteller] has counsel—not for a few situations, as the proverb does, but for many, like the sage. . . . His gift is the ability to relate his life; his distinction, to be able to tell his entire life. The storyteller: he is the man who could let the wick of his life be consumed completely by the gentle flame of his story. This is the basis of the incomparable aura of the storyteller, in Leslov as in Hauff, in Poe as in Stevenson. The storyteller is the figure in which the righteous man encounters himself. [274]

Should this observation be accurate, storytelling functions not merely by repeating what has been heard or by mimicking a known tradition, but rather as an existential act in which the storyteller's identity is caught up in, with great immediacy, the very process of transmission. This aspect illuminates the autobiographical dimension inherent in storytelling and thus in the transmission of truth and meaning to the reader.

Akin to these observations, Horowitz describes storytelling as indicative of the social and cultural experiences of the storyteller. For Horowitz, storytelling is:

> a quintessential human activity. Yet, where people tell stories; the ways people tell stories; the purposes served by stories; and the values, attitudes, and beliefs toward stories vary across communities. Historical, economic, class, social, religious, gender, and other factors also affect stories and storytelling. Without a doubt, storytelling is a complex, fascinating phenomenon. There are many ways to explore that complexity. One way is to study the work of a master storyteller.[275]

Both Benjamin's and Horowitz's observations are commensurate with the theses of this study. Important for the moment is the link that can be made between Wiesel's self-understanding as a storyteller on the one hand and a specific tradition of storytelling—the Hasidic—on the other. His conscious undertaking of

---

[274] Walter Benjamin, "The Storyteller," in *Illuminations: Essays and Reflections*, ed. Hannah Arendt, trans. Harry Zohn (New York: Schocken Books, 1968), 108-09; and Horowitz, "Introduction," in *Elie Wiesel and the Art of Storytelling*, 3.
[275] Horowitz, "Introduction," 3.

bearing witness must therefore be set in the context of his professed identity as a storyteller.

Drawing from the observations above, Wiesel's storytelling might well be understood as having two primary sources: the Holocaust and the Hasidic tradition of the shtetl. This observation aligns well with Young's theory of narrative formation. This theory recognizes Holocaust survivors as being impacted by two important series of events: formative events that have taken place before the Holocaust and those of the Holocaust itself. Although the latter constitute a break with the former, pre-Holocaust influences can be seen as having left their imprint on both firsthand subjective experiences of the Holocaust and on the ways in which these are reflected upon and later interpreted in narration.

In this theoretical context, the author's role as both storyteller and witness is made evident. One can therefore consider Wiesel as storyteller-witness or writer-witness. Zoe Trodd supports this claim in his exploration of Wiesel's continuing search for identity:

> After the war, [Wiesel] says, he felt "the obsession to tell the tale, to bear witness that every person shared and nourished and had to put forward," and so the autobiographical imperative becomes the witness imperative. . . . Wiesel's storytelling is inseparable from his philosophies of the self-as-subject and the self-as-witness.[276]

Within this context, the author's literary choices can be investigated with a view to the influences of tradition that permeate his texts. In the guise of stories, these texts bear witness to a larger, anguished tale.

Language, Metaphor, and Literary Field

Wiesel's exploration of the power of language inherent in literature is not unproblematic in a critical review of his works. His statements concerning the power of literature and the limits of language appear contradictory. To reiterate his claim: "There can be no literature of the Holocaust." How is this to explain the author's prodigious literary output? In what ways might his work be considered meaningful if it cannot be considered referential?

Arguably, Wiesel's existential struggle with both bearing witness and remaining silent is the reason for the apparent contradictions in his writing. A reading of his texts attentive to this tension reveals that this struggle is one that he never resolves. The collapse and exile of language; the silence imposed upon

---

[276] Zoe Trodd, "Mosaics and Mirrors: Wiesel, American Autobiographies, and the Shaping of the Storied Subject," in *Elie Wiesel and the Art of Storytelling*, ed. Horowitz, 29. Cf. Cargas, *Harry James Cargas in Conversation with Elie Wiesel*, 86, 87.

memory; the inaccessibility and unknowable character of what he considers to be an ontological, transcendent event; and the indifference of the world all speak against literary enterprise.

Wiesel's own understanding of his narratives as stories, as well as his narration process as storytelling, even in the face of the impotence of language, is helpful in this respect. In as much as the storyteller's life is involved in the transmission of the truths and meanings they have acquired, and in so far as that life continues to be impacted by their earliest influences, the storyteller is existentially engaged in a kind of truth-telling not immediately evident to the reader.

With this, we can begin to think through a reasonable application of Young's theory of literary representation to both Wiesel's narration process and his narratives. Young's concern is to explore testimonial narratives in terms of the plethora of factors that contribute to their formation. As such, he has maintained that the way in which a survivor comes to interpret and represent their Holocaust experience is influenced strongly by biographical factors that extend from events and circumstances that lie outside of the Holocaust. Accordingly, the language incorporated by testimonial narrative does bear marks—however furtive or obscured—of other influences. Indeed, this language never arises from a conceptual *tabula rasa*[277]; it always unfolds in connection with this broader interpretive context. Although Young's theory does display certain conceptual weaknesses,[278] it

---

[277] Meaning "clean slate."

[278] Young's theory of literary representation exhibits certain weaknesses, or, at the very least, a certain vagueness. His analyses focus on the nature, formation, and function of literary testimony. His primary concern, however, has been to understand testimony in the most all-encompassing manner possible so as to allow for an appropriate response to it. Thus, in conceiving the nature and purpose of testimony as being different from those of historical chronicling as such, his goal has been to ascertain how the readership of literary testimony reaches its interpretations, how interpretations eventually impact collective memory and how humankind then acts (or doesn't) upon this memory. It is in this sense that Young's theory has a powerfully practical, ethical thrust and intention. The vagueness in Young's assessment, however, is two-fold: first, he offers no extensive analysis as to what positive knowledge of the Holocaust might actually consist of, in spite of language's creative potential. Secondly, he offers no concrete suggestions as to what our responses might or even must be. Importantly, these two aspects are linked: it is only in the context of our knowledge of the Holocaust can we offer adequate responses to it.

Young's claim that our knowledge of the Holocaust lies in our knowledge of the influences exerted upon testimony, that is, in the knowledge gleaned from the historical exegesis of its narratives, does not, in my opinion, extend far enough. Should testimonial language actually affect its readers by way of its metaphors and the concrete ways in which they function, then some sort of knowledge of the Holocaust must ensue, however poor this knowledge might be. Should the forms, tropes, myths, legends, themes, etc. detectable in testimony not grant us any real knowledge beyond the knowledge of their original sources, then we would not ever be moved by testimony, and in not affecting us, it would neither change us nor call us to respond.

assists this study by proposing that the "historical exegesis" of testimonial narratives is indeed a meaningful undertaking. With respect to Wiesel, the theory helps to guide us in understanding how particular metaphors function in the author's writings, metaphors borne in the traditional forms, themes, myths, legends, and frames of reference drawn from his earliest influences. In this sense, Young's theory can aid us in better understanding better how metaphors function in Wiesel's writing, metaphors borne in the traditional forms, themes, myths, and legends of his earliest influences, his field. In turn, it also helps to identify better the ways in which Hasidism as a whole has come to impact his narratives.

Such an approach to Wiesel's texts complements and extends Bourdieu's theory of literary field. At the same time, it supports Young's exploration of how reading and interpreting texts function. Akin to the work of both critics, this study seeks to take seriously Wiesel's claim that his religious heritage has impacted his work in a fundamental way. Should his embrace of storytelling entail what he says it does, and should his religious heritage have come to impact his writing as he also claims, then our interests must turn to both his heritage and, subsequently, his texts. With this, an invitation to investigate his religious foundations has already been made.

Chapter Four

Hasidism: Foundations, Salient Features, and the Rise of the Shtetl

Hasidism as an Emerging Spiritual Landscape

The rise of Hasidism in eighteenth-century Eastern Europe represents a vital chapter in the history of Judaism in general and of European Jewish Mysticism in particular. Although space in this study does not allow for a more comprehensive examination of Hasidism, a view to the development of this religious-cultural movement aids this study in establishing Hasidism as a unique cultural and spiritual landscape within European Judaism up until the Holocaust.

Indeed, over the course of almost two centuries, Hasidim came to change the religious topography of Eastern European Judaism. Drawing from its complex beginnings and the equally complex factors that both incited and drove its unfolding, Hasidism eventually developed into a widespread movement. This development was indicative of (among other things) Hasidism's charismatic power to speak to the common folk, the capacity of its central figures to provide the folk with spiritual guidance and leadership, as well as its poignant message that advocated closeness to and unity with God in the hope of redemption—in other words, its powerfully compelling mystical component.

This chapter sketches the historical and theological roots of Wiesel's distinct *Sitz-im-Leben*. In the context of both the sociological and theological concerns that underscore and guide this study, such an examination is vital in positing the shtetl of Sighet as that field pivotal for Wiesel's post-Holocaust humanistic vision and literary undertaking and output. As such, the chapter poses as an important backdrop to the examination of the four texts central to this study.

Foundations

Earliest References to "Hasidim"

Among the earliest references to Hasidim as a specific group, party or sect are those that appear in the rabbinical literature of the second to the seventh-century BC. There, the name for the group known as *hasidim ha-Rishonim* can be translated from the Hebrew as "ancient Pietists" or "pious ones."[279] A number of texts link this designation to *Ansché Ma'assé*, which, meaning "men of the deed," refers to groups distinct from, but related to, *hasidim*.[280] In other contexts, an association is made to both *hasidim* and rainmakers.[281] Because all of these references are largely vague, it remains uncertain whether *hasidim* referenced pious, charismatic individuals, loosely associated groups or more formally organized groups constituting a religious movement.[282] In any case, what is clear in this literature is that the name *hasidim* actually referenced differing factional groups that had grown up within the region. Identifying which group the designation references is thus dependent on the literary source in which it is implemented.[283]

A significant reference to *hasidim* is found in the Jewish text Maccabees I from the second-century BC.[284] Known to modern scholarship as the "Hasideans," these *hasidim* constituted a group of learned Jews who chose to strictly adhere to the dictates of the Torah. The Hasideans formed a religious community during the Hellenistic era, from the fourth to the first century BC.[285] As a religious party with political affiliations, they fought together with Judas Maccabeus and his followers in the Maccabean Revolt (167-160 BCE) against the Seleucid Empire.[286]

A later group of *hasidim* was linked to the Sadducees, the religious faction out of which the Pharisees emerged.[287] As the "pious ones," these *hasidim* believed the "oral tradition, the ethic, conventions, to be as just as binding as the

---

[279] Gesenius translates *hesed* as "goodness" and "kindness," and *hasid* as "kind" or "pious." With this, the ethical dimension of the Hebrew original is underscored: "[A]s denoting the active practice of *hesed*, kindness." *Hasidim*, derived from *hesed*, relates to: "technically, the party of *the* pious who opposed the Hellenization of Judaea." See Gesenius, *Hebrew and English Lexicon of the Old Testament,* 338-39. Cf. Susanne Talabardon, *Chassidismus*, Jüdische Studien Band 2 (Tübingen: Mohr Siebeck, 2016), 18-19.

[280] Talabardon, *Chassidismus*, 19. Translation mine.

[281] Talabardon, *Chassidismus*, 20.

[282] Talabardon, *Chassidismus*, 19.

[283] Talabardon, *Chassidismus*, 20.

[284] The 1931 edition of the Zwingli Bible defines the *hasidim* as "fromme, gesetzeifrige Juden", meaning "pious Jews, jealous after the law." Excluded here are the frequent biblical references to *hasidim*, such as those found in the Psalms, where the word denotes simply "the pious ones." Our focus here is on those uses of *hasidim* which relate to particular groups whose members are bound together by some identifiable common denominator. See *Die Heilige Schrift des Alten und Neuen Testaments* (Zurich: Reutimann & Co., 1934), s.v. "1 Makkabäer 2." Translation above is mine.

[285] Georg Herlitz and Bruno Kirschner, eds., *Jüdisches Lexikon. Ein enzyklopädisches Handbuch des jüdischen Wissens* (Berlin: Jüdischer Verlag, 1927), 1:1338.

[286] John Bright, *A History of Israel* (Philadelphia: Westminster Press, 1981), 417-27.

[287] Herlitz and Kirschner, *Jüdisches Lexikon*, 1:1339.

written Torah."[288] Various rabbinic sources indicate the inclination of this group to adhere to traditions outside the Torah.[289]

European Jewish Mysticism

As can be inferred from the above, Jewish mysticism (as defined in the broadest of terms) extends as far back as the incipience of Judaism itself. Our next emphasis, however, is to isolate those trends in Europe that led to the development of, however indirectly, the Kabbalah, the predecessor of Hasidism.

These trends are often understood as constituting reactions to traditional Rabbinicism. As we shall see, during the course of the Middle Ages, the rabbinic approach to the written and oral traditions was perceived by many as too rationalistic, underemphasizing the spiritual and experiential components of faith. In this context, an increasing number of Jews were drawn to mysticism. This overall trend has been understood as having been at least partially responsible for the incipience of the "new" Hasidism of the eighteenth century.[290]

References to Hasidim during the Middle Ages

References to the *hasidim* of the eleventh century are the subject of scholarly speculation. Given the frequently equivocal use of the word *hasidim* in the literature of this period, scholars have had to differentiate between references to specific groups on the one hand and more general references to individuals of strong spiritual character with varying spiritual affiliations (such as the Kabbalah) on the other.

During this period, one important group, identified as having been pivotal to later developments, was the *Hasidei Ashkenaz*, otherwise referred to as the "German Hasidism," or "German Pietists."[291] Their numbers would increase during the twelfth and thirteenth centuries. This learned association of spiritually elite men was characterized by its strict adherence to the law. Its adherents believed that evil could be thwarted and spiritual perfection attained by living a life

---

[288] Herlitz and Kirchner, *Jüdisches Lexikon*, 1:1339. Translation mine.

[289] However, it remains unclear whether these references denote members of the organized religious party per se or the pious in general. See Herlitz and Kirschner, *Jüdisches Lexikon*, 1:1339.

[290] Talabardon summarizes the debate surrounding the movement's roots and beginnings, and offers a sketch of the research landscape past and present. In referencing the early Jewish Enlightenment critics of Hasidism, known as Maskilim, from historians such as Simon Dubnow, Martin Buber, and Gershom Scholem, and on to later scholars such as Moshe Rosman and Gershon D. Hundert, she traces the positions of three scholarly generations. The positions held by these diverge and thus divide, in greater and lesser ways. See Talabardon, *Chassidismus*, 7ff.

[291] Talabardon, *Chassidismus*, 21.

driven by the love of God and by way of prayers, repentance, penance, and ascetic practice.[292] With influences traceable to Christian sources,[293] their impact would be felt into the sixteenth and seventeenth centuries. Their sphere of influence ranged from Italy, into western and southern Germany, and then further west into northeastern France and the Iberian Peninsula.

Medieval philosophical and ethical texts most often implemented the word *hasidim* when referencing outstanding pious personalities in general. Additionally, they differentiated *hasidim* from *tzaddikim*. *Tzaddikim* were described simply as moderate, observant Jews. In particular contexts, however, these two designations were used interchangeably; both referenced pious individuals who had attained to a high level of spiritual advancement.[294]

In a similar way, Moshe Maimonides refers to *hasidim* as those who kept themselves far from pride and who adhered to the principles of humility, generosity to the poor, and moderation in both joyfulness and cheerfulness.[295]

Within the literature of the Kabbalah, the Sefer ha-Bahir, known as the "Book of Brightness," describes the *tzaddik* in biblical terms as the righteous man who serves as the "fundament of the world."[296] A small number of other early Kabbalistic works designate the followers of their teachings simply as *hasidim*.[297] The central text of the Kabbalah, the Zohar, mentions at times both *hasidim* and *tzaddikim*, although a clear delineation between the two groups is not offered. The employment of both these terms in the Kabbalistic context in particular, however, foreshadows their later usage within Eastern European Hasidism.[298]

In summary, although the term *hasidim* was not used unequivocally during the medieval period, its implementation is indicative of spiritual change and evolution in Jewish Europe. These changes are notable. Taken as a whole, these early religious trends preface the religious movements that follow.[299]

---

[292] Talabardon, *Chassidismus*, 21.
[293] Talabardon, *Chassidismus*, 21.
[294] Talabardon, *Chassidismus*, 23.
[295] Moshe Maimonides, *Hilkhot De'ot*, 1:4-5. Referenced in Talabardon, *Chassidismus*, 23.
[296] Talabardon, *Chassidismus*, 25. Translation mine.
[297] Talabardon, *Chassidismus*, 25.
[298] Talabardon, *Chassidismus*, 27.
[299] Talabardon: "This usage of both terms [*hasid* and *tzaddik*], as careful as their wide distribution over the entire Zoharian corpus might have been, already points to their specific use within Eastern European Hasidism." Talabardon, *Chassidismus*, 27. Translation mine.

German Hasidism as the Dawn of a New Mysticism

First published in 1941, Gershom Scholem's groundbreaking *Major Trends in European Jewish Mysticism*[300] provides an overview of German Hasidism. Scholem proposes that German Hasidism served as the forerunner to the Kabbalah. He then presents the Kabbalah as the mystical movement that nourished later Eastern European Hasidism.

According to Scholem, the roots of German Hasidism were complex.[301] Central to the movement, in any case, was an evolving understanding of religious devotion or piety "as a religious ideal which transcended all values derived from the intellectual sphere."[302] This trend was instrumental in moving European Judaism towards a deeper opening to mystical experience in general. The fledgling movement thus represented a growing set of values in which knowledge of the Bible, although important, became in some respects subsidiary to the spiritual dimensions of faith.

Scholem distinguishes three central features of German Hasidism, pivotal for its advancement: asceticism, serenity of mind, and altruism.[303] Here, the fear of and love for God formed the acme of the movement's spiritual ambitions.[304] Upon attaining spiritual advancement, the *hasid* was to act as the spiritual guide of the Jewish common folk. These priorities would come to impact European Jewry in the centuries that followed, bearing their marks on later mystical forms, particularly in the person of the Tzaddik.

According to Scholem, German Hasidism proved to be indispensable to the evolution of European Judaism in general.[305] Indeed, the rise of the movement would become decisive:

> Of all the factors determining the deeper religion of that community it was the greatest until the change which took place in the seventeenth-century under the influence of the later

---

[300] The edition used in this study is the 1946 edition. See Gershom Scholem, *Major Trends in Jewish Mysticism*, with a new foreword by Robert Alter (New York: Schocken Books, 1995).

[301] Scholem maintains that the rise of German Hasidism was not entirely removed from mystical trends emerging in Christian Europe around the same time. He insists, however, that other sources of mystical thought had infiltrated and impacted German Jewry long before. See Scholem, *Major Trends,* 80ff.

[302] Scholem, *Major Trends,* 91.

[303] Scholem, *Major Trends,* 91-95.

[304] Scholem, *Major Trends,* 95.

[305] Scholem, *Major Trends*, 81. Scholem maintains that although the movement's most creative period "was relatively short—about one century, from 1150 to 1250—its influence on the Jews of Germany was lasting; the religious ideas to which it gave rise and which it filled with life retained their vitality for centuries. It is to them that German Jewry largely owes the inner strength and devotion which it displayed when new storms of persecution arose." Scholem, *Major Trends,* 81.

> Kabbalism, which originated at Safed in Palestine. Strictly speaking, it was the only considerable religious event in the history of German Judaism. Its importance lies in the fact that it succeeded already during the Middle Ages in bringing about the triumph of new religious ideals and values which were acknowledged by the mass of the people. . . . So far from being isolated, the [German] Hasidim were intimately connected with the whole of Jewish life and the religious interests of the common folk; they were recognized as representatives of an ideally Jewish way of life even where their principles were never completely translated into practice.[306]

Scholem's interpretation of German Hasidism is commensurate with his thesis that Eastern European Hasidism was not a novelty or innovation in Jewish mysticism. According to Scholem, the later Hasidism embodied the culmination of a long succession of trends within the European Jewish context, emerging as the "last phase" of European Jewish mysticism.[307] Thus, in positing German Hasidism as the forerunner of the Kabbalah and, in turn, identifying the Kabbalah as the predecessor of Hasidism, he implies all three were linked.[308]

The Kabbalah

The roots of the Kabbalah as a distinct movement remain disputed;[309] the specificities of its beginnings depend on whom you consult. In spite of the wide-ranging theories of the Kabbalah, of its influences and inception, its rise and expansion, as well as its transmutations in modern times, the Kabbalah rose to evolve into one of the most influential movements within Judaism—and beyond.

The Kabbalah had a vital impact on its immediate successor, eighteenth-century Hasidism. As such, a brief overview of a number of the Kabbalah's salient features serves as a meaningful preface to an examination of Eastern European Hasidism.

The foundational work of the Kabbalah was the *Sefer haZohar*, otherwise known as the Zohar ("Book of Splendor" or "Radiance").[310] A multi-volume

---

306 Scholem, *Major Trends,* 81.

307 See Scholem, *Major Trends,* 325-350.

308 See Scholem, *Major Trends,* 118.

309 Although the designation "Kabbalah" would not be formally applied until the fourteenth century, the origins of the word *kabbalah* extend back to the Hebrew Bible. The Hebrew root of *kabbalah*, *kabbal*, "to receive,"(also widely translated as "tradition" or "acceptance") can certainly be linked to the later movement when "receiving" the secrets of the divine came to play a central and decisive role. See Gesenius, *Hebrew and English Lexicon of the Old Testament*, 867.

310 Scholem, *Major Trends*, 156.

midrashic commentary on the Pentateuch written in an unusual form of Aramaic, its exact origin and date are unknown—and debated. Discovered in Spain in the thirteenth century, it was first published by Moses de Leon, who ascribed the book to a second-century rabbi—a theory which modern scholarship has since rejected.[311] During the thirteenth century, the work became linked to the word Kabbalah. Influenced by the *Bahir* and other texts stemming from medieval rabbis and the *Hasidei Ashkenaz*,[312] the Zohar impacted emerging circles that would eventually spread the Kabbalah across medieval Europe. Arguably, however, the strongest impact would not be felt until after its publication in Mantua in the second half of the sixteenth century,[313] with the rise of the Lurianic Kabbalah.

The Zohar presents as a sophisticated, but highly obscure, compound work. It is widely understood as having both biblical and rabbinic sources. As a strikingly intricate, bold metaphorical work, its largely abstract language, convoluted, and at times conflicting images have subjected it to a plethora of interpretations and endless evaluation and critique.

Still, several theological notions found throughout the Zohar came to impact the theoretical and practical development of the Kabbalah. The first of these concepts addresses questions surrounding the creation of a finite world by an infinite Godhead. This notion, the *Ein Sof* (or "The Infinite"[314]), references the transcendent and infinite divinity that exists beyond all description and postulation. The ten attributes of the *Ein Sof*, known as *sefirot*, are understood as being directly involved in creation. In emanating some light of the divine, they bring the multi-layered finite world into existence.[315] This multifaceted, vital process unfolds sequentially, in a complex and dynamic fashion, birthing and sustaining the human being and, from there, the varied realms of the cosmos.

A remnant of the divine presence or power remains on earth, known in feminine terms as the *shekhinah*.[316] This remnant is engendered by the tenth and "lowest" *sefira* and remains unified with the transcendent divine through the ethical, spiritual acts of human beings. In striving to remain in harmonious contact with the Shekhinah, human beings can affect the flow between the finite and the infinite.[317] Due to the sensitivity of the Shekhinah caused by constant exposure

---

[311] Scholem, among others, attributes the book to Moses de Leon himself. See Scholem, *Major Trends,* 159.

[312] Scholem, *Major Trends,* 157.

[313] Harry M. Rabinowicz, *Hasidism: The Movement and its Masters* (Northvale, NJ: Jason Aronson, 1988), 16.

[314] Scholem, *Major Trends*, 208.

[315] Scholem, *Major Trends,* 208-9; and Joseph Dan, *Kabbalah: A Very Short Introduction* (Oxford: Oxford University Press, 2007), 43-47.

[316] Dan, *Kabbalah*, 47-51; and Scholem, *Major Trends*, 229-30.

[317] Significantly, Kabbalists sought to affect this aversion through adherence to the Torah and the Talmud. Dan, *Kabbalah*, 56-58.

to the separate, oppositional entity known as evil,[318] it is incumbent upon human beings to redeem the Shekhinah from evil. Here, the lower and higher realms, the realms of finite creation and of divine and infinite creation, emerge as linked. As the apex of creation, human beings have the potential to influence divine intentions and interventions on earth. With this, the evil that is a constitutive part of creation can be, to some extent at least, averted.[319]

This mystical, theoretical construct, impacted concretely the lives of its adherents. The constant striving towards ever-higher levels of moral and spiritual perfection expanded their mystical practices. These became imbued with magic rituals intended to overcome those demonic powers of evil understood to saturate the cosmos.

The Kabbalah spread through much of Europe during the Late Middle Ages. During this period, the Zohar became a familiar text in elitist circles. Reserved for the learned and spiritually advanced, the work was withheld from the common folk who were deemed unfit to grasp its esoteric content and fulfill its stringent practices. The long tradition prohibiting mystical investigation among the common folk was still adhered to; in this context, Kabbalists too, who considered themselves traditionalists, did not openly propagate their mystical affiliations. Their secret practices resulted in a blending of Kabbalistic teachings and traditional ones. These adherents were influential in the establishment of the theoretical framework of the later, Lurianic Kabbalah.

By the mid-fifteenth century, although the influence of the Zohar itself had slowed, the Kabbalistic worldview had begun to dominate mystical circles in Europe, North Africa, and the Middle East.[320] During this period, the messianic element in the writings of Kabbalists became more pronounced. This contributed to the spread of the Kabbalah in the century to follow.[321] Indeed, the sixteenth century would bring with it a renewal of Kabbalistic teachings. Eventually, these would become more accessible to common people and offer them some hope of relief for the sorrows of living in exile.

As we shall see, this revitalized Kabbalah assisted, over the course of its development, in making the general population receptive to the later Hasidic movement.

---

[318] Evil was understood by some medieval Kabbalists as having come into being through a distorted or defective process of emanation. As such, it was constitutive of a dualistic world view in which both good and evil vied for the upper hand in creation: the good, to redeem, and evil, to destroy. See Dan, *Kabbalah*, 51-52.

[319] Dan, *Kabbalah*, 54-61.

[320] Dan, *Kabbalah*, 36-37.

[321] Dan, *Kabbalah*, 36-37.

Transitions: Lurianic Kabbalah and the Hasidim of the "Old School"

The spread of the Lurianic (or "practical") Kabbalah throughout Europe and the Ottoman Empire from the seventeenth century onwards was to become decisive for the future of Hasidism. However, the impulses to this spread had begun a century earlier. During the years following the destruction of the Jewish center in Spain and the expulsion of the Jews from the region in 1492, the spiritual community in Safed, Upper Galilee, drew into its midst intellectuals and followers of the Kabbalah from Israel, the Iberian Peninsula, other parts of Europe—and beyond. This community was characterized by its search for spiritual refuge and clarity; its strict, orthodox adherence to the commandments of the Torah and the Talmud; its extreme acts of penance; as well as its spiritual determination and fortitude.[322]

In Safed, Moshe ben Jacob Cordovero (1522-1570) laid important ground with his innovative, rationalistic interpretation of the Zohar. Following him, Isaac Luria (1534-1572), who arrived in Safed in 1570, offered a seminal account of the teachings of the Zohar that would revolutionize the Kabbalah. Luria's disciple, Rabbi Hayyim ben Joseph Vital (1542-1620), acting as Luria's interpreter, voice, and scribe, compiled his master's teachings in such a way as to lend them compelling power.[323]

Luria's novel and extensive exegesis of the Zohar served to develop the work's most sublime concepts into a more clearly systematized, theoretical construct. This claimed to unravel the deepest mysteries of the divine, the universe, and humanity. The basic tenets of this construct impacted the path that the Kabbalah would take, extending beyond the borders of Israel, and eventually to North America and into modern times.

Luria postulated that the creation of the world was the result of voluntary contraction, constriction or self-withdrawal of the *Ein Sof* known as *tzimtzum*.[324] He envisioned the ensuing vacuum, known as *tehiru* (or "emptiness"[325]), as the very locus of creation. In the complex process of creation, thin rays of divine light shone into the vacuum; with this, the *sephirot* assumed the shape of "vessels" (*kelim*) whose content was divine light itself.[326] In as much as the vessels were unable to contain the greatness of the light, they broke (*shevirat ha-kelim*), scattering splinters of the vessels across creation.[327] While some of the shards returned to the higher spheres, others remain trapped in the lower ones, retaining "divine sparks"[328] of exiled light that stood in need of a kind of correction or

---

[322] Talabardon, *Chassidismus*, 27-28.
[323] Scholem, *Major Trends*, 252ff.
[324] Scholem, *Major Trends,* 260-264.
[325] Dan, *Kabbalah*, 75.
[326] Scholem, *Major Trends*, 252, 266-68.
[327] Dan, *Kabbalah*, 76.
[328] Dan, *Kabbalah*, 79.

rectification (*tikkun*).[329] When this correction occurred, the broken vessels would be mended. This restoration was understood to serve as, "the purpose of creation, of human existence, of the Torah, and of the people of Israel."[330]

The Godhead's attempt at creation had thus failed; indeed, the disequilibrium that ensued from the creative process between the infinite and finite worlds had given birth to evil. The redemption of the divine sparks that had the power to terminate the evil in the world could only be brought about by human obedience to the law. In striving to release the sparks into their original sphere by way of strict adherence to tradition, human beings could assist in transporting the sparks out of the lower spheres, thereby neutralizing evil.[331] Because the soul of the human being was deficient and perfect obedience was difficult to achieve, however, the possibilities of redeeming the sparks remained limited. Accordingly, only a soul free of sin was considered capable of escaping the endless cycle of reincarnation (*gilgul*), a cycle considered the fate of all until final redemption would take place.[332]

With its reflection on the themes presented by the Zohar, and in conjunction with the Kabbalistic theories and concepts proposed during the High and Late Middle Ages, Lurianic mysticism became concerned with similar questions of God, creation, the cosmos, humanity, and evil. More and more, these aspects were understood to be intrinsic to the complex unfolding of history and the universe. Later, in alignment with particular teachings surrounding the *tikkun*, teachings would develop that understood human beings as capable of hastening the coming of the Messiah through obedience to the written and oral Law.

All of this is important, for as Lurianic teachings were imported into Europe, they fell upon fertile ground. There, messianic expectations had already been growing among many exiled Jews following their traumatic expulsion from the Iberian Peninsula. As the coming of a messiah was deemed more and more necessary to liberate the Jews from their suffering, the new Kabbalah was swift to take hold. This development contributed to the intensifying of the messianic hopes of the people. With this, a new phase of mysticism had been ignited, one that would later come to impact Hasidism. With the rise of the heresies of Sabbateanism and Frankism, however, the Messianic component of the Kabbalah would be regarded cautiously.[333]

---

[329] Scholem, *Major Trends*, 273-78.
[330] Dan, *Kabbalah*, 78.
[331] Dan, *Kabbalah*, 78-84.
[332] Scholem, *Major Trends*, 280-84.
[333] Shabbatei Zevi's (1626-1676) apocalyptic message quickly secured a strong foothold in European Jewry, drawing large numbers of followers. But with the unmasking of the heresy on the occasion of Zevi's apostasy and conversion to Islam in 1666, European Jewry became unsettled once more. As Jacob Frank's (1726-1791) heresy was similarly exposed almost a century later, and as the crisis of faith deepened, the ground became fertile for revised visions of hope and deliverance. Many disillusioned Jews would eventually turn to the rationalism offered by the Enlightenment. However, others would

The gradual spread of the Kabbalah throughout Europe inspired the formation of smaller, offshoot groups of ascetics known as Hasidim (also referred to as the Hasidim of the "old school"), whose rigorous practices were based on esoteric Kabbalistic teachings.[334] Strict dietary guidelines, rules governing the observance of the Sabbath, rites of penance and prayer, the study of holy and esoteric texts, and extreme ascetic practices were modeled on those originally practiced in Safed, distancing its followers from the still widely-accepted teachings of Rabbinicism.[335]

During this period, Lurianic teachings gradually infiltrated the general population. Sacred rites intended to aid the coming of the Messiah, teachings of magic, as well as miraculous healing practices began to generate popular interest in the Kabbalah. By the end of the seventeenth century, groups of educated, spiritually elite Kabbalists known as "Masters of the Name" (*Ba'alei Shem*)[336] were sought after for spiritual guidance, cleansing, and bodily healing. The Masters kept demonic forces at bay by invoking the unspeakable "Name of God," conducting exorcisms, administering medications, and offering spiritual counsel. Increasingly, they were consulted as magicians, miracle-workers, and spiritual guides.[337]

By the mid-eighteenth century, Jewish communities across greater Poland had fallen into grave decline. In the hundred years following the Cossack Uprising, their socio-economic situation had worsened; the Golden Age of Eastern European Jewry was now past. Jews were stripped of economic privilege and status and were forced to live in the shadow of Christian landlords, clergy, and state officials. With antisemitism abounding, taxes needing duly to be paid, and

---

seek alternative sources within the by-now widely spread Kabbalah. In as much as Kabbalistic teachings were now deemed more accessible, even among the most uneducated of the common folk, many were drawn towards them. This swing towards a kind of grass-roots mysticism was to bear fruit in parts of Eastern Europe with the spread of Hasidism there. For more on the rise and fall of Sabbateanism and its link to Hasidism, see Scholem, *Major Trends*, 287-324, and 333-34. See also Pawel Maciejko, ed. *Sabbatian Heresy: Writings on Mysticism, Messianism, and the Origins of Jewish Modernity* (Waltham, MA: Brandeis University Press, 2017). For more on Frankism see Roberta Ascarelli and Klaus Davidowicz, eds. *Along the Road to Esau: Studies on Jacob Frank and Frankism* (Arezzo: Bibliotheca Aretina, 2011).

[334] Talabardon, *Chassidismus*, 30, 32-34.

[335] Talabardon *Chassidismus*, 32-34.

[336] The designation appeared as early as the thirteenth-century. See Talabardon, *Chassidismus*, 34.

[337] Immanuel Etkes maintains that the *Ba'alei Shem* have often been cast into dubious light due to their alleged status among the uneducated classes of their time. He attributes this view to the impact of the Haskalah literature of the nineteenth century. This literature, he suggests, overlooked how the *Ba'alei Shem* had become associated with all classes, including the highly educated. See Immanuel Etkes, *The Besht: Magician, Mystic, and Leader*, trans. Saadya Sternberg (Waltham, MA: Brandeis University Press, 2005), 43-45.

poverty among the lower classes rampant and on the rise, the lives of Eastern European Jews were ones of disillusionment and despondency.[338]

With these developments, deep divisions arose within the communities themselves. The chasms between the learned, powerful rabbis and uneducated Jews contributed to a pervasive atmosphere of tension and mistrust. By this time, many Jews had come to resent the spiritual authority of the rabbis who had increasingly distanced themselves from the plight of their constituents. Rabbinic teachings, the fruit of years-long academic study, were perceived by many as sterile and distant, divorced from day-to-day existence. Indeed, the dictates of strict religious practice placed upon the common folk only further burdened their lives of drudgery and servitude.[339]

This complex situation was arguably one important factor contributing to the receptivity of many Jews to the religious phenomenon that would soon appear. With the spread of the teachings of the new Kabbalah vying for the support of the people, the region was ripe to receive yet another mystical movement, one whose innovative founder would call the hearts of many to spiritual renewal.

Hasidism

The Besht

By the time Israel ben Eliezer, known as the *Baal Shem Tov* (ca. 1700-1760; "Master of the Good Name," popularly referred to as "The Besht") settled in Podolia around 1740, his forerunners had prepared the way for him. In spite of the popularity of the *Ba'alei Shem* as magicians and healers, they had continued as elitist and segregated groups; as such, their teachings had remained inaccessible to those outside their sphere. Indeed, the time was ripe for the folk to receive new teachings.

The Besht's appearance was timely indeed. The theological shift that his teachings represented embraced a compelling message—earthy and dynamic—that quickly drew the attention of other practicing Kabbalists.[340] Some of these would follow him and then, with time, form offshoot circles that would spread the Besht's teachings beyond their ranks to the common folk. It was with these groups in particular that a reform movement would begin.[341]

---

[338] Simon Dubnow, *Geschichte des Chassidismus*, trans. A. Steinberg (Berlin: Jüdischer Verlag, 1931; repr., Jerusalem: Jewish Publishing House, 1969), 1:30ff.

[339] Dubnow, *Geschichte des Chassidismus*, 1:47ff.

[340] Archives from the region indicate the Besht had been registered as a "practical Kabbalist."He is also thought to have practiced in the double role of *Ba'al Shem* and mystic, as a teacher of both the theoretical and practical Kabbalah. See Talabardon, *Chassidismus*, 36, 41-43.

[341] Talabaron identifies a dialectical relationship between "old school" Hasidism and the new movement. While the first group focused on ascetic Kabbalistic practices, the new

According to traditional sources, the Besht exuded extraordinary charisma, possessed gifts of healing, conducted exorcisms, and practiced ecstatic prayer.[342] More scholarly certainty can be lent to claims that, in possessing an undoubtedly strong personality, he laid aside the extreme asceticism of his contemporaries and opted for a more grounded approach to spirituality.[343] He is said to have insisted, for example, that joy, rather than grief and sobriety, was the key to understanding the divine realm. Instead of fasting, he propagated focused meditation on the holy alphabet.[344] Such spiritual admonitions would assist in shaping the new movement as it unfolded.

For the Besht, the Hebrew alphabet lay at the center of both creation and the cosmos. In as much as creation could be considered an emanation of the alphabet, the twenty-two letters were thought to embody the power of the creator. Layers of creation, understood as disparate worlds, were each formed by their respective letters, with each descending letter giving birth to ever more materialized worlds. With this descension, the powers of the divine became increasingly veiled and the spiritual nature of the Godhead more concealed. Here, the interpretations of the Genesis text "God spoke and it was," offered during late antiquity and the Middle Ages, were given new inflections.[345]

Proposing these notions as the cosmological basis for those teachings that posited each layer of creation, however concealing, as corresponding to the divine, the Besht maintained that no aspect of creation—and no place within creation—was "empty of God."[346] With this, the Hebrew alphabet took on enormous significance as the source of all that is; of all layers of creation, of all worlds, indeed, of the whole of the cosmos. Indeed, the whole of creation could be thought of as a text of God, created, upheld, and sustained by this one divine source.[347]

Hasidim would develop, over time, the figure of the *tzaddik*. The Tzaddik would help to bridge the gap between the common folk and the high ideals of the popularized Kabbalah. This development would be crucial to the spread of the movement across Eastern Europe. Talabardon, *Chassidismus*, 37.

342 Talabardon, *Chassidismus*, 37.

343 Whether and how the Besht is to be understood as the innovative founder of a "revolutionary" movement is debated. Traditional scholarship, based primarily on legends and hagiographic sketches, attests to his humble beginnings. He is believed to have drawn a circle around him distinct from his Kabbalist cohorts. Recent scholarship, however, posits him as a well-educated individual who rose to the ranks of the learned elite. As a man of influence and leadership, he is thought to have enjoyed the recognition of well-known personalities that extended into rabbinic circles. See Talabardon, *Chassidismus*, 44. Etkes offers a further investigation of the Besht with regard to his work as a *Ba'al Shem*. See Etkes, *The Besht*, 46-78.

344 Talabardon, *Chassidismus*, 49.

345 Talabardon, *Chassidismus*, 51.

346 Talabardon, *Chassidismus*, 51.

347 Talabardon, *Chassidismus*, 51.

The panentheism that emerged from this early Hasidic view is notable. Because no place or thing was considered to be absent of God, evil as such could not exist in an ontic sense.[348] As such, evil was only the veiled divine penetration of the lower levels of the cosmos, which were still full of God.[349] In this sense, evil could not be destroyed, only transformed; drawing from Kabbalistic notions, evil stood in need of being healed or "repaired" through human words and deeds. These could be lifted out of their immediate context and given back into their divine origin, the eternal good. With this, the letters of the alphabet could be realigned to correspond to their original positions.[350]

Drawing from this cosmology, human actions came to play a central role in overcoming evil. Meditative prayer known as *Yichud*, through which the devout sought to unite the male *sephira* with its female counterpart, the *shekhinah*, set free divine blessing to flow down into the lower realms. However, human actions needed to correspond to them; *Yichud* needed to be united with right-thinking, and right-thinking with right-speaking and acting, even in the most mundane of situations. Here, human behavior became integral to the transformation of evil; indeed, all actions were to be directed towards the Godhead's inner processes, which sought to restore order to the cosmos.[351]

In this context, human thinking emerged as central to the Besht's overall theological construct. United with human action, correct thinking set into motion those processes of the Godhead inextricably linked to and dependent on human action. With the letters of the alphabet capable of being rearranged correctly by way of *Yichud*, and thereby diminishing the powers of evil, this link becomes evident. Susanne Talabardon writes: "In the diction of the early Hasidic masters, this activity, which reaches well beyond the traditional duties of the human being towards the Eternal, is referred to as, "'service to God in corporeality (*Avoda be-Gashmi'ut*).'"[352] As such, any and all acts—including the most mundane—were enclosed within this "service" as long as they were directed correctly in terms of *Yichud*.

With evil capable of being overthrown by the realignment of the sacred letters through *Yichud* and *Avoda be-Gashmi'ut*, it is incumbent upon the human being to strive to overcome "the distance between him or her and the Eternal by cleaving to [the Eternal]."[353] This notion of intentionally directing oneself in body and spirit to the Godhead, known as *devequt*, was drawn from the Kabbalah. For the Besht, however, *devequt* comprised the cleaving of the entire person to the

---

348 Talabardon, *Chassidismus*, 51.
349 Talabardon, *Chassidismus*, 52.
350 Talabardon, *Chassidismus*, 52.
351 Talabardon, *Chassidismus*, 53.
352 Talabardon, *Chassidismus*, 53. Translation mine.
353 Talabardon, *Chassidismus*, 53. Translation mine.

spiritual being of the letters themselves.[354] Here, the extent to which early Hasidic teaching was absorbed with the mysteries of the Hebrew language is apparent.

In a strong sense, these teachings mirrored Kabbalistic ones. However, they were innovative by way of the fact that all persons, not merely the spiritually elite, could participate in the "service to God in corporeality."[355] By allowing for this in both the sacred and the mundane spheres of existence, the Besht's teachings represented an important first step towards in bringing the mystical thought of the time to the common people.

The Besht himself did not live to see the wider distribution of his teachings, and it would not be until the teachings surrounding the Tzaddik had become more widespread that the common folk would come to know and practice *devequt*. Just as these teachings became increasingly complex, so too would the situation of the Jewish laity.[356]

In what other ways can the teachings of the Besht be seen as innovative? Talabardon argues that the lines between the Besht's teachings and those of his forerunners blurred, in as much as the former flowed smoothly into the latter.[357] Still, several innovations can be highlighted here. First, the emphasis on vibrant joy in God contrasted starkly the at-times dark asceticism of the Kabbalah. Secondly, the *Avoda be-Gashmi'ut*, in which the entire physicality of the human being was caught up in the Eternal, was new in its advocation of a holistic, corporeal access to the divine. Thirdly, the panentheism embraced by the notion of "no place being empty of God" granted a novel twist to the idea of evil as having no ontic reality per se.[358] Fourthly, the relinquishment of the stringent study of the scriptures and the adherence to specific prayer forms and commandments in favor of the practice of ecstatic, often physically flamboyant styles of prayer, represented a clear divergence from Lurianic thought.[359] Finally, the mystical teachings surrounding the Hebrew alphabet revealed, to some extent, a return to notions that preceded the Lurianic Kabbalah while, at the same time, granting them new focus.

---

[354] Talabardon, *Chassidismus*, 54.
[355] Talabardon, *Chassidismus*, 53.
[356] Talabardon, *Chassidismus*, 54-55.
[357] Talabardon suggests that the disappointments incurred by the collapse of Sabbateanism and Frankism exacerbated the tendency of the new movement to avoid radical messianic theologies. With time, Hasidism would adhere much more to traditional, rabbinic messianic teachings. Talabardon, *Chassidismus*, 57.
[358] Moshe Idel argues that the panentheism of this phase of Hasidism was not entirely new: it was a theological paradigm that had existed before the rise of the Besht, handed down, ultimately, from the teachings of Rabbi Moshe Cordovero. See Moshe Idel, *Hasidism: Between Ecstasy and Magic* (Albany: State University of New York Press, 1995), 17-18.
[359] Friedrich Battenberg, *Das europäische Zeitalter der Juden. Zur Entwicklung einer Minderheit in der nichtjüdischen Umwelt Europas*, vol. 2. *Von 1650 bis 1945*, 2nd ed. Darmstadt: Wissenschaftliche Buchgesellschaft, 2000), 79.

Early Spread, Opposition, and Defiance

The early spread of the "new" Hasidism has been attributed more to the followers of the Besht, rather than to the Besht himself. At the time of his death around 1760, the Besht had attracted groups of followers, largely adherents of both the Kabbalah and rabbinic circles, who were drawn to his charisma, preaching, and teaching. As these dispersed throughout the region and beyond,[360] they began to establish the reputation of the Besht as, "a worker of miracles and a mystic of the highest rank, and as someone who paved a new path in divine worship."[361]

The Besht's most prominent follower, Rabbi Dov Ber, otherwise known as the "Maggid of Mezeritch" or "The Great Maggid," has most often been considered responsible for transforming the Besht's mission into a new movement. The transfer of the center of teaching from Podolia to Volhynia following the death of the Besht allowed the Maggid to institutionalize the teachings of his master. This resulted in the eventual spread of the teachings across Eastern Europe and into Central Europe.[362] With large numbers of students gathered around him, the Maggid came to develop and expand the teachings of the Besht. Within a relatively short amount of time, many of the Maggid's own disciples dispersed, forming smaller, tightly-knit groups whose teachings at times diverged theologically from their master's, a phenomenon that served to develop further the substance, cause, and direction of the fledgling movement. This development progressed until the death of the Maggid in 1772.[363]

However, the progression of Hasidism across the region was soon threatened from outside. Critique of the movement was inevitable. Many rabbis viewed the teachings of the Kabbalah, to which they now considered Hasidism to adhere, with suspicion. The unconventional practices of the Hasidim were cause for grave concern, and the suggestion that the study of the Talmud was secondary to the practice of prayer was considered an affront to traditional circles.[364] Most importantly, perhaps, the rabbinates began to feel their authority undermined as the role of the Tzaddik grew in importance.[365] In the context of the deepening conflict between the uneducated classes and rabbinic circles, and in light of growing political tensions across the region, it was inevitable that the rabbis viewed the new Hasidic teachings as an additional encroachment upon their authoritarian domain. Towards the end of the eighteenth century, the conflict became severe as the

---

[360] Battenberg, *Das europäische Zeitalter der Juden*, 2:78.
[361] Etkes, *The Besht*, 202.
[362] Battenberg, *Das europäische Zeitalter der Juden*, 2:79.
[363] Battenberg, *Das europäische Zeitalter der Juden*, 2:79.
[364] Battenberg, *Das europäische Zeitalter der Juden*, 2:79.
[365] Schmuel Ettinger argues that the issues of power and authority were central in the resistance against Hasidism at this time. Shmuel Ettinger, "The Hassidic Movement—Reality and Ideals" in *Essential Papers on Hasidism: Origins to Present*, ed. Gershon David Hundert (New York: New York University Press, 1991), 239-40.

movement began to take hold in Jewish communities across the wider region. This development has been deemed, "a rebellion of the poor masses against the learned rabbinate."[366]

The conflict between rabbinic circles and the Hasidim casts a shadow over the movement into the nineteenth century. Finding its center in Vilna, the so-called "Jerusalem of Lithuania,"[367] the counter-movement was led by Rabbi Elijah Ben Solomon Salman (1720-1797), otherwise known as the Gaon of Vilna. A leading Talmud scholar and prominent personality in rabbinic circles, the Gaon took it upon himself to crush the Hasidic communities that had grown up throughout the region.

The tale of this conflict is complex. By the time of the Gaon's death in 1797, Hasidism's influence across Lithuania and White Russia had weakened. Although the Russian state authorities decided to approve the existence of Hasidic communities in 1804, the conflict between the Hasidism and their opponents, the Mitnaggedim, raged on.[368]

Still, Hasidism continued to grow. Ironically, the conflict surrounding it had contributed to its "institutional stabilization."[369] In the communities where its adherents formed a majority, particularly in Ukraine, Eastern Galicia, and Hungary,[370] the powers of the rabbis diminished substantially. Ultimately, many rabbinates in these regions would become subservient to the Tzaddikim whose authority over communal life had already begun to take hold. With these developments, the Jewish communities, once seeped in crises of mistrust and suspicion, had strengthened yet again.[371]

In spite of the ongoing animosity between traditional Jewish communities and Hasidic ones, Hasidism became more and more integrated into Eastern European Jewry. However, by the time the Maskilim, proponents of the Haskalah (the Jewish Enlightenment) who had found a strong foothold in other parts of Europe, moved east, both traditional and Hasidic communities alike were beginning to recognize the threat that the new and "enlightened" ideas of the Haskalah posed to their conservative way of life. Ironically, in as much as the Maskilim advocated for new paradigms of study, faith, and lifestyle, both rabbi and Hasid came to view their struggle against the new ideology as a shared one.[372] This common cause, intensified by mounting fears generated by the encroachment of

---

366 Battenberg, *Das europäische Zeitalter der Juden*, 2:79. Translation mine.

367 Battenberg, *Das europäische Zeitalter der Juden*, 2:80. Translation mine.

368 Talabardon, *Chassidismus*, 126.

369 Battenberg, *Das europäische Zeitalter der Juden*, 2:81.

370 Battenberg, *Das europäische Zeitalter der Juden*, 2:81. See also Taladardon, *Chassidismus*, 133.

371 Battenberg, *Das europäische Zeitalter der Juden*, 2:81. See also Ettinger, "The Hassidic Movement," 241-42.

372 Shmuel Ettinger, *Geschichte des jüdischen Volkes*, vol. 3, *Vom 17. Jahrhundert bis zur Gegenwart. Die Neuzeit*, ed. Haim Hillel Ben-Sasson, trans. Christian Spiel (Munich: C. H. Beck, 1980), 147.

state authorities upon the existence of traditional communities,[373] allowed for a joining of ranks between the two camps in their fight for survival.

The saga of the Maskilim's struggle to win Eastern European Jewry is a bitter one. The attacks against both Hasidic and traditional communities from the side of the Maskilim were relentless and scathing.[374] By the 1870s, however, the cause of the Haskalah in Eastern Europe had weakened, which left the Maskilim questioning the efficacy of their struggle.[375] This would have a strong ripple-effect in the decades that followed. Although secondary to this project, all that ensued would contribute to the birth of Zionism. This movement too would have a strong impact on Hasidism.

A Movement of the Folk

Traditional scholarship has portrayed early Hasidism as a movement that encouraged a new spiritual direction for Jews of all social classes. The teachings of the Besht are seen to have embraced a faith-paradigm in which all could actively participate. During the first phase, at least, this was one element that came to impact the development and spread of the movement. However, the reasons that Hasidism took such strong hold are undoubtedly many: socio-political factors, economic realities, unjust power differentials, and widespread spiritual disillusionment all contributed to the rapid spread of the movement. Within a relatively short amount of time, Hasidism was able to spread throughout Eastern Europe, and transformed traditional Jewish life there. It secured its strongest footholds in parts of Russia, White Russia, Volhynia, Ukraine, Podolia, and Poland in particular.

Over the course of several generations, the new teachings passed through a number of critical phases. With time, Hasidic teachings came to represent a large and, at times, disparate body of thought. Eventually, however, the teachings surrounding the Tzaddikim came to dominate much of Hasidism. The Tzaddik came to exercise more and more power in Hasidic communities, creating a new dynamic within the movement. Some scholars identify these developments as the beginning of Hasidism's decline.

Central Teachings: The Examples of Great Maggid and J. Joseph

As was the case with the Kabbalah, Hasidism was, from its incipience, concerned with the nature of the divine, the creation of the world, and the origins of evil. Significantly, Hasidism's understanding of evil would become, with each new wave of the movement, constitutive of its understanding of the nature and

---

[373] Ettinger, *Geschichte des jüdischen Volkes*, 3:147.
[374] Ettinger, *Geschichte des jüdischen Volkes*, 3:149-151.
[375] Ettinger, *Geschichte des jüdischen Volkes*, 3:151.

destiny of the human being. Taken together, these themes would come to shape the unfolding of the movement.

In the nineteenth and twentieth centuries, Hasidic communal life centered on the numerous courts and dynasties of the Tzaddikim. The teachings of these courts and dynasties often diverged significantly. Given the number and diversity of these schools, a detailed overview of each reaches well beyond the parameters of this study. In light of this, I have chosen to examine the theoretical models of two early Hasidic teachers with the aim of highlighting several of the most notable features of their teachings. This examination provides insight into the ways in which the Besht's successors tended to modify his original teachings. While not exhaustive in its scope, it acts as a point of reference to examine the eventual mutation of particular themes and the strong sociological implications these then held for communal life.

Indeed, new formulations of the Besht's central teachings evolved following his death in 1760. Briefly, the Besht's cosmological theory centered on the Hebrew alphabet. According to the Besht, as God spoke the letters of the alphabet, creation—including all levels of the world and universe—was called into existence. In this process, God himself, embodied in emanations or *sephirot*, became present in multiple layers of creation; as such, nothing in creation was without God's indwelling presence. Be that as it may, the divine became increasingly veiled with each successively lower level. In the lowest levels, where the divine could no longer be perceived at all, this veiling resulted in what human beings perceived to be evil.

In this context, the duty of human beings was to break through the illusion of evil and behold the fullness of the divine. By inwardly cleaving to the letters (*devequt*) with full fervor, attention, and intention (*kavvanah*), and by all their actions (*avoda)*, both sacred and mundane, human beings could lift the veil of perceived evil to behold and be united with the divine. For the Besht, this possibility lay open to all.[376]

Due to the dispersion of the Besht's disciples, it was inevitable that these original teachings evolved. The Besht's best-known disciple, the Great Maggid of Mezeritch, Rabbi Dov Ber, has been considered, as previously indicated, largely responsible for the early development and spread of the movement. I will outline his theological program briefly here.

The Maggid overturned the Besht's panentheism, contending that, "the material world possessed no ontic quality, no independent reality."[377] To achieve the fullness of *devequt*, the world needed to be bracketed, worldly needs and enjoyments nullified, and the necessity for communal reform set aside.[378] With this,

---

376 Karl Erich Grözinger, *Jüdisches Denken. Theologie – Philosophie – Mystik*, vol. 2, *Von der mittelalterlichen Kabbala zum Chassidismus* (Frankfurt: Campus Verlag, 2005), 2: 856.
377 Talabardon, *Chassidismus*, 83. Translation mine.
378 Talabardon, *Chassidismus*, 83.

the Besht's "service to God in corporeality" was "transformed into a spiritual act."[379]

The problems inherent in creation preoccupied the Maggid, just as they did the Besht. In revising particular Lurianic concepts, the Maggid adapted the notion of *tzimtzum*, the elevation of the divine sparks, and reinterpreted it as a restriction of God's wisdom. This restriction was what had called all of creation into being, in particular, Israel and her election.[380]

With the world having been created *ex nihilo*, or "out of nothing," this Nothing posed as the divine Light that was ultimately responsible for creation in flowing from Wisdom itself.[381] In essence, all of creation was flowing back and forth into this Nothing; with this, Nothing symbolized for the Maggid the "absolute unity of the divine."[382] He came to understand Nothing as predicating all that is, indeed, as the precondition for and preface to the existence of everything.[383] Ultimately, he understood it as the vehicle through which God became immanent in all.[384]

Still, the Maggid had to reckon with the problem of evil in the world. He modified Lurianic teachings once again by positing a variation of the "breaking of the vessels" (*Sh'virat ha-Kelim*) that was to become the hallmark of his theory of creation. This complex teaching understood the "vessels" as having contained divine light that had then broken away and dispersed, their "splinters" (*K'lippot*) having been scattered throughout the cosmos. With this, God too had broken away from all he created, a devastating event that removed all of creation from its original roots, the Nothing. It was this detachment that was responsible for the endless variety found within creation. It was considered a process of individuation that, in contrast to Lurianic teaching, did not hinder the creation of the world, but rather served as the necessary condition and vehicle for it.[385]

With respect to this process, the Maggid noted how each individual entity claimed to be the "king of the world," to alone possess the title "I." This, the Maggid insisted, was a title only attributable to God.[386] This phenomenon of individuality had remained part and parcel of the "breaking of the vessels" that occurred; as such, it formed the very foundation of evil.

The Maggid understood this overall process as having been necessary in allowing anything to be created at all—as sinful and as evil as it must be.[387] Given

---

[379] Talabardon, *Chassidismus*, 88. Translation mine.
[380] Talabardon, *Chassidismus*, 85.
[381] Talabardon, *Chassidismus*, 86.
[382] Talabardon, *Chassidismus*, 86. Translation mine.
[383] Talabardon, *Chassidismus*, 86.
[384] Talabardon, *Chassidismus*, 90.
[385] Grözinger, *Jüdisches Denken*, 2:821-22.
[386] Grözinger, *Jüdisches Denken*, 2:822.
[387] This *felix culpa* remains an important trademark of the Maggid's cosmological model. See Grözinger, *Jüdisches Denken*, 2:823.

the necessity of the great break that gave birth to evil into the world, "Good and Evil are, in the thought of the Maggid, dialectically entwined."[388]

For the Maggid, the mission of the human being then was to penetrate the divine Nothing. With the origin of creation being Nothing, and Nothing being God, the human being needed to submit to God as the essence of all existence.[389] The purpose and destiny of humanity, then, its *devequt*, was nothing less than returning its broken self—indeed of the world itself—into the Light of the divine, whose source was Nothing.[390]

In contrast to the Besht, who stressed the joy found in serving God through all mediums of living, both sacred and mundane, the Maggid claimed that cleaving to the letters of the Torah and to God in prayer needed to be positioned above all mundane acts.[391]

As was the case with his master, the Great Maggid did not purport any specific teaching of the Tzaddik, although some elements of his teachings did impact later development of the teaching through his disciples.[392] Through them, the importance of the Tzaddik within the community would increase exponentially, eventually engendering a social dynamic that would prove problematic for the movement as a whole.

The Great Maggid was not alone in developing the teachings of the Besht. The Besht's personal scribe, Jacob Joseph of Polonne (1710-1784), was among the first to extend these teachings. As did the Besht, Joseph stressed the centrality of the Hebrew letters in the creation of the world. However, he diverged from his teacher in claiming that a division had occurred within the divine during the process of creation. This resulted in two poles within the divine: the masculine and feminine emanations (*sephirot*). Although existing in duality, these were actually a unity, though the masculine dimension was dominant.[393] Given the ongoing process of creation—the *creatio continua*—the whole of creation, in spite of its inherent duality of form and material, could be understood as a unity.[394] This "unity within duality" constituted a central motif in Joseph's teachings, in contrast to the monistic, panentheistic cosmology of his master.[395]

In extending the motif of duality, Joseph explained that the diversity experienced within creation, including all that is perceived to be evil, actually existed as a neutral reality. Sin and evil ensued only "when the intended solidarity and togetherness of the diversity are broken and their constitutive elements take

---

388 Grözinger, *Jüdisches Denken*, 2:823. Translation mine.

389 Talabardon, *Chassidismus*, 87.

390 Talabardon *Chassidismus*, 88. Grözinger highlights how this return references the "interior" or spiritual/mystical dimensions of the world, not its material. See Grözinger, *Jüdisches Denken*, 2:830ff.

391 Talabardon, *Chassidismus*, 88-89.

392 Talabardon, *Chassidismus*, 90. See Grözinger, *Jüdisches Denken*, 2:849-52.

393 Grözinger, *Jüdisches Denken*, 2:858.

394 Talabardon, *Chassidismus*, 62.

395 Grözinger, *Jüdisches Denken*, 2:856.

no notice of the fact that they are dependent upon each other."[396] Thus, "neither the material nor the form constitutes the actual source of evil, only their separation."[397]

Joseph reasoned that human beings, as a result of being created from both form and material, existed in deep duality as well. Persons born inclined to form were themselves form; they were drawn towards the spiritual spheres. Alternately, persons born inclined to material were themselves material; these were then assigned lower tasks related to the material world.[398] Joseph understood the Tzaddikim as human beings of form. Conversely, worldly persons, those men and women of the uneducated masses, were considered material human beings. All persons, however, were indeed human, and in being human, all existed as both individuals and as members of a larger community. Although the material human beings (i.e., the masses) were subservient to those of form (i.e., the Tzaddikim), both material and form human beings taken together formed a whole.[399] In this sense, Joseph's anthropological model illuminated the "individual and sociological dualism that cannot be eliminated, but can be seen to be transformed into a hierarchical, bipolar whole."[400]

These delineations were indispensable to Joseph's understanding of humanity's destiny, duty, and commission. In Karl Erich Grözinger's words: "In adhering to the bipolar laws of the world, there are consequences for the individual in terms of their ethical and mystical capacities."[401] Succinctly, Joseph envisioned the primary task of the human being as embracing the transformation of the materiality of the world into form; put differently, as ushering in the intended, but now broken unity, of creation.[402] By completing the task of opposing sin and evil, the human being approached the realm of the divine,[403] ennobling the soul within the body.[404]

Joseph's anthropology was woven carefully into his understanding of the tasks, functions, and forms of religious social contexts, that is, of spiritual community. As indicated, for Joseph, each individual was deemed a necessary part of a larger community. The community's existence hinged entirely on each individual fulfilling their role as either a material human being or a form human being. Crucial to the functioning of the community was the submission of material human beings to form human beings, that is, of the masses to the Tzaddikim.

It was only in the context of community that human beings could live out their roles as either material or form at all. Striking, too, was the notion that in

---

[396] Grözinger, *Jüdisches Denken*, 2:861. Translation mine.
[397] Grözinger, *Jüdisches Denken*, 2:865. Translation mine.
[398] Talabardon, *Chassidismus*, 63-64. See also Grözinger, *Jüdisches Denken*, 2:855.
[399] Talabardon, *Chassidismus*, 62.
[400] Grözinger, *Jüdisches Denken*, 2:855. Translation mine.
[401] Grözinger, *Jüdisches Denken*, 2:862. Translation mine.
[402] Talabardon, *Chassidismus*, 64, 72-73.
[403] Grözinger, *Jüdisches Denken*, 2:863.
[404] Grözinger, *Jüdisches Denken*, 2:864.

living out one's role as either material or form, one's deepest humanity would be realized.[405]

As both material and form human beings came together in community, they became a perfect entity, a whole. Sin and evil were then overcome, and transformed into goodness.[406]

With this model, Joseph had modified the Besht's teaching on the Tzaddik's relation to and role within the community. Given the duality inherent within humanity, both the Tzaddikim and the simple folk remained inseparable and interdependent. Still, the Tzaddikim's role was considered higher than that of the folk. According to Talabardon, "the Tzaddik was not only conceived by Jacob Joseph to be a mediator between the learned and the simple folk, he was also intended to enter the separation between heaven and earth, between God and humanity."[407]

The primary task of the Tzaddik was to cleave in *devequt* to the divine in the letters of the Torah, a task considered the "core and content of all the commandments of the Torah."[408] The task of both the simple Hasidim and the folk (all of whom, by nature, were incapable of sustaining the demands of *devequt*) was to cleave to the Tzaddik as he himself cleaved to the divine.[409] In this way, as the head of the community, the Tzaddik played a mediating role for the entire community. Evident here is the unique nature of *devequt*.[410]

For Joseph, the Tzaddik was first and foremost a mystic. However, his mysticism was expressed not only through his ascetic withdrawal from community, but also through his material presence *within* it.[411] Surprisingly, Joseph understood the composite needs of both the Tzaddikim and the folk as necessary for the life of all, in as much as they made possible the practice of *devequt*.[412] Just as the folk stood in constant spiritual need of the Tzaddik, and in so far as the Tzaddik was dependent on their constituents for the fulfillment of their material needs, an interdependent relationship between the two groups was inevitable.

It was with his understanding of the role of the Tzaddik that Joseph's teachings departed most distinctly from those of his teacher, the Besht. For Joseph, the abyss existing between the Tzaddik (as form) and the folk (as material) was indeed deep. Given this, and given the need for all human beings to take part in *devequt*, the Tzaddik would lower himself from the realms of the divine to the material realms of the folk in order to mediate between them and God. In so doing, the Tzaddik would draw close to the folk in "humility, compassion, and

---

405 Grözinger, *Jüdisches Denken*, 2:867.
406 Grözinger, *Jüdisches Denken*, 2:869.
407 Talabardon, *Chassidismus*, 66. Translation mine.
408 Talabardon, *Chassidismus*, 68. Translation mine.
409 Talabardon, *Chassidismus*, 69-70.
410 Talabardon, *Chassidismus*, 69-70. See also Grözinger, *Jüdisches Denken*, 2:877.
411 Grözinger, *Jüdisches Denken*, 2:873.
412 Grözinger, *Jüdisches Denken*, 2:875.

devotion."[413] The Tzaddik would then ascend once again, bringing up with him, at the same time, those who cleaved to him. Through this mystical act, the folk too were able to cleave to the divine, and thus participate in the *devequt*. For Joseph, ultimate salvation would occur when all of Israel reached a communal state of *devequt*. Without it, the holy sparks that were dispersed at the creation of the world would never be returned to their original source (*tikkun*).[414]

As offshoots of the teachings of the Besht, the Hasidic teachings of both the Great Maggid and Jacob Joseph represent only two models that came to impact the later evolution of Hasidism. However, they are helpful in understanding other vital aspects of the movement.

Hasidic Spirituality According to Martin Buber

The powerfully charismatic spirituality of Hasidism as a mystical movement was crucial to its intense and rapid development. Several key concepts have already been introduced in connection with this here. The composite paradigm these pose assists in understanding better the emotive character of Hasidism, its psycho-social power, as well as the ways in which it continues to attract followers today.

The legends surrounding the Besht strongly indicate that Hasidism at its earliest stage was so viscerally potent as to entice the learned and the unlearned to join its ranks. Indeed, it was a movement with compelling power. Its creative energy, purportedly set into motion by the charismatic personality of the Besht himself, appealed to folk who were desperately in need of refreshment. Intuitive, emotional, earthy, and potentially cathartic in its impassioned pronouncements, Hasidism was able to break through the at-times dark asceticism of the Kabbalah, offering its adherents a sense of liberation and closer proximity to God. With this, the movement possessed a dynamism and a magnetism arguably unparalleled in the history of European Jewish mysticism.

This section summarizes several central elements of Hasidic spirituality, and seeks to highlight how intricately these are interwoven in an overall paradigm. According to Martin Buber, [415] these elements include the notion of *hitlahavut* (ecstasy, fervor or bliss); *kavvanah* (intention); *shiflut* (humility) and

---

[413] Talabardon, *Chassidismus*, 71. Translation mine.

[414] Talabardon, *Chassidismus*, 71.

[415] I have chosen Martin Buber's interpretation of Hasidic mysticism to guide my analysis here, although the diagrams are my own. See Martin Buber, *Hasidism and Modern Man*, trans. and ed. Maurice Friedman (Princeton, NJ: Princeton University Press, 2016). In this volume, Buber examines Hasidism by focusing on four salient elements of Hasidic spirituality. While Scholem's consternation over Buber's portrayal of Hasidism may be persuasive, it brackets, often unfairly, Buber's insight into the uniqueness of the movement. Deferring to historical analysis, Scholem gives preference to the Kabbalah.

avoda (service). With *devequt* (cleaving to the divine) forming the center of this paradigm, one can visualize Hasidic spirituality in the following way (figure 4):

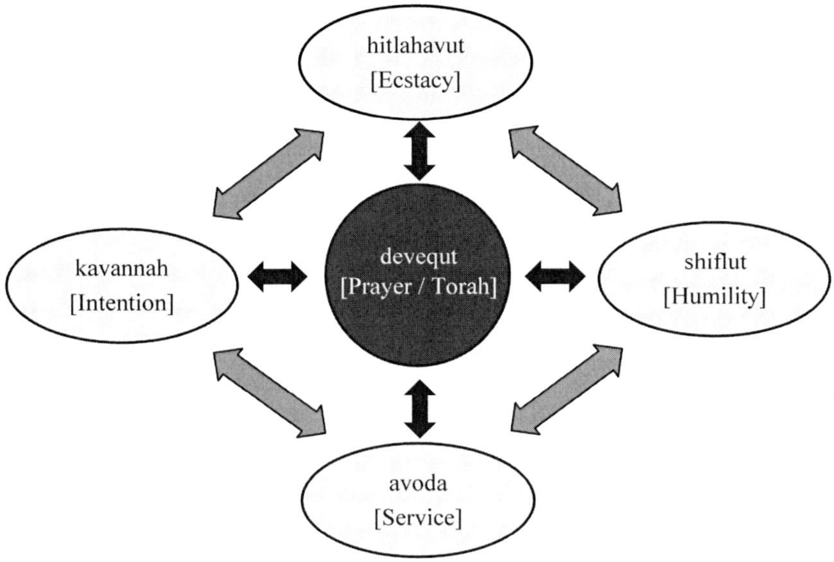

Figure 4 — Martin Buber's Model of Hasidic Spirituality

In this diagram, *devequt* can be seen as both forming the center of the model, and as being directly related to the other four elements. This constellation requires some elucidation.

As we have seen, the goal of *devequt* was to draw human beings into oneness with the divine (akin to the *unio mystica*). The Hasid understood that this was made possible through prayer and the study of the Torah. Through *kavvanah*, deeply-focused attention and intention, the Hasid, both in prayer and in study, yielded to the ecstasy of *hitlahavut*, experiencing bouts of fervent energy that led him to sing, dance, scream, and cry before God, and often falling into a stuporous, trance-like state of rapturous joy. Here, the link between *devequt*, *kavvanah*, and *hitlahavut* is made clear; *kavvanah* was the tool by which *devequt* was achieved and which gave way to *hitlahavut*, the ecstatic experience of God.

Important too is how *avoda* and *shiflut* were also linked to *devequt*, as well as both *kavvanah* and *hitlahavut*. For the Hasid, *avoda,* or service to God, was to be executed in all aspects of life, and always undertaken in the spirit of joy in, and love for, God. In this way, *avoda* was a constitutive part of the mystical journey. "Avoda is the mystic offering," writes Buber. "Avoda speaks, 'What am

I and what is my life that I wish to offer you my blood and fire?'"[416] Somewhat enigmatically, he continues: "Hitlahavut is as far from avoda as fulfillment is from longing. And yet hitlahavut streams out of avoda as the finding of God from the seeking of God."[417]

Avoda as service to God could be realized through both the most mundane and the most sacred of deeds. Given that all places, persons, and things everywhere were infused with the divine, all human action, even in the simplest of everyday settings, could be transformed into *avoda*. No deed was divorced from the life of the spirit and its quest to cleave to God, however simple it might have been. God himself was clothed in human deeds, in *avoda*; as such, all aspects of the Hasid's life flowed from and back into God. Again, Buber provides clarification:

> It was said of one zaddik, "With him, teaching and prayer and eating and sleeping are all one, and he can raise the soul to its roots."
>
> All action bound in one and the infinite life carried into every action: this is avoda. "In all the deeds of man—speaking and looking and listening and going and remaining standing and lying down—the boundless is clothed." . . .
>
> When through all action the rays of the universal sun radiate and the light concentrates in every deed, this is service. But no special act is elected for this service. God wills that one serve Him in all ways.[418]

The link between *hitlahavut* and *avoda* becomes evident:

> He makes his body the throne of life and life the throne of the spirit and the spirit the throne of the soul and the soul the throne of the light of God's glory, and the light streams round about him, and he sits in the midst of the light and trembles and rejoices.[419]

Within this model, *avoda* underscores the ethical dimension of Hasidism; the good and right deed, when done in the love of God and of others, possessed the power of opening up the way to the divine.

The humility of *shiflut* too highlights this same ethical dimension. While the ecstasy of *hitlahavut* and the intention of *kavvanah* were understood to be constitutive of the *avoda* that clothed the divine in *devequt*, *shiflut* assisted in

---

[416] Buber, *Hasidism and Modern Man*, 37.
[417] Buber, *Hasidism and Modern Man*, 37.
[418] Buber, *Hasidism and Modern Man*, 38.
[419] Buber, *Hasidism and Modern Man*, 44.

linking the Hasid to the community and to the world. As human beings came to assist in liberating the Shekhinah from its exile in the fractured cosmos, all tasks undertaken were always being performed in the context of that profound brokenness. In as much as the community was considered an inextricable part of the deep structure of the cosmos—and as such of God—service to the community was understood as a vital and necessary sphere where one could experience *devequt*. This service included the simplest, most humble, tasks needed to sustain the life of the community. Buber phrases this by stating that there is, "a high service [to God] that only the community can fulfill."[420]

Still, service in the physical world had its pitfalls; indeed, it could tempt one with visions of greatness. It was a temptation that needed to be resisted; haughtiness brought no blessing, only illusions.[421] The humility of *shiflut* had to be pure and unadulterated. This trait, according to Buber, was the key to true service to the community; in "disregarding" oneself, one mysteriously "regarded" the divine. He writes: "[W]hen a man rests in himself as in nothing, he is not limited by any other thing, he is limitless and God pours His glory into him."[422] Unforced and without compulsion, non-judgmental and in awe of the reality and uniqueness of each human being, *shiflut* was to flow from simplicity of spirit and, above all, from unrestricted love for all.[423] In this context, the "mystery of humility"[424] lay in the act of restraining oneself from the temptations of isolation and asceticism and to be truly present in the world.[425] [426]

---

420 Buber, *Hasidism and Modern Man*, 53.

421 Buber, *Hasidism and Modern Man*, 54.

422 Buber, *Hasidism and Modern Man*, 55.

423 See Buber, *Hasidism and Modern Man*, 55ff.

424 Buber, *Hasidism and Modern Man*, 55.

425 Buber, *Hasidism and Modern Man*, 54-56.

426 Buber's understanding of Hasidic mysticism, which has guided me in this section, came under direct fire from Scholem's keen pen. Hasidic mysticism, Scholem argues, was not an isolated spiritual phenomenon: it needed to be understood in those historical contexts that had had a decisive determining effect on its development. In my opinion, Scholem underemphasizes the extent to which the dynamic parameters of any mystical movement must always move it beyond its immediate historical context. In fact, in attempting to touch realities beyond the historical contingencies of human life, mysticism, by definition, embraces a decidedly ahistorical dimension. What is more, he overlooks how Buber approaches to this spiritual movement and the kinds of questions he poses. While Scholem approaches it through a historical lens, Buber has done so through a religious, theological, spiritual and phenomenological lens. The critique posed by Scholem then might in some sense also be taken up by Buber. In my opinion, the two bypassed one another for this reason.
Buber approaches Hasidic spirituality as one who has himself been impacted deeply by it; however, this cannot discredit his evaluation out of hand. He approaches the subject as from "within," rather than "without." Though Buber's reading of Hasidism may indeed reflect aspects of his own existential philosophy, it still engages with the most fundamental, definitive components of Hasidic spirituality, those that endowed it with such

With *devequt* as its primary motif, and by drawing its force from that one poignant center, the spirituality of Hasidism emerged as powerful and unique in Eastern Europe. Its influence at the grassroots level, at the level of actual, historical communities, was remarkable. Just how strong and compelling the movement was became evident in the phenomenon of the shtetl in particular. As small but dynamic enclaves of Jewish life and spirituality, the shtetlekh of Eastern Europe arguably represent the final concretization of the mystical journey of the European Jew.

Further Developments, Decline, and Extinction

Hasidism profoundly impacted Jewish communal life in Eastern Europe profoundly. Although Tzaddikism eventually came to cast a shadow over Hasidism, Hasidic spirituality was certainly the *tour de force* that ignited the movement at its onset, propelling it forward in such a way as to change the face of Eastern European Judaism, and this in spite of Hasidism's eventual, pre-World War decline.[427]

Considered sociologically, Hasidism's powerfully emotive dimension was one that assisted in its rapid spread and establishment. Indeed, it lent shape to the content, development, and distribution of its legends, language, and customs, as well as to the lively communal life of the shtetl. Hasidism also inspired the musical traditions of the shtetlekh, bringing to it new intonations of longing and belonging, of suffering and joy, of love and loss into communities. In the footsteps of the Kabbalah before it, Hasidism also influenced superstitions and preoccupations with magic, healing, and the supernatural. It impacted

---

strong psychosocial appeal. He reads it according to that frame of reference he has chosen and has guided all his examination of spirituality, philosophy, and religion—just as Scholem has done.

[427] Hasidism's decline had various causes, the problematic developments in Tzaddikism being but one. Geopolitics; the arrival of the Haskalah and the enlightened ideas of its Maskilim; emancipation, assimilation, and integration pressures from all sides; as well as the rise of Zionism and socialism—all came to play important roles in the waning of the movement. By the mid to late nineteenth century, modern antisemitism and pogroms were on the rise, and Eastern European Jewish life in general fell under threat. The first waves of emigration began. The First World War and the period between the two wars exacerbated these difficulties; more pogroms ensued, and more Jews began to flee Europe, heading to America, Israel, and other countries. Still, many shtetlekh remained, however impoverished, its people adamant to retain their traditions and culture. World War II was the ultimate and final blow in the destruction of Eastern European Jewry. For a concise overview of the developments of European Jewry during this period see Battenberg, ed. *Das europäische Zeitalter der Juden*, vol. 2, chaps. 3-4, and 6-10. See also Ettinger, *Geschichte des jüdischen Volkes*, vol. 3, chaps. 7-25.

significantly the ways in which men and women, communities and regions, all came to view and understand themselves.

By the nineteenth century, the role of the Tzaddik as a spiritual teacher evolved into that of a local lord with authority over all aspects of communal life. He judged legal matters with a compassionate or stern hand; received his constituents to hear their requests, settle their differences, or offer advice—both spiritual and worldly—and, if necessary, he provided for the material needs of the poor. In this way, a sense of dependency upon the Tzaddikim grew and intensified among the people who viewed them as their highest spiritual, moral, and social authority.[428] Seen as infallible, other-worldly, divinely-appointed beings capable of transmitting divine power, judgment, and goodness; as a blessing to the people; and last but not least, as virtual incarnations of the Torah, these men were both revered and feared.[429]

At this time, the powers of the Tzaddikim were transferred from father to son, rather than from teacher to disciple. With this, the complexity of Jewish communities deepened. Conflict and corruption within these prominent families were not uncommon, and the power struggles often enticed renegade sons to break off from their fathers to found schools of their own.

Amidst such changes, much of Jewish communal life in Hasidic-dominated regions was transformed. Even the most common member of the community fell under the authority of the Tzaddik, which came to override even that of

---

[428] Scholem writes: "The new ideal of the religious leader, the Zaddik, differs from the traditional ideal of rabbinical Judaism, the *Talmid Hakham* or student of the Torah, mainly in that he himself 'has become the Torah.' It is no longer his knowledge but his life which lends a religious value to his personality. He is the living incarnation of the Torah. Inevitably the original mystical conception of bottomless depths within the Torah was soon transferred to the personality of the saint." Scholem, *Major Trends*, 344. Scholarship surrounding the Tzaddik has at times mystified the role of the leader. Rabinowicz writes: "The role of the tzaddik was multifaceted. He was the attorney (*meilitz yosher*), who pleaded for his clients before the august assembly of the Heavenly Court; and he was *guter yid*, the friendly father figure, in whom his children could confide. Whether they needed spiritual strengthening or *gezunt und parnossa* (health and sustenance), the *rebbe*'s blessing and his assurance that 'the Almighty would help' fell like water on the parched lips of afflicted Jews sunk in the deep valley of despair. His power was far-reaching. His most casual utterances were invested with many levels of mystical meaning, and his considered judgments were counsels beyond cavil. He wore infallibility like a silken *kapote*, and his endorsement was thought to guarantee the success of any prophet." Rabinowicz, *Hasidism*, 171.

[429] The Tzaddik was understood to contain "the aspect of God" that enabled him to do all that God himself was capable of doing. In addition to his task of mediating between God and the folk, however, the Tzaddik provided the community with other needed spiritual and civil services. See Raphael Mahler, *Hasidism and the Jewish Enlightenment: Their Confrontation in Galicia and Poland in the First Half of the Nineteenth-Century*, trans. Aaron Klein, Jenny Machlowitz-Klein, and Eugene Orenstein (Philadelphia: The Jewish Publication Society of America, 1985), 249.

the rabbinate. With this, the Tzaddik's position was firmly established. And with many Tzaddikim living in relative luxury from the pocketbooks of their often-impoverished constituents,[430] the result was a power differential far removed from the intentions of the Besht.

Scholars such as Scholem and Buber view the greater structural changes of the movement—the expansion of the teachings surrounding the person of the Tzaddik in particular—as indicative of the movement's decline.[431] Ironically, other scholars have regarded the nineteenth century, with the widespread presence of Hasidic dynasties and the entrenchment of their teachings, as the movement's "golden era." The movement had a unifying effect on Jewish communities across Eastern Europe, and without doubt, the impact that the dynasties had on Jewish identity in the region was critical to their formation. Harry M. Rabinowicz writes:

> The nineteenth century was Hasidism's golden era. This was the time when many Eastern European villages had their own hasidic courts. Many a remote little *dorf* [hamlet] in Russia and Poland owes its immortality to the hasidic rabbi who lived there and adopted its name as its title. . . . From these hamlets, brilliant luminaries lit up the souls of men and added a new luster, a new richness, a new depth to the hasidic constellation.[432]

By the late-nineteenth century, Hasidism had become institutionalized across Eastern Europe. Hasidic courts and dynasties had long replaced small Hasidic

---

[430] The teachings surrounding the *Tzaddikim* that defended the accumulation of riches at the hands of the community were problematic. Based on passages found in the Torah, its proponents argued that supplying the Tzaddik with material goods was an adequate response to the spiritual aid provided by them to the community. See Mahler, *Hasidism and the Jewish Enlightenment*, 246-47.

[431] Scholem identifies a number of new developments in the second century of Hasidism as indicative of its departure from its original quest. The cult surrounding the personality of the Tzaddik was one that, in his view, divided the first half-century of Hasidism from its second phase. See Scholem, *Major Trends*, 336, 337-43, 343-44. Buber, whose literary interpretation of Hasidism clashed with Scholem's, agrees with Scholem in some respects. Buber writes: "The period which followed the first three generations of hasidism is usually treated as one of incipient decline. . . . There is no doubt that the crude power characteristic of the outset of hasidism lessened during this second epoch, which mainly occupies the first half of the nineteenth century, though certain exponents of hasidism lived past that time. . . . The real problems of the second period are not apparent in the sphere of the spirit and teachings of hasidism, but in that of its inner structure. They emerge in three different sets of relationship: that of the zaddik to the congregation, the zaddikim and their congregations to one another, and that of the zaddik to his school." Martin Buber, *Tales of the Hasidim*, trans. Olga Marx (New York: Schocken, 1948), 2:7.

[432] Rabinowicz, *Hasidism*, 153.

schools and had spread across the entire region, with Galicia and Podolia having almost entirely embraced the movement.[433] With the authoritative role of the Tzaddik strengthened and the teachings of their countless courts diverging, competition and even animosity between schools were not uncommon. Hasidic communal life differed from region to region, as economics, geopolitics and anti-Semitic sentiment began to impact Jewish populations to different degrees. The Hasidic movement had become heterogeneous.[434]

The situation for all of Eastern European Judaism, however, would soon change yet again. From the 1880s onwards, Eastern European Judaism would:

> experience an entire sequence of great catastrophes and violent disruptions. While antisemitism progressed in poisoning [Jewish] social life in Western Europe, a wave of pogroms rolled over and beyond southern Russia. Millions of Jews were driven to emigrate. The twentieth century, in particular the two World Wars, led to the near-extinction of Eastern European Judaism. In any case, the traditional life of the small hamlets and shtetls was extinguished. In the chaos of these incomprehensible events the Tzaddikim were forced to offer their followers help and orientation.[435]

The consequences of these events form the themes of this study.

The Shtetl of Sighet: Historical Context

Before turning to an exploration of Jewish lore, a few remarks can be made concerning the historical and social setting of the shtetl of Sighet at the onset of the Second World War.

The Jewish community of Sighet (known today as Sighetu Marmatiei)[436] possessed a degree of communal autonomy and economic self-sufficiency at the turn of the twentieth century.[437] However, following World War I, life in the shtetl

---

433 Talabardon, *Chassidismus*, 177-78.

434 Talabardon: "On the other hand, more than ever, *the* Eastern European Hasidism did not exist. During the course of the four generations very different types of *Tzaddikim* had developed and, resulting from this, very differently influenced communities." Talabardon, *Chassidismus*, 178. Translation mine.

435 Talabardon, *Chassidismus*, 179. Translation mine.

436 "Sighet," United States Holocaust Museum website, accessed January 23, 2018, https://www.ushmm.org/wlc/en/article.php?ModuleId=10008204

437 "By the late nineteenth-century, once it became possible for Jews to own land and timber, many Jews worked in the lumber industry. Sighet, with its sawmills, became a center in the forestry business. The town also functioned as a center for salt trade from nearby salt mines." See "Sighet," United States Holocaust Museum website.

was similar to many shtetlekh across Eastern Europe.[438] With antisemitism on the rise, [439] the rights and privileges of Jews in Sighet were eroding and acts of violence were increasing. According to Wiesel, abuses were suffered by the shtetl Jews at the hands of the Christian community outside its precincts.[440]

The structured hierarchy of the shtetl in Sighet was not unlike others of the region. A Jewish council had been put into place by the non-Jewish authorities to ensure that order was maintained in the shtetl. Practically speaking, the rabbinate held the highest position of authority and influence on both religious and secular matters. The schools of the shtetl, from the primary school *heder* to the schools of higher religious learning, the *yeshivoth*, performed the function of transferring knowledge and tradition from one generation to the next. The synagogues—of which there were five in Sighet[441]—served as centers not only for living out the traditions of faith, but also for drawing together the Jewish community and forming it into a tightly-knitted whole. Its leaders and elders played a vital role teaching and performing rituals that embraced all aspects of life from birth to death. This served to nourish the life of the shtetl, lending it structure, focus, and rhythm.

As was the case with many shtetlekh of the region, the shtetl of Sighet was strongly influenced by Hasidic traditions. A number of Hasidic schools were represented there: the line associated with Rabbi Yekuti'el Yehudah Teitelbaum (1912–1944), and later his uncle Yoel Teitelbaum (which would eventually become the Satmar sect); the Vizhnitzer tradition, which was predominant in Maramaros County, of which Sighet was a part; as well as newer dynasties such as

---

[438] "Sighet," United States Holocaust Museum website.

[439] Henry Eaton writes: "Between the world wars public institutions to which Romanian Jews had appealed for relief from persecution or support in their struggle for political rights declined or disappeared, or, like the government, church, law courts, and press had become united against them. Beneficial influences from the west, which had brought some advantages to Romanian Jews in the past, faded as Romania moved into the economic and political orbit of Nazi Germany. The underlying cause of this growing hostility was a volatile mixture of the old Christian mythologies, emerging pseudoscientific racism, militant nationalism, and a multitude of economic woes. In the rising tide of discontent, fascist antisemitic political parties flourished." Henry Eaton, *The Origins and Onset of the Romanian Holocaust* (Detroit: Wayne State University Press, 2013), 43. Wiesel also references his own angst in connection with the violence perpetrated against the Jews of Sighet during his childhood. See Wiesel, *All Rivers Run to the Sea,* 18-19.

[440] Wiesel writes: "In general, I accepted the outbreaks of anti-Jewish hatred as endemic to our condition. If they beat us on Christmas Eve or threatened us at Easter, it would pass soon enough. If drunks insulted us, cursing us for having 'profaned the Host,' 'poisoned the wells,' or 'killed the Lord,' it was only natural, to be expected. I faced these ordeals without astonishment, almost without sorrow, as though telling myself, it's their problem, not ours." Wiesel, *All Rivers Run to the Sea*, 19.

[441] See Sheldon Shreter, "Selected Facts on the Jews in Sighet, Maramuresh, Transylvania," accessed January 23, 2018, http://www.bigmeathammer.com/aushwitz1b.htm.

those associated with Spinka and Kretchnev.[442] A Sephardic ashkenazi congregation existed there as well.[443] Wiesel also indicates the presence of adherents to the Kabbalah.[444] Notwithstanding a growing number of Zionists and sympathizers of communism,[445] Sighet was by and large a community steeped in traditional religious fervor and zeal.[446]

Although Jewish communities had grown in larger centers due to the dynamics of immigration, economics, and geopolitics, many shtetlekh such as the one in Sighet continued to exist in smaller urban and rural centers. By the beginning of World War II, the Jewish population of Sighet had risen to about 10,500—approximately 37% of the town's overall population—from the 8,000 that had lived there at the onset of World War I. Following the war, Transylvania, the region in which Sighet was situated, had become a part of Romania, only to be transferred back to Hungary in 1940 with the Second Vienna Award.[447]

By the eve of World War II, the dark political cloud that had settled over Western Europe had moved eastward, and questions surrounding the region's future had exacerbated the tensions felt by Jews and non-Jews alike. Despite grave dangers, however, Sighet, as did other Jewish communities across the region, persisted as a relatively insular entity.[448] Its traditional life continued, and, as Wiesel indicates, religion and faith granted a sense of safety, distraction, and reprieve. Later, even as World War II was well underway, this sense would not dissipate entirely.[449]

During the interwar period, a contingent of non-Hungarian Jews had settled in Sighet as they had done in other parts of Hungary. However, not all of

---

[442] "Sighet," United States Holocaust Museum website.

[443] See Shreter, "Selected Facts on the Jews in Sighet, Maramuresh, Transylvania."

[444] Indeed, Wiesel himself was enticed to join a Kabbalistic circle, against the will of his father. See Elie Wiesel, *The Night Trilogy: Night, Dawn, Day,* trans. Marion Wiesel (New York: Hill and Wang, 2008), 22-23. For a more detailed account, see Wiesel, *All Rivers Run to the Sea*, 33-38.

[445] "Sighet," United States Holocaust Museum website. Later, Wiesel learned, by way of an encounter with Norman Podhoretz, that there had been an active community of Frankists in Sighet. See Wiesel, *All Rivers Run to the Sea*, 397-98.

[446] In addition to *Night* and *All Rivers Run to the Sea*, see Frederick L. Downing, *Elie Wiesel: A Religious Biography* (Macon, GA: Mercer University Press, 2008), 27-32.

[447] "Sighet," United States Holocaust Museum website. See also Eaton, *The Origins and Onset of the Romanian Holocaust*, 139-40.

[448] Wiesel's recollections of his early childhood in both *Night* and *All Rivers Run to the Sea* testify to the relative introversion of the shtetl. Still, with chaos of war growing all around it, the awareness of peril mounted. See Wiesel, *The Night Trilogy*, 27.

[449] Wiesel writes: "Tragedy loomed, but life went on. . . . We knew something of what was happening beyond the borders. . . . But we could not anticipate the horror of reality. . . . The truth is that, in spite of everything we knew about Nazi Germany, we had an inexplicable confidence in German culture and humanism. We kept telling ourselves that this was, after all, a civilized people, that we must not give credence to exaggerated rumors about its army's behavior." See Wiesel, *All Rivers Run to the Sea*, 26-27.

these Jews had been able to secure Hungarian citizenship, which resulted in the deportation of some 20,000 Jews to the camps at Kamenets-Podolsk in German-occupied Ukraine in 1941.[450] The deportations of the "foreign" Jews of Sighet took place in August of that year. According to Wiesel's account, many of the Jews remaining in Sighet dismissed this ominous sign, rejecting the possibility of further deportations.[451] According to the author, even in 1943, as reports of the bombings in Germany and of Stalingrad flooded in, the Jews of Sighet were convinced that better times were coming and that the end of the war was nigh.[452] As the Germans took possession of Sighet in the spring of 1944 and created two crowded Jewish ghettos there,[453] the Jews still continued to believe that the Germans would sidestep the deportation of the shtetl.[454] That did not happen, as Wiesel's testimony indicates.

Lore, Legend, and Literary Representation

The Hasidic Tale

Hasidic lore is saturated with legend. In a strong sense, this reflects the charismatic nature of the movement as having been founded by a spirited master around whom wondrous stories evolved. Still today, the Besht is considered its most central figure. However, Hasidism's large corpus of legends includes those extending well beyond the legends of the Besht and embraces countless stories of the many well-known and lesser-known Hasidic personalities whose legacies, however legendary, impacted posterity. For this study, a view to Hasidism as a tradition deeply impacted by its legends is helpful as it permits a better understanding of Hasidism as field.

Storytelling has always stood at the center of the Jewish faith. Extending from the myths of creation; to the legends of Adam, Abraham, Isaac and Jacob; to the story of the exodus referenced by the father's question at the Passover table, "What makes this night different from all other nights?"; from the parables and tales of the Talmud; to the legends of the Hasidim; and on to present-day Holocaust literature, storytelling has remained the primary vehicle of Jewish

---

450 "Sighet," United States Holocaust Museum website.

451 Wiesel, *The Night Trilogy*, 24-25. See also *All Rivers Run to the Sea*, 28-29.

452 Wiesel, *The Night Trilogy*, 25-26.

453 Wiesel, *The Night Trilogy*, 29.

454 Wiesel: "Most people thought we would remain in the ghetto until the end of the war, until the arrival of the Red Army. Afterward everything would be as before. The ghetto was ruled by neither German nor Jew; it was ruled by delusion." Wiesel, *The Night Trilogy*, 30.

memory.[455] Each of these stories has helped shape Jewish tradition and identity, allowing them to retain an identifiable core in all their diversity. Arguably, one might say that these stories comprise this core. In this sense, storytelling has been the driving force that has enabled Judaism to continue beyond all that has endeavored to extinguish it.

The Hasidic tale, often considered a hagiographic form, is an important component of that long storytelling tradition.[456] Tales of the Besht and his extended circles were handed down primarily through the sermons of itinerant preachers and through mouth-to-mouth transmission. Written accounts of these legends appear as early as 1780 and continue into the early nineteenth century.[457] Lily Kahn has identified two main genres in Hasidic literature: narrative and homiletical.[458]

Parables, hagiographic tales, and tales (allegedly) penned by the masters themselves serve as sub-categories within the narrative genre.[459] The first significant collection of tales of the Besht, the *Shivhei ha'Besht,* was published in 1814. That same year, Rabbi Nachman of Breslov's *Sippure Ma'asiyot* appeared in both Hebrew and Yiddish.[460] Although *Shivhei ha'Besht* contains some historical material, a large portion of this collection is comprised of legends of the supernatural, miraculous healings, and rescues.[461] The book exhibits influences of biblical, rabbinic, and kabbalistic sources.[462] This diversity of sources is demonstrative of its place within the expansive continuum of Jewish storytelling. Although less important publications were in circulation prior to this,[463] the *Shivhei ha'Besht*, although not uncontended in its time,[464] was intended to solidify the charismatic image of the Besht, particularly as the movement was finding an ever-stronger

---

[455] For a concise (but not exhaustive) account of the role and chronology of the Jewish legend, see Haya Bar-Itzhak, "Legend," in *Encyclopedia of Jewish Folklore and Traditions*, ed. Raphael Patai and Haya Bar-Itzhak, (Armonk, NY: Sharpe, 2013), 1: 327-28.
[456] For a more detailed account of the lineage Jewish hagiography, see Susanne Talabardon, "Judaism: Cross-Reading Hasidic Legends," in *Narrative Pattern and Genre in Hagiographic Life Writing: Comparative Perspectives from Asia to Europe,* ed. Stephan Conermann and Jim Rheingans, Narratio Aliena? Studien des Bonner Zentrums für Transkulturelle Narratologie, vol. 7 (Berlin: EB-Verlag, 2014), 281-86, 291-94.
[457] Lily Kahn, *A Grammar of the Eastern European Hasidic Hebrew Tale*, Studies in Semitic Languages and Linguistics, vol. 77 (Leiden: Brill, 2015), 1-2.
[458] Kahn, *Grammar*, 1.
[459] Kahn, *Grammar*, 1-2.
[460] Kahn, *Grammar*, 2.
[461] Joseph Dan, "Hasidic Tales," in *Encyclopedia of Jewish Folklore and Traditions*, ed. Patai and Bar-Itzhak, 1: 232.
[462] Gedalyah Nigal, *The Hasidic Tale*, trans. Edward Levin (Oxford: The Littman Library of Jewish Civilization, 2008), 18.
[463] Kahn, *Grammar*, 1-2.
[464] Nigal, *The Hasidic Tale*, 17.

foothold across an increasingly theologically and ideologically diversified and divided Eastern Europe.[465]

An interval of some fifty years followed the publication of the *Shivhei ha'Besht* before the next major work of Hasidic narrative literature appeared. In 1863, Michael Ha'levi Frumkin's *Kehal Hasidim* ended the hiatus,[466] beginning a new epoch in which the "Hasidic narrative tale genre, particularly hagiographic literature, flourished and grew into a substantial corpus."[467]

Unlike exegetical or homiletic literature, storytelling was directed at a largely uneducated audience seen to be in need of practical instruction. Gidalyah Nigal writes:

> While the theoretical exegetical literature was intended for the educated and therefore a relatively small circle of readers, the hasidic storytelling genre translated the practical portion of hasidic teaching into the language of the simple folk, women and children. There was, it seems, no propagandistic literature that spoke to the hearts of the Jewish masses in the villages and towns as forcefully as the storytelling genre, which had its origins in the oral tradition. The story enabled the materially poor, whose lives were replete with trials and tribulations, to find balm for their personal suffering in the miraculous acts that were performed for the wretched and the oppressed, to identify with them, and even to hope that their own problems would be solved by the merit of the exemplary individual of their own generation.[468]

Nigal sketches several typical attributes of the Hasidic tale or legend. The miracles conducted by the Tzaddikim most often form the center of a story in which other Hasidim play only secondary roles. In such tales, the Tzaddik is often approached to solve a problem or heal a disease. However, legends of miracles conducted by ordinary but virtuous people also pepper the literature, emphasizing the notion that even a simple, uneducated individual can claim a rank higher than that of a spiritually elevated person by the desire to live a life for God.[469]

Very generally, the Hasidic tale is simply structured and, at first reading, easy to grasp. Lacking in strong aesthetic quality, it is optimistic, pious, and pragmatic, with a decidedly moral focus. Hasidic, non-Hasidic and even non-Jewish

---

[465] The collector of these tales, Rabbi Dov Baer of Linitz, was concerned that the legends of the Besht were being harmed by opponents of Hasidism who saw in their discrepancies a basis for discrediting them. See Kahn, *Grammar*, 16, 61-62.

[466] Dan, "Hasidic Tales," 1: 232.

[467] Kahn, *Grammar*, 2.

[468] Nigal, *The Hasidic Tale*, 75.

[469] Nigal, *The Hasidic Tale*, 55.

motifs are at times present; references to nature or landscape play little or no role in shaping the story.[470] Its content is didactic, and intends to relay the message of one whose conduct was deserving of emulation.[471] A hidden message, however, is often present. With formal theoretical and theological teaching most often omitted, the listener or reader is meant to extract this message for him or herself. With this, the tale, frequently open-ended, tends to pose more questions than it does answers. As such, it functions as a kind of riddle to be solved. It is thus of "hidden, esoteric significance,"[472] embodying a message of ethical and spiritual consequence and importance.

Through storytelling, it was believed that the master could be lifted up to the status of an infallible saint who, in clinging to the divine in *devequt*, was capable of "standing in" for his followers. Importantly, the very act of storytelling was deemed holy, in as much as it was thought to assist in elevating the sparks of the divine that had been scattered throughout the cosmos at creation. In this sense, it was considered "a way of serving God, just like Torah study, prayer, and the observance of the commandments."[473] For the uneducated, storytelling was also thought to have had a sanctifying, if not miraculous effect, in the belief that the reiteration of a master's miracle was capable of inducing another.[474]

During the initial phase of Hasidism, tales were passed on by masters who intended to memorialize other masters. The masters, therefore, had a double role; they were at once the subjects of the tales as well as the tellers of them. As such, they were deeply ingrained in the lore of the movement and instrumental in its development and continuation.

The common folk were also instrumental in the oral transmission of tales. Images of piety, humility, wisdom, mercy, and neighborly love, as well as themes of magic, mystery, and the supernatural all enticed listeners to tell and retell. The role that intergenerational storytelling played in the rapid growth and the maturation of the movement was significant.

With time, the tale played an increasingly pragmatic, apologetic role in the history of Hasidism.[475] Hagiography was needed not only to entice others to join the movement, but also to ward off growing critique from outside its sphere.[476] By World War I, most Hasidic narrative literature was aimed at a non-Hasidic audience which, lured by the prospects of assimilation into greater European society in the wake of the Haskalah, had distanced itself from the tradition. Interestingly though, readers also consumed the publications for reasons of

---

[470] Nigal, *The Hasidic Tale*, 76.
[471] Nigal, *The Hasidic Tale*, 75.
[472] Nigal, *The Hasidic Tale*, 54.
[473] Nigal, *The Hasidic Tale*, 50.
[474] Nigal, *The Hasidic Tale*, 57, 59.
[475] Nigal, *The Hasidic Tale*, 3.
[476] Nigal, *The Hasidic Tale*, 64; Dan, "Hasidic Tales," 1:233.

nostalgia, and not of worship.[477] This trend increased during the interwar period, even among Jews living abroad who sought to either criticize or idealize.

The Image of the Shtetl

Following the Holocaust, the literary reconstruction of the by-now annihilated Eastern European Hasidism boomed. Strikingly, the image of Eastern European Jewry had become one of a pure, intact, yet irretrievable, world where shtetl Jews in particular had lived out deep, committed, albeit insulated lives of faith and practice.

In their 1952 publication, *Life is with People: The Jewish Little-Town of Eastern Europe*,[478] Mark Zborowski and Elizabeth Herzog presented their readers with an innovative account of shtetl life in Eastern Europe prior to the onset of World War II. They set out to sketch a composite, homogenizing picture of the traditions, customs, language, and self-identity inherent to life in the shtetl by interviewing immigrants and/or their family members and reviewing the literature, art music, and film of the period. Their goals were fuelled by the hypothesis that these incubated communities had possessed a common denominator that allowed them to be understood collectively as indicative of Eastern European Jewish life. The result of this undertaking is a vivid and illustrious volume that addresses a plethora of subjects. Sabbath customs; robust traditions of learning and study; Yiddish, the language which colored many aspects of everyday life; practices surrounding family life, marriage, and children; the role of women within the communities; and Jewish self-identity are all examined systematically. The work paints a pristine image of what it meant to be an Eastern European Jew.

Zborowski and Herzog's undertaking was significant. Indeed, their work—and that of like-minded scholars—contributed to growing perceptions of the shtetlekh as small, compact entities that had lent homogeneity to Eastern European Jewry despite some theological and cultural differences.

Due to its idealizing, often unrealistic images, the work eventually was subjected to serious critique.[479] This critique ignited debate surrounding shtetl

---

[477] Dan, "Hasidic Tales," 1:233.

[478] Mark Zborowski and Elizabeth Herzog, *Life is With People: The Jewish Little-Town of Eastern Europe* (New York: International Universities Press, 1952).

[479] Yohanan Petrovsky-Shtern critiques the work for accentuating the religious dimension of shtetl life while eclipsing other more dominant ones. His contention is that the shtetlekh—which were so distinct that any compression of their common denominator into religion alone must fail—were driven more by economics than other factors. The demise of the shtetl following its "Golden Age" from 1790-1840, he argues, was due largely to the impact of geopolitics. He offers a similar critique to Abraham Joshua Heschel's rendering of the shtetlekh. My view is that such critique, while highlighting correctly the economic and political factors involved in the decline of the shtetl, does injustice to its religious infrastructures in its underestimation of their centrality. See

literature in general. Indeed, much shtetl literature had come to portray the shtetl in ways not unlike *Life is With People*. Questions surrounding the "realities" of the shtetl intensified and persisted—until today.

Drawing from these at-times heated discussions, scholars have sought to find broader sociological and literary themes by sorting through historical documentation, as well as pre- and post-war forms of shtetl fiction and non-fiction. They have addressed how this gradual transformation occurred and the emergence of the image of the shtetl as a strong, enduring symbol of Jewish heritage, identity, continuity, and Jewish unity within Jewish collective memory above and beyond the Holocaust.[480]

In conjunction with this trend, questions of historicity, far from abating, have been complemented by literary questions.[481] What is the commensurability of the historical shtetl and the shtetl as a modern literary image subject to critical inquiry? What is the relationship between the two? What unites them, what divides? And, especially here: In what ways did the Holocaust promote a shift in the portrayal of the shtetl, and why? These questions are of interest to this study, not merely in terms of the role that the shtetl plays in Wiesel's writing, but also in terms of their focus, at the meta-level, on matters of historicity, literariness, the power of language, the literary representation of memory, and the impact of the image of the shtetl on collective memory. They also embrace themes related to cultural production, the interpretive nature of experience, and the complex processes of reality-building through narration.

The critique surrounding *Life is With People* also begs the question as to whether or not the shtetl can be unequivocally defined and, if so, with what criteria.[482] In as much as the image of the shtetl has continued to evolve as an image with multiple meanings, scholars have begun to reconsider whether the quest for

---

Yohanan Petrovsky-Shtern, *The Golden Age Shtetl: A New History of Jewish Life in East Europe* (Princeton, NJ: Princeton University Press, 2014), 9-12. For further critical investigation, see Jeffrey Veidlinger, *In the Shadow of the Shtetl: Small-Town Jewish Life in Soviet Ukraine* (Bloomington: Indiana University Press, 2013), 3.

[480] Jeffrey Schandler suggests that the "proliferating of the use of the term [shtetl] after World War II betokens a shift in how East European Jewish Life is understood, as well as how it is discussed." Also: "With this restriction of meaning [of the word shtetl] to a particular place, demographic, and time comes an expanded understanding of what values—religious, ethnic, ideological, affective—*shtetl* symbolizes." See Jeffrey Shandler, *Shtetl: A Vernacular Intellectual History* (New Brunswick, NJ: Rutgers University Press, 2014), 2, 3.

[481] For a more detailed discussion on the mythologizing role of the image of the shtetl in modern Jewish identity see Paula Giersch, Florian Krobb, and Franziska Schössler, eds., *Galizien im Diskurs. Inklusion, Exklusion, Repräsentation*, Inklusion/Exklusion. Studien zu Fremdheit und Armut von der Antike bis zur Gegenwart, Band 17 (Frankfurt am Main: Peter Lang Internationaler Verlag der Wissenschaften, 2012), 25-30, and chapter 3, "Erinnerung und Mythos," 223-362.

[482] Shandler, *Shtetl: A Vernacular Intellectual History*, 23.

such a definition is meaningful at all.[483] Whether implemented historically as a descriptive collective of a "center of an economic-cultural zone, linking Jews to Christians and Jews to Jews,"[484] or applied sociologically to designate a cultural invention "introduced into Jewish discourse in the nineteenth-century . . . [to become] in the narrative of the Jewish people one of the more lasting symbols of the life of the Diaspora,"[485] or executed literarily as an "imagined construct," "the product of historiographic reconstruction,"[486] the image of the shtetl has emerged as a powerful symbol in modern times.

The historical development of the literary image of the shtetl is of significance. Interest in the shtetl as a cultural phenomenon was first incited in the earliest decades of Hasidism. The translation of the word "shtetl" from Yiddish is inconsistent, but in most contexts, it means "town" or "small town."[487] The shtetl was not a solely Hasidic phenomenon; groups opposed to Hasidism understood the shtetl as the locus of Hasidic life. Many Maskilim divorced themselves from the shtetl as a living, human reality, referencing it "as if they were on the outside looking in."[488] In such a critical environment, the shtetl became the object of intense scrutiny and polemic in the by-then widely-accessible literature of the Haskalah.

The goal of the Maskilim was to portray the shtetl as an awkward center of Jewish life that needed redemption and enlightenment. The emerging trend in literature expanded rapidly, granting provincial images of the shtetl to a growing readership that reflected critically on the variations evident in European Jewish life. Within this context, early Maskilim novelists such as Yisroel Aksenfeld, Isaac Mayer Dik, and Sholem Yankev Abramovitsh came of age with works that scolded the backwardness of shtetl life in the guise of entertaining satire.[489]

---

[483] Shandler, *Shtetl: A Vernacular Intellectual History*, 23.

[484] Shandler, *Shtetl: A Vernacular Intellectual History*, 23.

[485] John Doyle Klier, "What Exactly is a Shtetl?" in *The Shtetl: Image and Reality, Papers of the Second Mendel Friedman International Conference on Yiddish*, ed. Gennady Estraikh and Mikhail Krutikov (Oxford: Legenda, European Humanities Research Centre, 2000), 26-27.

[486] Arnold J. Band, "Agnon's Synthetic Shtetl," in *The Shtetl: New Evaluations*, ed. Steven T. Katz (New York: New York University Press, 2007), 234.

[487] See Eva Hoffman, *Shtetl: The Life and Death of a Small Town and the World of Polish Jews* (London: Secker and Warburg, 1998), 11.

[488] Attributed to David Roskies, quoted in Shandler, *Shtetl: A Vernacular Intellectual History*, 27.

[489] Dan Miron underscores how writers of early shtetl literature, in their rejection of the relevance of shtetl life, were at the same time enamored with it. This ambiguity later contributed to the development of shtetl literature. He writes, "The deep, almost sensual love evinced by these writers for the colorful ethnographic detail—the need to record, anatomize, and 'immortalize' it—are pitted here against the overwhelming rejection of a folk civilization that is presented as atavistic, irrational, devious, and cumbersome, a heavy medieval encrustation limiting individual freedom and undermining orderly and rational behavior far more than the dour, restrictive rabbinical law. The ambivalence

Beyond the Haskalah, and towards the end of the nineteenth century, Hebrew and Yiddish writers began to push their own literary agendas forward. While Hebrew writers held the hope of igniting a new age of Jewish culture based on Western values and the revival of the Hebrew language, Yiddish writers had begun to produce prodigious works that reached a much wider, middle-class readership. Although critical of traditional Jewish life, this new literature sought to portray the shtetl as a starting point for modern Jewish living. This literary turn was important,[490] and as the nineteenth century merged into the twentieth century, the flourishing of the Yiddish press quickly became a vital factor contributing to the development of new ideologies and cultural practices.[491] The literary image of the shtetl had begun to contribute to new constellations of Jewish self-awareness.

Indeed, during the period leading up to World War I, the documentation of Eastern European Jewish life became a primary focus. With this, the image of the shtetl was introduced, in the context of the rise of Yiddish as a cultural "touchstone,"[492] and as an "imaginary construct" in literature, art, theater, visual arts, and music.[493]

During this time, artist Marc Chagall, shaken by the upheavals, yet still preoccupied by the world of the shtetl that had once been his own, began his project depicting the pre-World War I disintegration of the shtetl in modern images. His work reflects the sense of confusion and fragmentation felt within the shtetlekh during this time.[494] It remains a memorial to Eastern European Jewry in the face of its eventual extermination.

The evolving image of the shtetl eventually impacted America. In the context of the plethora of Jewish immigrant communities existing there, literature

---

with regard to folklore as aesthetically seductive yet morally repugnant perfectly illustrates the split or rift that Yiddish literature had to somehow overcome if it were to ever function as a unified literary system in which the aesthetic and the moral may coexist." See Dan Miron, *The Image of the Shtetl and Other Studies of Modern Jewish Literary Imagination* (Syracuse, NY: Syracuse University Press, 2000), xi.

[490] Shandler notes: "Though their work often critiqued aspects of *shtetl* life, some Yiddish writers positioned these towns not as sites of abjection but as defining points of origin—even if they were ultimately to be transcended."Shandler, *Shtetl: A Vernacular Intellectual History*, 30.

[491] Shandler, *Shtetl: A Vernacular Intellectual History*, 30.

[492] Shandler, *Shtetl: A Vernacular Intellectual History*, 30.

[493] Shandler, *Shtetl: A Vernacular Intellectual History*, 24.

[494] The exhibition "The Breakthrough Years, 1911-1918," displayed at the Museum of Art in Basel, Switzerland, from September 2017 to January 2018 set out to portray, in both text and art, this formative period of Marc Chagall's life and work. Tracing the evolution of his work of this period chronologically, the exhibition highlights the role Eastern European Jewry played in the life of the artist. Its pieces impart Chagall's distress over the first stage of dismantlement of traditional Jewish life in Eastern Europe. In a strong sense, his work augurs the ultimate eradication of this life during the Holocaust.

addressing shtetl life (and shtetl fiction in particular) flourished in both English and Yiddish. With this, "[p]opular culture soon became America's most widely familiar source of information about the shtetl."[495]

The role played by Yiddish writer Sholem Aleichem (1859-1916) during this period was decisive, particularly in America. He not only accelerated the establishment of Yiddish literature as literature in its own right, but developed the image of the shtetl more extensively. During his tenure in America, interest in the Jewish life of the "old world" peaked among Jews and non-Jews alike. The influx of works from abroad was increasing, as was their readership. Sholem Aleichem's writings impacted this trend, culminating, of course, in his *Tevye the Dairyman*, written between 1895 and 1914. This work would eventually find increased renown in its Broadway adaptation *Fiddler on the Roof* in 1964 and the film version *Anatevka* in 1971.[496] Within a relatively short span of time, American readers and audiences were gripped by nostalgic images of Jewish life in Eastern Europe, emotionally enticing enough·so as to grant them popular appeal.[497]

During the author's lifetime, Sholem Aleichem's works were considered to have made the life of Eastern European Jewry accessible to the "new" world. This became a matter of contention following Sholem Aleichem's passing in 1916. Critics observed how his works presented shtetl life as idyllic and intact. Critical questions regarding the historical accuracy of shtetl images had begun to emerge.

Within a relatively short period of time, however, the image of the shtetl would shift again. While in the 1920s American literature and art had embraced a decidedly satirical approach to shtetl life, the 1930s transformed the shtetlekh into "objects of longing."[498] In the wake of the news pouring in from Europe, the shtetlekh were now envisaged as "imperiled, at the mercy of larger forces."[499] With the rise of the works of Isaac Bashevis Singer (1902-1991), and with his portrayals of the shtetlekh as standing in the path of grave and uncertain dangers in particular, this image intensified.[500]

---

[495] Shandler, *Shtetl: A Vernacular Intellectual History*, 39.

[496] For a more detailed review of Sholem Aleichem and his works see Jeremy Dauber, *The Worlds of Sholem Aleichem* (New York: Nextbook, 2013); and Gennady Estraikh, et. al., eds. *Translating Sholem Aleichem: History, Politics and Art* (London: Legenda, 2012).

[497] For more on Sholem Aleichem's impact on the literary world and the revival of Yiddish storytelling see David G. Roskies, "Yiddish Storytelling and the Politics of Rescue,"in *Jewish Literature and History: An Interdisciplinary Conversation*, ed. Eliyana R. Adler and Sheila E. Jelen, (Bethesda, MD: University Press of Maryland, 2008), 17-22.

[498] Shandler, *Shtetl: A Vernacular Intellectual History*, 39.

[499] Shandler, *Shtetl: A Vernacular Intellectual History*, 42.

[500] Shandler, *Shtetl: A Vernacular Intellectual History*, 43. Miron writes: "Bashevis approached the act of literary creation with a base experience of underlying awareness that falls under the sign of fatalism and nihilism. Human existence and, certainly, Jewish

The most radical shift in the shtetl image occurred in the years following World War II. The inter-war image of the shtetl had constituted a "readily available idiom"[501] that proved useful in the hands of skilled writers. The concept of the shtetl as "world"[502] was transformed into the notion of a "lost" or "vanished world".[503] And as memoirs of Holocaust survivors began to be published, the motif of the shtetl intensified further as a strong symbol of Jewish identity, albeit now indelibly stained with the blood of the dead. In this context, the shtetl as motif was being transformed into one with "transcendental reference."[504]

Indeed, in the wake of the Holocaust, the shtetl began to be perceived as the "locus of destruction . . . [that was] an unprecedented rupture in European life in general, and for Jews in particular."[505] Much has been written that addresses this trend. Relevant here, however, is the strong sense in which post-Holocaust engagement with the shtetl was indicative of a change in discourse. In both fiction and non-fiction, the shtetl became the locus of both literary and scientific inquiry. Accordingly, whether portrayed accurately or not, the shtetl emerged as an inevitable symbol of an irretrievable, obliterated past, a past in which post-Holocaust generations of Jews would seek to understand themselves.[506]

Even today, the shtetl is portrayed with great fluidity. Authors, artists, and musicians alike have taken up the shtetl motif as they grapple with the Holocaust. The great and disparate influx of interpretations, pictures, and depictions of the shtetl across all genres is testament to this fact. These ever-fluctuating images of the shtetl have succeeded in positing the shtetl as an equivocal paradigm. Their ambiguous nature has, "afforded great flexibility to [the shtetl's] cultural engagements—indeed, its power as an icon lies, to a considerable extent, in its amorphousness."[507]

The discrepancies that exist between literary portrayals of the shtetl and its historical "realities" have been discussed at the beginning of this section.

---

existence appeared to him suffused with evil and suffering, torn apart from within by an absurdity both comical and tragic. . . . Bashevis 'understood' the twentieth-century as an age in which a suffering humanity was forced to follow lethal totalitarian ideological-eschatological agendas that gave birth to a murderousness unequaled in viciousness and horror by any evil known to man throughout all of history." See Miron, *The Image of the Shtetl*, 337.

501 Shandler, *Shtetl: A Vernacular Intellectual History*, 73.

502 Shandler, *Shtetl: A Vernacular Intellectual History*, 74.

503 Shandler, *Shtetl: A Vernacular Intellectual History*, 74.

504 Shandler, *Shtetl: A Vernacular Intellectual History*, 74.

505 Shandler, *Shtetl: A Vernacular Intellectual History*, 35.

506 See Jeffrey Shandler, "The Shtetl Subjunctive: Yaffa Eliach's Living History Museum" in *Culture Front: Representing Jews in Eastern Europe*, ed. Benjamin Nathans and Gabriella Safran (Philadelphia: University of Pennsylvania Press, 2008), 290-91. See also Jeffrey Shandler, "Shtetl" in *Encyclopedia of Jewish Folklore and Traditions*, ed. Patai and Bar-Itzhak, 500-01.

507 Shandler, *Shtetl: A Vernacular Intellectual History*, 47.

Important here is the inclination to cast the "lost world" of the shtetl as a trope of modern literature that "implies the loss of any visible traces of the past."[508] The void that ensued for the worldwide Jewish community after Auschwitz has been enormous. Artistic attempts to come to terms with that void have implemented the motif of the shtetl in myriad ways. While the meanings granted to this motif are many, all have been integral to the process of sorting through what it means to be Jewish in a world that has wanted to annihilate Jews. Indeed, "[f]ar from undermining the shtetl's symbolic importance, this disparity [of meaning] enhances it and has become essential to the shtetl's meaning in modern Jewish culture."[509] In as much as Jewish life has sought new definition following the Holocaust, the act of remembering the shtetl has certainly contributed to that process of self-definition.

Even in the face of the variations found in its literary portrayals, the image of the shtetl has emerged as referencing a special, but now-vanished, world. While it struggled with questions of identity, this world fought incessantly for survival from within and from without. The enduring presence of this image has lent force to remembrance in the wake of Auschwitz.

Synthesis

In the foregoing study, the foundations of, and developments within, Hasidism have been traced to illustrate how a plethora of historical factors converged to impact the complex development of Judaism's mystical traditions. Left neither untouched nor unscathed by the pressures of external politics, culture, and religion, Eastern European Jewish mysticism took a distinct turn. At the hands of the Kabbalah in particular, Hasidism was born. With this new movement, Eastern European Jewish lore changed its focus; it expanded and deepened, soon to be dispersed throughout the greater region. Hasidic lore both assisted in the spread of the movement and contributed to its evolution. Its forms, styles, and themes were shaped both by the long history of Jewish tradition in general, and the European social context in particular.

Within this broader context, the cultural production distinct to Hasidism was not a singular undertaking of the spiritual elite. Instead, it was embraced by all echelons of the movement and by all segments of society: by rich and poor; by the Tzaddikim and the Hasidim; and by the scholar and the uneducated laity. There arose, too, master storytellers and compilers of stories—from the Besht himself, to Buber and beyond—whose significant contributions have impacted the movement to the present day. All of these have played a role in shaping the story of Hasidism.

---

[508] Shandler, *Shtetl: A Vernacular Intellectual History*, 94.
[509] Shandler, *Shtetl: A Vernacular Intellectual History*, 136.

How adequately the tales and legends of Hasidism reflect the historical realities of the movement in Eastern Europe continues to be debated. However, the literary images, themes, and motifs of Hasidic legends still relay important information concerning the Eastern European Jewish context preceding World War II. The legends can be adjudicated with a view to the ways in which the shtetl is represented and portrayed literarily. However idealized their depictions of shtetl life may be, the legends do afford some sense of how followers of the tradition perceived themselves. Even in tales that display historical inaccuracies, the literary choices made by their authors are yet indicative of Hasidic self-understanding.

Exploring the evolution of the image of the shtetl in the literature of Eastern European Hasidism has proven meaningful for this study. Through the course of two world wars into the present day, the shtetl motif has emerged as a strong factor in the formation of external perceptions of Hasidism; indeed, the shtetl, in all its complexity, continues to be regarded as embracing the quintessence of traditional Jewish life in Eastern Europe in general.

Jewish self-identity has always been central to the Jewish faith. The new inflections supplied by Hasidism, strong and revitalizing, impacted the ways in which many Eastern European Jews would experience the horrors that lay ahead. Whether drawing strength from tradition or despairing the limitations of tradition in the face of moral and physical evil, this self-identity, in its myriad forms, would become their frame of reference, the lens through which they gauged their experiences of the Holocaust.

Chapter Five

Literary Investigations: Four Works by Elie Wiesel

"Night": The Core of the Oeuvre

Setting the Parameters

In May of 1944, the entire Jewish population of Sighet was deported to Auschwitz. The horrific chain of events that ensued, recorded in Wiesel's testimony *Night*, would come to shape his life in ways he could never have foreseen.

The account of Wiesel's time spent in Auschwitz is now well known. Still, *Night* continues to be regarded as a seminal work that, for many, personifies the horrors that befell European Jewry during World War II. It has also remained Wiesel's personal insignia, that work of his most deeply sketched into the conscience of the world. Indeed, it has contributed dramatically to the collective memory of humanity. Thus, any critical review of Wiesel's writing cannot bypass it. The textual analysis embraced by this study also begins with *Night*. An examination of how Wiesel's earliest influences came to impact his testimony provides clarity in examining subsequent works. Ultimately, it lends insight into his humanitarian agenda.

My proposal here is that Wiesel's childhood in Sighet forms a crucial starting point for his writing as a whole. Sighet can be understood to be informative of how Wiesel experienced Auschwitz (i.e., at the time of the experiencing) and of how he remembers it post-Auschwitz (i.e., at the time of writing and later). In his narratives, we discover the author maneuvering himself through memory with the shtetl continually behind him and with Auschwitz ever before him. In this way, Sighet can be seen to form the parameters within which he gauges and interprets his experience of trauma.

Indeed, both Sighet and Auschwitz prove to be indispensable to Wiesel's overall narration process. The difficult power dynamic, which exists between these two entities in memory, provides the palpable tension that permeates every page of his writing. The inner alignment of Sighet and Auschwitz in memory, representative of the struggle between good and evil is, at least in part, what distinguishes Wiesel's writing from that of other survivors such as Steiner, Levi, and Améry.

The suggestion that *Night* forms the core of Wiesel's oeuvre is not new. Wiesel himself writes:

> If in my lifetime I was to write only one book, this would be the one. Just as the past lingers in the present, all my writing

> after *Night*, including those that deal with biblical, Talmudic, or Hasidic themes profoundly bear its stamp, and cannot be understood if one has not read this very first of my works.[510]

A few introductory comments regarding my approach to *Night* may be made here. Most significantly, in my application of both social and narrative theory to Wiesel's texts, the aforementioned ellipse begins to emerge as an implementable theoretical construct. This construct, as we shall see, assists in visualizing better certain dynamics at work in Wiesel's narration of memory.

In this context, the kinds of questions I pose to *Night* in particular are novel; they peel back layers of the work, unmasking less obvious dimensions. In highlighting these dimensions, we can better observe the complexity of Wiesel's actual experience of the Holocaust and his subsequent narration of it.[511]

This undertaking exposes *Night's* own complexity; indeed, in identifying specific mechanisms at play in Wiesel's testimony, his unique narration process becomes evident.

In the sections to follow, particular consideration is given to Wiesel's literary portrayal of the shtetl of Sighet. The sense in which this portrayal of Sighet as a "small European Jerusalem"[512] correlates to Sighet's historical realities is somewhat problematic. It is a discussion to be taken up later in this study. Significant for now, however, is how Wiesel, in bracketing historical discrepancies, implements motifs and themes that intensify the tensions evident in his writing.

A number of these motifs and themes reappear in subsequent works. The image of the shtetl reappears and draws continually from the way Wiesel has portrayed it in *Night*. Tracing the presence and development of this central motif —which, as we shall see, corresponds to the first focal point of the conceptual ellipse—proves vital in assessing the role that the shtetl plays in both Wiesel's memory in general, and in his process of narration in particular.

In this broader context, it is possible to see how the image of the shtetl in *Night*, both as a literary image and as a motif, acquires a different function from the images of historians and literary critics. At particular junctures, Wiesel's image of the shtetl appears to touch particular historical inaccuracies; although this is the case, it continues to function as a vital component of his narrative.

My central claim is that *Night*, in functioning as the core of the oeuvre, sets particular interpretive parameters indispensable to the critical analysis of other texts of Wiesel. In addition to *Night*, I explore three of these works. There,

---

[510] Wiesel, *The Night Trilogy*, 5.

[511] Ellen S. Fine references too the complex nature of Wiesel's experiences: "In his literary universe, he seeks to assimilate the multiple levels of his encounter with history, to form legends and myth out of memory." Ellen S. Fine, *Legacy of Night: The Literary Universe of Elie Wiesel* (Albany, NY: State University of New York Press, 1982), 2.

[512] Downing, *Elie Wiesel: A Religious Biography*, 27.

arguments are posited incrementally that establish my central proposals and theses.

Setting the Stage: The Shtetl as a Microcosm of Field

To distill the hidden, "immanent structure"[513] of *Night,* we must begin by understanding the shtetl of Sighet as a microcosm of the author's primary field. As we shall see, the shtetl-as-field, together with all its inherent structures and actors, serves as the indispensable setting of Wiesel's testimony. There, Wiesel portrays the shtetl in vital and dynamic terms as that *field of power* that embraces the habitus, capital, and dispositions of all its actors.[514]

Wiesel's literary depiction of the shtetl-as-field is of interest here for several reasons. First, it assists in sketching out more fully the shape and content of his field. Secondly, and in alignment with Young's theory, it provides the protagonist of *Night*, Eliezer, with the interpretive parameters for gauging his immediate subjective experience of Auschwitz. Thirdly, it also suggests how Wiesel, as author of this narrative, has come to remember and narrate his experience of Auschwitz.

In this unfolding context, we can see how the field of the protagonist, in a sense akin to Bourdieu's analysis in *The Rules of Art*, serves simultaneously as the field of the author. From this analysis, insight is gleaned into how the shtetl functions as a motif in the author's overall literary agenda. This is elaborated upon in the examination of three further works by Wiesel.

The Shtetl as a Field of Power

The shtetl—as a field of power and as a first sphere of experience—proves indispensable to the narrative arc of the text, as well as the character arc of its protagonist. It supplies an interpretive frame of reference for Eliezer as the shtetl context is dramatically replaced by that of Auschwitz. Here, it is the emerging juxtaposition of the shtetl with Auschwitz—understood as "anti-field" or as the second focal point of the ellipse—that becomes indispensable to the powerful unfolding of the text.

Shtetl-As-Field: Protagonist and Author

The process of understanding the shtetl—the primary field—of *Night* entails isolating those structures within the field that comprise the habitus, capital, and dispositions of its actors or main players.

---

[513] See Bourdieu, *Rules of Art*, 3, and 14, for his sense of the term "immanent structure"of a literay work.
[514] Cf. Bourdieu, *Rules of Art*, 9-10.

Of necessity and by definition, the shtetl-as-field serves as the locus of the essential components of the field and of its cultural production. In so doing, it supplies the basic resources that all actors will draw upon as they live and interact with one another and as they contribute to the development of the field. The boundaries, or limits, of the shtetl-as-field are defined by its faith tradition, which in turn grants its actors their roles and trajectories and, as such, their respective positions within the narrative. Accordingly, these actors emerge not only as integral to the plot of the story, but also to the character development of Eliezer as the protagonist who is ultimately transformed—with Wiesel as author—into a witness of atrocity.

Central to this study, then, is the identification of the shtetl as a field that constitutes, in light of its written and oral traditions, a religious field of rich cultural production.[515] This field impacts both Eliezer "within" the story and Wiesel as the story's witness and author.

Jewish Faith: The Parameters of Field

Indeed, identifying the parameters of a field is essential to understanding how its rules impact the functioning of the field.[516] The parameters of the shtetl-as-field are marked by the physical, cultural, and religious parameters set by the shtetl itself. Indeed, the shtetl-as-field exists as a social context marked by a distinctive culture, ethnicity, language, and, most of all, faith tradition. Guided by the specificities of that tradition, it emerges as an entity distinct from those social contexts outside it.

Accordingly, *Night* positions the Jewish community of Sighet as set dramatically apart from the Christian community surrounding it. The shtetl-as-field exists as an autonomous cultural sphere contiguous to an external one; in being so, the demarcations between the two disavow any genuine integration of the Jewish population into its Christian surroundings. Rampant with antisemitic sentiment, the "world beyond" the shtetl proves to be "worlds apart," standing as its most imminent threat in the most concrete of ways.[517] Although interactions with

---

[515] Already in the 1970s, Bourdieu had implicated the religious field as one whose cultural instruction, at the hands of tradition, was determinative of both its parameters and the roles of its actors. These, in constant interaction, lent the field a dynamic that excludes a static existence. See Jurt, "Die Theorie des literarischen Feldes von Pierre Bourdieu,"6. See also Pierre Bourdieu, *Das Religiöse Feld. Texte zur Ökonomie des Heilgeschehens*, ed. Stephan Egger, et. al., trans. Andreas Pfeuffer (Constance: UVK Universitätsverlag Konstanz, 2000), 53.

[516] Bourdieu references the "structure of social space" which are indicative of its "deep and repressed structures." The anamnesis of these structures "supplies all the tools necessary for its own sociological analysis." See Bourdieu, *Rules of Art*, 3, 4.

[517] Antisemitic sentiment in Sighet frequently led to acts of violence against its Jewish population. As the time of the deportations drew near, humiliations became frequent.

the Christian population of Sighet are a normal part of life for many Jews living in the shtetl,[518] the lines of division between these two communities remain unremitting.

The boundaries between Jewish and Christian communities provide the shtetl's constituents with a sense of security. This dynamic allows them to continue their daily lives, despite the antagonism around them. However, the boundaries also prevent the community from grasping the grave drama that has been building beyond it. This reality is portrayed well in *Night*. Indeed, the insulated life of the shtetl impedes many Jews from realizing that the destruction of the shtetl is nigh. Even as Moishe the Beadle warns of the impending doom, the shtetl turns a blind eye. Wiesel writes:

> Thereafter, life seemed normal once again. London radio, which we listened to every evening, announced encouraging news: the daily bombings of Germany and Stalingrad, the preparation of the Second Front. And so we, the Jews of Sighet, waited for better days that surely were soon to come.
>
> I continued to devote myself to my studies, Talmud during the day and Kabbalah at night. My father took care of his business and the community. My grandfather came to spend Rosh Hashana with us so as to attend the services of the celebrated Rebbe of Borsche. My mother was beginning to think it was high time to find an appropriate match for Hilda.
>
> Thus passed the year 1943.[519]

The irony of this situation is telling. The community's delusion in the face of approaching atrocity is most adequately explained in terms of the rigid religious parameters set by the field.

The shtetl's living conditions also illustrate the shtetl's continued existence as a distinct religious and cultural community. The shtetl retains its relatively sequestered state until the Germans move into Sighet. Even as the Jews are forced into the ghettos, a degree of denial prevails; they continue with their Passover celebrations, continuing to hope for redemption and the end of the war. Even Eliezer's father does not completely relinquish his optimism.[520]

See Wiesel, *All Rivers Run to the Sea*, 18-19, and Wiesel, *Legends of our Time* (New York: Schocken Books, 1982), 25.

[518] Wiesel indicates elsewhere that the Jews' involvement in the lumber and salt industries evidences the strong economic dependence the Jewish population of Sighet had on its Christian counterpart. The Jewish market in Sighet supplied the town of Sighet with needed wares. Wiesel describes having had contact with Christian children, and that Christians regularly bought goods from his father's store. See Wiesel, *All Rivers Run to the Sea*, 22-23.

[519] Wiesel, *The Night Trilogy*, 25-26.

[520] Wiesel, *The Night Trilogy*, 27-30.

The juxtaposition of the shtetl with the Christian community prefigures the far more perverse juxtaposition of the shtetl with Auschwitz. Importantly, however, the physical dissolution of the shtetl will not succeed in obliterating the shtetl as the frame of reference by which Eliezer gauges and interprets his experience of Auschwitz.

In as much as Eliezer *is* Wiesel, the author of Eliezer's testimony, the narration of *Night* draws from this frame of reference as well. This will affect how the image of the shtetl functions *literarily* in *Night*—and beyond it.

The Players of the Shtetl-as-Field

a) The Jewish Community

Eliezer's story depicts Jewish life in Sighet as dynamic and colorful and, for the most part, as internally harmonious. The social hierarchy of the Jewish community of Sighet lends the shtetl the structure, order, and stability that ensure its harmony.[521] The Jewish authorities and elders ensure too that shtetl life remains organized and peaceful. The tenets of its faith and its rich traditions likewise impart a sense of cultural continuity and, as indicated, of divine protection from ills during times of peril.[522]

By and large, Wiesel portrays the shtetl as a congruous body of faithful orthodox Jews. With each having a particular role and task, the social hierarchy of the field is retained: from the matchmaker to the butcher; from the teacher to the housewife tending the home; from the Rabbi to the farmer and carpenter; and from the beggar and the fiddle-player to the madman on the street.

In the context of strict adherence to its religious calendar and its plethora of traditions and ritual observances, the shtetl community of *Night* understands itself as the elected people of Israel who, although living in exile, is defined by its relationship with God. Here, the rabbis and the teachers of the shtetl play an

---

[521] I reference here, once again, Wiesel's account as outlined in *Night*. Wiesel's *All Rivers Run to the Sea*, although providing more details surrounding the shtetl, loses little of its glossy tenor when referring to it, even as Wiesel admits to having been oblivious to the darker side of life there. "It had a secret life I never suspected," he writes. See page 32. In fact, the Jewish community of Sighet was familiar with internal conflict. Shreter writes: "Internal strife and controversy were always present among Sighet's Jews, as in virtually every other Jewish community, and around many of the same issues: religious organization, including the administration of the kashrut; education; competing Jewish ideologies (Zionism, anti-Zionism, etc.); domination of the community by various leading families and Hasidic dynasties; and, in effect, over modernization." See Shreter, "Selected Facts on the Jews in Sighet, Maramuresh, Transylvania."

[522] The blatant rejection of Moishe the Beadle upon his escape from execution reflects the extent to which the Jews of Sighet persist in their illusory belief in divine protection. See Wiesel, *The Night Trilogy*, 24-26. Wiesel's description of these events corresponds to the one he offers much later. See Wiesel, *All Rivers Run to the Sea*, 28-29.

important role in cultivating its religious life. They help ensure that future generations will be well-equipped to uphold their traditions, language, and heritage.

Although the rabbis of Sighet exert a certain influence over the shtetl, prominent personalities outside of the rabbinate, members of the Jewish Council and other community elders, hold important positions as well. These individuals, in whom much trust is placed, are pivotal in making decisions. They impact the life and fate of the shtetl, as is the case with Eliezer's father, Shlomo Wiesel.[523]

In the context of the literary representation of the shtetl provided by *Night*, a theoretical evaluation of the shtetl-as-field is now possible. The faith-parameters of the shtetl provide an internally stable milieu within which individuals are groomed for life there. The community is strong in its sense of solidarity and responsibility to tradition and faith. These social realities reflect the shtetl's nourishment of the habitus of *all* its members—its actors—in the context of their allotted roles. The shtetl allows for the cultivation of their individual patterns of behavior by providing the inherent laws or *lex insitia* that are constitutive of their individual habitus.

As is the case with most fields, the shtetl of *Night* offers rich ground for the provision of the variegated social positions within its sphere. Indeed, although the faith tradition of the shtetl stands as that aspect which determines its internal congruity, Sighet remains a differentiated context. There, social structures and hierarchy lend its actors a wide variety of roles. Eliezer's account of the dynamism of the shtetl in *Night* alludes to this underlying dynamic.

As we have seen, and congruent with the nature of habitus, social origin and upbringing are decisive for the development of the dispositions of its actors. Sighet, as the shtetl-as-field, can also be appraised in this light. In the context of its well-defined structures and social hierarchy and divisions, the shtetl provides the capital necessary for the growth and advancement of its individual constituents. Significantly, however, this capital is not always contingent upon the economic status of community members. Due to those parameters set by the shtetl's faith tradition, the educational opportunities offered by its religious institutions can be accessed by less privileged individuals. As such, the spirituality of the shtetl allows for a "spiritual capital" that can be drawn upon by those of greater or lesser means. This capital can thus be understood as a form of social and symbolic capital that is less dependent on economic resources than other forms.

The shtetl thus possesses a unique social dynamic in which persons of different economic standings have the opportunity to gain a certain degree of social importance—or at least acceptance—within the community. Those conversant with its heritage and who are immersed in its traditions have the potential of becoming persons whose opinions, wisdom, and intelligence are respected in

---

[523] Indeed, Wiesel's father, Shlomo Wiesel, has a strong voice in the community. See Wiesel, *The Night Trilogy*, 22, and *All Rivers Run to the Sea*, 5-6. However, Shlomo Wiesel's naivety has its consequences for the fate of both his family and the shtetl.

times of personal questioning, illness, and communal need.[524] With these dynamics present, the shtetl's constituents are continually shaped by the various kinds of capital made available to them.

Life in the shtetl of Sighet is dictated by the strict orthodox faith of its community. In particular, it is impacted strongly by Hasidism.[525] This tradition, deeply ingrained in the faith heritage of Sighet, retains its centrality in the shtetl-as-field.[526]

---

524 Shlomo Wiesel is one such example. Although a store owner and therefore not among the poorest of the shtetl, he is both a man of modest means and one held in high esteem. Although more a humanist than a spiritual leader, his opinions on matters concerning the shtetl are highly respected in the community. As one with valuable connections to the Hungarian police, he is sought out regularly for his advice concerning community matters. See Wiesel, *The Night Trilogy*, 22, 29.

525 Wiesel describes Hasidic influences more explicitly in works other than *Night*. *All Rivers Run to the Sea*, for example, references one of Wiesel's encounters with a local Rebbe, see 11-12. Wiesel's writings on Hasidism also lend credence to the extent to which the tradition impacted his upbringing. See his *Souls on Fire: Portraits and Legends of Hasidic Masters* and *Four Hasidic Masters and their Struggle Against Melancholy* (Notre Dame, IN: University of Notre Dame Press, 1978). Scholars have also noted that the shtetl of Sighet was a predominantly Hasidic one. Downing writes: "One of the most important treasures of this town . . . was its Jewishness, especially Hasidism. . . . Just as in Jerusalem, so in Sighet is one especially aware that the divine presence is everywhere, and that the faithful should be alert to recognize the holy in all things. In such a way, Hasidism taught faithful Jews to lead a life of total dedication to God." See Downing, *Elie Wiesel: A Religious Biography*, 31. Similarly, but in more differentiated fashion, Joel Berger traces the history of Hasidism in the region of Sighet and its impact on Sighet. Following the First World War, although Zionism and the Haskalah were expanding in other regions, new Hasidic influences (which Berger refers to as neo-Hasidic, a designation used equivocally today) were moving westwards, penetrating the Carpathian Mountains and Transylvania; there, they succeeded in winning over large parts of the population. Accordingly, Hasidism grew to have a strong impact on the religious life of the shtetlekh there. Other influences were certainly at work in Sighet, including Zionism and the Jewish Enlightenment, the Haskalah, which also impacted Shlomo Wiesel strongly. Despite varying theological and traditional influences in Sighet, what must be said is that Hasidic fervor, cultivated across Eastern Europe for over 250 years up to World War II, reverberated strongly there. Indeed, Hasidism was entrenched in the very life of the shtetl itself. See Joel Berger, "Spuren und Elemente jüdischer Volkskultur in den Werken Elie Wiesels" in *Kultur allein ist nicht genug*, ed. Boschki and Mensink, 183-184.

526 To extend the analyses of chapters two and five, those written and oral traditions constitutive of the religious heritage of the region evolved as factors contributing indispensably to the vibrant life of the shtetlekh. It is from within this broader context of the shtetl's fierce embrace of these traditions, that field emerges. With the lively, at times competitive interactions and struggles among its players—often among the spiritual leaders of the community in whose hands much of the responsibility for the written and oral traditions was placed—the shape and focus of the field, even in the context its

With the establishment of the shtetl-as-field, Sighet emerges, in the Bourdieulian sense, as a *field of power*. As such, and given the plethora of social positions and roles among its players, the struggles present there are constitutive of the power dynamics and differentials that have developed—as is the case with all fields. These struggles, viewed as points of collision or interactions, prevent the shtetl from becoming a rigid entity.[527]

b) The Family Wiesel-Feig Matrix

In evaluating Eliezer's family matrix, the family Wiesel-Feig, we arrive at a crucial juncture. Just as an analysis of the parameters and players of the shtetl assists in establishing the first setting of *Night* (the other being Auschwitz itself), an analysis of this family matrix identifies the center of the field within which Eliezer's story originates.

On first reading, Eliezer's mother, Sarah Wiesel-Feig, appears to figure less in the narrative than his father, Shlomo Wiesel. However, upon closer reading, she enters the story as an influential presence. Her role is that of a traditional Jewish woman; she tends to the home, raises four children, and assists in running the family store.[528] Even as the crisis beyond the shtetl intensifies, she is concerned with maintaining the stability of family life, even absorbed with finding a husband for her oldest daughter, Hilda.[529] In the evening before their expected deportation (they are then deported with the second convoy), she busies herself with preparing provisions for the journey. She sends her children to bed early, concerned they might otherwise be tired the next day.[530] The irony inherent in this naivety is palpable. Although this first part of *Night* suggests the strong presence of Sarah Wiesel in the Wiesel family, the most graphic scene in which she is present is the one in which she is selected for the gas chamber, alongside Eliezer's young sister, Tzipora.[531]

Background information to Sarah Wiesel extends Wiesel's portrayal of her in *Night*. Wiesel's autobiography describes her as a pious woman who, although educated at a secular school, possessed a faith that mirrored that of her Hasidic father, Rebbe Dodye Feig. Wiesel depicts Sarah as having been

---

structured parameters, can be considered as continually in motion, internally dynamic, and ever in flux.

[527] In reality, the interactions of all players contribute to the fluctuating, dynamic shape of the field. As Bourdieu indicates, "each of the behaviours of every single character will come to refine the system" in as much as each has a generative formula that contributes, however subtly, to the overall dynamism and development of the field. See Bourdieu, *Rules of Art*, 13.

[528] Wiesel, *The Night Trilogy*, 22.

[529] Wiesel, *The Night Trilogy*, 26, 29.

[530] Wiesel, *The Night Trilogy*, 38.

[531] Wiesel, *The Night Trilogy*, 47. It is not an event that Eliezer reflects upon extensively in *Night*; however, Wiesel as author will allude to the incident on other occasions.

concerned about his spiritual development as her only son. [532] There, she accompanies Wiesel to receive the blessing of the great Rabbi Israel of Vizhnitz, whose tradition her father is associated with as a respected, prominent Hasid.[533] Wiesel describes his enmeshed attachment to his mother at a tender age, describing his separation from her upon entering the *heder* at age three as having been distressing.[534] He remembers, too, her intense religious disposition: "She was a Hasidah, an extremely pious woman,"[535] he writes. And he recalls her messianic expectations:

> The Messiah. My mother never ceased to demand and await his coming. He was never far from her mind. At night, as she rocked me to sleep, she would sing of her deep conviction that nothing bad would happen to her child, since the Messiah would come to protect him. . . . The Jewish people would soon be delivered. . . . I don't know whether the Savior was awaited anywhere else with as much fervor and love as in Sighet.[536]

Sarah Wiesel's hope for her son to become a man of religious significance is alluded to in *The Town Behind the Wall*, contrasting his father's desire for Wiesel to secure a secular education:

> "Mother wants me to be a rabbi. Father would rather have me study for a doctorate in philosophy. . . . My mother lives body and soul for Hasidism: she devotes her actions and thoughts to God. My father adores reason: he devotes all his time to skepticism about the eternal verities. To make peace between them I promised to study religion *and* philosophy."[537]

Wiesel's father stands before the young Eliezer as a towering figure. In *Night*, his relationship with his father is distanced. He was "a cultured man," Eliezer notes, "rather unsentimental. He rarely displayed his feelings, not even within his family, and was more involved with the welfare of others than with that of his own

---

[532] Cf. Downing, *Elie Wiesel: A Religious Biography*, 25.
[533] Wiesel, *All Rivers Run to the Sea*, 11-12. See also Ellen Norman Stern, *Wo Engel sich versteckten. Das Leben des Elie Wiesel*, trans. Sibylle A. Niemoeller-von Sell (Freiburg i. B.: Herder, 1986), 33-34.
[534] Wiesel, *All Rivers Run to the Sea*, 10.
[535] Elie Wiesel, "Zum Geleit: Kultur allein ist nicht genug" in *Kultur allein ist nicht genug*, ed. Boschki and Mensink, 40. Translation mine.
[536] Wiesel, *All Rivers Run to the Sea*, 22.
[537] Elie Wiesel, *The Town Behind the Wall*, trans. Stephen Becker (New York: Holt, Rinehart and Winston, 1967), 25.

kin."[538] Thus, there exists a palpable discrepancy between Sarah Wiesel's spiritual temperament and her husband's intellectual disposition.

In *Night*, Shlomo Wiesel, as a man of reason, turns a blind eye to mysticism and discourages his son from its study, especially that of the Kabbalah.[539] Eliezer's delinquent interest in the movement irritates his father, who worries about his son's spiritual intensity.[540]

As the war rages on and tensions mount, Eliezer confronts his father about liquidating his assets and fleeing the shtetl. Shlomo Wiesel cites his age as a hindrance to such an undertaking.[541]

As a respected elder in the community who has connections with the Hungarian police, Shlomo Wiesel is consulted about the increasing restrictions on Jews. Wiesel writes: "[T]hey wanted to know what he thought of the situation. His view was that it was not all bleak. . . . 'The yellow star? So what? It's not lethal.'"[542] Shlomo Wiesel's surprise in learning of the coming liquidation of the ghetto is telling of his naivety.[543] As the deportations are announced, his concern is that all be ready to depart; he even accompanies the first deportees to the gate of the ghetto.[544] Surprisingly, his naivety persists as he continues to hope that a second deportation can be avoided. These hopes are dashed as he and his family are deported to Auschwitz a few days later.

According to other works by Wiesel, we learn that Shlomo Wiesel was indeed a man of reason and of letters. Wiesel describes him as a humanist who "enjoyed considerable renown in the community."[545] He writes affectionately of his father:

> My father was famous for his intelligence, his perspicacity, and his kindness. Patient and tolerant, he would see anyone, for any reason, listening with the same attentiveness to rich and poor, friend or stranger. His views mattered, his advice was invariably followed.[546]

Fine describes Shlomo Wiesel as:

> a middle-class shopkeeper who spent much of his time working for the community. In the early years of the war he helped save Polish Jews who had escaped to Hungary. Because of his

[538] Wiesel, *The Night Trilogy*, 22.
[539] Wiesel, *The Night Trilogy*, 22.
[540] Wiesel, *The Night Trilogy*, 22.
[541] Wiesel, *The Night Trilogy*, 27.
[542] Wiesel, *The Night Trilogy*, 29.
[543] Wiesel, *The Night Trilogy*, 31.
[544] Wiesel, *The Night Trilogy*, 36.
[545] Wiesel, *All Rivers Run to the Sea*, 5.
[546] Wiesel, *All Rivers Run to the Sea*, 6.

> efforts he spent a few months in jail. Shlomo instilled humanist values in his only son . . . and encouraged him to learn modern Hebrew and to read its literature. His father, Wiesel tells us, represented "reason" and his mother "faith."[547]

Indeed, Shlomo Wiesel plays a central role in Eliezer's growing self-identity. The distance between the two, however, follows them to Auschwitz. Although deficient, this relationship is to be impacted strongly by the enormity of Auschwitz. Ultimately, this has a determining impact on the arc of the story.

The figure of Dovid (Dodye) Feig, Wiesel's maternal grandfather, appears only peripherally in *Night*. He is mentioned there only once as having visited the Wiesel home in Sighet for Rosh Hashanah in 1943, with the intention of attending the services of the Rebbe of Borsche, a celebrated Hasid of the region.[548] Wiesel's descriptions of Dodye Feig elsewhere in his writing provide information regarding his grandfather's important role in the Wiesel family matrix. A fervent, impassioned Hasid living in the nearby town of Bichkev, Dodye Feig was a dynamic personality whom Wiesel loved and revered. Wiesel remembers:

> And how alive he was, my grandfather, alive and magnificent. . . . He allowed me—obliged me—to love life, to assume it as a Jew, to celebrate it for the Jewish people. A devout follower of the Rabbi of Wizhnitz, he was the embodiment of Hasidic creative force and fervor. His father, Getzl, a man who loved to go into the forest at night to play his violin under a tree, with God his only audience, lived to be ninety-four. My grandfather would surely have reached that age too . . . [549]

As a man also gifted in practical matters, working as a farmer off the land, Dodye Feig was known in the area and commanded respect there. When the Rebbe of Vizhnitz visited the region, he stayed at his home. He was a "cultured and erudite man" who was versed in the Bible and its commentaries, the Midrash, and in the words of the Musar. He was also familiar with Hasidic literature and music, along with the folk music of the region.[550]

Wiesel's relationship to Dodye Feig, although not elaborated upon in *Night*, is replete with affection. It is through Dodye Feig that Wiesel becomes most familiar with the tales of Hasidic tradition. Wiesel remembers:

---

[547] Fine, *The Legacy of Night*, 4. Cf. Cargas, *Harry James Cargas in Conversation with Elie Wiesel*, 62.

[548] Wiesel, *The Night Trilogy*, 26.

[549] Wiesel, *All Rivers Run to the Sea*, 41.

[550] Wiesel, *All Rivers Run to the Sea*, 41-42. Cf. Wiesel, *A Jew Today*, trans. Marion Wiesel (New York: Random House, 1978), 66-69.

> [Grandfather Feig] told stories too. Stories of miracle-workers, of unhappy princes and just men in disguise. It is to him I owe everything I have written on Hasidic literature. The enchanting tales of Rebbe Nachman of Bratslav, the parables of the Rebbe of Kotzk, the sayings of the Rebbe of Rizhin, and the witticisms of the Rebbe of Ropshitz: he knew them all, and he taught me to savor them. . . . "I'll never forget these stories," I told him, and he answered, "That's why I'm telling them to you. So they won't be forgotten."[551]

He writes:

> At one point [God] was my grandfather. . . . Almost literally. Not what he looked like—but I saw God's presence, God's spirit, on his face. Then he was my teacher, my rebbe.[552]

Although not decisive to the actual plot of *Night*, Dodye Feig will return in his other works. Significantly, the depth of this relationship contrasts starkly with the distanced relationship Wiesel has with his father in *Night*.

Wiesel's two oldest siblings, his sisters Bea and Hilda, play marginal roles in *Night*. They are present only in the background, although they too are deported with their family to Auschwitz. It is only Tzipora whose image is depicted with greater clarity. Just seven years old at the time of the deportations, Wiesel recalls her innocence in accompanying her family into the "small ghetto":

> I looked at my little sister, Tzipora, her blond hair neatly combed, her red coat over her arm: a little girl of seven. On her back a bag too heavy for her. She was clenching her teeth; she already knew it was useless to complain. Here and there, the police were lashing out with their clubs: "Faster!"[553]

Wiesel's last memory of Tzipora is of her walking towards extermination, hand in hand with her mother upon their arrival in Auschwitz. It is an image he would not forget and one that would come to haunt his testimony.

---

[551] Wiesel, *All Rivers Run to the Sea*, 42. For a more personal account of Wiesel's relationship with Dodye Feig, see Wiesel, *A Jew Today*, 65-70.
[552] Elie Wiesel, "Before the End of History—And After" in Abrahamson, ed. *Against Silence*, 3:267, adapted from Bonnie Remsberg, *Some of My Best Friends*, television interview, Chicago, Illinois, June 28, 1981.
[553] Wiesel, *The Night Trilogy*, 37.

c) *Moishe the Beadle*

The figure of Moishe the Beadle opens *Night*; however furtively, he plays a pivotal role in Eliezer's story. He also reappears as a key figure in Wiesel's other novels.[554] Although Moishe remains distant from his kinsfolk in the shtetl, speaking little and singing much, he still functions as an integrated member of the shtetl. He works in the Hasidic house of prayer or *shtibl* as a jack-of-all-trades.[555] At the age of thirteen, Eliezer comes to know him, and their first encounter leads to a strong bond between the two. Moishe proceeds to initiate Eliezer into the mysteries of the Kabbalah. Because this is of concern to his father, Eliezer secretly takes up his study of the Zohar. He is convinced that Moishe will assist him in entering into eternity, into "that time when question and answer would become ONE."[556]

This relationship is interrupted in 1942. Destined for extermination, all Hungarian Jews, including Moishe, are deported from Sighet. Months later, Moishe returns to Sighet, traumatized after miraculously escaping execution. However, his frantic warnings of the coming perils are ignored, and he is considered mad. Life in the shtetl quickly returns to normal and his voice is forgotten.[557] Even the young Eliezer, initially alarmed by Moishe's message, is soon transported back into the shtetl's illusion of security.

With this, Moishe assumes a prophetic role. His words are not understood, and his rebuke will carry with it dire consequences. [558] He is a link to the

---

[554] Moishe will not disappear from Wiesel's writings. He appears there again and again, wearing various garbs, often those of beggars and madmen, who then prove to be prophets in disguise. With Moishe in *Night*, Wiesel has introduced the theme of madness into his writing, a theme that will reappear throughout the oeuvre. Wiesel's novel *Twilight* focuses exclusively on this theme. See Elie Wiesel, *Twilight*, trans. Marion Wiesel (London: Penguin Books, 2013). For more on the role and function of madness in Wiesel's works, see Boshki, *Der Schrei. Gott und Mensch im Werk von Elie Wiesel* (Mainz: Matthias Grünewald Verlag, 1995), 166-71. See also Kirsten Nath, *The Function of Madness in Elie Wiesel's Works* (seminar paper, University of Hamburg, ebook: GRIN Verlag, 2013).

[555] Wiesel, *The Night Trilogy*, 21.

[556] Wiesel, *The Night Trilogy*, 23.

[557] Wiesel, *The Night Trilogy*, 24-26.

[558] Boschki identifies Moishe's role as prophetic in the most classic sense: "In all genres figures emerge that have a message for their surroundings. They are scouts, witnesses, and messengers who report of happenings which they themselves have experienced or which they have heard from others. They are a kind of prophetic caller or warner who desperately wishes to be heard. The tragedy of these characters, however, is that their message does not arrive at those addressed. The message cannot be conveyed and its transmission fails." Boschki, *Der Schrei*, 24. Translation mine.

universe of death that awaits the shtetl, and embodies the overlapping of two disparate universes. His very presence foreshadows the uprooting of the shtetl.[559]

Moishe's return to the shtetl quickly shifts the narrative. This transition is the first of four in Eliezer's story and serves to advance the first part of the story into the second. There, the shtetl hovers in relative delusion over and against the horrors of the world outside. Thus, the scene is set for the drama of deportation.

d) Eliezer: The Emerging Mystic

From the first pages of *Night*, Eliezer is portrayed as an adolescent immersed in an insulated social world. This world is determined by faith traditions that define all aspects of life there. As an only son, Eliezer is expected to carry on these traditions. Although obligated to pursue the study of the Bible and the Talmud, he is by nature a religious child, already caught up in the longings and hopes of his people. He feels drawn to unlock the secrets of the universe. When his time with Moishe the Beadle as a student of the Kabbalah comes to an abrupt halt, Eliezer continues his pursuit, intending to usher in the coming of the Messiah.[560] We observe here how Eliezer already holds a certain potential to extend his creative enterprise to the very limits of his field.

As we have seen, the social dynamics and religious infrastructure of the shtetl-as-field are requisite for forming the habitus of its constituents. In *Night*, the shtetl ensures that the capital necessary for the intellectual and spiritual formation of children and adults is provided through maintaining its schools and religious institutions. This infrastructure provides Eliezer with the resources necessary for the cultivation of his spiritual and intellectual dispositions. His development thus remains inextricably linked to the structures, institutions, and traditions made available to him; indeed, his intellectual and spiritual pursuits prove commensurate with the rules and structures inherent in the shtetl-as-field.

The Wiesel family matrix emerges as indispensable in this broader context. In their compliance with the rules of the shtetl-as-field, Sarah and Shlomo Wiesel are able to provide Eliezer with much of the economic, cultural, and symbolic capital necessary for the cultivation of his religious and intellectual inclinations. Grandfather Feig underscores these efforts through his spiritual bond with the boy. The intellectual humanism of Shlomo Wiesel and the spiritual influence of both Sarah Wiesel and her Hasidic father all assist in providing the stimulus necessary in fostering Eliezer's giftedness. Therefore, the trajectory of Eliezer's

---

[559] Bourdieu suggests that particular characters within any given narrative act as symbols within the text. In so doing, they mark pertinent positions within the social space. Here, they help define its overall shape, contributing not merely to its innermost functioning, but also to the unfolding of the story itself. Cf. Bourdieu, *Rules of Art*, 5.

[560] Wiesel, *The Night Trilogy*, 26.

character holds the promise of both spiritual and social advancement within the shtetl-as-field.[561]

The Wiesel family matrix thus plays a vital role in the first chapter of *Night*. As families in general are indispensable in transmitting the faith traditions of the shtetl to future generations, Eliezer's identity is linked to this matrix. Magdalena Fober notes:

> "Next to Moishe, the study of the Talmud and the visits to the synagogue, it is especially the family environment that influences Eliezer's Hasidic *Weltanschauung* and his identity. According to the Jewish tradition, it is . . . the family that encourages their offspring in the study of the Talmud and that secures the transformation of public knowledge into personal knowledge."[562]

Eliezer's identity as student-son is thus linked to knowledge of the traditions of the shtetl-as-field. This knowledge is imparted through the study of that tradition and its holy books, as well as through his full participation in the life of the shtetl.[563] It is an identity that comes to define him.[564] The opening page of *Night* reflects the intensity of that identity: "By day I studied Talmud, and by night I would run to the synagogue to weep over the destruction of the temple."[565]

The Emergence of the Shtetl as Motif

Eliezer's bond to the shtetl launches the shtetl as a vital literary motif. The shtetl is a fortress; it shields its inhabitants against the threats posed to it by

---

[561] For Bourdieu, character trajectories represent those dimensions of a player or actor in which his or her future will be "implicated in [the] past." See *Rules of Art*, 14.

[562] Magdalena Fober, *Identität und Wissen in ausgewählten Werken Elie Wiesels und William Styrons. (Wissens-)Grenzen des Selbst* (Frankfurt: Peter Lang Edition, 2017), 76. Translation mine.

[563] According to George Herbert Mead, it is in taking on or by acquiring the attitudes of a given social group that the identity of a self is solidified: "(The) getting of the broad activities of any given social whole or organized society as such within the experiential field of any one of the individuals involved or included in that whole is, in other words, the essential basis and prerequisite of the fullest development of that individual's self: only in so far as he takes the attitudes of the organized social group to which he belongs toward the organized, co-operative social activity or set of such activities in which that group is engaged, does he develop a complete self or possess the sort of complete self he has developed." George Herbert Mead, *Mind, Self, and Society: From the Standpoint of a Social Behaviorist*, ed. Charles W. Morris, 9th impression (Chicago: Chicago University Press, 1952), 155, quoted in Fober, *Identität und Wissen*, 69.

[564] Fober, *Identität und Wissen*, 78.

[565] Wiesel, *The Night Trilogy*, 21.

the outside world. Strikingly, however, this shielding is undertaken with a sense of optimism and hope—even as its fate is already sealed. Wiesel describes the community's move into two separate ghettos as inciting hope:

> The barbed wire that encircled us like a wall did not fill us with real fear. In fact, we felt this was not a bad thing; we were entirely among ourselves. . . .
>
> We would no longer have to look at those hostile faces, endure those hate-filled stares. No more fear. No more anguish. We would live among Jews, among brothers . . .
>
> Most people thought we would remain in the ghetto until the end of the war, until the arrival of the Red Army. Afterward everything would be as before. [566]

The shtetl will be unable to fulfill its intended mission in Eliezer's life; however, it will leave an indelible mark upon him. In his writing, the motif of the shtetl as fortress will remain, placed against the dark context of Auschwitz.

The Deportation of the Shtetl and the Uprooting of the Field

Just as the return of Moishe the Beadle to Sighet constitutes the first transition in the plot of *Night*, so too does the deportation of the community to Auschwitz constitute the second. It is a devastating uprooting, immediately obliterating the optimism that had sustained the community since Moishe's return. Tellingly, the shtetl community remains in a state of delusion until the deportations are actually underway—an occurrence that serves to accentuate the extremity of the event in the narrative. Eliezer, sent to awaken friends and acquaintances in preparation for the journey, is himself horrified by their obtuseness:

> "Get up, sir, get up! You must prepare yourself for the journey." . . .
>
> He had no idea what I was talking about. He probably thought I had lost my mind.
>
> "What are you saying? Get ready for the journey? What journey? Why? What is happening? Have you gone mad?"
>
> Half asleep, he was staring at me, his eyes filled with terror, as though he expected me to burst out laughing and tell him to go back to bed.[567]

---

[566] Wiesel, *The Night Trilogy*, 29-30.

[567] Wiesel, *The Night Trilogy*, 33.

On the journey to Auschwitz, not only is the shtetl left behind but its people are forced to descend into a netherworld contained in a "hermetically sealed cattle car."[568] Ironically, it is just as self-contained as the shtetl, though dominated by death rather than life. The tight enclosure of the train car prevents any return, physically or mentally, to what was.

> "There are eighty of you in the car," the German officer added. "If anyone goes missing, you will all be shot, like dogs." . . . The doors clanked shut. We had fallen into the trap, up to our necks. The doors were nailed, the way back irrevocably cut off.[569]

With the deportations, the metamorphosis of the shtetl's Jews has begun. They quickly become shadows of their past selves. Their image devastates Eliezer:

> They passed me by, one after the other, my teachers, my friends, the others, some of whom I had once feared, some of whom I had found ridiculous, all those whose lives I had shared for years. There they went, defeated, their bundles, their lives in tow, having left behind their homes, their childhood.
>
> They passed me by, like beaten dogs, with never a glance in my direction.[570]

The terrors experienced on the way to Auschwitz serve as Eliezer's initiation into the universe that awaits him. Mrs. Schächter, the mad woman whose vision of fire and smoke horrifies him, prematurely displaces the smoke stacks of Auschwitz to the confined space of the train car. Her violent subjugation by her fellow deportees marks the first point in the story where the innocent turn on each other. Her prophecy, revealed as such upon arrival at the camp, jolts both prisoner and reader alike. Wiesel's last remark in this segment is equally poignant; no one in the car had ever heard the word "Auschwitz" before.[571]

Significant, here, is the transition made by Eliezer himself; in witnessing the transformation of those he loves into beings unrecognizable to him, he enters that place where his innocence will be irreparably lost. His bubble of delusion, formed by the dynamics of the shtetl itself, is burst by the devastating violence of deportation. With this, the shtetl is exposed as having been powerless all along.

---

[568] Wiesel, *The Night Trilogy*, 42.
[569] Wiesel, *The Night Trilogy*, 42.
[570] Wiesel, *The Night Trilogy*, 35.
[571] Wiesel, *The Night Trilogy*, 45.

Eliezer's faith offers him no immediate remedy to appease his sense of horror. His faith is incommensurate with the train car. This incommensurability posits a stark juxtaposition of past and present, of the shtetl and evil.

Here we can detect, again for the first time, the sense in which Eliezer's immediate experience, poised against the context from which he has emerged, is simultaneously an interpretation. Indeed, the present moment can only be gauged from within his previous framework of faith. The forcible abandonment of the past has propelled Eliezer into a place he can adjudicate only by way of the physical loss of that primary framework.

Arguably, with this loss, Eliezer's identity begins to shift. His childhood innocence has been infringed upon for the first time. This loss of innocence evolves into a theme that permeates the whole of *Night*.[572] Fober argues:

> The deportation to the concentration camp . . . coincides directly with the end of (Wiesel's) childhood and marks therewith a break in his identity. . . . In *Night*, this loss of the "I" of his childhood is marked by the failure, at the hands of reality, of the knowledge he has acquired—Eliezer's personal knowledge offers no alternative for interpretation or for acting in the face of what is at hand.[573]

The extent to which Eliezer's faith tradition has been linked to his own adolescent identity is evident here. As he is forced out of his familiar sphere and as his faith proves powerless to thwart the evil he encounters, so too does his identity enter a place of crisis and inner conflict.

Within this context, the deportation scene is indispensable to the narrative. With the transition of its characters—in particular, Eliezer—to the next segment of the story, the shtetl-as-field has been violently dismantled. This dismantling engenders the deep fragmentation of its constituents as well, a fragmentation at both the intra- and inter-personal levels. Some characters succumb to madness (as is the case with Mrs. Schächter), as others, with time, take up the increasingly grim struggle for survival.

The two deportation scenes function on two levels in the narrative. First, as indicated, they transport the protagonist, his family, and his community to a place where most will not survive; the narrative shifts to the center of the plot. Secondly, they transfer the reader there as well. The juxtaposition of the shtetl with the cattle car is devastating for both the story's characters and the reader. Here, the power differential between the shtetl and Auschwitz—which is

[572] See Irving Halperin, "Loss of Innocence" in *Readings on Night*, ed. Wendy Mass, The Greenhaven Press Literary Companion to World Literature (San Diego: Greenhaven Press, 2000), 30-35.
[573] Fober, *Identität und Wissen*, 120. Translation mine.

yet to come—is first felt. It is felt both physically and psychologically by the deportees.

Ultimately, the juxtaposition of the shtetl with Auschwitz will impact how Eliezer as protagonist experiences Auschwitz from "within" the story. At the same time, Wiesel as author, looking on from "outside" through the perspective of memory, will slip into the character of Eliezer. There and then, he narrates his experiences through Eliezer in terms of the ways in which he himself, as Eliezer, had experienced them. This is indicative of a complex process that is both telling and central to this study.

The violence with which the shtetl is liquidated shocks the reader who has been instilled with the same sense of illusion as Eliezer. The latter's inability to receive Moishe's warning has become the reader's own. Hamaoui maintains: "Eliezer's rejection of the knowledge that Moshe brings back, literally, from the grave, predicts our own rejection of that knowledge. . . . The rejection of Moshe strips the reader of his own deafness in advance of the arrival at Auschwitz."[574]

Night has now fallen for both the shtetl community and the reader, all of whom remain unprepared for Auschwitz. With this, the theme of "night", which is central to the work, emerges.[575] The juxtaposition of past and present is exacerbated with the arrival of the train in Auschwitz. It devastates. Eliezer assesses this: "The beloved objects that we had carried with us from place to place were now left behind in the wagon and, with them, finally, our illusions."[576]

Auschwitz: L'univers concentrationnaire

a) The Emergence of the Anti-Field

With Eliezer's arrival at Auschwitz-Birkenau, his transition to *l'univers concentrationnaire* is complete. As Auschwitz's crass juxtaposition with the world of the shtetl is exposed, the reader is shocked. Here, for the first time, shtetl

---

[574] See Lea Hamaoui, "Historical Horror and the Shape of *Night*" in *Elie Wiesel: Between Memory and Hope*, ed. Carol Rittner (New York: New York University Press, 1990), 125.

[575] Fine identifies the theme of night as suffusing the volume: "The theme of night pervades Elie Wiesel's memoir as suggested by the title itself, which encompasses the overall Holocaust landscape—*l'univers concentrationnaire*—a world synonymous with methodical brutality and radical evil. The dark country presented to us is self-contained and self-structured, governed by its own criminal gods who have created laws based upon a death-dominated ideology. Wiesel uses the word *Night* throughout his writing to denote this strange sphere, unreal and unimaginable in its otherworldliness." See Fine, *Legacy of Night*, 11. Wiesel writes: "We were the children of Night" and "we knew more about truth and the paths leading to it than the wisest philosophers on earth." See Elie Wiesel, *From Holocaust to Rebirth* (New York: The Council of Jewish Federations and Welfare Funds, 1970), 32, quoted in Fine, *Legacy of Night*, 12.

[576] Wiesel, *The Night Trilogy*, 47.

and Auschwitz stand together as two fiercely defying, contrasting entities: one, a world of life that provides human beings with the structures and space necessary to develop themselves and their field; the other, a world of death whose internal machinery is intended to annihilate. Nothing is recognizable as human in the latter. In this sense, Auschwitz emerges as *anti-field*, a sphere of grave and deadly illogicalities and absurdities.

b) The Loss of Innocence: Becoming Witness

The second transition in the narrative, marked by the deportation of the shtetl to Auschwitz, parallels Eliezer's radical break in identity. Indeed, Eliezer has been propelled into the new role of camp inmate and slave.

The horrors that Eliezer witnesses upon arrival in Auschwitz lie beyond his grasp. What he first sees upon arrival—the smoke ascending from the crematoriums and small children being thrown alive into the flames—indicates to him that a definitive break with the past has occurred.[577] Eliezer's rhetoric is telling: "I pinched myself: Was I still alive? Was I awake? How was it possible that men, women, and children were being burned and that the world kept silent? No. All this could not be real."[578] As he realizes that his father's naivety too has been lost ("Today, everything is possible, even the crematoria . . ."),[579] Eliezer contemplates suicide. "I gathered all that remained of my strength in order to break rank and throw myself onto the barbed wire," Wiesel writes.[580] The boy begins to chant the Kaddish, but the idea of suicide is cut short as he and his father are directed away from the pit they have been encircling. Eliezer immediately takes his father's hand, childlike, the only gesture that grants some sense of familiarity.[581]

Evident here is the deep chasm that exists between the shtetl and the camp. It is one the reader cannot cross. But Eliezer does cross it. Thrust into the center of the juxtaposition of "before and after," he feels increasingly alienated from the shtetl. What transpires disorients and fragments him. Fober observes: "Robbed of the image he has of himself, Eliezer finds himself again in an environment that, in being significantly shaped by violence and death, stands diametrically opposed to the 'generalized other' of his childhood in Sighet."[582]

The stark dichotomy between these two worlds traumatizes Eliezer. This first layer of trauma is the locus of his break, "with the 'I' of his childhood."[583]

---

[577] Wiesel writes: "Yes, I did see this, with my own eyes . . . children thrown into the flames. (Is it any wonder that ever since then, sleep tends to elude me?)" Wiesel, *The Night Trilogy,* 50.
[578] Wiesel, *The Night Trilogy*, 50.
[579] Wiesel, *The Night Trilogy*, 51.
[580] Wiesel, *The Night Trilogy*, 51-52.
[581] Wiesel, *The Night Trilogy*, 52.
[582] Fober, *Identität und Wissen*, 90. Translation mine.
[583] Fober, *Identität und Wissen*, 90. Translation mine. According to Fober, this "I" has been defined by both his faith and his relationship to his father. See Fober, 78.

However, the extent to which this break is complete—holding no residue of what was—is something we will examine later.

Eliezer's shock upon arriving in Auschwitz incites anger and despair. During his first night at the camp, he comes to realize that the memory of Auschwitz will dictate the rest of his life; he already knows he has broken with the past. He vows never to forget. His faith tradition remains his reference point as he makes this vow. He promises:

> Never shall I forget that night, the first night in camp, that turned my life into one long night seven times sealed.
> Never shall I forget that smoke.
> Never shall I forget the small faces of the children whose bodies I saw transformed into smoke under a silent sky.
> Never shall I forget those flames that consumed my faith forever.
> Never shall I forget the nocturnal silence that deprived me for all eternity of the desire to live.
> Never shall I forget those moments that murdered my God and my soul and turned my dreams to ashes.
> Never shall I forget those things, even were I condemned to live as long as God himself.
> Never. [584]

With this vow, a fundamental change has occurred for the young Talmud student; he has now become *witness*.

c) *The Immanence of Hell and the Fragmentation of Faith*

Critics have examined Wiesel's experience of Auschwitz under a number of thematic and theological rubrics. Without undermining the importance of such studies, my central findings focus on how Wiesel's literary portrayal of Eliezer's experience is indicative of Wiesel's own primary point of reference and interpretation as author, which is to say, his *field*.

Strongly identifiable in the narrative surrounding Auschwitz in *Night* is its suffusion with language indicative of Wiesel's own faith tradition. It is exactly this language that is revealing of how that which has been experienced had already become an interpretation. This interpretation, implicit in Wiesel's text, was first born as the experience itself transpired and was "seen through" the lens of Eliezer's shtetl faith.

These observations represent a significant point of arrival. At the meta-level, they center on issues concerning the use of language and on the unique relation of language to field. Sketching out these issues assists in isolating the

---

[584] Wiesel, *The Night Trilogy*, 52.

mechanisms at play in constructing the narrative. These mechanisms are at play in both the text in a literary sense and its author as a narrator of memory.

We begin with the primary trauma of Auschwitz. The inhumane structure of camp life, the grotesque ideology, and, above all, the brutality of the SS, all complete the process of disintegration that began with the deportation from the ghettos. What began as humiliation, degradation, and subjugation has escalated to enslavement, torture, murder, and systematic annihilation.

Indeed, Eliezer experiences this acceleration in the first section of the text; he is thrust immediately into the train car, where human beings are reduced to mere objects.[585] Terrified, he witnesses how lightly life and death decisions are made. Upon arrival in Auschwitz, many are sent directly to the gas chambers. Although some sentiment to revolt against the SS is present among the inmates, this energy soon dissipates. Instead, the inmates begin their struggle to remain alive.[586] This struggle turns son against father, friend against friend, man against man, and, ultimately, men against God.

Eliezer enters the struggle for survival as well. Upon lying about his age and profession, he is horrified by the gravity of what he is experiencing.[587] His reaction, intensifying and filled with fury, finds expression in the language of *faith*. As his father begins to recite the Kaddish —"'May His name be celebrated and sanctified'"[588]), Eliezer's rage is directed at the Creator: "For the first time, I felt anger rising within me. Why should I sanctify His name? The Almighty, the eternal and terrible Master of the universe, chose to be silent. What was there to thank Him for?"[589] The poignancy of these questions, encapsulating the impasse of the theodicy dilemma at their heart, sheds light on Eliezer's immediate understanding of his experience. His experience is not evaluated within a cognitive vacuum, but rather is gauged against his tradition, which is understood within his interpretive framework: within that of the shtetl-as-field.

In recalling how the inmates are assigned their barracks and then sent to have their heads shaved, Eliezer continues to implement religious language. The

---

[585] Wiesel's portrayal of the objectification of the human being is, in some respects, reminiscent of Améry's personal account of torture. Telling, however, is the discrepancy in expression between the two writers. Whereas Améry, as an assimilated and atheist Jew, portrays his experience while bracketing the question of God, Wiesel's account arguably constitutes one large question concerning both God and humanity. The joining of these two areas of inquiry, of both theology and anthropology, marks the oeuvre. Boschki maintains: "In the oeuvre, the same emphasis put on theology is also put on anthropology. Wiesel's passion for God is always a passion for the human being—and vice versa. Herewith is his use of language in speaking of the human being just as pointedly as in his speaking of God . . . In his literature the human being is evaluated in a new light, in a new shadow." See Boschki, *Der Schrei*, 161. Translation mine.

[586] Wiesel, *The Night Trilogy*, 49.

[587] Wiesel, *The Night Trilogy*, 49-50.

[588] Wiesel, *The Night Trilogy*, 51.

[589] Wiesel, *The Night Trilogy*, 51.

present moment gives flesh to the idea of evil and a "Hell made immanent."[590] Eliezer observes the hell around him: "The barrack we had been assigned to was very long. On the roof, a few bluish lights. I thought: This is what the antechamber of hell must look like. So many crazed men, so much shouting, so much brutality."[591] There, standing mute in the face of violence, he is made acutely aware of his own moral disintegration and his powerlessness to prevent it:

> I stood petrified. What had happened to me? My father had just been struck, in front of me, and I had not even blinked. I had watched and kept silent. Only yesterday, I would have dug my nails into this criminal's flesh. Had I changed so much? So fast? Remorse began to gnaw at me. All I could think of was: I shall never forgive them for this.[592]

Here we observe how Eliezer's faith has quickly broken ranks with the piety he has known.

The violent shift in Eliezer's faith construct becomes more poignant as the narrative continues. This shift coincides with his change in identity: "The morning star shone in the sky. I, too, had become a different person. The student of the Talmud, the child I was, had been consumed by the flames. All that was left was a shape that resembled me. My soul had been invaded—and devoured—by a black flame."[593] This awareness quickly intensifies. The boy's inner protest against the attempts made by others to find comfort in faith are striking:

> Evenings, as we lay on our cots, we sometimes tried to sing a few Hasidic melodies. Akiba Drumer would break our hearts with his deep, grave voice.
>
> Some of the men spoke of God: His mysterious ways, the sins of the Jewish people, and the redemption to come. As for me, I had ceased to pray. I concurred with Job! I was not denying His existence, but I doubted His absolute justice.
>
> Akiba Drumer said:

---

[590] Steiner writes of his own experience: "The camp embodies, often down to minutiae, the images and chronicles of Hell in European art and thought from the twelfth to the eighteenth-centuries. . . . The concentration and death camps of the twentieth-century, wherever they exist, under whatever regime, are *Hell made immanent*. They are the transference of Hell from below the earth to its surface. They are the deliberate enactment of a long, precise imagining." George Steiner, *In Bluebeard's Castle: Some Notes Towards the Re-defintion of Culture* (New Haven, CT: Yale University Press, 1971), 53-54.

[591] Wiesel, *The Night Trilogy*, 52.

[592] Wiesel, *The Night Trilogy*, 57.

[593] Wiesel, *The Night Trilogy*, 55.

> "God is testing us. He wants to see whether we are capable of overcoming our basic instincts, of killing Satan within ourselves. We have no right to despair. And if He punishes us mercilessly, it is a sign that He loves us that much more."[594]

Even as Eliezer rebels against Akiba Drumer's reasoning (his heart too is "broken" upon hearing the Hasidic songs), he continues to stand in relation to the tradition. However, he has already deviated from the naïve faith of the shtetl. In raising his questions about and to God, Eliezer cannot bracket the enormity of his immediate experience. The Hasidic songs are no longer of comfort as they prove inadequate to meet this present reality.

As Eliezer is transferred to Buna and experiences torture, forced labor, starvation, and physical and mental exhaustion, his inner fragmentation becomes increasingly evident. Here, questions of faith no longer dominate the narrative: with the threat of death omnipresent, survival has become the focus of his daily existence.

The fragmentation of Eliezer's faith construct finds its culmination point in the much-reviewed passage of the *pipel's* hanging.[595] Not only does the young boy's death mark a decisive turning point for Eliezer, it also marks a third and thus penultimate transition in the story. The question posed by a nearby inmate as he witnesses the slow execution marks this transition: "For God's sake, where is God?" Eliezer's silent response reflects the definitiveness of the shift that has occurred within him: "Where is he? This is where—hanging here from this gallows . . ."[596] Although this ambiguous reply lies beyond any definitive interpretation—in particular, that of the Death of God—what can be maintained is that it marks the final breaking point of Eliezer's young faith. Strikingly, with this turning point, Eliezer's resolve to survive strengthens.

As the saga of *Night* unfolds, we observe how this break is not one with faith per se, but rather one *within* faith.[597] As Eliezer continues to raise his inner

---

[594] Wiesel, *The Night Trilogy*, 63.

[595] Wiesel denotes the word *"pipel"* was the term used at the camps by the SS for a young boy. See Wiesel, *The Night Trilogy*, 81.

[596] Wiesel, *The Night Trilogy*, 83.

[597] Wiesel himself has affirmed this faith dynamic. He writes: "[T]heorists of the idea that 'God is dead' have used my words unfairly as justification of their rejection of faith. But if Nietzsche could cry out to the old man in the forest that God is dead, the Jew in me cannot. I have never renounced my faith in God. I have risen against His justice, protested His silence and sometimes His absence, but my anger rises up *within faith and not outside it*." See Elie Wiesel, *All Rivers Run to the Sea*, 84, emphasis mine, quoted in Philipp Schweighauser, "Trauma and Utopia: Benjamin, Adorno and Elie Wiesel's *Night*," in *Haunted Narratives: Life Writing in an Age of Trauma*, ed. Gabriele Rippl, et. al. (Toronto: University of Toronto Press, 2013), 55-56. Questions surrounding how Wiesel has represented the death of God in his writings have generated debate. While

voice against God, we sense a breaking in, rather than the death, of faith. Indeed, he continues to address God with the very language of faith. "What are You, my God?" he cries during the inmates' celebration of Rosh Hashanah:

> How do You compare to this stricken mass gathered to affirm to You their faith, their anger, their defiance? What does Your grandeur mean, Master of the Universe, in the face of all this cowardice, this decay, and this misery?[598]

As the men present then begin to call out the words, "Blessed be God's name," Eliezer once again takes up his dialogue with God:

> Blessed be God's name?
>
> Why, but why would I bless him? Every fiber in me rebelled. . . . Blessed be Thou, Almighty, Master of the Universe, who chose us among all nations to be tortured day and night, to watch as our fathers, our mothers, our brothers end up in the furnaces?[599]

Finally, even as Eliezer shifts the question of God to that of the human being, he continues to question God—and still implement the language indicative of his tradition. However much he moves beyond that tradition to embrace a paradigm of questions and rage; he continues to *engage* with faith as he expresses his feelings of abandonment and loss:

> But now, I no longer pleaded for anything. I was no longer able to lament. On the contrary, I felt very strong. I was the accuser, God the accused. My eyes had opened and I was alone, terribly alone in a world without God, without man. Without love or mercy. I was nothing but ashes now, but I felt myself to be stronger than this Almighty to whom my life had been bound for so long. In the midst of these men assembled for prayer, I felt like an observer, a stranger.[600]

---

many images of the death of God haunt his texts—not the least of which has been inferred in the scene of the hanging of the *pipel* in *Night*—Wiesel has stated that, just as faith is not dead, so too is God not dead, contending here that not one of those assenting to the death of God were in Auschwitz. See Elie Wiesel, "Talking and Writing and Keeping Silent" in *The German Struggle and the Holocaust,* ed. Franklin H. Littell and Hubert G. Locke (Detroit: Wayne State University Press, 1974), 269-77. For more on the Death of God theme in Wiesel's works see Boschki, *Der Schrei*, 85-91.

[598] Wiesel, *The Night Trilogy*, 84.

[599] Wiesel, *The Night Trilogy*, 85.

[600] Wiesel, *The Night Trilogy,* 86.

Our sense in these observations is how Eliezer's language mirrors the change in his faith construct. However, even as his language begins to reflect what might arguably be considered a growing agnosticism, Eliezer does not abandon the syntax of the shtetl-as-field. Although his faith has been fragmented, his interpretive parameters remain intact.

This is an important juncture for several reasons. First, Eliezer's use of language is demonstrative of how he has continued to remain within the very sphere of his tradition in spite of his break within faith. Secondly, it is indicative of the way he interprets his experience as an event that concerns faith, as one that thus must be evaluated in terms of faith. Thirdly, and drawing directly from this, it reflects the extent to which that tradition remains the reference point by which Eliezer gauges his immediate experience. Accordingly, it also reflects the interpretive nature of Eliezer's experience, which is to say that his experience is itself an interpretation.

The ways in which this interpretation is expressed in *Night* are telling. Indicative of his field, Eliezer's language mirrors the vital dynamics of a context that never leaves his consciousness. Here, even as he breaks with the past, the event can only be understood *in terms of that past,* which is to say, in its dialectical relation to that past. Although hell is "immanent" in Auschwitz, the shtetl retains its place in Eliezer's cognitive and interpretive framework.

In summary, Eliezer's relinquishment of his traditional faith construct is an experience that finds expression in language indicative of the shtetl-as-field. It also clearly indicates the trauma he has experienced, of course. In this broader context, we observe how two disparate spheres—the shtetl and Auschwitz—collide and how interpretation arises in that moment of collision.[601]

d) The Death of Shlomo Wiesel and the Transfer of Power

Whereas the hanging of the *pipel* represents a third pivotal event in *Night*, it is not the work's final and most important transition. Nor does it represent the apex of the volume.[602] Both of these are embraced by the death of Elie's father,

---

[601] These observations are guided by both social and narrative theory. Bourdieu's theory isolates how a text is reflective of its field and the inner dynamics of that field. According to Young, whose theories can be understood as complementing Bourdieu's, every human experience is simultaneously an interpretation that, in all its complexity, reflects both the immediacy of the experienced event as well as those sources that lie behind the event.

[602] Importantly, scholars who have identified the hanging of the *pipel* as the pivotal point of *Night* tend, as a rule, to read the work as a theological treatise. While the book certainly gives credence to many theological themes, other readings grant other findings. Some of these have poignant literary and sociological implications. My analysis endeavors to seek the connections between theological, literary, and sociological aspects of *Night*. In so doing, it strengthens further how *Night* can be seen to function as the center of the oeuvre.

Shlomo Wiesel. Here, I contend that Wiesel's narrative has reached a vital point of arrival with Shlomo Wiesel's passing.

As Eliezer's story unfolds, and as the war approaches its end, its drama intensifies, moving quickly towards its culmination with the death march to Gleiwitz, Poland. A recounting of these details would be redundant here. Crucial to examining these final sections of the work is a reading that focuses on the father-son relationship theme. In the context of the father-son relationship, *Night* reaches its climax.

With Eliezer's move to the work camp, Buna, the plot progresses rapidly. Eliezer's complex relationship with his father begins to change. This relationship not only deepens in the most basic, human sense, but it also acquires a symbiotic dynamic; father and son have now become interdependent. Their enmeshment is indissoluble. Each has become obsessed with the task of keeping the other alive. Clinging to each other, they unconsciously believe that the survival of the one hinges upon the survival of the other. As the situation accelerates, however, as conditions in the camp worsen and as the inmates weaken, Shlomo Wiesel begins to deteriorate physically and psychologically. It is here that Eliezer enters into the role of caregiver. He is aware that their identities have merged, and that he has now become the stronger of the two. Eliezer recounts an incident in the summer of 1944:

> I ran to look for my father. . . . He was leaning against the wall, bent shoulders sagging as if under a heavy load. I went up to him, took his hand and kissed it. I felt a tear on my hand. Whose was it? Mine? His? I said nothing. Nor did he. Never before had we understood each other so clearly.[603]

It is at Rosh Hashanah, in the context of his growing sense of responsibility, as well as his intensifying rage against God and humanity, that Eliezer exchanges roles with his father. In becoming the keeper of what is now a broken faith, it is incumbent upon him to assume the upper hand, even with respect to God. From this perspective, the passage quoted above can be mentioned once again:

> [In days gone by], I fully believed that the salvation of the world depended on every one of my deeds, on every one of my prayers.
>
> But now, I no longer pleaded for anything. I was no longer able to lament. On the contrary, I felt very strong. I was the accuser, God the accused. My eyes had opened and I was alone, terribly alone in a world without God, without man. Without love or mercy. I was nothing but ashes now, but I felt

---

[603] Wiesel, *The Night Trilogy*, 86-87.

> myself to be stronger than this Almighty to whom my life had been bound for so long.[604]

Evident here is how the shift in Eliezer's traditional faith construct is linked to his perception of increased psychological strength. He has inwardly broken with past notions of God in which God is understood as a protector in control of the world. Eliezer now believes he is alone without God and thus responsible for his own survival and that of his embattled father. Thus, with his faith broken, he adopts the mindset of an adult.

In January of 1945, as Buna is evacuated in anticipation of the arrival of the Red Army, father and son are forced, along with thousands of others, to march their way to Gleiwitz under precarious conditions. The majority of prisoners die on route. Eliezer's sole purpose remains keeping his father alive long enough to reach their destination. Shlomo Wiesel, too, attempts to motivate his son to continue. The back and forth of this mutual struggle for survival permeates the final pages of *Night*. Although Eliezer at times feels the desire to end his life, his father's presence deters him: "My father's presence was the only thing that stopped me. He was running next to me, out of breath, out of strength, desperate. I had no right to let myself die. What would he do without me? I was his sole support."[605] Eliezer is quick to note the dramatic change in his father. "How he had aged since last night!" he remembers. "His body was completely twisted, shriveled up into himself. His eyes were glazed over, his lips parched, decayed. Everything about him expressed total exhaustion."[606] As a father would to a son, Eliezer encourages his father to rest:

> "Come, Father, let's go back to the shed . . . "
> He didn't answer. He was not even looking at the dead.
> "Come, Father. It's better there. You'll be able to lie down. We'll take turns. I'll watch over you and you'll watch over me. We won't let each other fall asleep. We'll look after each other."[607]

Astonishingly, the two arrive alive in Gleiwitz. Shlomo Wiesel's condition, however, has worsened. Barely escaping one of the final selections, he is permitted to stay near his son, but the end is clearly drawing near. Three days later, all remaining inmates are transported on to Buchenwald. The journey is harrowing. Although Shlomo Wiesel develops dysentery, Eliezer only intensifies his efforts to save him. All of his attempts at securing medical attention for his father fail. Eliezer's own strength is beginning to dissipate. Still, his bond to his father is

---

604 Wiesel, *The Night Trilogy*, 86.
605 Wiesel, *The Night Trilogy*, 104-5.
606 Wiesel, *The Night Trilogy*, 106.
607 Wiesel, *The Night Trilogy*, 107.

unrelenting. "I was riveted to my father's agony," Wiesel writes. "My hands were aching, I was clenching them so hard. To strangle the doctor and the others! To set the whole world on fire! My father's murderers! But even the cry stuck in my throat."[608]

Finally, after a restless night, Eliezer awakens to find his father, who had slept on the bunk below him, missing. He realizes that his father has perished during the night and that his corpse has been removed. The *Akeda* of Mount Moriah has been repeated, but in the most obscene terms. This time, the son has led his father to the altar, but the father is not spared.[609] With this, the young boy, now truly alone, is overcome with feelings of guilt. Still, he feels a paradoxical sense of relief and cannot weep.[610] Nor does he say kaddish.[611]

Eliezer spends the remainder of his time as a prisoner in Buchenwald in a fragmented, dissociative state, having lost all real will to live, even following the liberation of Buchenwald in April. As the memoir closes, Eliezer, upon viewing his reflection in a mirror for the first time since the shtetl was liquidated, is conscious of the fact that survival is and will remain, in the most unambiguous of terms, a grotesque paradox.

As the climax of Wiesel's testimony, the death of Shlomo introduces themes that will come to permeate many of Wiesel's works, themes associated with the presence and message of the dead, survivor guilt, and memory. These will become more apparent as we move forward in this study.

A closer analysis of the literary function of Shlomo Wiesel's death in the narrative is of interest as it assists in evaluating the work with a view to aspects of the theory of field. Specifically, Shlomo Wiesel's death indicates the indispensable transfer of power between generations within any given field.[612] This

---

[608] Wiesel, *The Night Trilogy*, 127.

[609] For more analysis on the *Akeda* theme present in the father-son relationship, see Fine, *The Legacy of Night,* 18-21. Fine references André Neher who suggests the notion of an "anti-*Akeda*" where "not a father leading his son to be sacrificed, but a son guiding, dragging, carrying to the altar an old man who no longer has the strength to continue." It is "a rewriting of the *Akeda* under the opaque light of Auschwitz."As quoted in *Fine, The Legacy of Night*, 21; see also André Neher, *L'Exile de la parole. Du silence biblique au silence d'Auschwitz* (Paris: Editions du Seuil, 1970), 235, 234. For more on the father-son relation in *Night*, see Ellen S. Fine, "Fathers and Sons" in *Readings on Night*, ed. Mass, 98-107. See also Boschki, *Der Schrei*, 98-103; and Greenberg, "The Hasidic Spark and the Holocaust," in *Elie Wiesel: Jewish, Literary, and Moral Perspectives*, ed. Katz and Rosen, 92-94.

[610] Wiesel, *The Night Trilogy*, 130.

[611] Wiesel, *The Night Trilogy*, 130. See also Wiesel, *Legends of Our Time*, 5. Wiesel's writing has often been understood to represent his ongoing kaddish to his father. Nearing death, Wiesel requested that his son Elisha Wiesel say kaddish for him after he passed. See Rick Lyman, "Elie Wiesel's Only Son Steps Up to His Father's Legacy," *New York Times*, May 12th, 2017.

[612] In as much as every field can be considered a *field of power* where particular rules dictate the lively interactions of its adherents, i.e., a "field of struggle" or a "field of

transfer can be considered a kind of "inheriting" by which the "social patrimony" (i.e., the inheritance itself) of the field is transferred from the hands of the older generation into those of the younger. According to Bourdieu, this act "always represents a critical moment" within which the younger generation and the "material, cultural, social and symbolic patrimony" of its field stand in a delicate position of "*reciprocal appropriation.*"[613] This notion implies that the heir inherits the inheritance and that the inheritance inherits the heir.[614] To apply this notion to *Night*, Eliezer inherits the shtetl with its social, intellectual, and spiritual legacy, just as the shtetl itself inherits Eliezer. In other words, as Eliezer is entrusted with the shtetl, he has, at the same time, been taken possession of by it.

This symbolic transaction has far-reaching implications for Eliezer, who has now assumed responsibility for and authority over the field. In both having inherited and having been inherited, he has involuntarily been placed under the banner of "survivor." The tasks implied in this role, including those of bearing witness, are yet far away from the mind of the boy, although nonetheless implicit in the very fact of survival. Eliezer has internalized the field, an act that will prove vital to his identity as survivor, witness, and storyteller.

We can now better judge the important literary role that Shlomo Wiesel plays in *Night*. As the father-son relationship theme ripples throughout the work, the father's (omni)presence in his son's life both before and during Auschwitz demonstrates the symbolic power of their relationship. Although Eliezer cannot process this relationship fully—its meaning and impact for the future—his father represents for him the heart of the shtetl. It is precisely within this context that the literary and sociological questions posed to the story converge. With the transfer of power inherent in the death of Shlomo Wiesel as the veritable "father of the shtetl," the complex legacy of the field—including its duties and responsibilities—are now passed over to his son who is his only direct surviving heir. It is here that Eliezer becomes the heir to the shtetl. The reversal of roles is now finalized; the child becomes the "father of the man."[615] Flung abruptly into adulthood,

---

forces" where "social forces, attractions or repulsions, are exercised," the power transferred from one generation to the next has to do exactly with the transmission of the field's deepest structures, its social legacy, its most deeply ingrained *dasein*, its way of being-in-the-world, its veritable way of life. See Bourdieu, *Rules of Art*, 9-13.

613 Bourdieu, *Rules of Art*, 11.

614 "The tendency of patrimony (and thus of the whole of social structure) to continue in its state cannot be realized unless the inheritance inherits the heir, unless, by the mediation notably of those who are provisionally responsible for it and who must assure their succession, 'the dead (that is, property), seizes the quick (that is, a proprietor disposed and able to inherit).'"See Bourdieu, 11.

615 See William Wordsworth's 1802 poem "My Heart Leaps Up"in *The Norton Anthology of Poetry*, ed. Alexander W. Allison et. al., 3rd shorter ed. (New York: W.W. Norton and Company, 1970), 285. Although interpretations of Wordsworth's phrase diverge, it can be best understood as the inner continuum existing between childhood and adulthood. Transferred to *Night*, I use the phrase twofold: to represent the role-reversal

Eliezer knows there will be no going home. This is to become the burden of his witness and memory.

Illuminating these inherent dynamics of *Night* brings us to an important juncture in this study. We can tease out yet deeper layers of the work. We can also begin to conjecture about the power the legacy of the shtetl may come to exert over Wiesel and how this power that comes to expression in other works of Wiesel.

Layering the Memoir: Further Analyses

a) Initial Remarks

Despite the clarity of the language of *Night*—its terse, lucid style; its distinct timeline; the clear transitions within its storyline; the intelligibility of the pictures and events portrayed—Wiesel conveys a world to the reader that remains unknowable. As indicated, the inherent inadequacy of language prevents those outside from knowing the world of the Holocaust. Ironically, language, a tool meant to relate, express, and convey, is exactly what prevents the reader from acquiring "true" knowledge of the Holocaust. It veils that which it attempts to convey. The source of this insufficiency is two-fold. It is founded in the impoverished capacity of language to transmit atrocity adequately and in the severe nature of the events themselves.

Sociology of literature also makes assertions about the inadequacy of language. It illuminates how little can be understood of a text without knowledge of its sources or its author. Although not applicable uniformly to the whole of Holocaust literature, its methods do assist in distilling elements of Holocaust texts that would otherwise remain hidden. To do so, we must examine the text's sources.

As is the case with other Holocaust testimony, *Night* is a work that conceals. The kinds of knowledge that we are able to receive from the text are limited. Despite this, there are still particular kinds of knowledge that are conveyed to the reader. This occurs despite their distance from the people and events that constitute the narrative.

A reading of *Night* that is attentive to its origins assists in distilling aspects of the work that are not obvious to the reader on first reading. While still unable to touch the ontological realities behind the text (here, the realities of the Holocaust), such a reading exposes how the text's origins impact both the text

---

between Shlomo Wiesel and Eliezer and to prefigure the manner in which Eliezer, as the child of the shtetl, will never leave Wiesel, the grown man and author, following the Holocaust. The main theses of this study hinge in part upon this claim.

itself and our interpretations of it. Such a reading helps to break the story's spell by "interrupting the complicity that unites author and reader."[616]

Our continued exploration of *Night* will serve as a starting point in examining three other works by Wiesel. Our next step is to view the complex relationship between Wiesel as author and his narrative *Night* and how this relationship reveals more clandestine aspects of both.

b) The Author and the Protagonist

Writing has the potential to transform the writer; indeed, the narration process does not leave the writer unchanged. However, author and text will always remain commensurable. Our quest here is to illuminate this commensurability in *Night* and to examine its implications.

Although the genre to which *Night* has been debated (e.g., whether it is autobiography, fiction, autobiographical fiction, memoir), more recent discussion understands it as *testimony*.[617] By this definition, the work does contain autobiographical elements.

The presence of this autobiographical content necessitates an anamnesis of the work's "deep and repressed structures."[618] The question to guide this anamnesis must address the relationship between Wiesel as author and Eliezer as protagonist.

---

[616] Bourdieu states: "The 'reality effect' is that very particular form of belief that literary fiction produces, through a disclaimed reference to the reality designated, which allows us to know everything by refusing to know what really is. A sociological reading breaks the spell. By interrupting the complicity that unites author and reader in the same relation of denegation of the reality expressed by the text, it reveals the truth that the text enunciates but in such a way that it does not say it; moreover, sociological reading *a contrario* brings to light the truth of the text itself." See Bourdieu, *Rules of Art*, 32.

[617] Fine writes: "The work [*Night*] defies all categories. It has been described as personal memoir, autobiographical narrative, fictionalized autobiography, nonfiction novel, and human document. Essentially, it is a *témoignage*, a first-hand account of the concentration camp experience, succinctly related by the fifteen-year-old narrator, Eliezer." Fine, *Legacy of Night*, 10. Colin Davis maintains that the designation of *Night* as testimony is linked inextricably to the identification of both the author and the protagonist of the story. "We are invited to read *La Nuit* as a *témoignage* (testimony), not a novel; for its impact, the text requires our belief in the literal truth of the facts that are described. In consequence, we should identify the Eliezer who narrates *La Nuit* with the Elie given on the title page as the author of the text. . . . If we do not accept the identification of Eliezer with Elie, then the direct link between the text and historical reality will be broken." Colin Davis, *Elie Wiesel's Secretive Texts* (Gainesville: University of Florida Press, 1994), 32.

[618] Bourdieu writes: "And should we not ask ourselves if work on form is not what makes possible the partial anamnesis of deep and repressed structures, if, in a word, the writer most preoccupied with formal research . . . is not actually driven to act as a *medium of those structures*?" Bourdieu, *Rules of Art*, 3-4.

I contend that this relationship is inextricable. It is a literary relationship in which Wiesel, the author, is simultaneously Eliezer the subject. This implies that, while the author tells the story, the story is also about the author. Wiesel is inscribed in the text as both its scribe and main player. Thus, he is involved with the production of the text while, at the same time, existing within the text. This also implies that Wiesel, although having separated himself from Eliezer by the act of writing, is yet bound to him.

With this in mind, two layers of the book can be identified. The first is the layer of the story, which is about the protagonist, Eliezer. The second is the layer of its narration, which is about the author, Wiesel. The link between these two is evident as we observe Wiesel acting as both the *mediator* of the story and the *mediated* of the story, as both subject *and* object. The subjective autobiographical dimension of the text implies the objectification that takes place. Because the text is relaying the author's own story, the author forfeits any claims to objectivity with respect to the narration of the story. The result is a dynamic literary enmeshment of Wiesel and Eliezer.

The implications of this fundamental relationship are striking. As much as Wiesel is indissolubly bound to Eliezer by way of the story, the story itself must mirror Wiesel as its author in the most basic ways. According to Bourdieu, the work's internal structure must of necessity reveal the internal structure of the author's mind,[619] which is to say, his social and mental structures.[620] In other words, the structure of Wiesel's social realities are recreated and reconstructed. As such, the author himself *mediates* the structures of the text. As the mind of the author is both mirrored and reconstructed in the story, the work is indicative of its source and therefore its field.

As we have seen, Eliezer continues to narrate his story within the interpretive parameters of the shtetl-as-field. At the same time, however, Wiesel's portrayal of Eliezer reflects those same parameters. Just as Eliezer, while in Auschwitz, has drawn on all the resources of the shtetl-as-field in "interpreting" his experience of Auschwitz as the experience itself unfolded, so too does Wiesel draw from these same resources in telling his story through Eliezer much later. This complex dynamic is reflected in the language that Wiesel uses to narrate the story, and through the literary character of Eliezer. It is in this context that we can

---

[619] In his analysis of Flaubert's *Sentimental Education*, Bourdieu writes: "In fact, *Sentimental Education* reconstitutes in an extraordinarily exact manner the structure of the social world in which it was produced and even the mental structures which, fashioned by these social structures, form the generative principle of the work in which these structures are revealed." Bourdieu, *Rules of Art*, 31-32. Bourdieu also indicates that "it is by means of and for the sake of the elaboration of a story that the author is led to uncover the most deeply buried structure—the most obscure because it is the most directly linked to his primary investments—which is at the foundation of his mental and his literary strategies." Bourdieu, *Rules of Art*, 25.

[620] Cf. Bourdieu, *Rules of Art*, 3-4.

consider how the world of the protagonist is simultaneously the world of the author.

This is a vital point of arrival. With Eliezer as the narrator or voice of the story, Wiesel *is* that voice.[621] It is a voice that reveals the past.[622] In his relation to the child that Wiesel once was, Eliezer stands for the trajectory of the future author. As with all trajectories, the future has been "implicated in the past,"[623] which is to say, Wiesel the author is prefigured in the character of Eliezer. At the same time, however, Wiesel projects himself back into Eliezer, revealing therewith his own internal structures. The mind of the author is thus unveiled as being one with the protagonist he has created. As a result, the author of *Night* is no uncreated creator. Instead, his relation to the trajectory of the child that once was is inextricable. As testimony, *Night* can be understood as auto-analytical. This implies its provision of a "socioanalysis" of Wiesel—of his *Sitz-im-Leben*, his social world, and its legacy.[624]

Both Wiesel and Eliezer function as witnesses. As author, Wiesel narrates Eliezer's story; in this particular context, he witnesses the witness. In this process of witnessing, that is, in the act of writing, his narrative becomes testimony. With this, Wiesel and Eliezer both fulfill the commission given at the death of Shlomo Wiesel, to remember the shtetl and to transmit its story.

c) The Narration of Night and the Evolution of the Ellipse

If *Night* can be seen to mirror the mind—the social and mental structures—of its author, the question arises as to the nature of that mirroring, which is to say, of those finer mechanisms at work within the process of narration. At the same time, we may consider how the images supplied by this process must be intrinsic to, or indicative of, the process itself. Whereas Bourdieu provides adequate grounds for an initial exploration of *Night* based on literary and sociological

---

[621] Fine writes: "This *voice from within* is the generative principle of the will to bear witness, source of survival, and residue of life in the kingdom of death. The narrator of *Night* has been reduced to a disembodied voice: the narrator *is* his voice." Fine, *Legacy of Night*, 29.

[622] Eliezer may also be understood in terms of his "will to faith." The notion "will to believe" is attributed to William James. See William James, *Varieties of Religious Experience* (Cambridge, MA: Harvard University Press, 1985), 174. See also William James, "The Will to Believe," in *The Will to Believe and Other Essays in Popular Philosophy*, ed. Frederick H. Burkhardt, Fredson Bowers, and Ignas K. Skrupskelis, vol. 6, *The Works of William James* (Cambridge, MA: Harvard University Press, 1979), 13-33.

[623] Bourdieu: "Agents temporalize themselves in the very act by which they transcend the immediate present towards the future implicated in the past of which their habitus is the product; they produce time in the practical anticipation of a still-to-come [à venir] which is at the same time the practical actualization of the past." Bourdieu, *Rules of Art*, 328.

[624] Bourdieu: "In place of the customary complacent and naïve projections of an autobiographical type, one should in fact perceive an enterprise of *objectification of the self*, of autoanalysis, of socioanalysis." Bourdieu, *Rules of Art*, 25.

inquiry, we discover that Young's theory of Holocaust representation aids in exploring its other layers.

In reference to Young's theory of how Holocaust literature is "indicative of its source," we are reminded of how our knowledge of Holocaust events, however limited that must be, is entirely dependent upon the ways in it has been represented. According to Young, the narration process is complex. Its images are drawn from cognitive and psychological interactions in which memory, succumbing to the sway of imagination as impacted by events past and present, portrays images of trauma in terms that reflect both one's earliest personal resources *and* the trauma itself. This process is, by nature, a highly interpretive one. The images conveyed tend to reflect, in obvious and tacit ways, events in a particular way, lending a narrative its language, its shape, form, content, and even literary style. In other words, it is indicative of its source.

My concern here is how *Night* is reflective of this fundamental process. I propose that *Night* not only aligns itself well with this theory, but also that, in so doing, it constitutes a crucial first extension of Wiesel's field, setting the stage for the works that follow.

To recall, in Young's model of the narration process, an event of trauma is experienced a priori within the interpretive framework of the one experiencing it. That framework is based on one's past influences: the language one has spoken and the ethnic, cultural, and religious traditions in which one has been raised. In other words, the ways one has grown to be-in-the-world, or in Bourdieusian terms, the ways one has drawn from all the capital provided by the field. This capital impacts the individual in the most basic of ways, emerging as a kind of filter through which trauma is experienced in one way, rather than another. This dynamic implies that trauma, as an experience, is always and simultaneously an interpretation—one that is made in relation to a complex nexus of factors and influences.

Wiesel's portrayal of events in *Night* can be examined under this rubric. Its structure is made visible by way of the four vital transition points. In directing us from the shtetl to its liquidation, from deportation to the experience of Auschwitz, from the hanging of the *pipel* to Wiesel's break in faith, and from the death of Shlomo Wiesel to Eliezer's appropriation of the legacy of his field, there is a movement within the text that mirrors directly that of the protagonist. Specifically, it constitutes the shift in Eliezer's faith construct. As his story unfolds, this is evidenced best by the rage and protest he expresses. Significant, however, is how this rage and protest continue to reflect his original faith construct. Specifically, Eliezer continues to converse with the God through whom his faith has been broken.

In observing this dynamic at work, one may begin to visualize *Night* in a new way. The dual nature of the narrative—which, on one level, relates the story of Eliezer as protagonist while, on a second level, clandestinely references the story of Wiesel as author who is engaged in the very process of remembering—produces a striking image, that of a trauma filtered through the same foundational faith construct that first interpreted it. Thus, although this construct has since been revised, it is still palpably present in the text.

This reveals, at its core, how both the shtetl-as-field and the trauma of Auschwitz have come to impact Wiesel's original interpretation of Auschwitz *and* his later recollection or memory of it. With this, we can sense how both of these entities have come to impact Wiesel's narration process.

Our observations of Wiesel's text thus align themselves with Young's model of the narration process. The shtetl is mirrored in the narrative process, the immediate experience of Auschwitz is at once an interpretation affected by the experience of the shtetl. In so far as that interpretation then proceeds to impact how the experience is remembered "after the fact," the narrative also bears the imprint of the shtetl.

In keeping with my discussion of Young's theory, we can depict the narration process evident in *Night,* as depicted in figure 5:

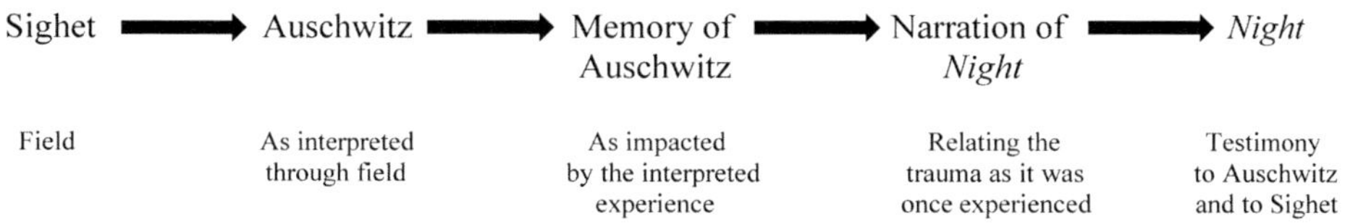

Figure 5 — The Narration Process

Evident here are the two abiding sources of *Night*: the shtetl of Sighet and Auschwitz.

With these two contradictory forces, the ellipse begins to take shape. By isolating Sighet, whose story demarcates the first and indispensable section of *Night*, which Wiesel portrays as a force of harmony, cohesion, and divine and human love, we may posit it as the first focal point of the ellipse. The second focal point is represented by Auschwitz, which stands diametrically opposed to Sighet. The power relationship is one of infinite tension. As Auschwitz itself seeks to overpower Sighet in Wiesel's memory, we find the author struggling to recover Sighet from the ashes of its destruction by way of testimony. Wiesel thus finds himself caught between the shtetl and Auschwitz as between two contradictory forces; indeed, each remains alive within memory and, as such, each continues to exert power over memory.

Memory itself is the center of the ellipse. After Wiesel encounters the void of Auschwitz, he remains, post-Auschwitz, caught between the annihilation and destruction embodied by Auschwitz and the goodness of Sighet. With memory standing mid-way between these two forces, we can begin to sketch the ellipse in the following way (see figure 6):

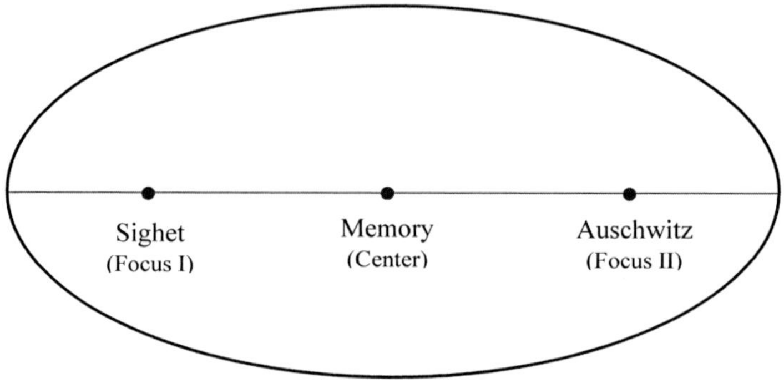

Figure 6 — Basic Ellipse Format

Here we observe that Sighet and Auschwitz are equidistant from memory. This is indicative of the power struggle between Sighet and Auschwitz in memory. We can observe how memory is constantly being pushed and pulled by both forces in its attempt to find expression through testimony.

However, as testimony, guided by memory, tends to draw more from one source than the other at different points in time, its distance to each of these can vary. For example, just as memory might be drawn more to Auschwitz than Sighet at any given point in time, testimony will be marked more by despair and the fallout of Auschwitz's evil. Conversely, when memory is drawn more to Sighet, as we observe in Wiesel's *Four Hasidic Masters,* testimony will reflect the hope of the shtetl, and its inherent constellations of goodness and love. In this context, testimony is represented as the various points of the ellipse. These two variations can be understood in the following contrasting models (figures 7 and 8):

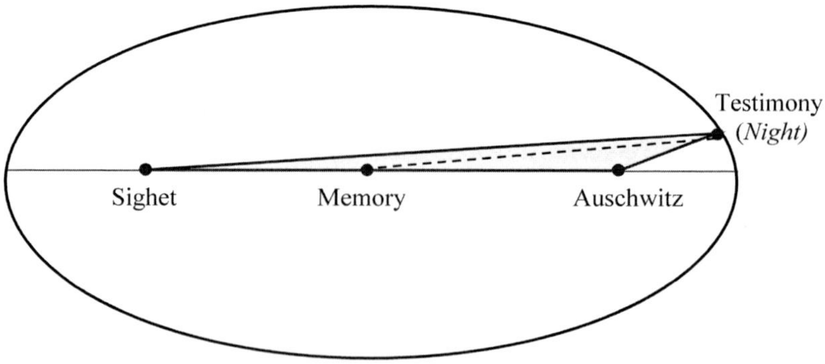

Figure 7 — Ellipse of *Night*

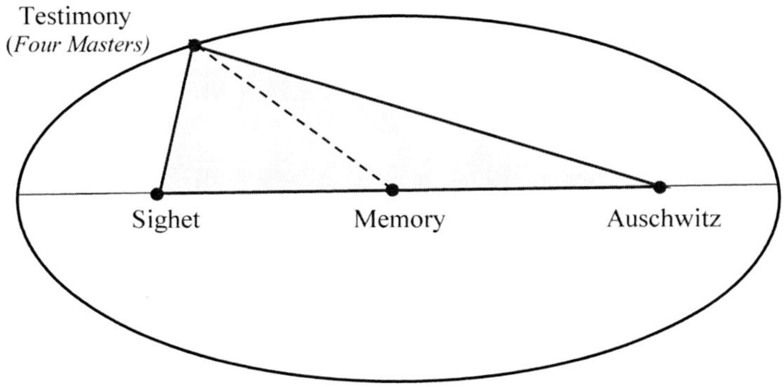

Figure 8 — Ellipse of *Four Masters*

Here we see that Sighet and Auschwitz remain simultaneously present. As such, Wiesel's testimony is constantly in flux and gravitates around the two focal points as memory interchangeably drawing more from one source than the other. This is indicative of the underlying, continuous struggle between good and evil.

In implementing these models, we note how *Night*, as testimony of the atrocities of Auschwitz itself, is best represented by Model I. While the shtetl is present in Sighet, it is all but eclipsed by the enormity of evil. As we consider other works that follow *Night*, our observations will shed light on Wiesel's attempt to mobilize memory to give life to the shtetl once more.

d) Night, Hasidism, and the First Extension of the Field

The terse narrative style of *Night* echoes that of a Hasidic tale. In his sparing of aesthetic detail, Wiesel relates his story laconically. With the exception of interspersed theological commentary on behalf of the protagonist, Wiesel eschews abstract reflection on the unfolding of events. Close to life, stark and exposed, his text reads as a tale that might be heard, rather than read. In the context of this simple and compact prose, we can underscore Boschki's suggestion that Wiesel's "language and choice of words are simple, in as much as they lean on the Jewish narrative tradition."[625]

Similar observations are possible with regard to the literary form of *Night*. While clear and succinct, Wiesel's testimony does not moralize, nor does it give away any message it may intend to convey. Instead, it recounts events in a manner that renders the reader responsible for extracting its message in the way that a Hasidic tale might. This is felt most poignantly at the end of the story; open-

[625] Boschki, *Der Schrei,* 75. Translation mine.

ended, it silently commissions its reader to discern the meaning of the mirror whose image is incapable of being expunged.

At the meta-level, we observe several themes with which Wiesel, speaking through Eliezer, struggles to come to terms. These center on the questions of good versus evil and God versus humanity. Tellingly, in Wiesel's testimony, these two questions are inextricably linked. In the wake of Auschwitz, they also assume new contours.

Indeed, theodicy's problem is exposed anew by *Night*. To revisit particular theological concerns of both the Kabbalah and Hasidism, the Kabbalah, in developing key concepts later central to Hasidism, sought to understand the creation of the cosmos, the emergence of evil, as well as humanity's struggle to overcome it.

Drawing from and developing these concerns further, Hasidism understands creation as an ever-deepening layering of the materiality of the cosmos which, at its most dense and opaque stratum, renders its creator imperceptible. Evil is understood as the place where the alignment of the holy letters responsible for creation has been disturbed. In this place, however, God is still considered present; indeed, there is no place void of God; all of creation is thus considered a text of God.

As we have seen, the central task of human beings is to correct the alignment of the holy letters and restore order in creation, to bring an end to the veiling of God. Thus, by way of its dynamic relationship with God—a relationship in which all acts, holy and profane, can potentially unite one to God—humanity is profoundly involved in *tikkun*. As such, humanity takes part in the liberation of creation from the entanglements of evil, in the deliverance of the Shekhinah from her exile, and in hastening the coming of the Messiah.

Elements of these themes tacitly permeate *Night*. Indeed, from the onset of Eliezer's story, beginning with Moishe's escape from execution, Wiesel's focus is the deviation of humanity from its intended course and the impact this deviation has on both humanity and God. In this context, Eliezer comes to despair of God. To inquire about the whereabouts of God in the face of human evil, he must cast into doubt the presence of God in all things. As a result, Wiesel renders the centermost claim of his faith untenable.

This point is important. While Wiesel rejects traditional claims of faith, he remains gripped by them. The basic framework within which he assesses the world, God, and his experience, does not change—in spite of how the conclusions he reaches do change. As such, although a theological shift occurs for Wiesel, his way of knowing and being-in-the-world retains its fundamental conceptual framework.

This is, of course, telling of Wiesel's relation to field. Eliezer's devastating conclusions with respect to God and his experience of trauma, even in their deviation from traditional faith claims, expose the sense in which Wiesel as author remains within the interpretive parameters of his tradition while, at the same time, advancing to the uttermost parameters of his field. In fact, with *Night*, he can be seen even to *extend* his field. In referencing Auschwitz as the unprecedented focus of his protest, this extension can be given the name *testimony*.[626]

Drawing on the ideas above, it is evident that Wiesel's traditional faith construct ironically retains elements of shtetl faith, exactly in its protest of them. His protest continues to implement the language and conceptual framework of faith. For Wiesel, the shtetl's efforts to commit all acts to God (*avoda*) as a way to reach God have failed. Not all acts, holy and profane, lead to God; indeed, they can lead away from God through the delusion they engender. The very acts of humanity have driven God out of his creation.

The clinging to God in *devequt* fails, too. The holy letters have not been realigned. Humanity assumes the place of God, and with this there is no restoration of the order of creation—no *tikkun*; as such, there is no retrieving of the shattered fragments of the divine from the world. The Shekhinah will not be liberated from her exile, and the Messiah will not soon return. In as much as all of these cosmic events remain dependent on human action and endeavor, redemption is thwarted.

By the end of his testimony, Eliezer, highly traumatized, succumbs to despair. Still, in his protest and lament, he takes up the commission given to him with the passing of his father. Wiesel too—as author—does not abandon faith, however much he is troubled by it. The parameters within which he continues to evaluate Auschwitz have thus not changed. Although scarred by Auschwitz, he has chosen to tell his story in terms of faith and its brokenness.

With this, Wiesel adopts another form of *devequt,* where cleaving to the divine transpires through language and by storytelling.

---

[626] *Night* has often been evaluated as a religious treatise. My contention here is that its story moves beyond that, embracing the status of a testimony that is guided by a particular religious reference point: the shtetl. It may also be understood as a kind of coming-of-age story— although one with grave and tragic parameters, consequences, and implications. The dark paradox of coming-of-age in this context is one that lends weight to the message. David L. Vanderwerken argues that the text represents a fundamental reversal of a coming-of-age story of the typical *Bildungsroman* in as much as its protagonist is not led into greater personal awareness but rather into "darkness and death."See David L. Vanderwerken, "Night is the Anti-'Coming-of-Age' Story," in *Readings on Night*, ed. Mass, 123-28. Langer, on the other hand, argues that "in its compressed imaginative power and artful presentation of the circumstances of the author's internment in Auschwitz, [*Night*] yields the effect of an authentic Bildungsroman—except that the youthful protagonist becomes an initiate into death rather than life." See Langer, *The Holocaust and the Literary Imagination*, 75. My contention here is that the story is indicative of Eliezer's coming-of-age exactly in terms of the forced and dreadful process of maturation into which he has been thrust. No less enlightened than the protagonist who enters into the bright light of day, Eliezer steps out into the night without any illusion that all is right with the world.

"Dawn": There Where the Night Reigns Forever

Exploring the Limits of Mind

In his second work, *Dawn*, Wiesel investigates the consequences of memory. The title reveals a deep irony. Even as dawn breaks upon a world post-Auschwitz, there will be no relenting of night; nor is there a balm for memory. Dawn proves to be but a grievous extension of night itself, revealing only another shade of the same, perpetuating darkness: a "grayish light the color of stagnant water."[627]

In many ways, *Dawn* resumes the testimony of *Night*.[628] First published in 1960 as *L'Aube*, just two years following *La Nuit*, it represents a further attempt by Wiesel to come to terms with his experiences. Notably, Wiesel does not explicitly recount any of these within his narrative. Instead, he circles about them furtively through the character of Elisha who, after having survived the camps, is tempted by hate to avenge his losses.[629] *Night* is thus present as the plot of *Dawn*

---

[627] Wiesel, *The Night Trilogy*, 221. With respect to *Dawn*, John K. Roth writes: "The shadows of the 'Final Solution' continue to destroy the longing for a positive solution. That is why the title *Dawn* is an ironic one, for following Auschwitz the night reigns on and the despair sneaks into the innermost existence of the survivor as would a snake. "See, John K. Roth, "Von „Nacht" bis „Abenddämmerung in der Ferne." Ein Philosoph liest das Romanwerk," in *Das Gegenteil von Gleichgültigkeit ist Erinnerung. Versuche zu Elie Wiesel*, eds. Mensink and Boschki, 82. Translation mine. Davis also highlights the irony inherent in the titles of the trilogy: "The progression implied in the titles of Wiesel's first three works (*La Nuit*, *L'Aube*, *Le Jour*), is not borne out by the texts themselves; there is no unambiguous movement from darkness to light, despair to hope. Wiesel's 'trilogy' appears to set itself a teleological program with which it fails to comply."Davis, *Elie Wiesel's Secretive Texts*, 62-63.

[628] While *Dawn* may be a work of fiction, it does retain autobiographical pieces of Wiesel's own story. In this sense, his novels can be understood as "fictional papers" rather than "fictional literature." See Boschki, "Zum Autor," in *Kultur allein ist nicht genug*, ed. Boschki and Mensink, 33. Davis contends: "The fictional status of *L'Aube* and *Le Jour* is acknowledged on their title pages. . . . Nevertheless, the divorce between fictional narrative and 'real' author remains incomplete; Wiesel names his principle characters 'Elisha' . . . and Eliezer . . . and thereby invites some degree of identification between author and narrator . . . even though the texts in which they appear are presented to the reader as fictional." See Davis, *Elie Wiesel's Secretive Texts*, 63.

[629] Just as Wiesel himself claims *Night* to be the core of his lifework, so too do his other works, in particular his novels, circle about that core. Without revisiting the camps explicitly in them, Wiesel sets out to explore themes associated with survival, with religious belief and tradition, and with the human condition. In this way, his writing offers a peripatetic view of the *univers concentrationnaire*. See Sidra DeKoven Ezrahi, *By Words Alone: The Holocaust in Literature* (Chicago: University of Chicago Press, 1980), 116. Mensink writes: "Most of the books of Elie Wiesel do not immediately concern themselves with the Holocaust. On the one hand, the relocation of literary happenings . . . grants him the necessary distance in order to present extreme experiences in a

opens and as it closes. In a nutshell, *Dawn* sets out to explore the psychological fallout of trauma in a most horrific setting.

I contend that *Dawn* constitutes an elongated exploration of the mirror theme of *Night*. Although liberated physically, the survivor is never able to escape memory. The story reveals how the survivor lives on two separate levels: the level of the present reality, and the level of the reality of the camps, now past.[630] The survivor remains trapped within a perilous inner divide where trauma dominates his or her dual existence. Psychologically conflicted, the survivor seeks to justify revenge. Detaching him or herself from the reality of the present, they become increasingly obsessed with the past. Psychological stigmata ensues. Despair is never far away, nor is insanity an impossibility.[631]

---

literary way at all. Second . . . memory for him means more than the literary documentation of his camp experiences. 'For this reason I [Wiesel] turned to the Hasidic epoch and then to the Kabbalah of the twelfth-century and then to the Talmud of the first-century and then to the prophets of the fifth-century BC. I simply wanted to expand the kingdom of memory and spread the voice of memory to every one of us—in the hope that memory, as a challenge to the enemy, would become our shield.'" See Dagmar Mensink, "Zur Einführung: Elie Wiesel lesen," in *Kultur allein ist nicht genug,* ed. Boschki and Mensink, 16-17. Translation mine. Mensink's Wiesel quotation is provided by Olaf Schwencke in *Erinnerung als Gegenwart. Elie Wiesel in Loccum* (Freiburg i. B.: Herder, 1987), 57.

630 Fine references Jean Cayrol's concept of "*le pouvoir de dédoublement*" as "the ability to live on two levels simultaneously." See Fine, *The Legacy of Night*, 33. Fine writes: "In the camps, prisoners developed this mechanism to detach themselves from the pain of the situation, . . . which enabled the inmates to mentally escape their suffering. However, the fluctuation between two levels of reality has the reverse effect on the survivor, who drifts in and out of his nightmares, continuing to relive the terror of the camps in his dreams as well as in his waking hours. . . . This perpetual state of vagabondage divides the survivor within himself." See Fine, *The Legacy of Night*, 33.

631 In his next novel, *Day*, Wiesel speaks to this theme through his unnamed protagonist: "Anyone who has been there has brought back some of humanity's madness. One day or another it will come to the surface." *The Night Trilogy*, 326. The theme of madness is one that pervades Wiesel's works. His novel *Twilight* in particular takes up the theme as its central concern. Set in a psychiatrist institution, a young doctor, himself a Holocaust survivor, seeks to understand his own story through his encounters with the insane. See Elie Wiesel, *Twilight*. Significantly, Wiesel also associates the theme of madness with Hasidism—though he understands Hasidism to be a holy madness. He writes: "All the first Hasidic masters were mad, and therefore I love them. . . . They had to be mad to try to transmit a message of humanism, a message of beauty, a message of compassion in a world that had none. Hasidism is madness—sacred, mystical madness." See Elie Wiesel, in Abrahamson, ed. *Against Silence*, 2:255, quoted in Friedman, *You Are My Witnesses*, 144. Still, as Friedman suggests: "[T]he *source* of Wiesel's fascination with madness is neither biblical nor Hasidic. It is the experience of the Holocaust."Friedman, *You Are My Witnesses*, 145. Ultimately, Wiesel embraces Hasidism in an attempt to thwart the threat of madness posed to the survivor. Indeed, for Wiesel, the line drawn between sanity and madness remains a thin one. Boschki writes: "The lostness of the

What is survival? Can it be equated with living? What role does memory play in the survivor's quest to continue to survive? What limits does the mind encounter in dealing with memory? These questions preoccupy Wiesel's second volume. Significantly, Wiesel sets out to investigate them in Hasidic fashion—by telling a story.[632] With this, he builds a bridge between himself and the reader, thus serving to link two disparate worlds.[633] As storyteller-witness, Wiesel engages with the reader in a unique writer-reader "pact" where the reader is challenged to grapple with the reality with which he or she is presented.[634]

With this, *Dawn* invites the reader to enter into a forbidden place. However, the realities clothed by the narrative remain barred off from the reader. The language of the narrative allows limited access only to small remnants of memory. Still, *Dawn* insists that memory must bear witness. Wiesel is unremitting in this respect; with *Dawn*, he hopes to move the reader by way of a message that is distinguishable beyond the content matter that remains veiled and impermeable.

Wiesel's continuous interweaving of Hasidic legends, themes, and motifs into *Dawn* grants some sense, however limited, of how horrific these events must have been. Wiesel's implementation of these traditional elements actually draws us into and binds us to his text. This assists in transliterating Wiesel's experiences into language and images that we are able to grasp better conceptually. As we enter the text as text by way of the metaphoric power of the images of the world of the shtetl, we begin to sense there is another place there too, one that terrifies.

Isolating these elements as a "continuity of cultural perspectives"[635] assists us in demythologizing the text. As we explore the influences that lie "behind" the narrative, we are better able to understand how these function in Wiesel's overall attempt to represent realities that remain incommunicable.

As was the case with *Night*, Wiesel implements the first-person perspective: Elisha is "I." This literary choice contributes to the reader's intense involvement with the text. The protagonist, the anguished Auschwitz survivor Elisha, has joined the Jewish armed resistance in British-occupied Palestine. Fighting for the

---

individual, the loneliness of the subject in a world that has become one without relationship, Kafkas great themes, became the leitmotif of [Wiesel's] own literature before the background of his experiences, which is to say, the lostness of the victims in the face of the machinery of death, the loneliness of the survivor in a world that doesn't understand him or her and does not want to understand, because he or she comes from "another universe." See Boschki, "Heimweh nach Sighet," 53. Translation mine.

[632] Cf. McAfee Brown, *Elie Wiesel: Messenger to All Humanity*, 43.

[633] Cf. McAfee Brown, *Elie Wiesel: Messenger to All Humanity*, 44.

[634] Ezrahi describes the pact between writer and reader with regard to Holocaust fiction as being unique. He writes: "Intensifying with the reader's familiarity with the Nazi system, and shifting with the degree of authorial intervention, a relationship evolves between maker and reader which is probably unprecedented in the history of Western literature." Ezrahi, *By Words Alone*. 8.

[635] Ezrahi, *By Words Alone*, 7.

birth of a Jewish nation, he has now been thrust into a role he never thought possible: that of executioner. As he remembers the past, however, and as the events and people of his past enter his present through memory, he is tormented by the reality of what will soon take place. As the time of the execution—dawn—draws near, his despair deepens. How is he to understand himself as a killer, knowing that, through murder, he will kill the fragment of spirit still left within him?

And the Shtetl Speaks: Hasidic Elements

a) Hasidic Legends and Motifs

As is the case with Wiesel's other novels, *Dawn* is replete with Hasidic legends and motifs. In this novel, they drive the entire thrust of the plot. They also form the very inner life of the protagonist.

In the extremity of the events that unfold—the core of which transpires in one single night—Elisha's anguish is exacerbated by one issue in particular: that of being able to distinguish night from day at the break of dawn. This motif is linked with the image of a window-mirror in the story, reminiscent of Wiesel's own experience upon his liberation from Buchenwald. This one motif functions as the novel's *leitmotif.* Other Hasidic elements are then woven into the story as it unfolds, in and about this leitmotif, serving to complement it, and, in so doing, to underscore its dreadful *pointe*.

b) The Beggar, The Dead, and the Face in the Window

The window-mirror motif is introduced in the first pages of *Dawn.* As Elisha prepares for the execution, the day is dying. The shutters of a house nearby are closed, and the room in which he finds himself is dimming. Gad, his comrade-in-arms, asks Elisha if he might turn on a light. As darkness has not yet settled upon them, Elisha declines. But the question is a trigger and ignites the memory of an encounter long ago when Elisha learned how to distinguish night from day as a boy in the shtetl synagogue.

The incident had been prompted by a beggar whose message would foreshadow Elisha's fate. The beggar had entered the synagogue where Elisha had been praying. Elisha is filled with fear; according to legend, beggars were potential messengers in disguise. Clothed as the prophet Elijah, they could offer reward and eternal life; if one were unlucky, however, they could be clothed as the Angel of Death who would bring death and destruction of the soul.[636]

Night had fallen; the candles of the synagogue were extinguishing. Elisha is afraid and flees the synagogue. He fears the dead as these were believed to rise from their graves at midnight to say their prayers there, and were always waiting to snatch away any visitor who might overhear their appeals. The beggar retreats with Elisha, who now knows that the beggar is a messenger not of this world.

---

636 Wiesel, *The Night Trilogy*, 144.

Indeed, the beggar's errand is mystical; he wishes to convey to the boy the deepest meaning of night and its juxtaposition to day. "Night is purer than day," the beggar reveals as he senses Elisha's fear of the darkness. "It is better for thinking and loving and dreaming. At night everything is more intense, more true. . . . The tragedy of man is that he doesn't know how to distinguish between day and night."[637] To make this distinction, the beggar continues, one must look to a window. Should it reflect a face, one knows that night has descended. "If you see a face, any face, then you can be sure that night has succeeded day. For believe me, night has a face."[638]

The beggar's instructions never leave the boy. He would continue to look, night after night, to the window as one would a mirror, seeing perpetually changing faces, among them the beggar's. Following his father's death, he saw his face there, too, "large with death and memory."[639] Years later, he would come to see his own. Indeed, Elisha would come to learn that the mirrored face of night is the face of death.

Elisha's recollection of the beggar introduces a number of themes central to *Dawn*. The theme of night becomes central once again, linked here to the window-mirror motif and the mirroring of night's many faces. The faces and, in particular, the watching eyes of those faces are recurrent images that saturate the work. As the tale continues, these images intensify until, at last, the very persons to whom they belong, the dead of Elisha's past, enter the tale. With their presence, Elisha's internal chaos grows.

As the night moves swiftly towards dawn, so too does Elisha's realization of his own approaching psychological execution. He is already in the process of dying; his inner torment has become unbearable. "Don't torture yourself," his colleagues admonish time and again. "This is war."[640] Ilana—the comrade whose voice for freedom is heard from radios across Palestine—continues this rationale by indicating that night holds the possibility of justifying evil deeds. "War is like night. It covers everything,"[641] she says. For Elisha, however, war and night are equated with death and destruction. Indeed, the night holds no merits; its covering of everything is indicative only of its propensity to annihilate all that crosses its path.

It is here that the night-window-mirror motif is introduced. It will weave its way through the entire narrative. At the end of the novel, upon John's Dawson's execution, Elisha envisions his own face in the window as belonging to one who has killed himself.

---

637 Wiesel, *The Night Trilogy*, 145.
638 Wiesel, *The Night Trilogy*, 145.
639 Wiesel, *The Night Trilogy*, 146.
640 The expression repeats itself throughout the novel, in varying forms and contexts. See, for example, Wiesel, *The Night Trilogy*, 143, 150, 165, 170, 193.
641 Wiesel, *The Night Trilogy*, 194.

c) The Messenger Meshulah

Like the beggar of the shtetl who functions as an other-worldly messenger who foretells a dark fate, Gad also assumes the role of Meshulah, a mythic figure commissioned to convey messages to chosen individuals. Wiesel writes:

> Having been brought up in the Hasidic tradition, I had heard strange stories about the Meshulah, the mysterious messenger of fate to whom nothing is impossible. His voice is such as to make a man tremble, for the message it brings is more powerful than either the bearer or the recipient. His every word seems to come from the absolute, the infinite, and its significance is at the same time fearful and fascinating. Gad is Meshulah, I said to myself.[642]

Gad's imposing presence captivates Elisha:

> "I am Gad," he said in a resonant voice, as if he were uttering some Kabbalistic sentence which contained an answer to every question. He said, "I am Gad" in the same way that Jehovah said, "I am that I am."[643]

In the role of a messenger, Gad fascinates Elisha—as would a Hasidic master—with his stories:

> I sat down on my bed, offering him the only chair in the room, but he remained standing. In the Hasidic legends the messenger is always portrayed standing, as if his body must at all times serve as a connecting link between heaven and earth. Standing thus, in a trench coat which seemed as if it had never been taken off and were an integral part of his body, with his head inclined toward his right shoulder and a fiery expression in his eyes, he proceeded to tell me about the Movement.[644]

Gad's stories are woven so subtly that Elisha becomes convinced that violence is the only path to Jewish liberation:

> Gad's stories were utterly fascinating. I saw in him a prince of Jewish history, a legendary messenger sent by fate to awaken my imagination, to tell the people whose past was now their religion: Come, come; the future is waiting for you with open

---

642 Wiesel, *The Night Trilogy*, 154.
643 Wiesel, *The Night Trilogy*, 153.
644 Wiesel, *The Night Trilogy*, 154-55.

> arms. From now on you will no longer be humiliated, persecuted, or even pitied. You will not be strangers encamped in an age and a place that are not yours. Come, brothers, come![645]

Elisha cannot resist Gad's persuasive, but shadowed, presence. Gad is possessed by hate towards the British and is convinced that only violence can free Palestine from their hands. He soon convinces Elisha to travel to Palestine and take up arms. Gad's role darkens as John Dawson's execution approaches. Gad is enigmatically bonded to Elisha—who knows no hate, only anguish. Tensions rise between the two as they discuss the prisoner's last meal, and Elisha feels powerless in Gad's presence:

> Perhaps I wanted to hear myself shout, to arouse my anger and see it reflected in the motionless shadows in the mirror and on the wall. Or perhaps out of sheer weakness. I felt powerless to change anything, least of all myself, in spite of the fact that I wanted to introduce a transformation into the room, to reorder the whole of creation. I would have made the Saint into a madman, have given John Dawson's name to Gad and his fate to David. But I knew there was nothing I could do. To have such power I should have had to take the place of death. [646]

Gad, the messenger who is Meshulah, now witnesses the accomplishment of his mission; in having delivered his ominous message at the onset of the tale, he has incited a sequence of events from which there is presently no escape. Fate's death-wielding sword will soon fall on the neck of Elisha.

d) "The Exchange"

Throughout the novel, Elisha remembers past events. As he remembers what transpired upon his arrival in Palestine, he recalls the admonishment of the masked leader of their group: one must hate the enemy. He had said that hate was to be their greatest source of strength in combating the British. Murder would be the method, akin to Hitler's own. No longer, he had insisted, would the Jewish people fall victim to the whims of those who detest them. They must resist:

> "If we must become more unjust and inhuman than those who have been unjust and inhuman to us, then we shall do so. . . . Murder will not be our profession but our duty. In the days and weeks and months to come you will have only one

---

[645] Wiesel, *The Night Trilogy*, 156.
[646] Wiesel, *The Night Trilogy*, 176-77.

> purpose: to kill those who have made us killers. We shall kill in order that once more we may be men . . ."[647]

Although shocked at what he had heard, Elisha had found the stranger's words stimulating. The stranger's justification of murder and revenge made sense—at least in the passion of the moment. Now however, as he deliberates on this fateful night, he draws a comparison to the tradition in which he was raised:

> I remembered how the grizzled master had explained the sixth commandment [do not kill] to me. Why has a man no right to commit murder? Because in so doing he takes upon himself the function of God. And this must not be done too easily. Well, I said to myself, if in order to change the course of our history we have to become God, we shall become Him. How easy that is we shall see.[648]

This particular scene is reminiscent of a legend Wiesel tells frequently. This legend, which I shall call "The Exchange," recounts a pact made between humanity and God in which both agree to exchange places for a short time to understand what it means to be the other. The tale takes on a dark twist when humanity, upon discovering the thrill of being all-powerful, refuses to relinquish its divine capacities. In the end, God is left weak and dependent, at the mercy of an evil counterpart.[649]

My suggestion here is that "The Exchange" serves furtively as the foundation of the novel. As Elisha assumes the role of murderer, he becomes increasingly aware of the gravity of what is at stake. In dictating over the life and death of a single man, Elisha, too, has taken on the role of God. Although he has, "killed before"[650] as a freedom fighter, he is now confronted with the coldly-calculated murder of a man he does not know and, above all, does not hate. "No, it was not

---

[647] Wiesel, *The Night Trilogy*, 162-63.

[648] Wiesel, *The Night Trilogy*, 163.

[649] In *The Town Behind the Wall*, Wiesel formulates the legend in this way: "Legend tells us that one day man spoke to God in this way: *'Let us change about. You be man, and I will be God. For only one second.' God smiled gently and asked him, 'Aren't you afraid?' 'No. And you?' 'Yes, I am,' God said. Nevertheless he granted man's desire. He became a man, and the man took his place and immediately availed himself of his omnipotence: he refused to revert to his previous state. So neither man nor God was ever again what he seemed to be. Years passed, centuries, perhaps eternities. And suddenly the drama quickened. The past for one, and the present for the other, were too heavy to be borne. As the liberation of the one was bound to the liberation of the other, they renewed the ancient dialogue whose echoes come to us in the night, charged with hatred, with remorse, and most of all, with infinite yearning.*" See Wiesel, *The Town Behind the Wall*, 179.

[650] Wiesel, *The Night Trilogy*, 161.

easy to play the part of God," Elisha reflects, "especially when it meant putting on the field-gray uniform of the SS. But it was easier than killing a hostage."[651] Despair sets in. Gad, upon sensing Elisha's psychological state retorts: "Don't torture yourself, Elisha. This is war."[652]

As the novel unfolds, the inflections of "The Exchange" become more complex. Set into its new context, and framed with the motifs of night and the window-mirror, it drives the novel, exacerbating its intensity and transporting its dire message to a theological-anthropological level.

e) "Open Sky"

In *Dawn*, Wiesel also reappropriates the legend of "The Open Sky." Ilana's presence incites a poignant memory in Elisha. The event had taken place in the period immediately following the war. Pensive and insecure, Elisha had gazed into the sky and recounted a Hasidic legend to his first lover Catherine:

> As we walked on I told her the legend of the open sky. When I was a child the old master told me that there were nights when the sky opened up in order to make way for the prayers of unhappy children. On one such night a little boy whose father was dying said to God: "Father, I am too small to know how to pray. But I ask you to heal my sick father." God did what the boy asked, but the boy himself was turned into a prayer and carried up into heaven. From that day on, the master told me, God has from time to time shown Himself to us in the face of a child. [653]

Elisha had been quick to realize that he was the child that, "had been turned into a prayer and carried up into heaven. [Catherine] knew that I had died and come back to earth, dead."[654]

The legend is poignant and suggestive of Elisha's fate. By positing the image of the child Elisha once had been, Wiesel tacitly resumes the father-son relationship theme that strongly dictates *Night*'s outcome. In so doing, the theme links the two works inextricably.

The plot unfolds. Elisha, walking the dangerous tightrope between sanity and madness, witnesses how the dead begin to enter the room as he awaits the dawn. When a small boy arrives, Elisha realizes that he strongly resembles the child he had been before the war. This boy, acting in the dream-vision as Elisha's gentle counter-ego, is assigned to answer "all [Elisha's] questions."[655] He is a

---

[651] Wiesel, *The Night Trilogy*, 165.
[652] Wiesel, *The Night Trilogy*, 165.
[653] Wiesel, *The Night Trilogy*, 180.
[654] Wiesel, *The Night Trilogy*, 183.
[655] Wiesel, *The Night Trilogy*, 186.

quiet companion who will remain present with Elisha till dawn, when the murder is committed. It is the boy who admonishes Elisha to grant John Dawson a final meal. As Elisha justifies his actions and as he admonishes the dead for casting their judgment upon him, the boy falls silent. His fear appears to mirror Elisha's own:

> Only when I perceived the silence of the boy, a silence eloquent in his eyes, did I decide to speak. He had a look of anxiety which made him seem older, more mature. I shall speak up, I said to myself, I have no right to condemn the little boy.[656]

Elisha's identification with both the boy in the sky and the boy of his vision is telling; he sees himself mirrored in the boy's eyes. He recognizes in the child not merely his own pre-war innocence, but also his post-war woundedness, his own deep and entrenched silence. As he considers himself to have already died in the camps, Elisha knows that the boy, when he witnesses Elisha commit murder, will also witness his being killed a second time.

f) "The Goat Beside your Bed"

Ilana reminds Elisha not only of Catherine, but also of his own Hasidic mother. We observe how Ilana assumes a motherly role towards Elisha as his torment mounts. "Poor boy, poor boy!" she laments, echoing his mother's words. Strangely, they had been Catherine's, too. Later, falling silent, Ilana attempts to soothe her comrade: "You torture yourself, Elisha." Elisha recalls the moment: "I was reminded of my own mother. She talked in the same moving voice and used almost the same words in the same places." This "mirroring" subtly touches the window-mirror motif once again.

Incited by Ilana's presence, Elisha recalls a story once told him by his mother long before:

> There is a goat beside your bed, she used to tell me, a goat of gold. Everywhere you go in life the goat will guide and protect you. Even when you are grown up and very rich, when you know everything a man can know and possess all that he should possess, the goat will still be near you.[657]

The irony in this traditional image is that manhood has brought Elisha neither knowledge nor wisdom nor the possessions conducive to both, but only death and the capacity to kill. The little goat accompanies him, perhaps, but does not protect him.

---

[656] Wiesel, *The Night Trilogy*, 197.
[657] Wiesel, *The Night Trilogy*, 194.

The Shtetl Enters the Room

In one of *Dawn*'s most dramatic scenes, the dead enter the upper chamber where Elisha is preparing to execute John Dawson. They begin to shuffle in, making the small room unbearably stifling. The entire shtetl is there. Among those present are Elisha's father; his mother; his spiritual master, the rabbi; Yerachmiel, his school friend and spiritual companion in the practice of the Kabbalah; a beggar; as well as the boy mentioned above.[658] Their presence overwhelms Elisha. In attempting to converse with them, however, more chaos ensues.

The dead say little. Elisha's deceased father, drained of life and full of grief, remains silent as his son demands to know the reason for their coming. At this moment, Elisha recalls his father's death. He had deceived the Angel of Death, for he had "stolen away a minute before the Angel of Death came to take him; in cheating the Angel he had taken with him the human sorrow which he endured while he was alive." [659] That grief is now present once again, and his father's sorrowful gaze grants Elisha no solace. Elisha's mother, full of compassion and sorrow, laments the plight of her now-adult son. "Poor little boy, poor little boy!" is all she can murmur, echoing both Catherine's and Ilana's words.[660] His master, full of wisdom and tradition, is silent too, as so often he had been in life. However, his present gaze is one of fire, which incites fear in Elisha.[661] Yerachmiel, with whom Elisha had attempted to hasten the coming of the Messiah, remains as still as the others.[662] Only the boy converses with Elisha and the beggar, who stands tall above the rest. It is he who will, in the end, gently remind Elisha that the time to murder has arrived.[663]

Faces from the past, both familiar and distantly familiar—faces from a childhood steeped in traditions—all are present in the room. These presences perform the vital function of rousing Elisha's awareness of the proximity of the past. Taken together, they assume a strong symbolic role in the novel. The dead have come to witness him commit murder. They are linked, inextricably bonded to him. The dead are all that Elisha is, and his actions will be their own. "You are the sum total of what we have been. . . . In a way, we are the ones to execute

---

[658] Wiesel, *The Night Trilogy*, 184.
[659] Wiesel, *The Night Trilogy*, 197.
[660] Elisha appears to conflate the identities of his mother with those of Ilana and Catherine. Indeed, all three take on the role of his caregiver. Both Ilana and Catherine are somewhat older than he is and speak to him as ones who have known much suffering. Both express the need to care for Elisha. Wiesel, 178, 180, 183, 185, 187. Ilana, known as the "Voice of Freedom" throughout Palestine, is especially attentive to Elisha, exhibiting at times an erotic attraction to him. See *The Night Trilogy*, 158-159, 191, 193.
[661] Wiesel, *The Night Trilogy*, 185.
[662] Wiesel, *The Night Trilogy*, 198-99.
[663] Wiesel, *The Night Trilogy*, 219.

John Dawson. Because you can't do it without us,"[664] the boy indicates. However, the dead do not judge him, however much their fate is a part of his:

> "We're not here to sit in judgment. We're here simply because you're here. We're present wherever you go; we are what you do. When you raise your eyes to heaven we share in their sight; when you pat the head of a hungry child a thousand hands are laid on his head; when you give bread to a beggar we give him that taste of paradise which only the poor can savor. Why are we silent? Because silence is not only our dwelling place but our very being as well. We *are* silence. And your silence is us. You carry us with you. Occasionally you may see us, but most of the time we are invisible to you. When you see us you imagine that we are sitting in judgment upon you. You are wrong. Your silence is your judge."[665]

The boy's comment is telling. The dead are Elisha's witnesses. Because Elisha, as a survivor of both Auschwitz and Buchenwald, is himself a witness, the dead are witnessing the witness. They are not absent, nor are they aloof; they are omnipresent as God would be. As a constitutive part of all that Elisha is and does, they too will assume the title "murderer" as Elisha executes John Dawson. Their bond exists on a mystical level that can only be explained by a common fate and by the force of memory.

The dead are Elisha's memory. In him, they remain alive. He is their mouth, their hands, and their feet. They watch, and they witness through him. Ultimately, he is accountable to them alone. Elisha has not separated himself from the shtetl, although it now lies in dust and ashes. He carries its dead within him; in so doing, memory becomes what defines and drives him.[666]

This point of arrival is essential. The presence of the shtetl's dead is indicative of the grave conflict that rages on in Elisha. It also reveals the profound juxtaposition of the shtetl with Auschwitz, one that reaches deep into the psyche of Elisha and serves to exacerbate the torment he feels there.

---

[664] Wiesel, *The Night Trilogy*, 187.

[665] Wiesel, *The Night Trilogy*, 200.

[666] Wiesel's sense of accountability to the dead never dissipated. In his foundational essay, "Warum ich schreibe" (Why I write), Wiesel maintains: "To snatch the victims away from being forgotten. To help the dead claim victory over death." Elie Wiesel, *Den Frieden Feiern*, ed. Reinhold Boschert-Kimmig (Freiburg i. B.: Herder, 1991), 28. Translation mine. He resumes the theme in *From the Kingdom of Memory*: "I owe [the dead] my memory. I am duty-bound to serve as their emissary, transmitting the history of their disappearance, even if it disturbs, even if it brings pain. Not to do so would be to betray them, and thus myself." See page 16.

Elisha, the Broken Hasid

Just as the window-mirror image builds the central motif of *Dawn*, and just as the legend of the exchange between God and humanity serves as the novel's subtle but vital foundation, so too do night, death, and the dead emerge as important themes that help guide the work. Strikingly, each of these—the motif, the legend, the themes—is intricately woven into the novel so as to deepen its intensity while, at the same time, serving to further complicate the anguished inner journey of Elisha. This journey is one of identity-seeking, for although Elisha's identity as a Hasid persists, it has shifted into that of a broken Hasid.

The "I" who is Elisha has continually sought his identity as a survivor of Auschwitz in a post-Auschwitz world. Elisha's post-war period in Paris had been marked by his search to understand who he is in light of his story. Immersing himself in the study of philosophy, he sought to "understand the meaning of the events of which [he] had been the victim."[667] The existential search was framed by abstract questions:

> Where is God to be found? In suffering or in rebellion? When is a man most truly a man? When he submits or when he refuses? Where does suffering lead him? To purification or to bestiality? Philosophy, I hoped, would give me an answer.[668]

The mysterious entrance of Gad had quickly thwarted Elisha's goal of plummeting the deepest truths of God and humanity. Seduced by the prospect of revenge and the possibility of devoting himself to a noble cause, Elisha decides to abandon his intellectual pursuits. Ironically, Elisha soon enters a world of violence and murder all over again. To his horror, of course, he finds himself newly entangled with the problem of evil—albeit with the evil within himself. Ironic, too, is his belief that all of this will grant his life meaning and even free him in the end. [669]

During that fated night in Palestine, Elisha's questions wreak havoc within him. Confronted with the very necessity of hating—for executioners must hate their victims[670]—he comes into immediate conflict with memory. As the

---

[667] Wiesel, *The Night Trilogy*, 152.

[668] Wiesel, *The Night Trilogy*, 152.

[669] Davis writes: "Elisha lives in anticipation of meaning, and he seems justified in his anticipation when he abandons philosophy in favor of direct intervention in the struggle for the foundation of Israel. . . . Nevertheless, such a meaning is never revealed. John Dawson turns his failure to understand the meaning of death back onto Elisha: "I don't even know why I am dying . . . Do you know why? "The question remains unanswered, and thereby the text refuses to confirm the authority of meaning for which the narrator is searching." See Davis, *Elie Wiesel's Secretive Texts*, 66.

[670] "I didn't hate him at all," writes Wiesel, "but I wanted to hate him. That would have made it all very easy. Hate—like faith or love or war—justifies everything." See Wiesel, *The Night Trilogy*, 214.

dead enter the room where Elisha is preparing himself for the execution, the shtetl comes to life once more. The dead send out a silent message that he cannot help but hear, for they remind him of all he has ever held sacred.

The legends of the past take on new poignancy and relevance as memory is activated. Under the solemn, watchful gaze of the dead, Elisha must justify the evil crime he is about to commit. The questions he once posed to philosophy, questions of God and humanity, now return to him existentially with brute force. He realizes that Gad has deceived him and, as a result, he has fallen into a role he did not intend to assume:

> It flashed across my mind that in speaking of John Dawson's imminent death Ilana was speaking of me also, since I was his killer. Who was to kill David ben Moshe? For a moment I had the impression that I was to kill both of them and all the other Johns and Davids on earth. I was the executioner. And I was eighteen years old. Eighteen years of searching and suffering, of study and rebellion, and they all added up to this. I wanted to understand the pure, unadulterated essence of human nature, the path to the understanding of man. I had sought after the truth, and here I was about to become a killer, a participant in the work of death and God. I went over to the mirror hanging on the wall and looked into my face. I almost cried out, for everywhere I saw my own eyes.[671]

The dead draw Elisha back into the world of the shtetl. Confronted by them, he realizes he has never truly left that world. The shtetl has not ceased to define who he is, not ceased to grant him the orientation point from which he interprets every moment and every memory, regardless of his present torment. As the dead enter the story and fill the room, Elisha tacitly alludes to the fact that deep within, he can never be anything other than what he once was and has since remained:

> As I let my eyes wander about the room I realized that all of those who had contributed to my formation, to the formation of my permanent identity, were there. Some of them were familiar, but I could not pin a label on them; they were names without faces or faces without names. And yet I knew that at some point my life had crossed theirs.[672]

The mere presence of the dead in the room is telling. Elisha knows that the shtetl can never truly leave him. He will always be a Hasid. The shtetl's presence contrasts starkly with the evil he is about to commit, providing the theological

[671] Wiesel, *The Night Trilogy*, 159.
[672] Wiesel, *The Night Trilogy*, 184.

framework for his anguished deliberations. Indeed, it is precisely here that Elisha's crisis exacerbates and deepens. The violent discrepancy between the shtetl and the present moment—one could even say, the vicious conflict arising between these two disparate entities—hinders Elisha from distinguishing reality from unreality. His vision of the dead sharpens and becomes all-consuming. Whether Elisha has entered a psychotic state is a question the text leaves open.

In the context of his strong identification with the dead, with the plight of the shtetl, Elisha knows that he will soon betray their memory. The dead will not forget his betrayal. "[T]he dead never forget," Elisha reflects. "[T]hey would remember. In their eyes I should be forever branded a killer."[673] In his vision of them—in these moments of tense, unholy madness—Elisha knows that the dead are about to be victimized for a second time; just as "they are what he is" and "do what he does," they too are about to become murderers. This realization devastates. Although still unable to hate John Dawson, Elisha is, for complex psychological reasons, rendered powerless to loosen his grip on the task set out before him.

By the end of the novel, Elisha turns to John Dawson himself to justify his deed. John Dawson cannot give it to him; he grants Elisha no opportunity to hate. Instead, Elisha finds John Dawson (ironically, the "son of dawn") likable, a father with a son back home.[674] Very quickly, Elisha bonds with Dawson, knowing their fates are grotesquely bound to each other. Elisha, however, has deteriorated too far to retrace his steps; there is no turning back.

Upon murdering John Dawson, Elisha ascends to the room where his comrades await him. There, he sees his darkened face mirrored in the window one last time. Although dawn has broken, Elisha's inner night draws its death-bearing cloak around him more tightly than before. He has betrayed the memory of the dead, and with them, himself:

> The night lifted, leaving behind it a grayish light the color of stagnant water. Soon there was only a tattered fragment of darkness, hanging in midair, the other side of the window. Fear caught my throat. The tattered fragment of darkness had a face. Looking at it, I understood the reason for my fear. The face was my own.[675]

---

673 Wiesel, *The Night Trilogy*, 195.

674 The father-son relationship is a theme that Wiesel resumes in *Dawn* with John Dawson's execution. Dawson's mention of his son affects Elisha who has lost his own father in the Holocaust. Dawson's stories ignite in Elisha feelings which exacerbate his psychological impasse. "And he went on to tell me more about this son who was "studying at Cambridge." Every sentence was a tongue of flame which burned my body. With my right hand I patted the revolver in my pocket. The revolver too was incandescent, and burned my fingers. I mustn't listen to him, I told myself. He's my enemy, and the enemy has no story." *The Night Trilogy*, 209-10.

675 Wiesel, *The Night Trilogy*, 221.

Who is Elisha? Is he survivor, victim, witness, or executioner? The text addresses these questions at the level of the story and at the meta-level beyond the story. At both levels, Elisha plays all three roles. The grave atrocities he had witnessed in the camps had robbed him of family, community, and psychological well-being; indeed, they have transported him to a place of inner chaos and perpetual night. Even in Palestine as a young "freedom-fighter," his sense of disorientation does not dissipate; even there he still cannot distinguish between day and night. His thirst for truth is not quenched. Instead, his questions of God, humanity, and evil are framed by a context that reflects back to him, as would a mirror, his own inherent evil. In fulfilling his role as executioner, Elisha succumbs to that evil. It is in this sense that Elisha kills Elisha, casting him into the role of victim once again.[676]

Further Considerations

Both thematically and stylistically, *Dawn* functions as an extension of *Night*. In its strong juxtaposition of the shtetl with Auschwitz, it mirrors its predecessor. Once again, a terse, compact style confronts the reader. Its themes devastate and its warning of the power of evil distresses. Although fiction, the text references elements of Wiesel's biography. However, its focus remains Wiesel's existential search for answers and, concomitantly, his concern for a world after Auschwitz.

The novel does not merely display Hasidic themes and motifs, but is also guided by them. Wiesel has not relinquished his task of not-forgetting. By way of memory, he understands the shtetl's dead, though deeply wounded, as bearers of an urgent message. In the context of the seductive lure of revenge, the shtetl symbolizes a lost world in need of resurrection. Dramatically, Wiesel resurrects it literarily in the troubled mind of Elisha.

---

[676] Berenbaum notes the poignant irony inherent in Elisha's name, which references the prophet Elisha who raised the dead to life: "The interpretation of this passage [of the killing of John Dawson] beyond the literal level hinges on the meaning of the name Elisha. It is obvious that in killing another person Elisha has also killed a part of himself." See Michael Berenbaum, *The Vision of the Void: Theological Reflections on the Works of Elie Wiesel* (Middletown, CT: Wesleyan University Press, 1979), 23. Horowitz emphasizes that the killing of Dawson produces in Elisha the opposite of what he originally intended: "Killing Dawson, while perhaps useful to the political and military cause, makes Elisha an executioner. By killing his enemy, Elisha turns himself into the type of person he detests. In effect, he symbolically kills his innocent self when he kills Dawson. Thus, carrying out the orders does not bring Elisha relief. On the contrary, it brings him tremendous anguish. . . . He has exchanged places with the enemy and gains no peace." See Rosemary Horowitz, "Creative Ambiguity in Wiesel's Storytelling," in *Elie Wiesel and the Art of Storytelling*, 41.

As we have observed in *Night*, Wiesel has constructed *Dawn* while working at the uttermost parameters of his field. Wiesel infuses its Hasidic elements with new meanings that move the reader. While the reader remains incapable of understanding survivor-authors' experiences, *Dawn*'s poignant message is replete with ethical implications. Revenge and hate only lead back into the grip of evil; indeed, revenge and avengement only induce new evil, and render the healing of past atrocities impossible.

Within this interpretive context, we can better assess how Wiesel has reworked trusted legends into the story in ways that lend them new force and potency. These legends are now disconnected from past meanings due to their dark, new context. Auschwitz changes everything in its wake—even language and its capacity to describe, convey, and transmit knowledge. So too must the legacy of the shtetl change.

The plot of *Dawn* unfolds through Elisha's act of remembering Hasidic legends. The themes and images evoked by these legends captivate the reader and, in their poignancy, draw her or him more deeply into the narrative. In this sense, Wiesel, the Hasid, transliterates Hasidic elements into language vigorous enough to allow the reader to be shocked by their relevance. With this, Wiesel has succeeded in integrating the ancient legacy with a modern setting to resonate with the modern reader.

This particular use of Hasidic imagery renders language capable of relating the text to the reader at all. At the same time, however, it is exactly this language that bars the reader from entering the realities that lie beyond the text—realities that only the dead and the survivor can know. Indeed, the reader remains removed from the universe of Auschwitz.

It is in this context that we can sense how Wiesel's language functions metaphorically. Although it references realities that the reader cannot access, its images and themes indicate something of the power of evil and the necessity of resisting it. By being reminded of things and realities to which the reader can relate, some past message becomes discernable. *It is in this sense alone that Wiesel's language can be thought of as metaphorical.*

In light of the power and powerlessness of language exhibited in *Dawn*, we can better understand how the work remains veiled and highly enigmatic.

Drawing on this discussion, several final observations can be made. As was the case with *Night*, *Dawn* posits the symbolic encounter of the shtetl with Auschwitz as indicative of the universal struggle between good and evil. Indeed, they function as two juxtaposing universes. Unlike *Night*, however, *Dawn* postures the struggle between good and evil in the survivor's mind. Auschwitz as a physical entity has been eliminated, and its surviving prisoners liberated; Auschwitz as an ontological entity persists in the survivor's psyche as trauma and memory. The inner divide evident in Elisha's psyche, a divide that forces him to choose between good and evil, is one imposed on him by the enduring evil of Auschwitz itself. Thus, although the attempts of the shtetl to lure Elisha to the good are strong, Auschwitz does not relinquish its grip on him. As both entities vie for his allegiance, the shtetl's dead, who watch and witness, collide with the real world of murder and revenge. In this world, John Dawson is not a mythic or fantasy figure, but a man of flesh and blood whose life stands at the mercy of another.

Thus, touching on survivor themes, the novel bravely explores how a human being can remain caught in the embrace and perpetuating cycle of evil. Wiesel presents the survivor's inner world—memory—as a psychological purgatory in which they wander, seeking orientation, direction, and meaning.[677] Along this excruciating journey, revenge and hate can appear justified.[678] But, Wiesel contends, the traumas of the past do not release—even in the face of a noble cause—an individual from his or her responsibility to choose and uphold life.[679]

The message to choose life is simultaneously a warning. It embraces the questions of God, humanity, and evil. These are questions that bring us to concerns central to this study once again. They assist in considering how *Dawn* furtively embraces other Hasidic themes.[680] According to Hasidic thought, all human actions are of divine significance; as such, all contribute to the functioning or malfunctioning of the cosmos. Wiesel's efforts to arrive at new constellations of

---

[677] Wiesel's presentation of Elisha is that of one—as is the case with so many survivors—hovering psychologically between life and death. Hannah Arendt describes survivors as "inanimate men, i.e., men who can no longer be psychologically understood, whose return to the psychologically or otherwise intelligibly human world closely resembles the resurrection of Lazarus." Hannah Arendt, *The Origins of Totalitarianism* (New York: Harcourt, Brace and World, 1951), 441, quoted in Fine, *Legacy of Night*, 32.

[678] Wiesel, *The Night Trilogy*, 214.

[679] Elisha attempts to justify his deed to the dead by referencing the biblical dictum that God proclaimed to the Jewish people of choosing life over death, as recorded in Deuteronomy 30:19: "I call heaven and earth to witness against you today that I have set before you life and death, blessing and curses. Choose life that you and your descendants may live. "*The Holy Bible Containing the Old and New Testaments with the Apocryphal/Deuterocanonical Books: New Revised Standard Version* (Nashville: Thomas Nelson Publishers, 1989), 186. Elisha says to the dead: "I haven't betrayed you. . . . If I were to refuse obey orders I should betray my living friends. And the living have more rights over us than the dead. You told me that yourself. *Therefore choose life*, it is written in the Scriptures. I have espoused the cause of the living, and that is no betrayal." See *The Night Trilogy*, 198. Elisha is aware, however, that his first duty is to the dead and that through the fulfillment of that duty, one's duty to the living is fulfilled as well. His accountability to the dead is clear to him: "In their frozen world the dead have nothing to do but judge, and because they have no sense of past or future they judge without pity. They condemn not with words or gestures but with their very existence." And, "But the dead never forget; they would remember. In their eyes I should be forever branded a killer." See pages *The Night Trilogy*, 196, 195.

[680] Friedman suggests that Wiesel views Hasidism as a "protest against divine indifference, an attempt to shake God out of His seventh heaven and bring Him closer to man." See Friedman, *You Are My Witnesses*, 169.

these sacred principles are evident in *Dawn*. In particular, he extends the Hasidic exploration of humanity by querying how human beings, though created by God, can incite the very evil over which they are meant to prevail.

Ultimately, Wiesel is concerned with the redemption of humanity and the world. In *Dawn*, however, the final restoration of the world, the *tikkun*, is not accomplished—in spite of the fact that Elisha would indeed, as Hasidic teaching emphasizes, like to "reorder the whole of creation."[681] What is more, the Shekhinah—the female essence of God entrapped in the cosmos since the creation of the world—has not been released from her exile. [682] And as the Messiah's coming is dependent upon human actions, he too remains absent. Humanity has not learned from the radical evil inherent in the atrocities of Auschwitz; instead, the individual perpetuates it. With this dark conclusion, Wiesel struggles to find meaning in a world after the Holocaust.

The ellipse that forms the core of *Night* can be sketched anew when considering *Dawn.* The personification of memory in Elisha's vision of the dead reveals not only the extremity of the atrocities committed, but also the shtetl's dramatic opposition to Auschwitz. The dead of the shtetl in *Dawn*, however, are frail and unable to prevent Elisha from committing murder. The fight between the shtetl and Auschwitz for control of memory is lost by the shtetl in *Dawn*. This might well be suggestive of how Wiesel's own memory has continued to gravitate towards the bleak reality of night.

This being said, the shtetl remains a powerful presence in memory. In *Dawn*, Elisha—and therefore Wiesel—remembers the shtetl, and this memory, though painful, does counteract the power of Auschwitz in some fashion. For Wiesel, the memory—and with it the testimony—that determines the shape of the ellipse has moved closer to the shtetl since his writing of *Night* (see figure 9).

---

[681] Wiesel, *The Night Trilogy*, 177.

[682] Wiesel writes, "In mystical terms, man must seek out the lost sparks, gather them, and deliver them to their sacred source. Everywhere there are souls waiting to be called. Everywhere, and especially beneath the ashes, sparks exist only for this call. What is required is for man to find these souls and save them; when all have been 'restored,' the divine flame will become the messianic light." See Elie Wiesel, *Sages and Dreamers: Biblical, Talmudic, and Hasidic Portraits and Legends* (New York: Summit Books, 1991), 353-54.

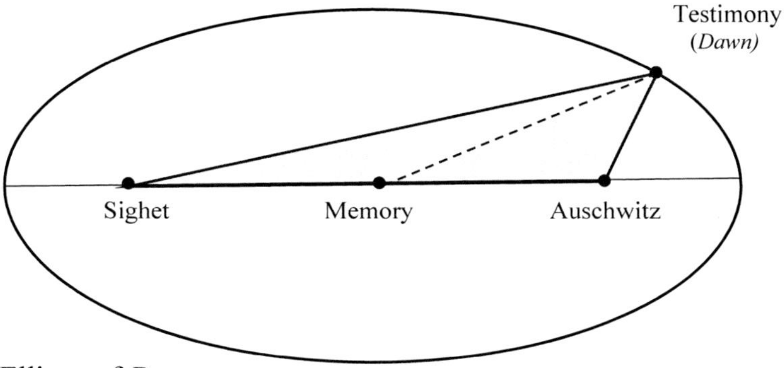

Figure 9 — Ellipse of *Dawn*

Dawn beckons the reader to consider more deeply the extent of Auschwitz's atrocities. And it warns of future ones. With this, the reader is subtly confronted with universal truths reflected in the ellipse, in particular with humanity's struggle to choose between good and evil.[683] Having been drawn into the existential choices that the protagonist must make, the reader is challenged by the choices set before them to choose life, or deny and destroy it.

Dawn presents itself as a pessimistic work. The reader asks: Is there no hope for the world after Auschwitz? Wiesel offers a clue to answering this question. As his tale draws to an end, we observe John Dawson scribbling a note to his faraway son. He commissions Elisha, his murderer, to have it delivered. Elisha consents to the request and then proceeds with the execution. In this one short exchange, however, something significant has taken place; once again, as was the case in *Night*, the dead succeed in passing on their legacy to the living. The necessary transmission of power between generations has occurred once again. The content of John Dawson's letter is unknown, but we assume it to contain a message of consolation and human love. The prospect of this message reaching the hands of one so far removed from these events grants the reader some remnant of hope. With John Dawson (as the "son-of-dawn") having been allowed to die with

[683] As previously noted, McAfee Brown emphasizes the stark contrast between the evil of Auschwitz and the good of Sighet. To reiterate McAfee's words: "Auschwitz . . . Sighet. Irreconcilable realities. Incapable of existing in the same world. At first the destructive flames of hatred and dispassion in Auschwitz extinguished the creative flames of love and ardor in Sighet. But they could not fully do so. For although the flames of Sighet are searing, seeking to revive a people destroyed by other flames, they also contain foretastes of healing, as Wiesel recreates that world of his childhood for us—glancing references here, allusions there, stories *of* Sighet on one page, stories *from* Sighet on another, this character reanimated, that character redrawn. The rest of us are beneficiaries of his anguished creativity." See McAfee Brown, *Elie Wiesel: Messenger to All Humanity*, 113.

a semblance of dignity—and not in hate—the reader might glean a vague confidence in humanity's survival, even in the face of atrocity.

The final scene of *Dawn* thus presents itself, however furtively, as indicative of Wiesel's struggle to find hope in the face of all that is without meaning. Indeed, with the extension of *Night*'s father-son theme to Elisha's encounter with John Dawson, we sense the author's continuing effort to make sense of life in the aftermath of Auschwitz. The legacy of the shtetl remains present, reminding him of his own accountability to truth and life.[684] It may also be considered as constitutive of his battle against despair.

"Four Hasidic Masters and Their Struggle Against Melancholy"

An Intermezzo of Hope

In 1978, Elie Wiesel released his second volume of Hasidic tales, *Four Hasidic Master and Their Struggle Against Melancholy*. Distinct from his first work of this genre, *Souls on Fire: Portraits and Legends of Hasidic Masters* (1972),[685] a more comprehensive collection of Hasidic tales and legends, *Four Hasidic Masters* examines just four masters, each of whom, in his own way, struggles against despair. Wiesel sets out to investigate how the masters' existential struggles might shed light on our own. To do this, he retreats into their respective worlds to seek solace and hope for a world post-Auschwitz.

Still, our interest here lies in exposing deeper dimensions of the work. Essentially, these dimensions are contingent upon how Wiesel represents these masters literarily. Specifically, we observe how Wiesel, by identifying strongly with the masters, does not simply re-tell their stories, but succeeds in re-interpreting them. In doing so, he offers suggestions that he hopes will be helpful to modernity. Here, at the most basic level of the text, Wiesel's own interpretive parameters become evident. The author appears to be aware of these biases. In the epilogue of the text, he confesses:

> *These great Masters whom we have just encountered, it is with reluctance that the story-teller [Wiesel] considers leaving them; their hold on him has never been stronger.*
>
> *Such is the power of legends; their intense and moving beauty stays with you and involves you. A Hasidic story is about Hasidism more than about their Masters; it is about*

---

684 Wiesel, *The Night Trilogy*, 198.

685 Elie Wiesel, *Souls on Fire: Portraits and Legends of Hasidic Masters*. New York: Simon and Schuster Paperbacks, 1972.

> *those who retell it as much as about those who experienced it.*[686]

With *Four Hasidic Masters*, Wiesel deviates from the dark pessimism expressed in his first three works, *Night*, *Dawn,* and *Day*. In so doing, he seeks a place that might grant inner orientation following Auschwitz. By descending into the world of the Hasidic masters, Wiesel reframes their legends, using the perspective of memory to re-interpret the Holocaust. This illustrates his particular post-Auschwitz understanding of Hasidism as well as his ongoing attempt to come to terms with Auschwitz.

Wiesel hopes not merely to re-evaluate and revive Hasidism, but also *to recover the shtetl itself.* Wiesel's search for the lost shtetl is one that shall occupy the remainder of this study, as it touches on themes related to literary representation and narrative formation.

These investigations are well supported by Wiesel's own statements regarding his relationship with Hasidism. Tellingly, Wiesel alludes to Hasidism as supplying the needed vantage point from which he writes:

> How to define Hasidism? A group in revolt against the establishment? A mystical sect? A religious movement with social overtones?
>
> In my novels Hasidism becomes framework and vantage point; the Besht (the Baal Shem Tov) or Rebbe Levi-Yitzchak of Berditchev comes to the rescue of my characters, just as they responded to my requests long ago . . .
>
> As the apotheosis of an evolving humanism, Hasidism places the emphasis on the sacred aspect of man and that which makes him human. In a society dominated by the awesome magic of technology, young people discover with wonder the Beshtian precept that the mystery of the universe resides in man, just as the secret of life resides in life itself.[687]

Meaningful here is Wiesel's conception of Hasidism as "an apotheosis of evolving humanism." With this, he links his particular interpretation of Hasidism to humanism, and therefore to ethics.

As Wiesel sets out to remember legends of the masters, he seeks to draw his readers into this same sphere of memory. This goal is certainly constitutive of his overall commitment to keep memory alive. He references this goal in his recollection of writing *Souls on Fire*. During that formative experience, his Hasidic grandfather and mother had become present to him once more:

---

[686] Wiesel, 121. (Original text in italics).

[687] Wiesel, *And the Sea is Never Full*, 28-9.

> I put into [the text] everything I received from my grandfather Reb Dodye: his love of his people, his passion for songs and stories. As I write, I see him on a Friday night as he enters the light-filled house with dancing steps. He sings and I sing along with him into my very prayers and silences. It is with him and his youngest daughter, my mother, in mind that I compose my Song of Songs in homage to the Hasidic tradition; it was their tradition and it remains mine.[688]

Four Hasidic Masters is testament to an author seeking comfort in his tradition—the tradition of the shtetl—in his quest for truth and direction. One might thus view the work as a kind of intermezzo among so many other distressing and dark texts he has written.

Each of the four personalities Wiesel chooses to review struggles against sadness, despair, and depression—and this, despite their own popularity among their disciples and the common folk. Wiesel seeks reasons for their melancholy and, in so doing, comes to conclusions that do not surprise, as we shall see.

In my survey of this book, my concern is not simply to flesh out the salient features of its stories (which are largely character sketches), but also to determine how Wiesel's particular renditions of the stories are revealing of his interpretation of them, of the questions he poses to them, and of how he reads back into the stories his most urgent concerns. In other words, I set out to evaluate just how Wiesel's own dictum might be true, which is to say, how the story itself may be just as much about the one who re-tells it as it is about those who first experienced it. Here, new perspectives emerge that assist in understanding how the Hasidic shtetl as motif and metaphor rises in Wiesel's thought, and the role it plays there.

Rebbe Pinhas of Koretz: The Sadness in Truth-Seeking

a) Synopsis: The Yoke of Truth

We begin where Wiesel begins, with Rebbe Pinhas of Koretz. The Rebbe is wise, intelligent, erudite, compassionate, reserved, modest, kind, and generous—the images Wiesel provides comfort and console. For the author, this Rebbe is deserving of honorable mention in the history of Hasidism. Although the master neither officially joined the movement nor adhered to a particular clan or dynasty,[689] his credentials lie in the strength of his character, his commitment to truth, and in his care for the simple folk of the shtetlekh.

---

[688] Wiesel, *And the Sea is Never Full*, 28.

[689] Wiesel writes: "Withdrawn, reserved, modest, with individualistic tendencies, he refused to be crowned Rebbe. He held no court, proposed no doctrine, promised no

Wiesel's sketch of the Rebbe is significant on two levels: first, concerning the personality traits he as author chooses to highlight—that is, what proves to be of particular interest to him; and secondly, in terms of the author's subjective interpretation of the Rebbe's life—and with it, the meanings he attaches to that life. Both of these levels are inextricably linked, and taken together, we can better understand Wiesel's attachment to Hasidism. In this context, the question arises as to how Wiesel's own experiences have impacted his interpretation of the Rebbe's story and legacy.

Who was Rebbe Pinhas of Koretz for Wiesel? A close friend of the Besht, the Rebbe is considered first and foremost a truth-seeker.[690] All attributes of his personality prove to draw from this singular, focused orientation. In seeking truth, and in close proximity to both the concrete realities and the mystical truths of life, Rebbe Pinhas possessed a clear vision of humanity and God.'

Indeed, the Rebbe was a practical man who understood his mission as one directed to the common folk, those suffering under the yoke of poverty and oppression.[691] The people came to him for counsel and spiritual direction; the Rebbe wisely granted advice and consolation in his compassion. Still, he attached no value to his popularity; in fact, he expressed disdain towards the Tzaddikim who so vehemently strove after power and prestige. He mistrusted authority figures,[692] perceiving the grave pitfalls of vanity[693] and the ambiguity inherent in fame—even in his own. He came to recognize the intrinsic worth of every human being and the value of friendship, which he considered the heart of Hasidism.

---

miracles, established no dynasty, declined honors and privileges." See Wiesel, *Four Hasidic Masters*, 5.

[690] See Wiesel, *Four Hasidic Masters*, 1-4. Here, Wiesel opens his evaluation of the Rebbe with a legend. The Rebbe offers direction to a truth-seeking young man who has come to him for spiritual counsel. We find that the Rebbe did not fear questions; instead, he advocated them: "The moral of the story: In the first place, young people ought not to fear questions—provided they have studied before and . . . go on studying after. Secondly, doubts are not necessarily destructive—provided they bring one to a Rebbe." See page 3. Later: "' If all men would speak the truth, there would be no further need to bring the Messiah; he would be here already. Just as the Messiah brings truth, truth brings the Messiah.' Truth: Rebbe Pinhas' total obsession and all-consuming passion." See page 20.

[691] At times, the Rebbe resented his popularity among the people: "Rebbe Pinhas, too, became popular, and resented it. Too many people visited him for too many reasons, taking too much of his time away from study and meditation." See Wiesel, *Four Hasidic Masters*, 15-16. Wiesel queries as to whether or not the Rebbe's involvement with the community was the reason that sadness befell him at the end of his life: "Or was it that, like the other Masters, he had heard too many tales of sorrow and pain? People were coming to him with their doubts and regrets, sharing with him their anguish and misery. Was it that, at one point, he could take it no more?" See pages 25-26.

[692] Wiesel, "In his own gentle way, Pinhas distrusted all leaders. That is why he refused to become one himself." Wiesel, *Four Hasidic Masters*, 10.

[693] See Wiesel, *Four Hasidic Masters*, 11-12.

Despite his practical approach to life, the Rebbe was a devoted teacher and spiritual master. His teachings stressed the presence of God in all of creation;[694] the holiness of the Torah;[695] the possibility of redemption inherent in following the most basic commandments;[696] the link between one's personal fate and that of the Messiah;[697] and the closeness of God to his people.[698] He eschewed the Kabbalah in favor of Hasidism's more accessible, life-oriented teachings that granted simple folk confidence in their own place within creation.[699] For the Rebbe, all spheres of life and every person mattered to God. And since all persons could play a role in restoring order to the cosmos and in hastening the Messiah's coming, all were indispensable.[700] On the Day of Judgment, all would be judged according to the principles of living rightly in the context of one's faith in God.[701]

At the heart of these theological precepts lies the Rebbe's concern for the common folk to uncover the joy and hope to be found in fulfilling one's duty to the world and to God. Rebbe Pinhas' search for truth was embedded in both his practical approach to life and people, and in his theology; he thus understood the reality of God to be inextricably linked to the life of the individual and the community.

Still, beneath the Rebbe's noble endeavors lay a man who struggled with the most profound questions of God and the human condition. Unexpectedly, and

---

[694] Wiesel: "God is everywhere, even in pain, even in the search for faith." Wiesel, *Four Hasidic Masters*, 3.

[695] Wiesel: "'Go and study,' said Rebbe Pinhas of Koretz. 'It is the only remedy I know. Torah contains all the answers. Torah *is* the answer.'" Wiesel, *Four Hasidic Masters,* 1.

[696] Wiesel: "Instead, he stresses the importance of each individual, no matter how saintly or how ignorant. It is enough to fulfill certain basic and practical commandments to enable the Redeemer to appear in our midst for one hour—to one other human being, and then to more and more." Wiesel, *Four Hasidic Masters*, 19.

[697] Wiesel: "Redemption occupied his thoughts and dreams. What Hasid does not wait for the Messiah? To be Jewish is to link one's fate to that of the Messiah—to that of all those who are waiting for the Messiah." Wiesel, *Four Hasidic Masters*, 19.

[698] Wiesel: "God *is*, and that means that He dwells in every human being. In the unlearned too? Yes, in the unlearned too. In the sinner too. In the humble, the humble most of all, He can be found. And he can He perceived by everyone. Sitting on his throne, said Rebbe Pinhas, He can be approached both through the tears of the penitent and the fervor of the worshipper. God *is*, God is *one*; and that means He is the same to people who turn to Him in different ways." Wiesel, *Four Hasidic Masters*, 14-15.

[699] Wiesel: "How is one to accelerate events? Never mind the Kabbalistic methods. They are too complicated, involved, and inaccessible; and then, they have not proved too successful in the past. No, better try simpler ways. Better appeal to simpler people." Wiesel, *Four Hasidic Masters*, 19.

[700] Wiesel: "Every person may change the course of history; it is in power of every individual to shorten exile." Wiesel, *Four Hasidic Masters*, 19.

[701] Wiesel: "On Judgment Day, he would say, even the lectern will be judged, and sentenced to serve either for study or for feeding the stove." Wiesel, *Four Hasidic Masters,* 18.

for reasons only he knew, the Rebbe succumbed to a deep and lasting melancholy during the final phase of his life. Filled with anxiety in the wake of all his dashed dreams, he was overwhelmed by feelings of deficiency and failure. In the end, he longed to escape to the Holy Land. He died just before he set out for the journey.

b) Analysis: Rebbe Pinhas and the Holocaust

Wiesel's affection for the Rebbe of Koretz is palpable. Wiesel describes him as, "one of the most human, one of the most gracious and beautiful characters in the Hasidic gallery."[702] Wiesel investigates this luminous personality in terms of his relationship to truth, God, and humanity amidst great existential questions.

Wiesel's synopsis of Rebbe Pinhas' life and person is indeed telling. The author links the practical wisdom and human compassion of the Rebbe to his quest for truth. It is in this context that Wiesel reveals, however indirectly, the ethical dimension of the Rebbe's teachings. Service, duty, and integrity are key concepts; personal authenticity, truth, and humility are guides. According to the Rebbe, the individual stands at the center of God's creation. Their commission was to be in solidarity with others and to love God. Through service to the community, loneliness could then be combated.[703]

We find traces of Wiesel's own penchant for humanism here, for marrying truth with love, for living out one's personal truth in the world. Indeed, Wiesel's interpretation of the Rebbe's teachings, stressing above all friendship, human solidarity, and love for God, echoes aspects of his own thought.

Our question to Wiesel's text then concerns how the author has approached the legends and whether he has simply identified in them aspects that conform to his own post-Auschwitz agenda and concerns. The answer must be a differentiated one. First of all, Wiesel demonstrates that he is familiar with the historical circumstances surrounding Rebbe Pinhas' life and times. Here, he sketches not only the legends of the Rebbe, but also historical aspects of the Hasidic movement: the rise of the movement in Eastern Europe and the social and spiritual milieu in which it arose; the historical situation in Europe at the time of its development; the tensions and strife between the Tzaddikim; and the life and teachings of its founder, the Besht. These inclusions—which act as excursions within the text—indicate Wiesel's familiarity with the material.[704]

Wiesel's inquiry into Rebbe's unexpected melancholy, however, suggests a subjective interpretation of the legends; indeed, the themes he highlights reverberate with his own concerns. This is most apparent toward the close of his sketch

---

[702] Wiesel, *Four Hasidic Masters*, 5.

[703] Wiesel: "This, too, is part of the Hasidic message: there is a solution to loneliness—and loneliness is no solution. What is the significance of the *Tikoun* (mystical reparation)? Rebbe Pinhas would ask. It is to be concerned not only with yourself but with everything that goes on around you; help others and you will help yourself. You want to serve God? Start with serving His children." Wiesel, *Four Hasidic Masters*, 16.

[704] See Wiesel, *Four Hasidic Masters*, 12-15.

of the Rebbe, where Wiesel looks to the Holocaust for answers pertaining to the enigmatic melancholy of the Rebbe. In considering all probable causes for the Rebbe's sadness (he had perhaps heard too many difficult stories, was despondent over the spiritual decline of the movement, had felt spiritually inadequate, or had despaired over the state of the world),[705] Wiesel questions whether or not the master may have had a premonition of the end of Koretz in 1941, which is to say, of the Holocaust. He writes:

> Or was it that [Rebbe Pinhas] had a premonition of what would be the end of Koretz?
>
> The end occurred on Succoth, 1941. The Germans liquidated the ghetto. The last of its Jews disappeared in the tempest. Was it Reb Pinhas' tragic intuition, or tragic imagination, that induced him to set the example and move away—away from Gentile hate and Jewish laxity, away from quarreling factions and their leaders, away from unfulfilled dreams? Did he simply want to leave everything behind him and go . . . ?[706]

Whether Wiesel's query is far-fetched can be bracketed here. However, a critical reading raises these questions: How might Wiesel's suggestions be reflective of his own existential concerns? In what sense has he subjected them to his personal biases? How is his highlighting of particular legends—and omission of others—indicative of his own agenda, of his own struggle against melancholy?

Posing such questions advocates reading the text with an eye to the author *behind* the text. Without having to answer the questions definitively (we cannot enter the author's mind), we observe how Pinhas' existential, theological, and anthropological perspectives do in fact mirror Wiesel's own. Here, we suspect that Wiesel's reading of the legends has, in a most straightforward way, been guided by his subjective experience of both the shtetl and Auschwitz.

Tellingly, Wiesel concludes this first chapter by alluding once again—however subtly—to the Holocaust:

> His mystery remains intact. We don't know what happened to him at the end of his life—we never will. He who was always composed, calm, serene—why was he possessed by such fear at the end? What had he glimpsed? What visions did he have—and about whom? . . . Did he suddenly realize that Jews have no friends—anywhere? Or that the Messiah would be

---

[705] See Wiesel, *Four Hasidic Masters*, 22-28.

[706] Wiesel, *Four Hasidic Masters*, 26.

> late in coming—much later than he had anticipated, much later than he had feared?[707]

Wiesel's final words reference his overall concern to draw strength from the memory of the dead:

> [Rebbe Pinhas] died—and Koretz died with him. And now he has become a sacred letter, a fascinating tale, an evocative name: a key to wisdom and compassion.
> His longing is our longing, his questions remain ours . . . and *we* must continue.[708]

Rebbe Barukh of Medzebozh: The Melancholy of Rebellion

a) Synopsis: The Anger, the Doubt, the Faith

Wiesel's portrayal of Rebbe Barukh of Medzebozh contrasts starkly that of Rebbe Pinhas of Koretz. While both Hasidim struggled, particularly towards the end of their lives, against melancholy, Rebbe Barukh poses perhaps the greater challenge to Wiesel: that of reconciling images of the Rebbe's melancholy with those portraying his hostility and rage.

Indeed, the Rebbe's rage can challenge and upset; he is not immediately likeable. However, Wiesel's presentation of the Rebbe—gracious and conciliatory—invites other considerations. The author attempts to endear the Rebbe to us through his own interpretation of both the Rebbe's antics and—perhaps most importantly—his spiritual quest.

The legends prompt poignant questions for Wiesel. How can anger and faith be considered compatible? And what about faith and doubt? Might psychological, spiritual constellations exist that allow for the coexistence of all three? If so, how might these coexist without tension, without psychological conflict? These queries serve to guide Wiesel's exploration of the Rebbe.

Wiesel begins by describing Rebbe Barukh as a "strange man."[709] Hostile, power-hungry, dominating, arrogant, authoritarian, and obsessed with wealth and the comforts it provides, he resembles very little the picture of a faithful Hasid. Anger was his trademark. Feared by strangers, colleagues, and friends alike, he lived a life of utter tyranny.[710]

Rebbe Barukh was a well-known character in his day. Son of the Besht's beautiful, legendary daughter Oudil, he commanded respect if only by way of his

---

[707] Wiesel, *Four Hasidic Masters*, 27.
[708] Wiesel, *Four Hasidic Masters*, 28.
[709] Wiesel, *Four Hasidic Masters*, 32.
[710] Cf. Wiesel, *Four Hasidic Masters*, 36.

holy lineage.[711] The Besht himself loved him, as did his mother. She preferred him to her first son, the humble and erudite Rebbe Ephraim.[712] Unlike his brother, Rebbe Barukh was lax with regard to study,[713] concerned instead with privilege and power.

Wiesel maintains that Rebbe Barukh—although full of vice—still came to advance the cause of Hasidism in his region. He writes:

> Thanks to him Medzebozh became a capital for the second time, attracting Hasidim from all over the Beshtian provinces. Medzebozh, the small village in Podolia, again became a center for pilgrimage, a glorious symbol of a glorious kingdom.[714]

The Rebbe is portrayed as one who was feared by his own disciples, by the Mitnagdim, and even by other Hasidic leaders. Indeed, he incited anger in them all.[715] Wiesel admits that even tradition displays a "certain reticence" toward him, revealed too by the sparcity of material devoted to him:

> Few books are devoted to him; and his place in other Master's legends is surprisingly modest. One could say that there he is known only by the hostility he aroused. They found him quarrelsome, arrogant, moody, and would have preferred not to deal with him. But how could they avoid it? He was the Besht's grandson and his impact on Hasidism could not be denied.[716]

Wiesel's curiosity regarding the Rebbe is certainly piqued by the impertinence of this character. Ultimately, however, Wiesel is concerned about the Rebbe's legacy—his memory—and wonders if posterity has done him some injustice. This inquiry is prompted by the astonishing reports of the Rebbe's eventual fall into despondency and depression. Wiesel's fascination with the Rebbe centers on this mysterious turn in the story. As Wiesel's analysis of this enigma deepens, we witness him attempting to fill in the blanks left open by the legends.

---

[711] See Wiesel, *Four Hasidic Masters*, 33ff.

[712] The legend of Rebbe Barukh is linked to one surrounding his mother, the proud daughter of the Besht, Oudil. Oudil had not been content with her one son, Rebbe Ephraim, who was a "future author and scholar." She "wanted a Rebbe, not a writer." See Wiesel, *Four Hasidic Masters*, 35-6.

[713] The Rebbe had married into wealth, allowing him to bypass the necessity of study. Wiesel, *Four Hasidic Masters*, 38.

[714] Wiesel, *Four Hasidic Masters*, 33.

[715] Wiesel, *Four Hasidic Masters*, 33.

[716] Wiesel, *Four Hasidic Masters*, 36.

Whereas the controversy associated with the Rebbe fills the first segment of Wiesel's reflections, the onset of the Rebbe's depression marks the beginning of the second:

> It was in Medzebozh that melancholy took hold of Rebbe Barukh, though we do not know what provoked it nor when it was first noticed. All we know is that it invaded him one day—and that it remained unexplained. How could anyone teach the Hasidic idea and not receive its message of joy? How could one claim to continue the Besht's mission and yield to sadness? How could Rebbe Barukh be a Hasidic Master and look on creation with anger?[717]

Wiesel's questions address the mystery of the Rebbe. According to Wiesel, this mystery must be indicative of the Rebbe's secret life of longing. This longing can be best observed in the Rebbe's existential questions of God, life, and humanity. These questions seem to intensify as his sense of despair deepens:

> Weeping over God and man alike, Rebbe Barukh could not help but sink into melancholy. Like other Hasidic Masters before him and after him, he knew that the secret of redemption lies in the union between the Creator and creation. But what if Creator and creation were to remain strangers forever? Reb Barukh's despair was of an existential nature. Divine severity frightened him less than divine separation. Let God be our king, our father, or even our judge—but let Him not be estranged from us![718]

Concerned about the Rebe's radical shift in priorities, Wiesel takes up the Rebbe's cause. He suggests that the Rebbe, "[f]orever misunderstood,"[719] needs reconsideration. Wiesel proceeds by exploring possible reasons for the Rebbe's despair. Had he questioned the very efficacy of the Hasidic movement, its teachings, its personalities? Had he doubted his self-worth? Wiesel suspects that the Rebbe's deep "love of God, love of Torah and love of Israel"[720]—as well as his disappointment in the failure of these loves to change the world—were the cause for both his anguish and anger:

> Perhaps [the Besht's] grandson, Reb Barukh, understood all of a sudden that love alone—in a world without love, filled with

---

[717] Wiesel, *Four Hasidic Masters*, 40-1.
[718] Wiesel, *Four Hasidic Masters*, 53.
[719] Wiesel, *Four Hasidic Masters*, 46.
[720] Wiesel, *Four Hasidic Masters*, 57.

> violence and crowded with strangers—is not enough to assure the survival of his people . . . Perhaps he thought that a certain measure of anger, of rage, was necessary for the people of Israel . . . Hence his sadness, hence his despair: how can one not despair of a world where rage is needed for redemption?[721]

Preoccupied with these questions, Wiesel suggests that the Rebbe is worthy of our forgiveness by merit of the questions with which he allegedly struggled:

> [The Rebbe] tried to explain—others did not. They did not even seem to mind. Do we? No, not really. We try to understand him, and love him. Others forgave his taste for luxury and power; we forgive his anger. Perhaps he wanted to teach us something about the Tzaddik, namely: that though the Tzaddik must be revered and feared, he must also be measured in human terms. The Tzaddik is human—and must be. No true greatness, no real holiness can be attained at the expense of one's humanity.[722]

Wiesel maintains that by granting him forgiveness in the end, we are left not so much with the Rebbe's anger, but with his "Song of Songs,"[723] his love of God. He suggests the Rebbe's rage was but a mask after all, one that intended to hide his uncommon admixture of anger, faith, and doubt:

> The beauty of Rebbe Barukh is that he could speak of faith not as opposed to anguish but as being a part of it. "Faith and the abyss are next to one another," he told his disciple. "I would even say: one within the other. True faith lies beyond questions; true faith comes after it has been challenged."[724]

Whether this (re)interpretation is problematic is a matter we will examine briefly at the end of the analysis to follow. There we must pose, once again, pertinent questions about the author.

b) Analysis: Projections of Rage and Love

Wiesel's portrayal of Rebbe Barukh strongly displays interpretation. In light of the shortage of historical material pertaining to the Rebbe,[725] Wiesel's attempt to reconstruct the Rebbe's inner life in particular appears forced. As we

---

[721] Wiesel, *Four Hasidic Masters*, 57.
[722] Wiesel, *Four Hasidic Masters*, 56-7.
[723] Wiesel, *Four Hasidic Masters*, 58.
[724] Wiesel, *Four Hasidic Masters*, 59.
[725] See Wiesel, *Four Hasidic Masters*, 36.

have done with Wiesel's sketch of Rebbe Pinhas, we speculate about Wiesel's personal exploration of this master. Which of his own concerns has he projected onto Rebbe Barukh? Does he not address these concerns once again in and through the legends to find answers for himself?

The answer might well be yes. In his pursuit of the Rebbe behind the mask, the author discovers that the face mirrored back to him is akin to his own. In fact, out of the four portraits of Hasidic masters he has supplied, Wiesel's depiction of Rebbe Barukh resembles most strikingly the author and his own existential preoccupations.

Once again, we can sense how closely Wiesel identifies with the Rebbe. This grants further insight into how Wiesel's religious influences and past experiences have come to impact his post-Auschwitz memory. We see how Wiesel's experience of Auschwitz has impacted his understanding of Hasidism. Within this context, we might consider, once again, how both Hasidism and Auschwitz remain linked in Wiesel's memory by way of their very juxtaposition and dominant place in memory.

The vital link between Hasidism and Auschwitz in Wiesel's memory is crucial to this study. Wiesel does not envisage Rebbe Barukh without bias; rather, he comes to understand him in terms of his experience of Auschwitz and in the light of his longing for the shtetl. His portrayal of the Rebbe displays aspects of himself—rage, doubt, faith, and love—and, in so doing, is suggestive of those particular mechanisms of memory, interpretation, and narration at work in both *Night* and *Dawn*.

Wiesel's fascination with the Rebbe of Medzebozh is revealing. Akin to his assessment of Rebbe Pinhas of Koretz, the author sets before himself a brave task: to retrieve a lesser-known Rebbe from the annals of history and ingratiate him to the reader. However much Wiesel's account of the Rebbe may provoke disapproval, it is still able to entice the reader. The reader, confronted once again with very basic questions surrounding what it means to be human and to live a life of poignant longing, is drawn to the Rebbe—or, at least, to Wiesel's portrayal of him. Indeed, in Wiesel's portrayal of the pain in becoming truly human, the Rebbe is made more accessible to the reader. With this, the reader may, as Wiesel suggests, forgive the Rebbe all of his rage.

Wiesel closes his portrait of Rebbe Barukh with the same legend with which he began. There, the Rebbe, quite out of character, reaches out to a young seeker who is not only at the brink of despair, but also in the throes of losing his faith. As the Rebbe's strong hand is able to pull the man out of his anguish, he recognizes that both doubt and faith are two sides of that same one coin, and that anger can be found in both. Wiesel suggests that the Rebbe's anger was not based in hostility after all, but rather had grown out of his sense of fundamental concern, his care. Wiesel cites the Rebbe as saying:

> I know there are questions that have no answers, there is a suffering that has no name; there is injustice in God's

> creation—and there are reasons enough for man to explode with rage. I know there are reasons for you to be angry. Good. Let us be angry. Together.[726]

Wiesel's relationship to Hasidism has grown more intriguing. More will be said about this theme a little later. For the moment, we let stand, as is, this portrait of a Rebbe—a "keeper of the Hasidic flame"[727]—who both vexes and consoles.

The Holy Seer of Lublin: The Anguish in the Vision

a) Synopsis: Igniting the Flame—Inciting the Fall

Reb Itzikl had almost made the jump. Standing at the precipice of the mountain at Lizensk and contemplating the grandeur of God ("God is God and man is small"[728]), the soon-to-be Seer of Lublin had felt the need to offer himself up to the Creator as a gift of thanks and praise—and to cast himself into the abyss. In the "nick of time," Reb Salke had pulled him back from the edge, saving Reb Itzikl from what otherwise would have been a holy fate. Was Reb Itzikl happy with Reb Salke's deed? The legends leave that matter open. But rumor has it that, for many years, the Seer would recall the incident and say to Reb Salke: "Yes, Salke, we remember what you have done for us in Lizensk—that is why our love for you is not whole."[729]

The Holy Seer of Lublin: one of the most exuberant, charismatic personalities of Eastern European Hasidism. A favorite of the great Maggid of Mezeritch and renegade protégé of Reb Elimelekh, the Seer impacted the movement like no other, leaving posterity with countless legends attesting to his wondrous powers.

What is Wiesel's attraction to this Hasidic master whose legacy is replete with such fantastical images? As was the case with both Rebbe Pinhas and Rebbe Barukh, it remains the Seer's clandestine struggle with despair—and how he combatted that despair. Shrouded in mystery, this painful dimension of the master's story forms the center of Wiesel's inquiry. Around this center, the author spins the legends and tells the tales. The result is a portrait of a master whose shining legacy is tinged with both the dark shadows of melancholy and the joys of Messianic hope.

Wiesel describes the Seer as a rising star of Hasidism. Although he formed no dynasty of his own, his renown spread across Eastern Europe. "Tall, robust, tense, extremely perceptive,"[730] the Seer possessed a personality that laid bare the hearts of the people. Wiesel writes about his presence reverently:

---

[726] Wiesel, *Four Hasidic Masters*, 60.
[727] Wiesel, *Four Hasidic Masters*, 33.
[728] Wiesel, *Four Hasidic Masters*, 78.
[729] Wiesel, *Four Hasidic Masters*, 78-9.
[730] Wiesel, *Four Hasidic Masters*, 71.

> In his presence, one felt shaken, purified . . . transformed. What struck people most were his eyes—one bigger than the other—which often took on a disquieting fixity when looking at someone. Hasidim were convinced that he was searching their inner depths. Nothing resisted his gaze, neither time nor space. He would go to the window and observe what was happening continents away, centuries before. It is said of him that he was able to trace one's soul back to Cain or Abel, and determine precisely how many times it had migrated since—and where.[731]

Allured by his magnetism, drawn by his miracles, people flocked to Lublin from near and far—critics, skeptics and seekers alike, all hungry for his presence and all wishing to partake in the drama. With him, the city dazzled with the brilliance of celebration and joy. Indeed, due to the Seer, Lublin was ablaze with Hasidic fire.[732]

But was the Seer's charisma constitutive of him? Wiesel says no. Tracing the master's journey, Wiesel weaves together tales that bear the secret of a man inwardly driven to the margins of the very world he served. "Though he was accessible, generous and compassionate, there existed between him and his followers a kind of barrier which prevented them from coming too close, from lifting the veil,"[733] Wiesel writes. The Seer's intensity was pervasive, his presence on occasion forbidding—and yet he remained withdrawn. "Serious, at times melancholy" and compared by some to an angry lion,[734] his life, according to Wiesel, appears to have been marked by sadness and moments of uncertainty:

> And yet, he who gave so much to others was himself longing for change. He gave joy to others but rarely to himself. Often he would remark: "Strange—people come to me sad and leave

---

[731] Wiesel, *Four Hasidic Masters*, 71. Wiesel appears here to reference the Kabbalistic notion of the transmigration of souls, *gilgul*. The notion would later be more thoroughly developed by the Lurianic Kabbalah. See Dan, *Kabbalah*, 83. See also Erwin K.J. Hilburg, *Der Chassidismus*, Germania Judaica 7:2/3 (Cologne: Kölner Bibliothek zur Geschichte des Deutschen Judentums, 1968), 28. For a more detailed account of reincarnation in the Kabbalah, see Dina Ripsman Eylon, *Reincarnation in Jewish Mysticism and Gnosticism,* Jewish Studies, vol. 25 (Lewiston, NY: Edwin Mellen Press, 2003). See also Brian Ogren, *Renaissance and Rebirth: Reincarnation in Early Modern Italian Kabbalah*, Studies in Jewish History and Culture, vol. 24 (Leiden: Brill, 2009).

[732] Wiesel: "People go to Riminov to get sustenance and to Kozhenitz to get cures. But they come to Lublin to get the Hasidic fire." And: "In Lublin, Hasidim were urged live not only in fear of God but also in fear for God and, above all, in joy with God." See Wiesel, *Four Hasidic Masters*, 86, and 90.

[733] Wiesel, *Four Hasidic Masters*, 72.

[734] Wiesel, *Four Hasidic Masters*, 72-3.

> happy; whereas I . . . I stay with my sadness; mine is a black fire." In moments of doubt he would groan: "Woe to the generation whose leader I am."[735]

For Wiesel, the Seer remained far more inaccessible than his followers realized. He longed for the coming of the Messiah, believing, above all, that he would come only at the occasion of the joy of his people.[736] Although sadness was a state with which he was familiar, he himself tolerated it very little. "I prefer a simple Jew who prays with joy to a sage who studies with sadness,"[737] he claims. And in reference to a "notorious sinner in Lublin" with whom the Seer liked to spend time, he says: "I like him because he is cheerful. When *you* commit a sin you immediately regret it; you repent for the pleasure you have felt. Not he. His joy continues."[738] More poignant still, he admonishes his disciples to abandon their despondency: "Do you know the real sin of our forefathers in the desert? Not their rebellious behavior, but their ensuing depression."[739]

Thus, the secret of the Seer lies in his quest to combat despair—even his own. Wiesel writes:

> Like other Masters, the Seer advocated passion and compassion, and enthusiasm, fervor—*hitlahavut*—fervor, above all. "I prefer an opponent—a passionate Mitnagged—rather than a lukewarm Hasid," he said. For absence of fire, absence of passion, leads to indifference and resignation—in other words, to death. What is worse than suffering? Indifference. What is worse than despair? Resignation—the inability to be moved, to let oneself go, to let one's imagination catch fire.[740]

If Wiesel's assessment is correct, we discover in the Seer one whose life was marked by a certain paradox. With clairvoyant clarity, he saw the despair of his struggling fellow Jews and wished to mend it. His remedy for despair was the fervor found in loving God, remaining close to nature (where God was ever-present), and retaining one's loyalty to the masters, friends, and community.[741]

Still, as Wiesel speculates, the Seer exhibited signs of the sadness that come when one spends one's life listening to the pain of the people, waiting for the Messiah and for the liberation of the Shekhinah. In this sense, the Seer was

---

735 Wiesel, *Four Hasidic Masters*, 89.
736 Wiesel, *Four Hasidic Masters*, 94.
737 Wiesel, *Four Hasidic Masters*, 89.
738 Wiesel, *Four Hasidic Masters*, 89.
739 Wiesel, *Four Hasidic Masters*, 89.
740 Wiesel, *Four Hasidic Masters*, 81.
741 Cf. Wiesel, *Four Hasidic Masters*, 83.

no different than other masters—including the Besht. Wiesel compares them, writing:

> But then [other masters], too, seem to have been subject to similar spells of depression. From the Besht to the Maggid, to Reb Levi-Yitzhak, to Reb Barukh, to Reb Elimilekh, to the Kotzker—all endured pain and anguish. The reasons were manifold. Mystically inclined, they constantly thought of the Shekhinah suffering in exile, and if the Shekhinah suffered, how could *they* not suffer with her? The Seer of Lublin said: "A Hasid, like a child, should cry and laugh at the same time." And he explained how he managed to combine the two when lamenting over the Shekhinah's suffering every night at mid-night: "Imagine an exiled king who visits his friend; the friend is sad that the king is in exile, but still he is happy to be seeing him."[742]

Near the end of the Seer's life, his unfulfilled Messianic longing led to his spiritual collapse—later known as the "Great Fall." The Seer, along with his two friends, Reb Mendel of Riminov and the Maggid of Kozhenitz, forged a pact to incite the Messiah's coming. On the evening of the Simbat Torah of 1814, in Lublin, the three gathered with a multitude of Hasidim for a celebration of singing, dancing, and joy in God. As the fervor intensified and the Hasidim lost themselves in bliss-ful ecstasy, the great Seer of Lublin retreated to a back room—and then disap-peared.[743] He was later found outside the venue on the ground, weeping and in despair, calling out repeatedly: "And the abyss calls for another abyss."[744] His cryptic words caused the Hasidim—and posterity—to despair. Strangely, the Seer and his two conspirators all died soon after. The mystery of the event remains unsolved to this day.

b) Analysis: Joy, Melancholy, and a Vision of the Holocaust

Wiesel's account and interpretation of the life of the Holy Seer of Lublin illuminate, once again, a number of his own preoccupations: the struggle against melancholy; the ambiguity of fame; the fight against indifference; and the need to change the world. Still, there may be more to Wiesel's attraction to the Seer than is first apparent. The author appears drawn to him as one whose remedy for sadness—the sadness that hovers over all humanity—is found in joy in God. Alt-hough all four of Wiesel's masters emphasize this remedy, it is the Seer of Lublin above all who allows joy to shape him, and adapts it as his personal maxim, his creed.

---

[742] Wiesel, *Four Hasidic Masters*, 90-1.
[743] Wiesel, *Four Hasidic Masters*, 61-5.
[744] Wiesel, *Four Hasidic Masters*, 64.

With this, Wiesel considers the Seer to have been both "dazzling and . . . secretive,"[745] thus presenting the master as a paradoxical figure. Wiesel asks: how are we to understand the great sadness that the Seer felt within? The legends suggest the depth of his pain, the extent of his spiritual exhaustion, the enduring anguish of lost friendships, and the abyss left behind by longing left unfulfilled. Might any or all of these have been the occasion for his anguish— ultimately, for his Great Fall? Wiesel's answer is complex, as are the legends from which he draws his conclusions.

Ultimately, Wiesel wonders whether the Seer's struggles are more profound than previously assumed. Wiesel deepens his inquiry to address the Great Fall itself:

> [W]hat did happen on that Simhat Torah evening in Lublin? What caused the accident? Was it an accident? What kind of an accident?
>
> Why did the Seer leave the exuberant festivities? Why did he stop dancing? . . . Was he afraid? And if so—of what, of whom?
>
> Was it a sudden attack of sadness, of depression? Was it his way of telling God: Either You save Your people—or erase me from Your book? I no longer wish to go on living—unless You put an end to Jewish suffering?
>
> Could it be that, having failed to bring the Messiah through joy, he thought of trying . . . despair?[746]

Wiesel continues this line of thought, asking whether the Seer realized that redemption would be postponed at the cost of more suffering. Did he have a vision of atrocities to come? Wiesel's extends his questions—and offers possible answers.

> Could it also be that in a sudden flash of fear the Seer had a glimpse of the distant future when night would descend upon the Jewish people and particularly upon its most compassionate and generous children—those of the Hasidic community? Was that why he strayed outside? To wait under the somber sky, abandoned and shattered, to wait and wait through several generations, if necessary, for other victims of other catastrophes?[747]

---

[745] Wiesel, *Four Hasidic Masters*, 65.
[746] Wiesel, *Four Hasidic Masters*, 93-94.
[747] Wiesel, *Four Hasidic Masters*, 94-95.

Once again, Wiesel links a master to the Holocaust; only by looking to the Holocaust can he look to the master. This tendency provides a clue to understanding Wiesel's preoccupation with the masters in general.

Wiesel is drawn to the Seer of Lublin not merely in terms of his identification with the Seer's melancholy but also—perhaps above all—with the Seer's solution to it. We sense in this chapter, more than in the others, Wiesel's prolonged attempt to find a balm to ease the pain incurred by Auschwitz. In some sense paradoxically, Wiesel is fascinated by the prospect of joy.

Wiesel concludes his chapter on the Holy Seer with an excursion on the fate of Lublin. Ultimately, he is thoughtful about humanity:

> Lublin, during the darkest hours, became a center for torment and death. Lublin, an ingathering place for condemned Jews, led to nearby Belzec. Lublin meant Majdanek. Lublin meant the great fall not of one man, nor of one people, but of mankind.
>
> And yet, and yet . . . [748]

Wiesel's renowned "and yet" now finds a place in Lublin. Drawn by Hasidism, but also haunted by the memory of Auschwitz, the author reveals his attempt to console one by remembering the other.

Rebbe Naphtali of Ropshitz: The Mask to Hide the Despair

a) Synopsis: When Only Laughter Will Save the World

Who *was* Rebbe Naphtali of Ropshitz? As is the case with the other three masters discussed, the legends provide contradictory information that lends inconsistent images. Was he a man of laughter, the court jester of the movement, as so many tales portray him to have been? Was he the secluded wise man, the humble Just Man, the seeker of truth who lacked confidence in his own abilities, his own worthiness? Or was he simply a "nostalgic and unhappy visionary"?[749] Wiesel hopes to unravel the mystery of the Rebbe as one whose enigma rivals those of his colleagues from Koretz, Medzebozh, and Lublin.

Wiesel begins, as always, by telling the story. Born in Linsk, Galicia, in 1760 (the year the Besht died), Rebbe Naphtali's father was hostile to Hasidism—but his mother was its friend. At his bar mitzvah, Rebbe Mekhal of Zlotchov, a disciple of the Besht, helped him with his first tephillin.[750] "I have just tied his

[748] Wiesel, *Four Hasidic Masters*, 95.
[749] Wiesel, *Four Hasidic Masters*, 115.
[750] Wiesel, *Four Hasidic Masters*, 101-2.

soul up there; the knot will be a lasting one,"[751] the Rebbe had said. The premonition was correct: the boy became a Rabbi.

But he remained a Rabbi distinct from all others. Humor was his trademark, laughter his tool. It disarmed all those around him. It is even said that God forfeited hearing the prayers of the celebrated Maggid of Kozhenitz because Rebbe Naphtali distracted God by telling jokes at a wedding.[752] The Rebbe had little patience for false humility, and exposed the hypocrisy of self-acclaimed ascetics. "Life is given to man to be lived," Wiesel quotes him as saying. "To mutilate life is to offend its source; to choose suffering is to reject a gift both rare and irreplaceable. The path to paradise leads through the world of reality."[753]

Rebbe Naphtali also loved to provoke. He gave no heed in aggravating those around him with his witticisms. Wiesel writes:

> Original, picturesque, amusing, Rebbe Naphtali is a friend, an equal, of the greatest—with a difference: he dares to antagonize the holy Seer of Lublin, who dislikes his sense of humor, and Rebbe Mendel of Riminov, who distrusts his political views. He even dares respectfully to mock the founder of a school, the reverend Elimelekh of Lizensk. He is Hasidism's *enfant terrible*. Other Masters speak of God; he discusses everyday down-to-earth matters. Other Rebbes cry; he laughs. Better yet: he makes people laugh. Others tend to take life seriously, if not tragically; there are but few things *he* takes seriously. . . . For him, laughter performs a philosophical, quasi-religious function. With him, laughter becomes an integral part of the Hasidic experience and its tales.[754]

Indeed, Rebbe Naphtali differed from other masters in his fundamental disposition to celebrate life. Pragmatic, witty, cheerful, spontaneous, and frequently in trouble, he gained a reputation as one who provoked through humor – and cleverness. He lost no time on vanity or stupidity, emphasizing intelligence instead. He did not conduct miracles—nor did he want to. He was happy to obtain no great following. He gave credence to no one master; in fact, he was a disciple of several—an anomaly in Hasidism. He gained popularity in many circles, but found enemies too, among the Mitnagdim and even among other Hasidim. Loved and hated, revered and despised, Rebbe Naphtali sought life through being alive, by being human.

---

751 Wiesel, *Four Hasidic Masters*, 102.
752 Wiesel, *Four Hasidic Masters*, 100-101.
753 Wiesel, *Four Hasidic Masters*, 110.
754 Wiesel, *Four Hasidic Masters*, 98-99.

However, just as was the case with Rebbes Pinhas and Barukh and with the Seer of Lublin, Rebbe Naphtali possessed another side. He also struggled against melancholy.

Wiesel's interest in the Rebbe relates to exactly this enigma. How might one unlock his secret? To answer this question, Wiesel references the rubric also associated with the Rebbe: *hokhma*, or wisdom. The irony here is evident. Wiesel wonders how the Rebbe was considered wise:

> We smile, we laugh—but we do not cry out in wonder. We are struck by neither the depth of his perception nor by his erudition. On the contrary, his metaphors, though brilliant, lack the anguish of a Kotzker saying and the fire of a Bratzlaver tale. Where is his *hokhma*, his wisdom, of which one speaks so much in Hasidic literature?[755]

Wiesel concludes that the answer to this riddle must be found in his humor—the very place where the Rebbe undoubtedly hid his melancholy:

> For this complex and complicated Tzaddik was, in spite of appearances, profoundly humble—and sad. But his humility s hidden under arrogance and pride, just as his melancholy was covered with exuberance.[756]

He acknowledges the disbelief caused by the Rebbe's outward appearance:

> The Ropshitzer—sad? Unhappy? He whose gaiety was as legendary as was the Kotzker's depression? People saw his laughter but not the torment beneath it; he ranks among the most misunderstood figures in Hasidism.[757]

How might wisdom be associated with one who masked his self-doubt and humility with cleverness and laughter? The leap that Wiesel makes in his sketch is tacit; the wisdom of the Rebbe lay exactly in his ability to hide his pain—and in his desire to do so:

> That is what he wanted: not to be understood. Not to be pitied. He concealed his pain—and that was his wisdom. He laughed so as not to cry; he chose exhibitionism so as to hide his

[755] Wiesel, *Four Hasidic Masters*, 110-11.
[756] Wiesel, *Four Hasidic Masters*, 113.
[757] Wiesel, *Four Hasidic Masters*, 115.

> anguish, his lack of confidence in himself, in his own powers, in his own words. [758]

Be that as it may, Wiesel maintains, the Rebbe's humor served not merely as his persona, but also as his answer to the sadness of the world. Indeed, he believed in the power of laughter and joy to open the human heart to the world of God:

> "What is a Hasid? Someone who possesses a precious key, a key that opens all the doors, even those that God keeps closed. And that key is . . . the *Nigoun*, the song of joy that makes our hearts thrill. The *Nigoun* opens the gates of heaven. Melancholy closes them."[759]

For Wiesel, the clue to understanding the Rebbe is found in his mask. It held the dual purpose of concealing his own pain while, at the same time, healing that of those around him.

Not unlike his colleagues, the Rebbe of Ropshitz fell into a deep silence as he neared the end of his life. He retreated into seclusion, away from all who knew him. At his deathbed, when asked by his son as to the reason for his silence, he could only say: "I . . . am . . . afraid."[760] The mystery of his person continues.

b) Analysis: Letting the Pain Stand

Wiesel's interpretation of the life of Rebbe Naphtali of Ropshtiz is indicative, yet again, of the author's own desire to find solace in the past. Unlike his portraits of Rebbes Pinhas and Barukh and the Seer of Lublin, however, Wiesel attributes no vision of future atrocities to Rebbe Naphtali; instead, he simply lets his pain and his silence stand. In place of any long excursions addressing the nature of his despair, Wiesel focuses on the joy that the Rebbe exuded. Undoubtedly, this is a Rebbe whose legacy challenges Wiesel at a profound level.

What draws Wiesel so deeply into the tale of this master? Is it the Rebbe's ability to hide his fear behind a mask of his own making? Is it the fact that he had found a way to reach out to others despite his pain? Or is it merely the message that the Rebbe has to give: that joy, laughter, and humor are necessary in a world full of darkness? Undoubtedly, it is the last. Wiesel's portrait is—unsurprisingly so—constructed to emphasize exactly this necessity. For Wiesel, the Rebbe's deepest struggle lay not in his need to hide, but rather in his desire to use his mask for the good of others. This was his secret and his *hokhma*.

Wiesel's attachment to Rebbe Naphtali is the strongest of all the four Rebbes he portrays. His portrait is replete with hope in the message of Hasidism. For Wiesel, even though the mystical quest is often beset by anguish, pain, rage

---

[758] Wiesel, *Four Hasidic Masters*, 115.
[759] Wiesel, *Four Hasidic Masters*, 117.
[760] Wiesel, *Four Hasidic Masters*, 120.

and despair, it is Hasidism's vision of a world replete with God that beckons his people to joy and hope. Essentially, this message represents the core of the Rebbe of Ropshitz's spiritual legacy.

Is Wiesel's assessment correct? Is it not reminiscent of Wiesel's own quest? Wiesel himself appears to support this suggestion by stating simply that a Hasidic story, "is about those who retell it as much as about those who experienced it." Should this statement hold, we may consider Wiesel's account of Rebbe Naphtali's life to reveal the author's own tragic sense of longing. As he clutches onto the Rebbe's vision of hope, his own vision for humanity is made clearer. Indeed, Rebbe Naphtali's agenda of saving the world through laughter grants the Rebbe this final place of honor in Wiesel's text. Whether Wiesel's journey truly resonates with Naphtali's is a matter open for discussion.

Reflection: The Return Home to the Shtetl

To begin this section, I recall a scene from Wiesel's biography. It is autumn of 1964: Wiesel is returning to Sighet from America for the first time since his liberation from Buchenwald. He has been preparing for the visit since the deportations. He is anxious knowing that "that town . . . no longer existed. It had followed the Jews into deportation."[761] He knows that the trip will be "a watershed. From that time on there would be a 'before' and an 'after.'"[762] What would be waiting for him when he arrived?

As Wiesel predicts, the visit is re-traumatizing. Another family—of non-Jews—is now living in his family home. Wiesel debates whether he should knock on the door or not. He relents. He ponders, full of grief:

> Like a blind man, I let my fingers wander over the fence that surrounded the garden, over the walls of the house, over the windows; I was waiting for them to return to me the things that had strayed, the images that had dissolved. I felt vulnerable and invincible at the same time: I could do everything, I could do nothing. I could evoke the past, I could not bring it to life again. Nothing had changed. The house was the same, the street was the same, the world was the same, God was the same. Only the Jews had disappeared.[763]

Wiesel goes home to find Sighet. He returns home to America, knowing that the Sighet of his past cannot be retrieved.

---

[761] Wiesel, *Legends of Our Time*, 112.
[762] Wiesel, *Legends of Our Time*, 111.
[763] Wiesel, *Legends of Our Time*, 120.

The scene of Wiesel's return to Sighet is striking, and it is one I wish to take up in concluding my exploration of *Four Hasidic Masters*. Specifically, I wish to extract from the scene the motif of the search for Sighet and relate it specifically to Wiesel's retelling of Hasidic legends.

My suggestion is that Wiesel's re-examination of the history and legends of Hasidism is indicative of his search for the lost shtetl. For Wiesel, Sighet is always present in the story of Hasidism. Sighet represents for him the sum total of Hasidism's long and complex past; in fact, it *is* that past. Upon entering the stories of Hasidism, he re-enters a part of his own story—he *returns* to Sighet. This movement within memory grants him consolation and orientation after Auschwitz.

This observation permits us to better understand how the shtetl functions as a powerful literary motif for Wiesel. As memory merges with legend, the shtetl arises powerfully from the ashes of Auschwitz as an entity that juxtaposes and contradicts. It holds the possibility of bearing witness, of speaking truth. As such, it emerges as the *conditio sine qua non* of Wiesel's being able to approach Auschwitz at all.

In the context of these dynamics, the search for the lost shtetl proves to be constitutive of Wiesel's overall pursuit of memory.

Wiesel has come to express that search literarily, that is, through narration. Wiesel can only find and return to the shtetl in and through storytelling, through reconstructing the shtetl in narrative.[764] Even if only in stories, the journey of seeking and returning proves painful. The backdrop to this journey is always Auschwitz. The return home is always overshadowed by its dark presence.

In *Four Hasidic Masters*, as Wiesel enters the ancient legends, he is aware that he is walking on sacred ground. This "sacred space"[765] constitutes a place within his kingdom of memory that beckons him away from Auschwitz to contemplate all that is good—in spite of all that is evil. Wiesel's relationship to Hasidism is reflected in this very contemplation. Hasidism is Wiesel's *refugium*, his place of refuge, that vantage point in memory from which he attempts to make sense of a world that has, since Auschwitz, become foreign to him. In remembering the shtetl and re-telling its story, he returns there once again—not to a Sighet

---

[764] Polen writes: "Childhood memories are intimately intertwined with the sense of self, one's feeling of place in the world. It is true that every return to a childhood home is fraught with disappointment brought about by the inevitability of change. But typically change is incremental, accretive, usually most visible at the margins. In Sighet and hundreds of other towns of Jewish Europe, however, the rupture was sudden, total, irreversible. Everything ended in the course of a day. . . . There was almost no "back" to go to; the erasure was nearly complete. If there was to be a future, it had to be constructed somewhere else, yet it could be done only by telling the tale of what had once been." See Polen, "Yearning for Sacred Place," in *Elie Wiesel: Jewish, Literary, and Moral Perspectives*, ed. Katz and Rosen, 76-77.

[765] Phrase taken from the title to Polen's article, "Yearning for Sacred Place," 69-82.

where strangers live in his home, but to the Sighet of his childhood and of his dreams.

It is in this context that the ellipse revises its previous form (see again figure 8 below). Here, as Wiesel's memory gravitates closer to the shtetl, the burden of the memory of Auschwitz eases. Although Auschwitz can be neither bracketed nor erased, the memory of the shtetl remains. In so doing, it retains its poignant relevance even in the wake of atrocity. This relevance allows Wiesel to continue his task to remember, to not-forget.

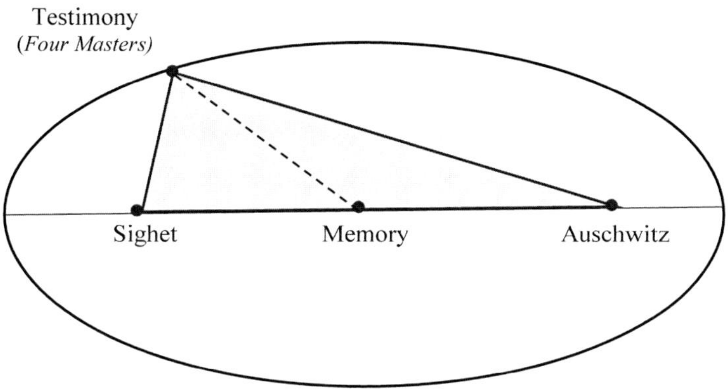

Figure 8 — Ellipse of *Four Masters*

"The Forgotten": When Memory Alone is Not Enough

Introductory Remarks

Although Wiesel's writings on Hasidism evoke a sense of reprieve from his often dark and conflicted fiction, his struggle to remember and to understand is observed best in his fiction. Wiesel's novels, full of anguish, yet marked by traces of hope, explore the depths of memory as the author attempts to span the bridge between the power and powerlessness of language. Although it is a task that ultimately cannot be completed, Wiesel never relinquishes his goal of trying to relate something of his experiences, of bearing witness.

In *The Forgotten*, Wiesel resumes his existential search for the lost shtetl. The work is arguably the novel that best embodies this search. However, the search is cleverly sheathed in a plot whose storyline and characters may appear at first reading removed from the testimony of *Night*. Still, a reading of the work guided by the theses of this study reveals the extent to which Wiesel seeks not only to resurrect the shtetl of his youth but also—and above all—to distill and reclaim its message for humankind. Borne of the Hasidic tradition out of which the shtetl grew, this message is simultaneously one of hope and one of warning. In *The Forgotten,* it is embedded in a story where the pain of trauma, tragedy, grief, and loss is offered a provisional balm as particular characters are granted a remnant of healing.

The Forgotten requires subtle reflection. Unlike in *Dawn*, Wiesel omits an extended inclusion of Hasidic legends in the text. He chooses instead to extend the lost shtetl motif. In so doing, however, Hasidic themes leap up from the text. Ultimately, though, it is the shtetl's radical ethic that best reveals the impact of Hasidism on this one text.

Wiesel's concerns in *The Forgotten* are similar to those of his other works. He remains preoccupied with the problem of good versus evil, with the price to be paid for hate and revenge, and with the message inherent in memory. Within these parameters, we observe Wiesel skirting the outermost edge of his field. He addresses themes borne in tradition and offers them a radically new context that grants them pressing, universal relevance. With this, his story assumes—however obliquely—the form of a revised and extended Hasidic legend. Here, we observe Wiesel drawing skillfully from those resources—from that capital—provided to him by the shtetl-as-field. The tradition of the Hasidic tale emerges as a literary form that Wiesel appropriates and then transforms as he attempts to convey yet another story of darkness and light.

Plot

First published in 1989 as *L'Oublié*, *The Forgotten* appeared in English in 1992.[766] With this novel, Wiesel carefully weaves together the stories of Elhanan and Malkiel Rosenbaum, a father and son, allowing their stories to converge into one unbroken, unified whole. The epicenter of their common story embraces an event of trauma and atrocity that has impacted both characters' lives in ways in which they are not entirely aware.

Elhanan Rosenbaum, a renowned psychotherapist in New York City, is a Romanian Holocaust survivor who has devoted his post-war life to the care of his adult son Malkiel, an obituary journalist with the *New York Times*, and to listening, as a therapist, to the stories of other Holocaust survivors. But Elhanan carries within him a secret of a dark past. During the war, as an adolescent, having managed to escape the shtetl before the deportations, he had taken up arms with the Hungarian resistance against the German and Hungarian forces in Poland. Upon his eventual return to the shtetl, he learns that all was lost. He then witnesses his closest friend Itzik, in an act of hate and revenge, rape a non-Jewish woman, the innocent widow of Zoltan. Zoltan had been a notorious tyrant who committed heinous crimes against the shtetl Jews. Elhanan is unable to prevent the rape—a circumstance that inwardly holds him prisoner for decades after the event.

Following the war, Elhanan emigrates to Israel, marries his love Talia, and joins the new Israeli army, the Haganah. Over the course of time, he again

[766] Elie Wiesel, *The Forgotten* (New York: Schocken Books, 1992).

meets Itzik—and confronts him about the rape. The latter remains unmoved. Shortly afterwards, Itzik is killed by Arab forces. Elhanan is taken prisoner by the Arabs and sent to an internment camp in Jordan. During his imprisonment, Talia dies while giving birth to Malkiel. Upon Elhanan's release and return to Israel, he learns of the tragedy and is bereft. He eventually leaves for America with his son in the hope of a new life there where wounds might be closed and memories forgotten.

But Elhanan never forgets. Now growing older, he has been diagnosed with Alzheimer's disease. In danger of forgetting his darkest memory—of the crime he was powerless to avert—he is desperate to pass his story on to Malkiel before his memory fades entirely. In scattered, piece-meal moments of clarity and of pain, Elhanan relates the tale to Malkiel. Elhanan instructs Malkiel to return to the location where everything had taken place—to Bozhoi, a small town in Romania, in the Carpathian Mountains, a town which once bore the name of the shtetl of his youth, *Feherfalu*.

Malkiel travels to Romania and finds Bozhoi. There he meets people whose stories had once intersected with his father's own. Although the shtetl has long since been annihilated, Malkiel finds, by chance or by fate, the rape victim, who is now old, sick, and decrepit. He confronts her with the story of the rape; she breaks down in Malkiel's presence. In her distress, however, she recounts to him the memory of a kind bystander who had witnessed the crime, a memory that had given her the strength to face the years of hardship that followed. As Malkiel reveals himself to her as the son of that man, the woman collapses in disbelief—and gratitude.

The end of the novel finds Malkiel back in New York. Elhanan's memory has now receded all but completely. Finally, he is unable to recall the "essential thing" he has wished to convey to Malkiel and Tamar, Malkiel's wife-to-be, who are both at his side. In mid-sentence, the novel closes open-ended, with Elhanan's final words slipping away into forgetfulness.

Title

A critical consideration of the title of *The Forgotten* provides direction for investigating the fundamentally enigmatic character of the novel. This enigma develops from within the narrative itself, which, as is common with Wiesel's works, functions on many levels.[767] Although these levels are not immediately

[767] Davis contends that the element of secrecy is one that permeates all of Wiesel's work and that the motif "secrets" forms the enigmatic basis of *The Forgotten*. See Davis, *Elie Wiesel's Secretive Texts*, 176-184. My suggestion is that "secrets"—Elhanan's secret past, Malkiel's "avoidance of direct questions," Tamar's love of secrets, Lidia's "right to have secrets," etc.—while not constituting the *leitmotif* of the novel in itself, do contribute to its enigmatic dimension. Indeed, while each character has his or her secrets, not all are disclosed, a fact that leaves aspects of character development and plot open.

evident, they act, in their complexity, as vital building blocks in developing the story.

The Forgotten: The title serves as an epigraph for all that follows. Still, its reference is equivocal: Who or what is being forgotten? Is it Elhanan in New York, whose memory of the past is quickly dissipating? Is it the widow and the crime committed against her, a crime that led her to a life of poverty, misery, sickness, and pain? Is it the shtetl, defiled by atrocity from without and from within? Or might the title be an intentional misnomer, given that nothing and no one in the story has ever truly been forgotten? Or might it be a combination of all of these: events forgotten, not forgotten, in danger of being forgotten—all of them together?[768]

My contention is the latter. In as much as the rape forms the epicenter of the narrative, the other elements of the plot relate to this center and function only in conjunction with that center. As all of the elements eventually converge, not only is memory of the past transmitted and preserved, but the message of Feherfalu is also heard and heeded.

In light of the complexity of the novel, its title may indeed mislead the reader. This possibility demands a sensitive reading of the text with a keen eye to the themes of forgetting, remembering, and seeking. As the plot unfolds, however, a sense of ambiguity remains: the tale retains, to the end, an element of secrecy and hiddenness.

Wiesel's existential concern for memory comes to full expression in his protagonist. Elhanan, his mind dying and memory fading, is forced to confront the past in its totality. He knows the past is about to be forgotten. It must now be transmitted to those who will listen to its story and honor it as testimony. It must be entrusted to those who will act upon it as message. With this, Elhanan knows that memory itself is not enough—the message demands a response.[769]

---

[768] The original title of the novel, *L'Oublié*, leaves open whether or not "the forgotten" is masculine or gender-neutral. As masculine, it might indeed give reference to a man—perhaps Elhanan; as neutral, perhaps a thing, a state of being, or a situation. The English title leaves even more possibilities open as the word is gender-neutral.

[769] Boschki suggests that, in connection with Wiesel's humanist agenda, remembering and transmitting that memory are one and the same, bound to one another in so far as they are "complementary, interchangeable terms," in as much as "the one who remembers is continually the one who passes on his or her memory, who tells his or her story or stories." Boschki, *Der Schrei*, 205-06. Translation mine. *The Forgotten*, however, highlights the dangers found in remembering but not speaking, as indicated by Elhanan's unresolved trauma. This trauma is one that remains until he finally bears witness to the past. For Wiesel then, transmission cannot be taken for granted (it is indeed possible to remember without speaking). Only the vital combination of memory and transmission can thwart the repetition of the past, of history. However, the temptation of the survivor to remain silent is strong given the psychological impact and social ramifications of speaking. Rosenfeld has suggested that this speaking or telling, while certainly "enlarging [his or her] vision" can have detrimental consequences for the

The Shtetl Motif Revisited

Although Hasidic elements and themes are less explicitly prevalent in *The Forgotten* than in other works by Wiesel, they still furtively assist in underscoring the author's enduring bond with and commitment to his Hasidic past. His shtetl motif is therewith newly accentuated and strengthened.

Indeed, Wiesel's shtetl is sketched anew through Elhanan's poignant longing for the shtetl. This longing is indicative of Wiesel's own view of the shtetl as kind of a "Paradise Lost"[770] which, although it is lost, is ever-present in memory. For Wiesel, the shtetl is always evolving. Just as *The Forgotten* offers an alternate portrayal of the shtetl as having been violated from within, so too does Wiesel draw new conclusions and, with them, glean new ethical insight. By unleashing his own, experiential-based categorical imperative, Wiesel successfully extends his own shtetl motif, fine-tuning it to his humanistic agenda.

Here we come to observe, first of all, how the shtetl persists in impacting Wiesel, even in the face of Auschwitz, and, secondly, how Wiesel is maturing and has evolved as a writer. Indeed, the variations of his shtetl motif are indicative, in one way or another, of the continuing impact that the author's religious and cultural roots have had upon him following Auschwitz. With this, the shtetl is posited, once again, as diametrically opposed to Auschwitz.

Recovering the Shtetl

In *The Forgotten*, Wiesel frames his search for the shtetl by exploring the consequences of trauma anew.[771] In particular, he is consumed by questions of

---

survivor. See Alvin H. Rosenfeld, *A Double Dying: Reflections on Holocaust Literature* (Bloomington: Indiana University Press, 1980), 32. Although Wiesel is aware of this dilemma, he also knows that only testimony can save the world: "I believe, first of all, that if we remember what human beings have done to other human beings, we can prevent other tragedies from happening." Elie Wiesel and Richard D. Heffner, *Conversations with Elie Wiesel*, ed. Thomas J. Vinciguerra (New York: Schocken Books, 2003), 146.

[770] Cf. Frunză, "Elie Wiesel and Nostalgia for a Lost Paradise," 101.

[771] Strikingly, Wiesel's portrait of Elhanan corresponds in many ways to those profiles of Holocaust survivors sketched by clinical study. Felman and Laub's study of the testimonies of survivors' highlights, among other aspects, both the survivor's paradoxical need to bear witness and his or her fear of actually doing so. Laub offers a clinical evaluation of the dilemmas inherent in both giving testimony and in listening to it. See Laub, "Bearing Witness *or* the Vicissitudes of Listening" in Felman and Laub, *Testimony: Crises of Witnessing*, 57-74.
Since the 1990s, trauma theory has developed into a broad field of ongoing research, instigated, at least in part, by clinical work with Holocaust survivors. Susannah Radstone maintains that many problems that researchers encounter stem from their focus on survivors whose trauma renders them vulnerable to research studies and clinical treatment. For an overview of the controversies and politics surrounding trauma theory, see

personal identity and inner development in the face of trauma.[772] He pursues these questions while sketching out his main characters and telling their stories.

In his fiction, Wiesel's protagonists all exhibit some relationship to the lost world of the shtetl, either as survivors or as children of survivors. In *The Forgotten,* we encounter two individuals, father and son, who fulfill both roles. Whereas Elhanan has never forgotten his religious and cultural roots, Malkiel knows nothing of his father's past; in the wake of this unknowing, he finds himself unable—and unwilling—to replicate his father's deep faith.[773] Still, Malkiel stands as the grandchild of the shtetl, and as much as his father's trauma remains unresolved, it profoundly affects his own life. In essence, Elhanan has bequeathed to his son his trauma, but not (yet) his memory.[774]

Susannah Radstone, "Trauma Theory: Contexts, Politics, Ethics," *Paragraph* 30:1 (2007), 9-29.

[772] Reeve Robert Brenner highlights the unique relationship between trauma and identity with respect to Jewish Holocaust survivors. He maintains that in as much as Jewish identity in general tends to be based more on memory than on theology, the ways in which the trauma impacts Jewish identity must be evaluated in light of the Jewish memory tradition. He suggests that the plethora of religious, theological, and personal responses to the Holocaust is telling of the individuality of the experience and the idiosyncrasies of being both human and Jewish. "Each survivor . . . is an entire world," he states. See Reeve Robert Brenner, *The Faith and Doubt of Holocaust Survivors*, (New Brunswick, NJ: Transaction Publishers, 2014), xviii. For an introduction into his theses, see his Introduction to the Transaction Edition, "Imaging the Jewish Past," in *Faith and Doubt*, ix-xxxi. With respect to *The Forgotten*, Elhanan arguably does not appear so much to be in a crisis of faith as in a crisis of identity, perpetuated by the trauma he has left clothed in silence.

[773] Although Malkiel has always been careful to respect his father's faith tradition, his deepest experiences of that tradition are made while in Romania. His encounter with the widow represents his most dramatic faith experience, perhaps a kind of conversion. At the end of his journey, Malkiel finds himself at the grave of his grandfather, despairing over his forthcoming return to his father. He takes an oath not only to remember, but also to bear witness. In so doing, he promises to remain within the faith and, with Tamar together, raise his own children within that faith. Wiesel, *The Forgotten*, 307-10.

[774] Malkiel resents the abstruse suffering of his father and the life he has to live in its shadow. Malkiel recalls: "Why did I sometimes feel that perverse need—even if it was unconscious—to wound him? To be like other kids? To punish him for bringing me into a world that is ugly, unjust, stupid, doomed? To break free from his hold on me? To put an end between his nightmares and me?" Wiesel, *The Forgotten*, 131-32. The extent to which Malkiel is suffering from secondary trauma is left open. Hadas Wiseman and Jacques P. Barber highlight the discrepancies present in trauma theory concerning whether or not trauma can, in fact, be transmitted to the next generation. The findings of clinical studies and empirical research are debated. Wiseman and Barber do, however, highlight recurrent relational and emotional themes and psychological phenomena in the "second generation." See Hadas Wiseman and Jacques P. Barber, *Echoes of the Trauma: Relational Themes and Emotions in Children of Holocaust Survivors* (New York: Cambridge University Press, 2008), 1-12.

An examination of the problematic father-son relationship between Elhanan and Malkiel is vital to unlocking the novel's message.[775] As we learn of Elhanan's remarkable journey of survival, we begin to understand Elhanan as being bound inextricably to Malkiel. Their symbiosis is unremitting; their identities intersect, they blend and clash. Elhanan is aware of this and acknowledges it to his son:

> "You're the center of my life, Malkiel. It's you who makes me invincible. But it is you who also makes me vulnerable: if anything happened to you I couldn't stand it—I'd die."[776]

In this, Elhanan is also aware of his son's suffering:

> "You know, my son, no one can suffer in another's place. All I can promise you is that when you suffer, I'll be present." What an irony, Malkiel mused. Our roles are reversed. He's suffering and I can't suffer for him.[777]

Malkiel is not unaware of his father's anguish: "His father's natural element was suffering and the memory of suffering."[778] The suffering of Malkiel has been suffused with that of his father's. Both are bound to a past that they only partially share. Both suffer for and with one another, imprisoned by the memory that Elhanan has withheld.

Upon learning that he is ill and will soon forget all, Elhanan decides to tell Malkiel his story. He asks Malkiel to remember the story and to give witness to it later.[779] Malkiel promises, but is frightened by the prospect:

> Overwhelmed, blinded by emotion, he saw himself walking a tightrope over an abyss: one false step, one awkward word, and he would fall, dragging his father with him. "Listen to me, Father. You've always been at the center of my existence; and you always will be, to the end of my days."[780]

The Forgotten's plot unfolds as Malkiel sets out to fulfill the promise made to his father. The novel proceeds by relating the story that has made this promise

---

[775] Simon P. Sibelman underscores this suggestion. See Simon P. Sibelman, *Silence in the Novels of Elie Wiesel* (New York: St. Martin's Press, 1995), 164ff.
[776] Wiesel, *The Forgotten*, 132.
[777] Wiesel, *The Forgotten*, 24.
[778] Wiesel, *The Forgotten*, 44.
[779] See Wiesel, *The Forgotten*, 29-30, 91-92, 102-103, 129-30.
[780] Wiesel, *The Forgotten*, 65.

necessary. In so doing, it also exposes the psychological processes that both characters must embrace as they finally come to terms with the past.

a) Remembering

Elhanan's post-war identity is determined by his perpetual sense of guilt concerning the rape. Long after events have passed, Elhanan realizes that his strained efforts at coming to terms with the past have borne no fruit. The psychological wounds of his trauma have not healed. His therapeutic work with Holocaust survivors has offered no relief from the pain, and his compulsion to proactively direct the course of his troubled son's life has only added to his sorrow. Even the attention given to uphold his faith tradition has offered him little escape from the perpetual cycle of distress and despair. All of his efforts at mitigating his grief fail; indeed, time has been no healer.[781]

The onset of Elhanan's illness triggers an acute re-traumatization.[782] Confronted with his rapidly advancing dementia, Elhanan knows that what he has strained to forget must now be fully remembered. Sensing the urgency to make his story known, he realizes that his memory must be transmitted to the one bound to him by the very story he has consciously withheld: to his son, Malkiel.[783]

Elhanan's story is dark. During his time in the Resistance, he was catapulted from the innocence of youth into the role of a vengeful warrior tempted by the logic of hate.[784] Upon witnessing the rape of the widow, however, he

[781] Elhanan's chronic depression, his self-imposed isolation, his angst with respect to his son's future—all but a few indicators of his ongoing sense of trauma. For example, see Wiesel, *The Forgotten*, 43-44, 59-60, 70-71, 76.

[782] Elhanan's sense of desperation to relay his past to his son is an indication of his re-traumatization. As Elhanan's memory fades, this desperation intensifies. Finally, he becomes delusional. See Wiesel, *The Forgotten*, 146-47. Laub highlights the possibility of survivor re-traumatization triggered by later trauma. See Laub, "Bearing Witness *or* the Vicissitudes of Listening," in Felman and Laub, *Testimony: Crises of Witnessing*, 65-67.

[783] In announcing his intention to bear witness, Elhanan warns Malkiel of the dangers of remembering and of the need to remain grounded in the face of memory—something he himself had not accomplished. See Wiesel, *The Forgotten*, 70. Laub identifies the sense of urgency often exhibited by survivors to tell their stories. He calls this the "imperative to tell." He observes a relation between the survivor's desire to transmit memories and their need to survive. See Dori Laub, M. D., "An Event Without a Witness," in Felman and Laub, *Testimony: Crises of Witnessing in Literature, Psychoanalysis, and History*, 78-79. It can be argued, however, that, in *The Forgotten*, Elhanan becomes more concerned about the survival of memory for the next generation than about his own physical survival. This is plausibly reflective of Wiesel's own decision to bear witness.

[784] Elhanan states: "I know I seem young, but in wartime young people are old." Wiesel, *The Forgotten*, 106. During his odyssey while serving in the Hungarian resistance, Elhanan never leaves Itzik's side. Itzik, known as "the Avenger" teaches Elhanan not merely how to hate, but also how to kill. See pages 155-79.

experiences a revulsion and a disgust which incite within him a kind of conversion towards compassion.[785]

In spite of this, decades later, Elhanan continues to believe he is co-responsible for the crime. The onset of his illness exacerbates his feelings of guilt. Elhanan believes that he would not have become ill if he had responded to the rape as tradition dictated. He confesses:

> "I am a guilty man. That is why I am being punished. Like Abuya's heretical sons, I gazed when I should not have gazed and turned my eyes away when I should not have. I saw a sin committed . . . a crime. . . . I could have, I should have, done something, called out, shouted, struck a blow. I forgot our precepts, our laws, that require an individual to struggle against evil whenever it appears. I forgot that we can never simply remain spectators, we have no right to stand aside, to keep silent, to let the victim fight the aggressor alone. I forgot so many things that day. . . . That is why I am forgetting other things now. Can there be anything worse than that?"[786]

Strikingly, as the novel unfolds, Elhanan's identity begins to shift again. In daring to confront memory—even more, in daring to transmit it—he assumes the tentative role of healer. The act of transmission initiates Malkiel's journey to the lost shtetl, to Feherfalu, and, ultimately, to the rape victim whose identity has remained entangled with Elhanan's own.

In Feherfalu, Malkiel stands in, by proxy, for his absent father.[787] Elhanan is reunited with Zoltan's widow through Malkiel. In this instance, although far away and oblivious to the fact, Elhanan participates in the pivotal, cathartic moment of the story. The widow finds a balm for her wound.

---

785 Wiesel, *The Forgotten*, 190-93. Elhanan's witness of the rape of the widow not only breaks his bond with Itzik, but also his own spirit. Revolted by Itzik's actions as well as his own powerlessness, he knows that what he has seen is atrocity. Elhanan never forgets the scene, as is evident in his confrontation with Itzik later in Israel. During this confrontation, Elhanan is vehement: "And the divine image we all bear within us—what did you do to it? And the letter of the Torah that every one of us embodies—where did you leave it? And the Law that demands of us justice as much as mercy—how did you get around that?" Wiesel, 229. The imagery implemented here is drawn from Hasidic spirituality, referencing the divine sparks scattered about creation at the time of the breaking of the vessels.

786 Wiesel, *The Forgotten*, 51.

787 As Malkiel decides to journey to Feherfalu to seek out the widow, Elhanan pronounces: "*Keep your eyes and ears open, look and listen: you must represent me. I want to see everything with your eyes, and hear everything with your ears.*" Wiesel, *The Forgotten,* 92.

b) Returning

As the son of a survivor whose deepest secrets have remained hidden, Malkiel participates in the trauma of his father. Indeed, Malkiel exhibits an existential anxiety that mirrors Elhanan's own.[788] As he matures, drifting from relationship to relationship, he attempts to avert his father's angst by distancing himself from his father's faith and its traditions. Within this context, Malkiel's identity as Elhanan's son is complicated by his identity as seeker.

As his father's memory fails, and upon learning of the trauma that has haunted him all these years, Malkiel travels to Romania. Malkiel's aim is to seek out the widow and reconcile his father to her. With this, Malkiel becomes the seeker *par excellence*. In fulfilling his father's final wishes, he also sets out on a mission to understand his own story.

Soon after his arrival in Romania, Malkiel discovers that the shtetl Feherfalu no longer exists. Instead, the community of Bozhoi has taken its place.[789] It has erased all but one piece of evidence of its Jewish past, namely, the Jewish cemetery. It is here where Malkiel's journey in Romania begins.

Malkiel's encounter with the gravedigger Hershel, witness of the dramatic fate of the shtetl during the war, provides the first pivotal point of the novel.[790] Hershel is a madman, and he intrigues the young journalist as he seeks clues to the past. As is the case with the madmen of Wiesel's other works,[791] the madman-gravedigger of *The Forgotten* acts as catalyst for events to come; as the

---

[788] Wiseman and Barber, in outlining the debate as to whether the trauma of survivors can in fact be transmitted to the "second generation," have highlighted the idiosyncratic element at play. They stress that how particular emotional states and "motifs" are present in the next generation tends to correlate with how such persons define themselves as children of survivors. Here, the themes of vulnerability, adjustment, and resilience come to the fore. Attachment theory has investigated too the impact of Holocaust trauma on parenting effectiveness. Within this context, Wiseman and Barber set out to explore complex relational themes present between children and their survivor parents. See Wiseman and Barber, *Echoes of the Trauma*, 1-12. Importantly, in *The Forgotten*, Malkiel's attitude towards his vulnerable father plays into his own vulnerability, drawing him close to his father during his childhood and away from him as he enters adulthood. During that time, he seeks his identity beyond the confines of his father's unspoken sorrow. Still, he is unable to fully escape his father's trauma. However much he may be unaware of it, he is in fact the child of a survivor.

[789] Wiesel, *The Forgotten*, 16.

[790] Wiesel, *The Forgotten*, 12-15.

[791] The motif of madness recurs frequently in both Wiesel's fiction and non-fiction. Wiesel himself relates this directly to the impact of Hasidism on his thought: "[A]ll the first Hasidic masters were mad, and therefore I love them. They were mad, they had to be made to try to transmit a message of humanism, a message of beauty, a message of compassion in a world that had none. Hasidism is an act of madness—sacred, mystical madness." See Elie Wiesel, "Hasidism and Man's Love of Man," in Abrahamson, ed. *Against Silence*, ed. Abrahamson, 2:255-56, quoted in Friedman, *You Are My Witnesses*, 144. For Friedman's reflection on madness in Wiesel's thought, see Friedman, 142-61.

only survivor of Feherfalu, he *is* the shtetl's *memory*. He relates the story of the shtetl and its annihilation to Malkiel. While Hershel's connection with the dead of the shtetl may be disturbing,[792] Malkiel is left strengthened in his resolve to fulfill his mission in Feherfalu. Through the efforts of his Romanian translator, Lydia, Malkiel is able to locate the widow and extend to her the olive branch provided by his father.[793] With this encounter, Malkiel the seeker now takes on the identity of finder.

c) Reconciling

Although Zoltan's widow occupies only small sections of text in *The Forgotten*, she plays a central role in the novel; indeed, she is an integral part of its epicenter. In as much as Elhanan's sense of guilt draws from what he feels has been his complicity in the rape, his trauma has remained linked to that of the widow. As is the case with Elhanan, her sorrow has not abated, nor has her sense of trauma dissipated. Elhanan's anguish has been exacerbated by the onset of illness; the widow's has been aggravated by an endless, vicious cycle of tragedy and woe.

Wiesel's placement of the widow at the heart of his narrative is ironic: she, a non-Jew, represents the shtetl as its last living remnant. She embodies, in her woundedness, the dark, last moment of Feherfalu's story. This fact deepens and intensifies the novel's evolving message and warning.

As the widow is reconciled with Elhanan through the person of Malkiel, a remnant of the shtetl is recovered at last. With this, its holy commandment to choose life above hate and death cries out from within the story.

Although the wounds of all three characters can never be fully healed, and the past cannot be undone, there is some degree of personal closure, reconciliation, and redemption at the end of the novel. As the novel closes, the reader is aware that, even in the absence of complete healing, what has been accomplished is, in fact, enough. In the wake of evil, good may indeed be granted the last word, and old identities can be transformed from that of victim to survivor.

d) Receiving

In *The Forgotten*, Wiesel explores a father-son relationship once again.[794] Unlike *Night*—which casts Wiesel's relationship with his own father in the

---

[792] In a cryptic passage in the text, Hershel relates his encounters with dead Rabbis and Hasidim around the time of the deportations. They had come to the cemetery to grieve the fate of the shtetl. The scene echoes the Kabbalistic/Hasidic belief in *gilgul*. See Wiesel, *The Forgotten*, 119-27.

[793] Wiesel, *The Forgotten*, 286-98.

[794] The father-son relationship is a theme of recurrent exploration in Wiesel's writing. For more on this theme, see Davis, *Elie Wiesel's Secretive Texts* 142-58; Fine, *The Legacy of Night*, 18-26; Fober, *Identität und Wissen*, 92-96; and André Neher, *The Exile of*

shadow of ambivalence, guilt, unresolved grief, the loss of paternal authority, and the impairment of meaning[795]—*The Forgotten* suggests the possibility of healing such relationships through the telling of story, through memory and its transmission. However complex it may be, the relationship between Elhanan and Malkiel becomes the catalyst for a journey that will have healing consequences.

Wiesel's longing to recover the shtetl from the ashes of its annihilation remains poignant throughout *The Forgotten*. He achieves his goal literarily not merely through Elhanan's transmission of memory to Malkiel, but above all through Malkiel's cathartic encounter with Zoltan's widow. The shtetl is found as the widow is found, as she is confronted and is asked to forgive. With this singular act of both contrition and compassion, the trauma of the past, while not forgotten, is made more tolerable in the present.

Malkiel, too, makes peace with the past by receiving his father's memory as both burden and gift. He is released from the trauma of his father, equipped to return home to New York, to both Elhanan—now dying—and to Tamar, Malkiel's lover, to begin anew.

Upon Malkiel's return, Elhanan is still bearing witness. However, their relationship has been transformed, and their roles are reversed. Malkiel is on the brink of becoming witness himself:

> (Elhanan was talking and Malkiel was listening. With a full heart he heard his sick father recall a time long ago, a world long gone. There was perfect harmony between father and son: the more the father let himself go, the more the son took in. In proportion as Elhanan felt his memory diminish, Malkiel felt his own expand.)[796]

The pathological dimension of the father-son relationship is resolved, healed through the transmission of memory. Malkiel will not only be the new teller of the story, but also the bearer of its humanitarian message.

Although the shtetl may never be recovered in a literal sense, its message can be. Guilt is still guilt, the dead remain dead, but the message of the shtetl remains relevant and urgent. Through remembering and receiving, hope for the future is retrieved. Still, that hope is a cautious hope, for it also embraces warning

---

the Word: From the Silence of the Bible to the Silence of Auschwitz, trans. David Maisel (Philadelphia: The Jewish Publication Society of America, 1981), 216-18.

[795] For more on the emotional residue left to Wiesel upon the death of his father, see Davis, *Elie Wiesel's Secretive Texts*, 142-44.

[796] Wiesel, *The Forgotten*, 234. Before leaving Romania for New York, Malkiel realizes what his father had intended in having sent him to Romania. He speaks once again at his grandfather's grave: "Did [my father] know what would strike him down? That he might explain why he agreed to open up, why he undertook a kind of memory transfusion as one has a blood transfusion? Was it his wish that my memory substitute for his own? That I do the remembering for him? Is that even possible?" Wiesel, *The Forgotten*, 309.

and admonition. Indeed, memory alone is not enough; in its transmission, it must embrace an ethic that actively walks the path towards peace.[797]

It is exactly this hope and urgency that Wiesel wishes to convey. Elhanan's memory, however grievous, is transformative for the next generation.[798] True engagement with memory is not theoretical and theological, but rather existential and ethical. Although Elhanan's journey represents but a small stone in the larger mosaic of peace work, Wiesel is adamant that such encounters are replete with meaning.

---

[797] Frunză investigates the correlation between memory and ethics in Wiesel's writing. He stresses that, in the Jewish tradition, memory is linked to one's sense of responsibility to God and to community. He attributes Wiesel's understanding of the link between memory and ethic to his Talmudic studies, in particular under the Talmudic master, Chouchani, while in Paris. Frunză compares Wiesel to Emmanuel Levinas who also studied under Chouchani. See Sandu Frunză, "Ethics, Religion and Memory in Elie Wiesel's *Night,*" *Journal for the Study of Religions and Ideologies*, 9:26 (Summer 2010), 94-113. In a similar vein, Fackenheim, in arguing for the necessity of a "Midrashic existence," has maintained that one "acts as though all depended on man and prays as though all depended on God." Still, he continues, this ethic is not based on mysticism, but rather on the contingencies of human existence in the world in the wake of Auschwitz. See Emil L. Fackenheim, "Midrashic Existence after the Holocaust: Reflections Occasioned by the Work of Elie Wiesel," in *Confronting the Holocaust*, eds. Rosenfeld and Greenberg, 109. For Fackenheim's entire article, see 99-116.
Mensink investigates Walter Benjamin's focus on the biblical notion of *zachar*, "to remember" as referencing the "experience of experienced time" in the present moment. The ethical dimension of this notion is strong in as much as the prophet acts as the messenger of the present moment, not of the future. See Dagmar Mensink, "Erinnerung ist das Gegenteil von Gleichgültigkeit," in *Das Gegenteil von Gleichgültigkeit ist Erinnerung*, ed. Mensink and Boschki, 165-71. Similarly, Wiesel stresses that the past must always stand in relation to the present, and is as such of ethical significance. "Memory," Wiesel states, is the "opposite of indifference and everything that it conceives and which belongs to it." Memory thus stands as an "ethical notion." Wiesel cited in Mensink, 168, but with incomplete bibliographical reference. Translation mine. See also Stéphane Moses, "Eingedenken und Jetztzeit—Geschichtliches Bewusstsein im Spätwerk Walter Benjamins," in *Memoria—vergessen und erinnern*, eds. Anselm Haverkamp and Renate Lachmann, with Reinhart Herzog (Munich: William Fink Verlag, 1993), 385-405.

[798] Just before he leaves Romania, Malkiel's reveals at his grandfather's grave his intention to marry Tamar and to carry forward his father's memory to his own children. Given Malkiel's previous anathema to having children at all, his words are reflective of the reconciliation and healing that have taken place. See Wiesel, *The Forgotten*, 46-47, 309-10.

The Shtetl's Categorical Imperative

a) Rejecting Hate, Doing What is Good

Elements of *The Forgotten* mirror aspects of Wiesel's own journey. The shtetl and its annihilation serve as a starting point of Elhanan's memory, as with Wiesel. Elhanan's story is thus rooted in a time and place where faith and tradition act as the touchstone of human duty and responsibility. Elhanan's need to remember, to not-forget, was born in Feherfalu. He has not forgotten that world and, in not-forgetting, he continues to claim it as his own. Through the person of Elhanan, Wiesel claims it as his own as well. From this vital, vigilant base, both protagonist and author fulfill not only their commission to remember, but also their duty to live humanely in the world.

Within this context, we see how Wiesel's quest to remember is linked to his need to transmit the shtetl's urgent categorical imperative to a world that he fears is incapable of learning from its past.[799] Wiesel has subtly woven this imperative into the novel as its clandestine but most pressing theme.[800]

The forms that this imperative assumes in *The Forgotten* merit closer attention. It appears significantly in Elhanan's return to the humanist morals of the shtetl upon witnessing the rape of the widow. From that moment forward, Elhanan knows that answering hate with hate can only result in an unending, inescapable cycle of retaliation and violence.[801]

---

[799] Ozick highlights the inextricable link between Wiesel's Jewishness, his call to remembrance, and his humanism. "*The Forgotten* is, aptly, the name of one of his novels. It is a remarkable and tragic story of the necessity, the urgency, the inescapable humanity of Jewish remembering. What makes us Jews? We have chosen the One God of *Shema*; and we have chosen historical memory. We inscribe, we do not erase. We do not forget, we strive to remember. And it is for this reason that Elie Wiesel earns his extraordinary place among us. He is our generation's great Memory Teacher. He helps us remember not only what has happened, but who we are and what we are intended to *mean*." Cynthia Ozick, "Afterword," in *Celebrating Elie Wiesel: Stories, Essays, Reflections*, ed. Alan Rosen (Notre Dame, IN: University of Notre Dame Press, 1998), 337. Wiesel has often reflected on the link between memory and humanism. He states: "I believe, first of all, that if we remember what human beings have done to other human beings, we can prevent other tragedies from happening." See Wiesel and Heffner, *Conversations with Elie Wiesel*, 146.

[800] Here, Wiesel's ethic is reminiscent of Adorno, who has reformulated—and thus rejected—Kant's categorical imperative. Adorno's imperative is based in experience, not in metaphysics. Boschki writes: "[Adorno's] imperative for human thinking and acting is based not on a Kantian theory but on history. The *memory* of the terror of the extermination of the Jews should protect people in the present and future from a repetition of Auschwitz." See Reinhold Boschki, "Towards an Ethics of Remembrance after the Shoah" in *Celebrating Elie Wiesel*, 212.

[801] Here, we sense the strong pull of Feherfalu's Hasidic legacy upon Elhanan, the pull of an ethic that seeks to repair and uphold life rather than destroy it. In as much as Hasidism is concerned with humanity's proximity to the divine and, concomitantly, with

The imperative is, of course, best expressed through Malkiel's encounter with the widow whose story is so profoundly entangled with Elhanan's and Malkiel's own. Here, Wiesel powerfully explores the possibility of humanism by recovering and reclaiming, even from the ashes of atrocity, the shtetl's call to choose life. By the close of the novel, the author's conviction of the efficacy of this vital message becomes evident by the measure of healing granted to his characters.

Several other passages in the novel give further indication of its ethical thrust. The novel opens with Malkiel's journey to Romania and withvisit to his grandfather's grave. There, Malkiel discovers that he bears his grandfather's name. He is devastated by this knowledge. This vital link to the past propels Malkiel forward in his quest to uncover the secrets of the past and, above all, to make amends with them. The call of the shtetl to repair, restore, and redeem life has now taken hold of him as well.

The sacrifice made by the elder of the shtetl, who was murdered in refusing to betray the people of the shtetl, provides another clear image of the shtetl's stringent ethic.[802] His death stands as a powerful symbol of the shtetl's call to life, duty, honor, and community.[803]

The dead also play a central role in underscoring this ethic. The dead of the shtetl, with whom the gravedigger still communes; grandfather Malkiel, whose sacrifice for the shtetl remains vibrant in the gravedigger's memory;

---

the central role it plays in the reparation of the cosmos, this ethic makes sense: it is commensurate with the acute sense of the humane implicit in Hasidism's composite theological constructs. Alan L. Berger supports this view: "Memory requires one to act in a way that seeks at least a partial tikkun (repair) of the world, while simultaneously asking questions of both the divine and human covenantal partners." Alan L. Berger, "Transfusing Memory: Second-Generation Postmemory in Elie Wiesel's *The Forgotten*," in *Obliged by Memory: Literature, Religion, Ethics; A Collection of Essays Honoring Elie Wiesel's Seventieth Birthday*, eds. Steven T. Katz and Alan Rosen (Syracuse: Syracuse University Press, 2006), 117-18, quoted in Sandu Frunză, "Ethics, Religion and Memory in Elie Wiesel's *Night*," 106. McAfee Brown states, "The journey to the past does not end there. It leads back to the present, empowering those on the journey to refashion the present in ways not possible before. The agenda is clear: responding to human need wherever it confronts us." See McAfee Brown, *Elie Wiesel: Messenger to All Humanity,* 129.

[802] Wiesel, *The Forgotten*, 112-13.

[803] The sacrifice of the community elder appears to echo that of Wiesel's father, Shlomo Wiesel. Silber connects Wiesel's sense of the priority of the community to Shlomo Wiesel's refusal to be separated from his community, even at the urgency of the family's domestic help. See John Silber, "From Thebes to Auschwitz: Moral Responsibility in Sophocles and Wiesel," in *Celebrating Elie Wiesel*, ed. Rosen, 176. Wiesel writes: "'My father was right.' If what one does will be done by all, and if what happens to one will happen to all, does that not only involve suffering and death, but also responsibility and, consequently, innocence or guilt?" Elie Wiesel, *Night*, trans. Stella Rodway (New York: Hill and Wang, 1960), 122.

Elhanan's deceased wife, Talia; the pious child, Absalom, who is killed in combat against the Arabs in Palestine;[804] and even, in negative fashion, Itzik and Zoltan—all of these speak from the realm of the dead into the conscience of posterity. Together, they help facilitate the novel's intense moral thrust.[805]

b) Humanism and Theology

The Forgotten speaks far more of humanism than of theology. Indeed, it forfeits the role of theological treatise outright, offering no overt credo or extended technical theological reflection. Although the kinds of agonized questions posed to God by the young Eliezer in *Night* are certainly Elhanan's own, they are, for the most part, clothed in silence.[806]

While *The Forgotten* avoids all explicit forms of theological problem-solving, the narrative is replete with theological themes in typical Wieselian style. These themes include, among others: the presence and/or absence of God; the possibility of evil; humanity's role in evil; and the necessity of, and path to, humanity's redemption.

The text addresses these themes only in the context of Wiesel's larger, ethically-focused literary agenda. Implied here is the necessity for theology and even spirituality to remain within the practical sphere of human experience; indeed, should theological reflection omit its indispensable experiential parameters, it is destined to thwart the moral possibilities inherent in memory, in remembrance.[807] The novel contends, in Jewish fashion, that the theological and the

---

[804] Wiesel, *The Forgotten*, 230.

[805] At the entrance to Yad Vashem in Jerusalem, it is written: "Redemption Lies In Remembering." Attributed to the Baal Shem Tov, the words imply the dynamic link between memory, memorial, and Jewish ethics. See Rosenfeld, *A Double Dying*, 185. In a similar vein, Wiesel recognizes the memorializing status of memory, testimony, and writing—all of which have ethical implications. "But for me, writing is a *matzeva*, an invisible tombstone, erected to the memory of the dead unburied." See Wiesel, *Legends of Our Time*, 8.

[806] Greenberg understands silence in the Hasidic tradition as constituting a human reaction to those contradictions existing between creation and the human condition. He quotes Wiesel: "'Hasidism never claimed to resolve contradiction—rather, it assumed they were there.'" See Greenberg, "The Hasidic Spark and the Holocaust," in *Elie Wiesel: Jewish, Literary, and Moral Perspectives*, ed. Katz and Rosen, 84; and Wiesel, *Somewhere a Master: Further Hasidic Portraits and Legends*, trans. Marion Wiesel (New York: Summit Books, 1982), 179.

[807] Boschki writes: "The lack of a role for experience in philosophy and theology results in a lack of remembrance." See Boschki, "Towards an Ethic of Remembrance" in *Celebrating Elie Wiesel*, 214. Here, Boschki also suggests the need to develop a "theology of remembrance" in which memory, in being bound to experience, may provide a remnant of hope for a human world. See page 216. McAfee Brown writes, "The journey to the past does not end there. It leads back to the present, empowering those on the journey to refashion the present in ways not possible before. The agenda is clear: responding to

ethical must always be linked; they must merge and meld as one and the same foundation for human life and endeavor.[808] Together, they communicate a humane message that, while Jewish in nature, is simultaneously universal.[809]

Within the ethical matrix of the shtetl's legacy, human evil is exposed as a grotesque deviation from humanity's intended vocation. Still, by way of this same evaluation, hope is possible. The shtetl's humane vision offers concrete alternatives to the destructive course that humanity has taken. Hope remains that the human being just might, in the end, learn to choose life above hate and revenge.[810] It is this longing that lies at the heart of *The Forgotten*.

In this overall context, the shtetl's spiritual ethic can be seen to function as the foundation of *The Forgotten*'s theological and existential inquiry into the nature of both God and humanity—in the wake of Auschwitz. With this in mind, the novel can be considered an attempt on behalf of Wiesel to explore anew his own religious-humanist agenda. The results of his efforts are stunning. We learn that authentic faith and humanism preclude any diametrical relationship; they neither cancel nor invalidate each other. Rather, they underscore and enhance each other. With this, both ethics and faith remain options, even in the face of

---

human need wherever it confronts us. Cambodia, Russia, Israel, Washington, wherever . . ." McAfee Brown, *Elie Wiesel: Messenger to All Humanity*, 129.

[808] Katz highlights the intrinsic link between theology, spirituality, and the ethical in the Hasidic tradition in terms of its emphasis on the "religious deed." He states: "The theurgical power of the mitzvah (religious deed) has the capacity to alter the cosmic order and bring redemption. . . . The keeping of the mitzvot was a form of dialogue with heaven, an encounter between God and man. And therefore the life of mitzvot had to have a human dimension beyond the obligation of obedience, one that entailed, at its highest, grace and love." See Steven T. Katz, "Reflections on Wiesel's Hasidic Tales" in *Elie Wiesel: Jewish, Literary, and Moral Perspectives*, ed. Katz and Rosen, 62.

[809] Wiesel maintains that Judaism serves as a microcosm of humanity. Within this context, he adheres to an ethic he considers valid for all of humankind. He links the universality of this ethic to the universal nature of the Holocaust as being first and foremost a Jewish event. "Was the Holocaust a universal event or solely a Jewish and therefore unique one? My answer: it was both. Because it was Jewish, it was universal. Its universality lies in its Jewishness, in its uniqueness." See Elie Wiesel, closing statement, transcript, *Proceedings, President's Commission on the Holocaust*, Commission Meeting, Washington DC, February 15th, 1979, 174. Cited in Abrahamson, ed. *Against Silence*, 1:43.

[810] Boschki suggests that Wiesel's "and yet" is linked paradoxically to his focus on memory and hope. See Boschki, *Der Schrei*, 219-20. My contention is that it is linked to his ethic as well. In spite of memory, one hopes (however cautiously), and because of hope, one acts. This coincides with aspects of Hasidic thought where song and joy are considered to be appropriate responses to painful paradoxes inherent in creation and humanity. See also Greenberg, "The Hasidic Spark and the Holocaust," 86-87; and McAfee Brown, *Elie Wiesel: Messenger to All Humanity*, 117-22.

unanswerable theological questions. Without having to submit to the death of God, one is freed to lament against God.[811]

c) Upholding the Not-Forgotten

The Forgotten begs the question as to whether anything is ever really forgotten. Can it be? How is it possible that history—even its most distressing chapters—can be forgotten?

The author provides no modest answers to these questions. By claiming that only those closest to atrocity can never forget, Wiesel warns that dangers remain when memory lies dormant, frozen in the spirits of survivors. These dangers can be thwarted only through actively transmitting memory to posterity, and, subsequently, by translating memory into a responsible ethic. The course of history can only be altered by upholding the not-yet-forgotten in a revised vision of humanity and the world. Such an ethic presupposes and builds upon testimony.

The Forgotten stands as one of Wiesel's most poignant narratives in driving home this truth. As Elhanan relates his story, though piecemeal, to Malkiel, he bequeaths to his son not merely memory, but also a key to intercept, in however small a way, the vicious cycle of evil which has perpetuated since the events occurred. It is here that Malkiel allows himself to enter the story of his father's past by returning to the shtetl and making peace with Zoltan's widow.

According to Wiesel, the power of transmission cannot be underestimated. Not only are the dead honored,[812] but future generations are granted one last chance at redemption. As Elhanan speaks his truth, and as the past becomes real once again, Malkiel, in receiving his father's story, and in a resolute act of courage and strength, frees his father's memory from its disempowering prison and utilizes it for the cause of good. Although unable to change what is past, he can imbue memory with hope both for himself and the generations to follow. With this, the shtetl's ethic—its own not-forgotten—has been upheld, holding the potential of being preserved for posterity.

[811] Berenbaum maintains that Wiesel's intimations of the death of God do hold some affinity to Rubenstein's own; however, Wiesel's observance of tradition—even in the face of his reformulation of that tradition—remains that essential dimension which distinguishes him from Rubenstein. See Michael Berenbaum, *Elie Wiesel: God, the Holocaust, and the Children of Israel* (West Orange, NJ: Behrman House, 1994), 161-80. Boschki suggests that Wiesel implies instead the death of a "particular" God, vis., the God of his naïve, childhood faith. See Boschki, *Der Schrei*, 91.

[812] Again, Wiesel has alluded to his writing as a tombstone to the dead: "For me, writing is a *matzeva*, an invisible tombstone, erected to the memory of the dead unburied." Wiesel, *Legends of Our Time*, 8.

Hasidic Elements

a) Narrative as Legend

As is often the case with Wiesel's fiction, *The Forgotten* embraces a Hasidic legend's terse, condensed literary style.[813] The narrative, sparse on description and supplying only the most basic, formal necessities in character development, challenges the reader to attend to the novel's less obvious dimensions, particularly those engendered by the enigmatic biographies of its characters. Just as the Hasidic legend embraces deeply human stories told in minimalistic fashion, stories whose interpretations most often remain open, so too does *The Forgotten* convey a story that probes the human condition. It, too, admonishes the reader, particularly at its conclusion, to extract its central meaning or meanings. Both the work's style and form may be seen to reflect those of the Hasidic legend where minimalism, secrecy, and mystery play an important role.[814]

Indeed, within these parameters, the undertones of legend are felt most. Each of *The Forgotten*'s central characters live out some element of secrecy in their suffering: Elhanan's deepest despair in remembering the rape and his (supposed) complicity in it; the psychological confusion of his son Malkiel who is entrapped in his father's trauma without understanding how or why; the pain and yet strength of Tamar, Malkiel's lover, who is drawn to this troubled family and, ultimately, into its trauma; the mysterious Lidia, whose difficult biography is felt, but unknown; and finally, the defiled widow whose traumatization has not dissipated and whose life represents one long, unbroken attempt at survival.[815] The secrecy of the novel's characters—the gaps in their stories—contributes to the narrative's opaqueness. Even as the story concludes, and with the breaking of

---

[813] Fine echoes this position: "[Wiesel's] narrative structure is often fragmented: characterized by shifts in points of view, disjointed images, contradictory statements, and a blending of fact and fiction, of history and imagination. The effect produced is similar to the mode of the *Nouveau Roman* and, at the same time, is in keeping with the tradition of the Jewish storyteller who weaves folktales, anecdotes, and parables into the fabric of his texts, transmitting messages that are highly ambiguous." See Fine, *Legacy of Night*, 6-7.

[814] Cf. Friedman, *You Are My Witnesses*, 134-41. Wiesel himself has stressed that, even in the context of Hasidism's lively, dynamic existence, the element of silence is, in fact, of central importance. In his *Four Hasidic Masters* as well as *Somewhere a Master*, Wiesel attends to those masters whose devotion to silence had been instrumental to their dedication to the community.

[815] In his fiction, Wiesel tends to offer more insight into his male characters than into his female ones. In *The Forgotten*, the primary female characters, Malkiel's lover Tamar and his translator in Romania, Lidia, although both central to the plot, lack the depth of character development that have been provided to Elhanan and Malkiel. In other works of Wiesel, many of his female characters tend to fall into similar roles: strong, beautiful, independent—but most certainly vulnerable and wounded. Further study is warranted in examining Wiesel's inclination to portray women in this way, indeed, in his propensity to focus on male protagonists in general.

certain silences and taboos that provides each character with his or her sense—however provisional—of closure, the reader's concern for the fates of these individuals does not necessarily dissipate.

In this context, Wiesel's narrative can be understood to contain another vital dimension of legend. It retains a sense of clandestineness where ethical implications and trajectories must be discerned. In the context of developing his story through the secret lives of his characters, the author purposely leaves the story open-ended, in some sense inscrutable. Elhanan, having already announced his intention of relaying to Malkiel "one essential thing" in and through his testimony, is prevented from doing exactly that as Elhanan's memory fades for good. The reader is left in suspense, compelled to guess what that essential thing might be. This poignant omission serves to deepen the mystery of the novel.

b) Motifs

Wiesel's careful weaving of specific motifs into the narrative lends insight into his religious and cultural framework. I will isolate here a few of these to support this claim.

We find the first of these in Elhanan's opening prayer in which he, in lamenting his fate, calls upon his creator to thwart the encroaching loss of memory. With this motif of lament, he evokes the tradition of the shtetl, recalling its past and its martyrs, requesting that his bond to its dead be retained through sustained memory. He fears being cast into the realm of the dead, "the *kaf-ha-kallah*, the chasm where all life, hope and light are extinguished by oblivion."[816]

Wiesel also alludes to Hasidic folklore in referencing beliefs and superstitions surrounding death and the dead. This is particularly evident in the character of Hershel the gravedigger who explains to Malkiel that the Angel of Death's task is to remove the living from the world and cast them into the realm of the dead. The dead, in turn, protect the living, and rise from their graves after midnight to consult each other. Hershel indicates that he himself had been witness to such a consultation at the time of the Feherfalu's deportation.[817]

---

[816] Wiesel, *The Forgotten*, 10. Patterson isolates the *kaf-ha-kallah*, as referenced in the Midrash, as a realm of the afterlife in which the dead are confronted with the life they have lived, and with the fates they have endured. It is thus a place of deep regret and longing for what could have been, and a "time of reckoning." See David Patterson, "Life and Afterlife: Judaism's Contribution to the Jewish-Christian Muslim Trialogue," in *Trialogue and Terror: Judaism, Christianity, and Islam after 9/11*, ed. Alan L. Berger (Eugene OR: Cascade Books, 2012), 44.

[817] See Wiesel, *The Forgotten*, 15, 114-28. Wiesel's ongoing conversation with the dead may be indicative of his childhood belief in the activities of the dead beyond death. His entire two-volume autobiography (*All Rivers Run to the Sea* and *And the Sea is Never Full*) is framed by conversations with his dead father. In a striking passage in *And the Sea is Never Full*, Wiesel recounts seeing his father sitting in a chair just behind his son, Elisha, as he gives his Nobel Peace Prize address. See page 270. Whether or not these

Wiesel resumes his frequent mystical madness motif in Elhanan's recollection of a mysterious itinerant preacher in Feherfalu who, upon returning there after a lengthy absence, had strangely fallen strangely silent. While the community believed him to have gone mad, Elhanan queries as to whether or not his silence had somehow been "imposed."[818] This story is reminiscent of the mystic Moishe in *Night*, who returned to the shtetl as a madman-messenger following his escape from execution in 1941. This motif is one that recurs in all of Wiesel's novels.[819]

The motif of study and learning appears in the novel as well. Elhanan is consumed with nurturing his spiritual and intellectual roots. He preoccupies himself with the study of the scholarly traditions of the shtetl he once knew—from the Talmud to the Midrash, to Hasidic tales and legends. He converses with past masters, compares their schools and their teachings, and hears their answers in their texts.[820] Elhanan's focus on Rabbi Nachman in particular is reminiscent of Wiesel's penchant for this Hasidic master.[821]

Elhanan is also concerned with transmitting his memories of the shtetl and its teachings to his son.[822] Malkiel resents these efforts, and attempts to slacken his emotional dependence upon his father. He also distances himself from the tradition. Ultimately, it is Malkiel's journey to Feherfalu that provides the catalyst necessary to complete his process of individualization. Ironically, it is

---

passages are indicative of Wiesel's proclivity to the mystical notion of *gilgul*, the Kabbalistic notion of reincarnation, remains an open question.

[818] See Wiesel, *The Forgotten*, 151-54.

[819] The theme of mystical madness is addressed in his works on Hasidism, his essays as well as in his simple admission that he writes, "in order not to go mad." See Wiesel, *From the Kingdom of Memory*, 13. See Boschki's exposition on the understanding of madness in Jewish mysticism, *Der Schrei*, 169-70. Wiesel has maintained that the "madness" of the Hasidic masters drew not from clinical insanity but from their "intoxication" by God which drove them to service, community and, ultimately, to the vanquishing of evil and to the hastening of the Messiah's coming. McAfee Brown elucidates the theme of madness evidenced in a number of Wiesel's early works, where Wiesel deliberates whether madness epitomizes the state of the world following the Holocaust. See McAfee Brown, *Elie Wiesel: Messenger to All Humanity*, 74-79.

[820] Wiesel, *The Forgotten*, 74.

[821] Wiesel, *The Forgotten*, 85-86. Wiesel, in identifying himself as a Vizhnitzer Hasid in terms of his childhood upbringing, confesses his love for Rabbi Nachman, particularly in light of the Rabbi's capacity to overcome sadness in times of pain. Tellingly, in this same video, Wiesel ambiguously identifies himself as Nachman's follower, as a Breslover Hasid. See Mr. Yeshiva Guy, "Elie Wiesel on Rabbi Nachman of Breslov," welcoming remarks, posted on the internet on January 9, 2017, https://youtu.be/YJ7nWgz7bLw. No further information provided. Accessed 30 January, 2019.

[822] Wiesel, *The Forgotten*, 75-76.

exactly this process that leads him to fully embrace his father's memory and spiritual legacy.[823] The shtetl has now become a part of him, too.

c) *Hasidic Themes*

The Forgotten presents a tale that is made "accessible" to the average reader by way of its modern context. However, a closer view of the narrative through the lens of Hasidic thought permits an interpretation that reveals other, less obvious layers of the narrative. These indicate how Wiesel, either consciously or unconsciously, has been able to weave important Hasidic themes into his text. Three of these themes will be explored next.

Elhanan as the "Broken" Just Man

Elhanan's story of profound pain and trauma, his post-war life of humanism and study, as well as his desire to "put right" the things of the past, of memory—all of these may justifiably raise the question as to whether Wiesel has sketched in Elhanan a modern portrait of the Hasidic "Just Man."

While originating beyond the parameters of Hasidism, the idea of the Just Man (*tzadikim nistarim*) fills the legends of the Hasidim. Traditionally, the idea references those thirty-six Tzaddikim who, while living mystically close to God, wander the earth, seeking, by way of humility or of miracle, to alleviate suffering and transform evil into good. Corresponding to particular teachings of Hasidism, such feats constitute the elevation of the divine sparks scattered at the creation of the cosmos. In seeking the good even in that which is evil (for no place on earth is utterly devoid of the divine), the Just Man participates in those attempts at redeeming creation (*tikkun*) from its entanglement in the lowest layers of creation, where the godhead has been completely veiled.[824]

My suggestion is that Elhanan Rosenbaum's life corresponds to this profile. Following the Holocaust, Elhanan remains dedicated to alleviating human suffering. His *avoda* may be observed in his therapeutic work with Holocaust survivors as he seeks to open avenues to ease the pain of memory. At the same time, he seeks to assuage the burden of his own memory—carefully concealed but ever-present—by cultivating his spiritual tradition and by scholarly study. His *devequt* and *kavvanah* can be felt in exactly that loyalty; in his persistent cleaving to ethics, faith, and tradition—even in the face of great sorrow and painful questions.

As his *Avoda be-Gashmi'ut*—his "service to God in corporeality"—Elhanan's life of simple, earthly deeds and endeavors is reminiscent of one who has sought, however unconsciously, to diminish the power of evil present in the lower

---

[823] Before leaving Romania, Malkiel promises at his father's grave to both uphold the testimony of his father and to pass on the memory of the shtetl to his children. Wiesel, *The Forgotten,* 309-10.

[824] For more on the Hasidic understanding of the Just Man, see Hilburg, *Der Chassidismus*, 23-25.

levels of the cosmos. Elhanan is Wiesel's Just Man, a humble mystic incognito who, in his desire to create a small island of reprieve in a world that still causes him to tremble, refuses to abandon the call to humanism entrenched in the tradition in which he was raised. Although broken, Elhanan remains aware of the fact that even brokenness carries with it profound human responsibility.

Elhanan's humanism is rooted indeed in his own brokenness. We remember here his conversion from hate to love while witnessing the rape of Zoltan's widow. Strikingly, it was this devastating experience that set him out on the path to wisdom. As illness then befalls him, he wisely realizes that one more task stands yet before him: he must bear witness to the past and testify to his son.

Elhanan's testimony functions as a legend of a master whose message must be distilled, and as a tale whose transmission is needed to ensure the future of the tradition. The result is a kind of legend-within-a-legend. With Malkiel at his side, Elhanan's memory becomes part of the larger story of *The Forgotten,* with far-reaching ethical implications.

Elhanan is no miracle worker, nor must he be. He neither heals nor changes the world. However, by way of humility, courage, and faith, he sets a process into motion that has significant consequences for others. It is exactly here that we find him drawing just a little closer to setting free those divine sparks once locked into the lowest strata of creation.

Liberating the Shekhinah: The Widow of Feherfalu

In adopting these proposals, I wish to focus now on Zoltan's widow, around whose story Wiesel's tale is actually centered. My suggestion is that this unnamed woman functions in Wiesel's narrative as a metaphor for the mystical Shekhinah.

Indeed, the widow's fate echoes elements of the notion of the Shekhinah. In so far as the Shekhinah remains in exile, divorced from the godhead of which she is a part, and locked into the evil strata of the cosmos, she stands in need of liberation, of being released back into the divine.

In Wiesel's text, the widow's trauma has left her separated from any semblance of the life she could have known, a life that would have been characterized by human love, security, children, and wisdom in old age. Instead, she has remained imprisoned within the atrocity that was committed. Like the Shekhinah, she must be set free. Only her memory of the "kind man"—one could say, of the "Just Man"—has permitted her to bear the weight of the past at all. Indeed, her bond to Elhanan has continued, at great distance, for all those years.

As we have seen, Elhanan's commission to Malkiel to return to Feherfalu and seek out the widow sets into motion a series of events that transforms all those involved. Through liberating the widow from the trauma of memory, those around her are changed. This has a ripple effect; Malkiel returns to New York and, in relaying what has transpired, a final healing takes place in his relationship with both his father and his lover, Tamar. Although the "one essential thing" which Elhanan has wished to reveal remains "under lock and key" in his now-closed, inner world, the widow's catharsis causes a chain-reaction in places and persons far removed from herself.

My claim that the widow of Feherfalu functions as a metaphor for the Shekhinah in *The Forgotten* is one worthy of further consideration.

The Messiah Postponed: Forgetting the "One Essential Thing"

Just as no part of creation, even that which is evil, can be truly devoid of God, so too does Elhanan's life journey—as the journey of the Just Man—reveal traces of the divine. Through his compassion towards one whose innocence was broken in an act of vile evil, something of the divine is unveiled. In alignment with Hasidic spirituality, Elhanan's compassion, as a deed done rightly, holds the potential for saving the world.[825]

In this context, *The Forgotten* appears to contain clandestine Messianic constellations. In Hasidic spirituality, through an ethic born in *devequt*, human beings are able to hasten the Messiah's coming, and it is incumbent upon them to do so. However, according to the legends, this coming is often thwarted by small or simple acts, oversights, or omissions on the part of a human being (in the legends, most often a master or other Hasid). Redemption is thereby often postponed, awaiting that one moment when all prerequisites have been fulfilled.

A similar constellation is presented as metaphor at the conclusion of *The Forgotten*. With Elhanan's forgetting of the "one essential thing," ultimate redemption has been postponed once again; the world has been left just as vulnerable as it had been. Although some closure has been provided by the events that have taken place in Feherfalu, the world still stands in danger of repeating its past. Here, the reader is left wondering not only about what Elhanan's final message might have entailed, but also about how it might have changed those present—and the world beyond them. Might the Messiah have come? Might the path to redemption have been revealed? Wiesel leaves these vital questions open. However, by provoking his readership in this way, he exposes the urgent need to both listen and adhere to the message inherent in memory.

Although final salvation has not taken place, Wiesel's text, although revealing a dark tale, embraces the Hasidic hope that human beings, in the end, may come to fulfill their ultimate commission; that is, to live according to the laws of love and responsibility and not to those of hate and revenge.

With this, we return to the title of the novel. Might not "the forgotten" of the tale refer to Elhanan's forgotten message, that message which, though now in danger of slipping away forever, is urgently needed to liberate the world from the grip of evil?

---

[825] According to Kabbalistic thought, *tikkun* would occur when all human prerequisites were fulfilled. One could therefore never know if a particular deed might be the last one needed to usher in redemption. Cf. Dan, *Kabbalah*, 78-80; and Hilburg, *Chassidismus*, 27-29.

Relation to "Night": The Ellipse Revisited

In *The Forgotten,* Wiesel returns to the shtetl once again, this time in the person of Malkiel. Wiesel's search for the shtetl is symbolized by Malkiel's literal search for the lost Feherfalu. However, Malkiel discovers that the shtetl has been annihilated and that its memory has been desecrated by a crime committed from within—by a fellow Jew whose hunger for revenge had been insatiable. Within this setting, the themes of recovering and rehabilitating the shtetl are extended. Malkiel awakens the shtetl from its deathly sleep by finding and confronting the widow who is its last true remnant. She symbolizes the violated shtetl, which now warns of the ills implicit in hate, of the evils hidden in revenge.

The backdrop to this dramatic course of events remains the Holocaust. The shtetl must be sought always and only because of Auschwitz, in the wake of Auschwitz. With this, we see how the darkness of *Night* permeates *The Forgotten*. Again, we find that Wiesel has built upon that one foundation, that single core. In *The Forgotten,* he revisits themes and motifs present in *Night*, but from new angles through a new setting, new characters, and a new story. Night, death, the lost shtetl, the father-son dilemma, the intergenerational transfer of power, madness, memory, faith, despair—all resound throughout *The Forgotten*. And although the word "Auschwitz" is omitted in the narrative, it stands within its silent, silenced center as that primary event from which all other events unfold. The rape of the widow is subsumed by Auschwitz, too, swallowed up by it, becoming a part of that center. Auschwitz has murdered the shtetl, and the last blow of its blade was the widow's rape. We observe how *Night* functions as its core by approaching the work from these perspectives, from that of the murdered shtetl.

With this, we return once again to the model of the ellipse. I have suggested that, because memory remains the center of Wiesel's overall work, the shtetl and Auschwitz stand as the necessary focal points equidistant to that center. These are pitted powerfully against one another as each competes for control of memory; indeed, their relationship is indicative of a powerplay of immense proportions. Within this context, Wiesel's individual works function as those testimonial forms which, in drawing from memory, dynamically form the points of the ellipse's curve. According to Wiesel's viewpoint in constructing each work and the distance each work assumes with respect to the memory of either the shtetl or Auschwitz, the ellipse emerges.

How might the ellipse be constructed with respect to *The Forgotten*? This work presents us with a more difficult task. I would suggest that the novel be placed at equidistance between the shtetl and Auschwitz. We might thus sketch the ellipse in this way (see figure 10):

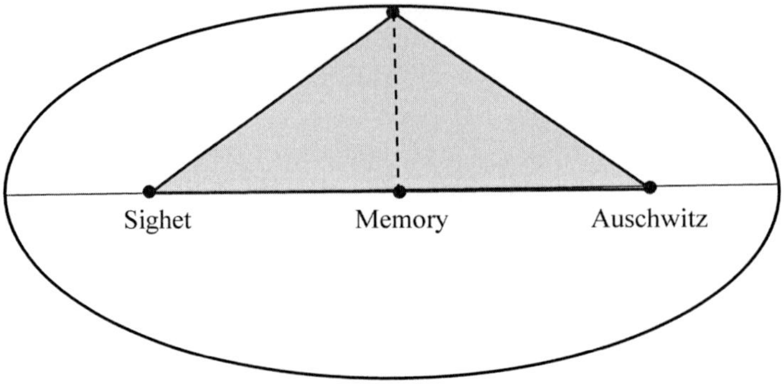

Figure 10 — Ellipse of *The Forgotten*

We see the ongoing struggle between the evil of Auschwitz and the goodness of the shtetl as *both* occurring within the sacred walls of the shtetl itself. Indeed, the rape of the widow serves to relocate Auschwitz *to* the shtetl. They merge, they conflate. The pull of the memory of both emerges as equally strong. Within these parameters, the testimony presented in the novel may be seen as hovering equidistant between the two. The battle in memory rages on as both vie for the upper hand there.

Whichever side wins the upper hand is the deciding factor between clinging to hope or succumbing to despair. Auschwitz continues to wound as its evil extends beyond the historical events in which it was created. However, the shtetl remains the place to which Wiesel is continually drawn as he searches for good in the face of evil. As such, the shtetl is for him a solid counterpoint of meaning and orientation against the chaos of Auschwitz, even as the threat of evil continues; indeed, for Wiesel, even the shtetl, sometimes strong, sometimes frail, retains its integrity and its message. [826]

---

[826] On occasion, Wiesel admits to his idealizing of the shtetl: "How does one commemorate [the death] . . . of an entire community? What must one say? How many candles should one light, how many prayers should one recite, and how many times? Perhaps someone knows the answer. I don't. I am still searching and I still do not know what one must do to keep alive the image of a town which seems more and more unreal to me each day. . . . That is why I describe and embellish it so often, and often more than it deserves. I did not know it in its ugliness but at its most exalted, as it appeared to a young Jew for whom its outlines fused with those of his imagination." See Elie Wiesel, *One Generation After*, 27. This consolidates Frunză's observations: "Within each person's memory there is a special place, a place we view as an original and authentic structure, like the Happy Isles or Paradise Lost. In religious and symbolic terms, one may say that in his books Wiesel speaks like a beloved son exiled from Paradise. . . . The hostile world in which he must live is scarred by another world, lost too soon and

Legend, Literary Field, and the Language of the Shtetl

In closing this section and this chapter, we address *The Forgotten*'s relationship to field and, concomitantly, Wiesel's use of language. Drawing on the foregoing discussion, I propose that the novel stands as both a continuation of the literary-oral tradition of Hasidism (a continuity), as well as a creative extension of it (a discontinuity). It is in this overall context that
Wiesel's innovative use of language becomes evident.

In exploring this novel, I have highlighted how Wiesel implements elements of literary style and form that present the novel as an extended Hasidic legend. I have shown how the author incorporates constructs that echo Hasidic spirituality and theology. Wiesel has woven the image of the shtetl subtly into his text, bringing to life literarily far-away people and far-away places. From this final act of care and concern, the message of the shtetl is revived once more. In light of all of this, a Hasidic reading of the text can be deemed not only tenable, but meaningful.

In a strong sense, Wiesel has set out to explore what an attempt at unveiling God might reveal. Ultimately, central characters learn, however unconsciously, to practice *devequt;* they subtly cleave to that which is divine in the world. They learn about *avoda*, a living-out of that ethic that draws one more closely into the divine. In this context, they also practice *kavvanah*, a life focused intentionally on the good existing in the world, and on God, even at the most mundane level of human existence, even as evil must inevitably be confronted. Within this overall context, the meaning of life is found in one's living out a dynamic ethic, one aimed at countering the fallout of the veiled-ness of God.

In light of all these findings, Wiesel's text can be seen as continuous with aspects of the Hasidic tradition. We can conclude that the work strongly exhibits elements of Wiesel's original field.

However, the work also and inevitably exhibits discontinuity with that field. This discontinuity is necessarily born of Auschwitz. Indeed, the tale's setting is unique with Auschwitz ever-present and ever-evil. The story emerges from another plane of human existence and experience, one that is far removed from the Besht. Themes such as human evil, human suffering, the necessity to repair the broken aspects of the cosmos, etc., are now thrust into this hitherto unknown context. They deepen and darken. They are no longer the same. Auschwitz means that nothing will ever be the same again, and that even ancient ways of knowing, understanding, and describing the world must be re-evaluated and redefined.

Ontological evil haunts the narrative; the Holocaust remains, as Wiesel has asserted, a transcendent, ontological event with no precedents.[827] In this way,

---

forever. In this context, memory and testimony become principles that nurture both the nostalgia for a lost world and its restoration in the living conscience of generations to come." See Frunză, "Elie Wiesel and Nostalgia for a Lost Paradise," 101-02.

[827] Wiesel: "The event remains unique, unlike any other product of history, it transcends history. The burden of its horror weighing upon all aspects of the human experience, it

his tale retains a dimension of separateness from those influences that have assisted in its formation.

The discontinuity with the shtetl is that which, ultimately, renders the hidden realities behind the text inaccessible to the reader. Indeed, the reader is granted no access to them. On the other hand, the text's continuity with the shtetl renders aspects of the story discernable.

This point of arrival is pivotal in concluding this study. Indeed, at the meta-level of all of Wiesel's texts, Auschwitz and the shtetl stand in stark juxtaposition. Their struggle becomes clear. In as much as this struggle remains unresolved, however, and in so far as evil continues to threaten humanity with extinction, humanity must rethink its commission. With this, a new vocabulary for old ways of being, thinking, and speaking must be sought—a language for memory powerful enough to avert further catastrophe.

For Wiesel, this language is, ironically perhaps, the language of Hasidism, of the shtetl-as-field. Although it still proves insufficient in allowing the reader access to the dark realities behind his tale, Wiesel has nonetheless chosen this language in his attempt to remember and to testify.

The emotive, evocative power of the language of the shtetl functions powerfully in all of Wiesel's tales. It does so by accessing the reader's imagination and drawing them into his stories. While continuing to keep historical realities at bay, this language still links the reader with the writer by portraying images to which the reader, in however limited a way, can relate. The most important image is that of the shtetl itself. Although the shtetl remains far away from our own experiences, its image—however idealized—does remind us of other images with which we, not only as reader, but also as human beings, have become acquainted. In fact, the shtetl is that image in the story with which we relate most of all, just as Auschwitz remains entirely *concentrationnaire*. The abyss between the two is infinite. As such, we grasp onto the shtetl as our own place of orientation and sanity in the face of a dark universe we can never know. We only learn to gauge our experience of hearing and reading testimony by orienting ourselves against the image of the shtetl, a metaphor for the good.

At the meta-level, only this metaphorical use of language allows us to enter Wiesel's text at all. Although metaphor always has limits, it does nonetheless provide its readers with some kind of knowledge—however vague, however far away from reality. With respect to the Holocaust, which is so infinitely other, it must be another kind of knowledge. My contention has been, and still is, that this knowledge is and must be *ethical* knowledge—knowledge that embraces the categorical imperative of the shtetl.

---

goes beyond everything. Auschwitz: the ultimate mystery. Impossible to enter it from the outside. . . . Treblinka: kingdom of another world, symbol of total defeat. There, man finds himself condemned, robbed of all hopes, all illusion." See Elie Wiesel, "The Christian Conscience, "Foreword to Harry James Cargas, *Shadows of Auschwitz: A Christian Response to the Holocaust* (New York: Crossroad, 1990), iii.

This ethical knowledge must be cultivated and translated into ethical awareness and human duty. In having been gleaned from the metaphor of the shtetl, it is adequate enough not only to admonish and warn but, ultimately, to effect change in the world.

With *The Forgotten*, Wiesel presents us with a highly enigmatic work. It is a work that epitomizes Wiesel's own search for the lost shtetl. His existential longing and his hope for ultimate redemption are palpable. However, he makes clear that there can be no redemption without the active involvement of humanity. This involvement is humanity's way of cleaving onto the highest good, its *devequt*; it is devotion, *kavvanah*. Ultimately, it is service, its *avoda*.

Chapter Six

God in the Shtetl: Concluding Reflections and Trajectory

Reclaiming the Shtetl in a World After Auschwitz

In this study, I have explored Wiesel's attempt to find a new language to remember the Holocaust. I have proposed that this pursuit is linked inextricably to the author's existential "search for the lost shtetl." For Wiesel, although language has been rendered lame in the wake of Auschwitz, the need to uphold the memory of Auschwitz and the shtetl in some practical, responsible way remains poignant.

Indeed, just as Wiesel is concerned that Auschwitz is not forgotten, so too is he concerned that the world of the shtetl is remembered. His writing reflects a consolidation of these two concerns in his portrayal of both the shtetl and Auschwitz as two dynamic, but conflicting entities that clash and vie for the upper hand in memory. This striking image becomes discernible in his writing through a critical reading of his texts with an eye to the Hasidic elements he has integrated there. It is by way of these Hasidic elements that Wiesel succeeds in recovering, reclaiming, and recreating the shtetl as a powerful force of goodness, a force meant not only to serve as a juxtaposition to the memory of Auschwitz—indeed, with the persisting, relentless evil of Auschwitz—but also to temper ongoing anguish and despair. In this search to recover and reclaim Sighet, a movement towards hope arises, even in the presence of broken faith,

It is within this context that I have established my two-fold thesis. By exploring how Wiesel's texts, in exhibiting Hasidic influences, recreate the shtetl literarily, I have shown how this image rises to oppose Auschwitz in memory in what might be considered a cosmic struggle meant to determine the fate of the world.

Ultimately, the shtetl serves as the point of departure of Wiesel's writing. This is evidenced in particular in *Night;* Sighet prefaces all that will follow, providing as such the interpretive parameters—in this case, parameters of faith—of his Auschwitz experience. With *Night* serving as the center of the oeuvre, we are then able to observe how both Sighet and Auschwitz dominate all of his post-Auschwitz memory.

Wiesel rises from the ashes of Auschwitz as a Hasidic storyteller par excellence. However, as Benjamin suggests, storytelling consists not of reiterating legends of the past, but rather of recreating them in the present through memory.[828] And, as the Jewish tradition emphasizes, memory itself is about "making real in the present what was real in the past." [829]

In this attempt to make real and recreate, the teller's life and influences shine through; as such, the story told succeeds in revealing as much about the teller as it does about its subject matter. Wiesel has indeed told stories in ways that embrace the religious heritage and spiritual legacy that are his own. His stories invoke ancient times and more recent times, times of joy and faith, as well as times of atrocity and ensuing existential doubt. In this sense, he has indeed become the Maggid of Sighet.

Literary Representation of the Holocaust: New Perspectives

As we have seen, Wiesel, as so many others have done, takes issue with post-Holocaust language. In the anguish of memory, silence is his preferred response. However, in light of the dangers inherent in the present moment and in all of the evil that has followed Auschwitz, he remains aware that something *must* be said. However cautiously, Wiesel again and again makes the decision to embrace language and literature as his medium for memory.

This task has undoubtedly proven to be daunting. If Adorno is right, Auschwitz has invalidated all artistic expression; indeed, poetry becomes obscene in the face of genocide. Should one dare to temper Adorno's dictum, however, which Wiesel arguably appears, however tacitly, to have done, the tasks of speaking, narrating, and writing become acts carrying with them unparalleled responsibility. The result is the need for a responsible ethic of literature and language within whose parameters one might dare address atrocity at all.

Wiesel remains mindful of the ethics involved in the combined effort of remembering and narrating. Consciously aware that what needs to be said cannot be said, he opts to tell stories that relay complex images that circle about that one dark, inaccessible center. Although poignant and powerful, these images will always remain incapable of transmitting the "realities" of Auschwitz. The path to the past is barricaded to all who have not already walked it.

No, language is not enough. And it will always be insufficient to say what really needs to be said. Language will always veil that which it desires most to

[828] Benjamin writes: "In fact, one can go on and ask oneself whether the relationship of the storyteller to his material, human life, is not in itself a craftsman's relationship, whether it is not his very task to fashion the raw material of experience, his own and that of others, in a solid, useful, and unique way. It is a kind of procedure which may perhaps most adequately be exemplified by the proverb if one thinks of it as an ideogram of a story. A proverb, one might say, is a ruin which stands on the site of an old story and in which a moral twines about a happening like ivy around a wall." See Benjamin, "The Storyteller," in *Illuminations*, 108.

[829] I attribute the expression to Rev. Dr. Timothy R. Ashley, as recalled from his lecture series "Introduction to the Hebrew Bible" at Acadia University, Fall Semester, 1988.

portray. Still, it remains the most immediate, everyday medium we can use in attempting to express things—even those things we cannot.

What, then, are these images that Wiesel that supplies? How do they function and what can they mean? These questions have directed, at least in part, this study. My suggestions have relied upon aspects of the theory of literary field and narrative theory. Although these are theoretical constructs, both function as thoroughly practical guides not only in thinking through what it means, very generally, for us to be-in-the-world, but also in considering how our specific social context and formative influences might affect our ways of being-in-the-world. Literature—indeed, all art forms—are indicative of these ways of being; our concerns for the meaning of literature and what it intends to express are crucial. This is all the more reason for this maxim to be applied to literature of the Holocaust.

The theory of literary field has lent shape to this study by offering a new lens through which to read Wiesel. Through my exploration of the history of Hasidism, Hasidic spirituality, the rise of the shtetl, and the emergence of the literary image of the shtetl as one of strong symbolic power in the Jewish world, I have established Hasidism as field. The larger field of Hasidism finds its microcosm in Sighet, which I have designated as shtetl-as-field. *Night* gives evidence of how the shtetl provided the young Wiesel with the capital necessary to fulfill his future role as storyteller. In having been provided with a very specific framework for interpreting life and the world around him, Wiesel came to experience Auschwitz within this framework, which is to say, within the parameters of faith. Much later, in remembering Auschwitz, these parameters would also impact how he narrated his experiences. Put differently, the way that Wiesel experienced Auschwitz at the time helped to form how he remembered, interpreted, and, ultimately, wrote about it much later. *Night*, above all, evidences this dynamic process. My analysis of this process leans on Young's theory of narration and literary representation.

The shtetl thus comes to assume a powerful and determining role in Wiesel's narratives. It emerges as a vital literary image with unique staying power in confronting the evils of Auschwitz. For the reader, this confrontation is a literary one; for Wiesel, it is existential, psychological, spiritual, ontological—in a sense, *real*.

Identifying the discrepancy between the literary and the real is important; it assists in discerning better the core problems surrounding literary representation. In addition to—indeed, in conjunction with—the most basic problem of expressing what is inexpressible, literary representation is concerned with the matter of bridging the gulf between reader and writer.

In precisely this context, Young's theories continue to be helpful. In my investigation of three other works by Wiesel, I have highlighted how the shtetl-as-field has continued to form and inform his ongoing narration process. In *Dawn*, by integrating a variety of Hasidic legends and mythical figures into his text, the author has narrated a dark confrontation between the goodness of the shtetl and the universe of evil. However, while the dead of the shtetl display their concern and have a message to relay, the power of Auschwitz is still strong.

In *Four Hasidic Masters*, Wiesel's existential search for the shtetl becomes poignant. The author seeks the past by taking to task traditional Hasidic legends, and by retelling and reinterpreting them as a survivor. In so doing, he seeks a balm for his wound. There, past masters become his own, which is to say, they become his guides, his comforters, indeed, fellow witnesses for life—just as if they, too, had known the camps.

In *The Forgotten*, Wiesel seeks the lost shtetl anew. Indeed, the motif of seeking emerges as that which drives the thrust of the plot. Ultimately, the shtetl is found through the cathartic encounters of its primary characters. A remnant of hope is offered, even in the face of unspeakable loss. Hasidic themes deepen the text, resounding the shtetl's appeal to abhor hate and revenge and seek reconciliation and new paths to peace. The shtetl emerges as that metaphor to which the reader can relate in terms of its juxtaposition to Auschwitz and the acute ethical awareness that this juxtaposition generates. While this metaphor can relay no real knowledge of Auschwitz, the categorical imperative that emerges from it is strong enough to provide direction in a post-Holocaust world.

In conclusion, the transliteration and integration of Hasidic themes, legends, motifs, and images assist Wiesel in representing literarily his own existential confrontation with evil. These Hasidic elements move us. Taken together, they serve to link us as readers to Wiesel as writer. They stand together as Wiesel's medium, as his way of reaching out to us. Indeed, they converge to form the very fabric of testimony; in so doing, they constitute that which permits us, in however limited a way, to access testimony at all. Although we cannot enter the darkest realities he portrays, testimony does affect us. It activates our imagination. It upsets, it disturbs, it enrages and, ultimately, it demands from us an ethical response. It is in this overall sense that the metaphor of the shtetl, in particular, reaches us. Although incapable of making real all that lies behind it, it is visceral and evocative, eliciting from us reactions that challenge us to "go out and change the world." With this, we discover that we have come to witness the witness, and in so doing, discover we have possibly become, as Fine has suggested, witnesses ourselves.[830]

Trajectory: From Broken Vessels to the Restoration of the World

Combatting Collective Evil: Life Within the Ellipse

In the legend of "The Exchange", both God and humanity have, post-Auschwitz, renewed their "ancient dialogue." At its heart, this dialogue is about humanity resuming its ethical responsibilities on the stage of its own, yet-unfolding drama.

---

[830] See Fine, *Legacy of Night*, 9.

Wiesel's writings are testament to both his acute struggle against despair, as well as his attempt to warn humanity of its inherent evil. In light of my exploration of several of his texts, I would like to propose a model of human duty, one based on the ellipse I have sketched in my own encounter with Wiesel's texts. I reference this model with the phrase: "Life within the ellipse."

Although the ellipse is a conceptual construct intended to portray strains of tension in Wiesel's thought, it can also be understood as symbolizing the very real, historical phenomena of his experiences and as mirroring his dynamic narration process. We can also understand the ellipse as symbolizing the very same power dynamic at work in the legend of "The Exchange"; humanity, in possessing absolute power, has the possibility of either granting and nurturing life, or of destroying it.

Should my sketches of the ellipse prove reasonable, we might begin to consider what life lived between both focal points could look like. My suggestion embraces aspects of what Abraham Joshua Heschel has called "elliptic thinking"[831] and what Irving Greenberg has termed "dialectical thinking and living."[832]

With these two notions, Heschel and Greenberg are concerned with the idea of *polarity*. Heschel explains his understanding of polarity by comparing it to the phenomena of philosophy of religion. There, as both theology and philosophy encounter one another, a dialogue ensues in which one becomes informative of the other. Heschel writes:

> Philosophy of religion is involved in a polarity; like an ellipse it revolves around two foci: philosophy and religion. Except for two points on the curve that stand in equal distance to both foci, the more closely its thought comes to one, the more distant it is from the other one. The failure to sense the profound tension of philosophical and theological categories has been the cause of much confusion.
>
> The unique situation of being exposed to two different powers, to two competing sources of understanding, is one that must not be abandoned. It is precisely that tension, that elliptic thinking which is a source of enrichment to both philosophy and religion.[833]

---

831 Abraham Joshua Heschel, *God in Search of Man: A Philosophy of Judaism*, second edition (New York: Farrar, Straus and Giroux, 1983) 12-13.

832 See Irving Greenberg, "Dialectical Living and Thinking: Wiesel as Storyteller and Interpreter of the Shoah" in *Elie Wiesel: Jewish, Literary and Moral Perspectives*, 173-189.

833 Heschel, *God in Search of Man*, 13.

For Greenberg, Wiesel's writings exhibit polarity as he presents Sighet and the Holocaust as opposing paradigms. First, Greenberg identifies Sighet as the paradigm of Jewish redemption and existence. He writes:

> Wiesel, as a teacher, offers his own understanding of the impact of the Shoah on the classic Jewish paradigm of Exodus and redemption. Before the Holocaust, Wiesel lived in Sighet in accordance with that classical Jewish paradigm. In that universe, however, life was of infinite value; human beings were meant to be free and would be redeemed; ultimately, all was well with the world, and suffering was really a deviation.[834]

The Holocaust, Greenberg indicates, shattered this classical paradigm as would a "sledgehammer,"[835] calling forth a second paradigm, one of infinite death, murder, and atrocity.

Greenberg suggests that the presence of these two, diametrically opposed paradigms results in several deeply-entrenched contradictions in Wiesel's thought. With respect to these paradigms and contradictions, Greenberg considers Wiesel a touchstone for human responsibility; ultimately, they serve to make clearer humanity's duty to combat evil—even when the temptation to succumb to madness can be so strong. Indeed:

> Madness is an appropriate protest and a form of truth telling in response to these evil phenomena. But as an overall policy or policy guide, madness constitutes an evasion of responsibility and loss of hope, which leads to a victory for evil. Reason and responsibility must be upheld—although they are often inadequate to the crisis.[836]

Should this observation be accurate, Wiesel's dialectical living and thinking entails living dutifully within all of the existential tensions left by the Holocaust. These tensions, however, are *necessary* if humanity is to survive at all. Although they come at a cost, they incite the acute sense of duty that is needed:

> There is another element that makes this dialectical tension necessary. . . . Living in these tensions—rather than resolving them—is to live in constant angst. One can never come to rest or complacency or neutrality—because the pull of the two sides is continuous and never relaxes. This means that the people who live these tensions experience a constant unease—which carries

[834] Greenberg, "Dialectical Living and Thinking," 179.
[835] Greenberg, "Dialectical Living and Thinking," 179.
[836] Greenberg, "Dialectical Living and Thinking," 184.

> with it awareness and a pang of mourning for those who were lost. This mourning is not necessarily expressed in overt grief or in articulated sentimentality of loss. Rather it is reflected in an absence of tranquility and in permanent heightened moral awareness. Therefore, this dialectical tension is in itself a powerful ritual of memory (more powerful in that it is hidden).[837]

If we consolidate Greenberg's with Heschel's claims, we discover that dialectical living and thinking are, at one and the same time, elliptic living and thinking. Memory, although traumatized by the evil of Auschwitz, still draws from the paradigm of redemption found in the shtetl. Within the ellipse, in the face of existential fragmentation, some sense of moral orientation can be acquired once again. However anguished, this sense is enough for one to continue with a provisional hope and with the "heightened moral awareness" that must be cultivated and nurtured through remembering and bearing witness.

Within the context of these tensions, within this deep, lasting dialectic, language emerges as a tension and a paradox in its own right.[838] For Wiesel, bearing witness does not necessarily relay the "full story of the Holocaust."[839] Life lived within the ellipse, however, constitutes both not-forgetting Auschwitz and remembering the shtetl. Both Auschwitz and the shtetl are constituent parts of memory, and the polarity of these, the tensions engendered by these, are what makes life so difficult. Be that as it may, as it is a morally-focused life, and even in the face of the loss of meaning, it can be lived meaningfully.

Only this kind of life has the possibility of combatting, on any level at all, collective evil. Elliptic thinking and living is to think and live dutifully in the embrace of memory.

A Cautious Hope

Wiesel's life represents a life lived at the edge of his field. By retelling and reinterpreting Hasidic tales and legends; by addressing Hasidic themes in modern settings, plots, and characters; and by weaving his powerful image of the shtetl tacitly into his narratives, he has succeeded in transliterating the universal message of the shtetl. He has used language that provokes and evokes. With this, he emerges as a Hasidic storyteller in the garb of post-modernism.

For Wiesel, however, ancient images of breaking vessels and restoring the world in *tikkun* are not fairy tale pictures intended to act as moral reminders. Much more, they correspond to the realities of human existence and to all of the unseen realities of the cosmos. Brokenness is not abstract for Wiesel, but concrete

[837] Greenberg, "Dialectical Living and Thinking," 185.
[838] See Greenberg, "Dialectical Living and Thinking," 185-86.
[839] Greenberg, "Dialectical Living and Thinking," 186.

and real. Restoring the world is about evoking change in the real world, in the world as we know it. Only by remembering and continuing to bear witness and living in relation to these can humanity find its way out of the complex labyrinth of collective evil.

Wiesel insists on the uniqueness and the universality of the Holocaust. It is universal, he has said, exactly because it was uniquely Jewish. The Jewish hope, the hope that was tested in the crucible of Auschwitz, emerges as a cautious hope. For readers of Wiesel, the image of the shtetl embodies that hope. Although the shtetl cannot be resuscitated nor its dead resurrected, they can be *remembered*, and it is in the act of remembering that their message can be reclaimed.

Beyond Auschwitz, our "knowledge of the Holocaust" can *only* be the ethical awareness evoked by the message of the shtetl. As the voice of the shtetl, Wiesel's voice has contributed to the collective memory of humanity—and seared its collective conscience. That this has exposed him to both praise and critique is unsurprising. His voice stands inevitably in danger of being over-heard, dismissed, or—ironically—forgotten. Be that as it may, as an admixture of hope, despair, and his incessant *ani ma'amin*, his voice still invites change and renewal—at the feet of the dead and in honor of their memory.

Bibliography

Selected Bibliography of Elie Wiesel

Wiesel, Elie. *Adam oder das Geheimnis des Anfangs. Legenden und Porträts.* Translated by Hanns Bücker. Freiburg i. B.: Herder, 1980.

———. *Against Silence: The Voice and Vision of Elie Wiesel.* Edited by Irving Abrahamson. 3 vols. New York: Holocaust Library, 1985.

———. *All Rivers Run to the Sea: Memoirs Volume One, 1928-1969.* London: Harper Collins Publishers, 1997.

———. *And the Sea Is Never Full: Memoirs, 1969-.* Translated by Marion Wiesel. New York: Alfred A. Knopf: 1999.

———. *Ani Maamin: A Song Lost and Found Again.* Music for the cantata composed by Darius Milhaud. Translated by Marion Wiesel. New York: Random House, 1973.

———. *A Beggar in Jerusalem.* New York: Random House, 1970.

———. "The Christian Conscience." Foreword to *Shadows of Auschwitz: A Christian Response to the Holocaust*, by Harry James Cargas. New York: Crossroad, 1990.

———. *The Fifth Son.* Translated by Marion Wiesel. New York: Schocken Books, 1985.

———. *The Forgotten.* Translated by Stephen Becker. New York: Schocken Books, 1992.

———. *Four Hasidic Masters and their Struggle Against Melancholy.* Notre Dame, IN: University of Notre Dame Press, 1978.

———. *Den Frieden Feiern.* Edited by Reinhold Boschert-Kimmig. Freiburg i. B.: Herder, 1991.

———. *From Holocaust to Rebirth*. New York: The Council of Jewish Federations and Welfare Funds, 1970.

———. *From the Kingdom of Memory: Reminiscences*. New York: Schocken Books, 1990.

———. *The Gates of the Forest*. Translated by Frances Frenaye. New York: Schocken Books, 1982.

———. *The Golem: The Story of a Legend*. Illustrated by Mark Podwal. Translated by Anne Borchardt. New York: Summit Books, 1983.

———. "The Holocaust as Literary Inspiration." In *Dimensions of the Holocaust: Lectures at Northwestern University*, by Elie Wiesel, Lucy S. Dawidowicz, Dorothy Rabinowitz and Robert McAfee Brown, 5-19. Evanston, IL: Northwestern University Press, 1977.

———. *A Jew Today*. Translated by Marion Wiesel. New York: Random House, 1978.

———. *The Jews of Silence: A Personal Report on Soviet Jewry*. Translated by Neal Kozodoy. 2nd ed., with a new introduction by the author. New York: Schocken Books, 2011.

———. *Legends of Our Time*. New York: Schocken Books, 1982.

———. *Macht Gebete aus meinen Geschichten. Essays eines Betroffenen*. Translated by Hanns Bücker and Ursula Schottelius. Freiburg i. B.: Herder, 1986.

———. *A Mad Desire to Dance*. Translated by Catherine Temerson. New York: Schocken Books, 2009.

———. "The Madmen of Sighet: A Story." *Commentary* (May 1968): 38-41.

———. *Messengers of God: Biblical Portraits and Legends*. Translated by Marion Wiesel. New York: Random House, 1976.

———. *Night*. Translated by Stella Rodway. New York: Hill and Wang, 1960.

———. *The Night Trilogy: Night, Dawn, Day.* Translated by Marion Wiesel. New York: Hill and Wang, 2008.

———. *La Nuit*. With a preface by François Mauriac. Paris: Les Editions Minuit, 1958.

———. *The Oath*. Translated by Marion Wiesel. New York: Random House, 1973.

———. *One Generation After*. Translated by Lily Edelman and Elie Wiesel. New York: Schocken Books, 2011.

______. *Open Heart*. Translated by Marion Wiesel. New York: Alfred A. Knopf, 2012.

———. "Prologue." In *God, Faith & Identity from the Ashes: Reflections of Children and Grandchildren of Holocaust Survivors*, edited by Menachem Z. Rosensaft, xv-xvii. Woodstock, VT: Jewish Lights Publishing, 2015.

———. *Rashi: A Portrait*. New York: Nextbook, 2009.

———. *Sages and Dreamers: Biblical, Talmudic, and Hasidic Portraits and Legends*. New York: Summit Books, 1991.

———. *Somewhere a Master: Further Hasidic Portraits and Legends*. Translated by Marion Wiesel. New York: Summit Books, 1982.

———. *Souls on Fire: Portraits and Legends of Hasidic Masters*. Translated by Marion Wiesel. New York: Simon and Schuster Paperbacks, 1972.

______. *Souls on Fire: Portraits and Legends of Hasidic Masters*. Translated by Marion Wiesel. Northvale: Jason Aronson, 1993.

———. "Talking and Writing and Keeping Silent." In *The German Struggle and the Holocaust*, edited by Franklin H. Littell and Hubert G. Locke, 269-77. Detroit: Wayne State University Press, 1974.

———. *The Testament*. Translated by Marion Wiesel. New York: Summit Books, 1981.

———. *The Time of the Uprooted*. Translated by David Hapgood. New York: Alfred A. Knopf, 2005.

———. *The Town Behind the Wall*. Translated by Stephan Becker. 2nd edition. New York: Holt, Rinehart and Winston, 1967.

———. *The Trial of God (as it was held on February 25, 1649, in Shamgorod): A Play in Three Acts*. Translated by Marion Wiesel. New York: Random House: 1979.

———. *Twilight*. Translated by Marion Wiesel. London: Penguin Books, 2013.

______. "The World of the Shtetl." In *The Shtetl: New Evaluations*, edited by Steven T. Katz, 290-306. New York: New York University Press, 2007.

———. *Zalmen, or The Madness of God*. Based on a translation from the French by Nathan Edelman. Adapted for the stage by Marion Wiesel. New York: Random House, 1975.

———. "Zum Geleit: Kultur allein ist nicht genug." In *Kultur allein ist nicht genug. Das Werk von Elie Wiesel—Herausforderung für Religion und Gesellschaft,* edited by Reinhold Boschki and Dagmar Mensink, with Britta Frede, 38-42. Religion – Geschichte – Gesellschaft. Fundamentaltheologische Studien Band 10. Münster: LIT Verlag, 1998.

———, and Richard D. Heffner. *Conversations with Elie Wiesel*. Edited by Thomas J. Vinciguerra. New York: Schocken Books, 2003.

———, and Albert H. Friedlander. *The Six Days of Destruction: Meditations Towards Hope*. Oxford: Pergamon Press, 1988.

Secondary Sources Bibliography

Abrahamson, Irving, ed. *Against Silence: The Voice and Vision of Elie Wiesel*. 3 vols. New York: Holocaust Library, 1985.

———. "Introductory Essay." In *Against Silence: The Voice and Vision of Elie Wiesel*, 7-74.

Abramowitz, Molly. *Elie Wiesel: A Bibliography*. Metuchen, NJ: Scarecrow Press, 1974.

Abromeit, John. *Max Horkheimer and the Foundations of the Frankfurt School*. Cambridge: Cambridge University Press, 2011.

Adler, Eliyana R., and Sheila E. Jelen, eds. *Jewish Literature and History: An Interdisciplinary Conversation*. Bethesda, MD: University Press of Maryland, 2008.

Adorno, Theodor W. *Aesthetic Theory*. Edited by Gretel Adorno and Rolf Tiedemann. Translated by C. Lenhardt. London: Routledge and Kegan Paul, 1984.

———. *Ästhetische Theorie*. Frankfurt am Main: Suhrkamp, 1973.

———. "Cultural Criticism and Society." In *Prisms*, translated by Samuel and Shierry Weber, 17-34. London: Neville Spearman, 1967.

———. "Kulturkritik und Gesellschaft," in *Gesammelte Schriften*. Edited by Rolf Tiedemann. Band 10.1: *Kulturkritik und Gesellschaft I. Prismen. Ohne Leitbild*. Frankfurt am Main: Suhrkamp Verlag, 1977.

———. *Minima Moralia: Reflections from Damaged Life*. Translated by E. F. N. Jephcott. London: Verso, 1978.

———. *Negative Dialectics*. Translated by E. B. Ashton. New York: Continuum, 1973.

———. *Negative Dialektik. Jargon der Eigentlichkeit*. Edited by Rolf Tiedemann. Frankfurt am Main: Suhrkamp Verlag, 1973.

———. *Prisms*. Translated by Samuel and Shierry Weber. London: Neville Spearman, 1967.

———, and Max Horkheimer. *Dialektik der Aufklärung. Philosophische Fragmente.* Frankfurt am Main: Fischer, 1969.

Agamben, Giorgio. *Was von Auschwitz bleibt. Das Archiv und der Zeuge.* Translated by Stefan Monhardt. Frankfurt am Main: Suhrkamp, 2003.

Aleichem, Sholem. *Tevye the Dairyman and the Railroad Stories*. New York: Schocken Books, 1987.

Allison, Alexander W., Herbert Barrows, Caesar R. Blake, Arthur J. Carr, Arthur M. Eastman, Hubert M. English, Jr., eds. *The Norton Anthology of Poetry.* 3rd shorter ed. New York: W.W. Norton, 1970.

Améry, Jean. *At the Mind's Limits: Contemplations by a Survivor on Auschwitz and its Realities*. Translated by Sidney Rosenfeld and Stella P. Rosenfeld. Bloomington: Indiana University Press, 1980.

———. *Jenseits von Schuld und Sühne: Bewältigungsversuche eines Überwältigten*. Munich: Szczesny Klett-Cotta, 1966.

Arendt, Hannah. *Eichmann in Jerusalem. Ein Bericht von der Banalität des Bösen*. Munich: Piper Verlag, 2013.

———. *The Origins of Totalitarianism*. New York: Harcourt, Brace and World, 1951.

Arnold, Heinz Ludwig. *Die Gruppe 47*. Reinbek: Rowohlt, 2004.

Ascarelli, Roberta, and Klaus Davidowicz, eds. *Along the Road to Esau: Studies on Jakob Frank and Frankism*. Arezzo: Bibliotheca Aretina, 2011.

Aschheim, Steven E. *Brothers and Strangers: The East European Jew in German Jewish Consciousness, 1800-1923*. Madison: The University of Wisconsin Press, 1982.

Assaf, David. *Untold Tales of the Hasidim: Crisis and Discontent in the History of Hasidism*. Translated by Dena Ordan. Waltham, MA: Brandeis University Press, 2010.

Assmann, Aleida. *Erinnerungsräume. Formen und Wandlungen des kulturellen Gedächtnisses.* Munich: C. H. Beck, 1999.

———. *Der lange Schatten der Vergangenheit. Erinnerungskultur und Geschichtspolitik*. Munich: C. H. Beck, 2014.

______. *Das neue Unbehagen an der Erinnerungskultur. Eine Intervention*. Munich: C. H. Beck, 2013.

———, and Jan Assmann, eds. *Schweigen.* Archäologie der literarischen Kommunikation 11. Munich: Wilhelm Fink, 2013.

———, and Sebastian Conrad, eds. *Memory in a Global Age: Discourses, Practices and Trajectories*. Basingstoke: Palgrave Macmillan, 2010.

———, and Ute Frevert. *Geschichtsvergessenheit—Geschichtsversessenheit. Vom Umgang mit deutschen Vergangenheiten nach 1945.* Stuttgart: Deutsche Verlags-Anstalt, 1999.

———, and Linda Shortt, eds. *Memory and Political Change*. Basingstoke: Palgrave Macmillan, 2012.

Assmann, Jan. *Das kulturelle Gedächtnis. Schrift, Erinnerung und politische Identität in frühen Hochkulturen*. Munich: C. H. Beck, 1992.

Atkins, Stephen E. *Holocaust Denial as an International Movement*. Westport, CT: Praeger, 2009.

Baasner, Rainer, and Maria Zens, *Methoden und Modelle der Literaturwissenschaft. Eine Einführung*. 3rd edition. Berlin: Erich Schmidt Verlag, 2005.

Bachmann, Michael. *Der Abwesende Zeuge. Autorisierungsstrategien in Darstellungen der Shoah*. Tübingen: Francke Verlag, 2010.

Band, Arnold J. "Agnon's Synthetic Shtetl." In *The Shtetl: New Evaluations,* edited by Steven T. Katz, 233-42. New York: New York University Press, 2007.

Barboric, Antonia. *Der Holocaust in der literarischen Erinnerung. Autobiographische Aufzeichnungen von Udo Dietmar und Elie Wiesel*. Vienna: Böhlau Verlag, 2014.

Barnouw, David. *Das Phänomen Anne Frank*. Translated by Simone Schroth. Essen: Klartext Verlag, 2015.

Bartlett, Steven James. *The Pathology of Man: A Study of Human Evil*. Springfield, IL: Charles C. Thomas, 2005.

Battenberg, Friedrich. *Das europäische Zeitalter der Juden. Zur Entwicklung einer Minderheit in der nichtjüdischen Umwelt Europas.* Vol. 2, *Von 1650 bis 1945.* 2nd ed. Darmstadt: Wissenschaftliche Buchgesellschaft, 2000.

Bauer, Yehuda. *The Death of the Shtetl*. New Haven, CT: Yale University Press, 2009.

Ben-Chorin, Schalom, and Verena Lenzen, eds. *Lust an der Erkenntnis. Jüdische Theologie im 20. Jahrhundert. Ein Lesebuch*. Munich: Piper, 1988.

Benjamin, Walter. *Illuminations: Essays and Reflections*. Edited and an introduction by Hannah Arendt. Translated by Harry Zohn. New York: Schocken Books, 1968.

———. "The Storyteller." In Walter Benjamin, *Illuminations: Essays and Reflections*, edited and with an introduction by Hannah Arendt, and translated by Harry Zohn, 83-109. New York: Schocken Books, 1968.

Benz, Wolfgang, ed. *Lexikon des Holocaust*. Munich: C. H. Beck, 2002.

Berenbaum, Michael. "The Additional Covenant." In *Confronting the Holocaust: The Impact of Elie Wiesel*, edited by Alvin H. Rosenfeld and Irving Greenberg, 169-85. Bloomington, IN: Indiana University Press, 1978.

———. *Elie Wiesel: God, the Holocaust, and the Children of Israel*. West Orange, NJ: Behrman House, 1994.

———. *The Vision of the Void: Theological Reflections on the Works of Elie Wiesel*. Middletown, CT: Wesleyan University Press, 1979.

Berg, Nicolas. *Luftmenschen. Zur Geschichte einer Metapher*. Göttingen: Vandenhoeck & Ruprecht, 2008.

Berger, Alan L. "Transfusing Memory: Second-Generation Postmemory in Elie Wiesel's *The Forgotten.*" In *Obliged by Memory: Literature, Religion, Ethics; A Collection of Essays Honoring Elie Wiesel's Seventieth Birthday,* edited by Steven T. Katz and Alan Rosen, 117-28. Syracuse, NY: Syracuse University Press, 2006.

———, ed. *Trialogue and Terror: Judaism, Christianity, and Islam after 9/11*. Eugene, OR: Cascade Books, 2012.

Berger, Joel. "Spuren und Elemente jüdischer Volkskultur in den Werken Elie Wiesels." In *Kultur allein ist nicht genug. Das Werk von Elie Wiesel—Herausforderung für Religion und Gesellschaft,* edited by Reinhold Boschki and Dagmar Mensink, with Britta Frede, 181-89. Religion – Geschichte – Gesellschaft. Fundamentaltheologische Studien Band 10. Münster: LIT Verlag, 1998.

Berger, Peter L. *The Sacred Canopy: Elements of a Sociological Theory of Religion*. New York: Anchor Books, 1990.

———, and Thomas Luckmann. *The Social Construction of Reality: A Treatise in the Sociology of Knowledge*. New York: Anchor Books, 1967.

Bormuth, Matthias, and Susan Nurmi-Schomers, eds. *Kritik aus Passion. Studien zu Jean Améry*. Göttingen: Wallstein Verlag, 2005.

Boschki, Reinhold. "Heimweh nach Sighet. Einführung in die literarische Welt Wiesels." In *Das Gegenteil von Gleichgültigkeit ist Erinnerung. Versuche zu Elie Wiesel,* edited by Dagmar Mensink and Reinhold Boschki, 38-64. Mainz: Matthias Grünewald Verlag, 1995.

———. "Reden und Schweigen sind unmöglich. Das Werk Elie Wiesels als Beitrag zu einer Kultur der Erinnerung." In *Das Judentum kann nicht definiert werden. Beträge zur jüdischen Geschichte und Kultur,* edited by Reinhold Boschki and René Buchholz, 253-272. Forum Christen und Juden 11. Berlin: LIT Verlag, 2014.

———. *Der Schrei. Gott und Mensch im Werk von Elie Wiesel.* With a foreword by Elie Wiesel. Mainz: Matthias Grünewald Verlag, 1995.

———. "Towards an Ethics of Remembrance after the Shoah." In *Celebrating Elie Wiesel: Stories, Essays, Reflection*s, edited by Alan Rosen, 203-22. Notre Dame, IN: University of Notre Dame Press, 1998.

______. "*Die Zeit der Entwurzelten*. Zur Aktualität und bleibenden Bedeutung des Werks von Elie Wiesel." *Zeitschrift für Jüdisch-Christliche Begegnung im Kontext*, 1/2 (2017), 17-24.

———. "Zum Autor: Elie Wiesel im Spiegel seiner Autobiographien." In *Kultur allein ist nicht genug. Das Werk von Elie Wiesel—Herausforderung für Religion und Gesellschaft,* edited by Reinhold Boschki and Dagmar Mensink, with Britta Frede, 22-37. Religion – Geschichte – Gesellschaft. Fundamentaltheologische Studien Band 10. Münster: LIT Verlag, 1998

.

———, and René Buchholz, eds. *Das Judentum kann nicht definiert werden. Beiträge zur jüdischen Geschichte und Kultur*. Forum Christen und Juden 11. Berlin: LIT Verlag, 2014.

———, and Dagmar Mensink, eds. *Kultur allein ist nicht genug. Das Werk von Elie Wiesel— Herausforderung für Religion und Gesellschaft*, with Britta Frede. Religion – Geschichte – Gesellschaft. Fundamentaltheologische Studien Band 10. Münster: LIT Verlag, 1998.

Bourdieu, Pierre. "Champ de pouvoir, champ intellectuel et habitus de classe." *Scolies,* no. 1 (1971): 7-26.

———. *Entwurf einer Theorie der Praxis auf der ethnologischen Grundlage der kabylischen Gesellschaft*. Translated by Cordula Pialoux and Bernd Schwibs. Frankfurt am Main: Suhrkamp, 1976.

———. *Outline of a Theory of Practice*. Translated by Richard Nice. Cambridge: Cambridge University Press, 1977.

———. *Les règles de l'art. Genèse et structure du champ littéraire*. Paris: Éditions du Seuil, 1992

.

———. *Das Religiöse Feld. Texte zur Ökonomie des Heilgeschehens*. Edited by Stephan Egger, Andreas Pfeuffer, and Franz Schultheis, and translated by Andreas Pfeuffer. Constance: UVK Universitätsverlag Konstanz, 2000.

———. *The Rules of Art: Genesis and Structure of the Literary Field.* Translated by Susan Emanuel. Cambridge: Polity Press, 1996. Reprint. Cambridge: Polity Press, 2017.

———. *Sozialer Sinn. Kritik der theoretischen Vernunft*. Translated by Günter Seib. Frankfurt am Main: Suhrkamp, 1987.

Braese, Stephan, and Holger Gehle. "Literaturwissenschaft und Literaturgeschichte nach dem Holocaust." In *Literatur und Holocaust*, Heft 144, edited by Heinz Ludwig Arnold, 79-95. Munich: Edition Text & Kritik, 1999.

Brenner, Reeve Robert. *The Faith and Doubt of Holocaust Survivors*. New Brunswick, NJ: Transaction Publishers, 2014.

Bright, John. *A History of Israel*. 3rd edition. Philadelphia: Westminster Press, 1981.

Brocke, Michael, and Herbert Jochum, eds. *Wolkensäule und Feuerschein. Jüdische Theologie des Holocaust*. Translated by Gaetano Hassdenteufel and Michael Brocke. Munich: Kaiser Taschenbücher, 1993.

Buber, Martin. *Deutung des Chassidismus. Drei Versuche*. Bücherei des Schocken Verlags 43. Berlin: Schocken, 1935.

———. *Die Erzählungen der Chassidim*. Zurich: Manesse Verlag, 1949.

———. *Hasidism and Modern Man*. Edited and translated by Maurice Friedman, and with a new introduction by David Biale. Princeton: Princeton University Press, 2016.

———. *Mein Weg zum Chassidismus. Erinnerungen*. Frankfurt am Main: Rütten & Loening, 1918.

———. *Schriften zum Chassidismus*. Munich: Kösel, 1963.

———. *Tales of the Hasidim*. Translated by Olga Marx. 2 vols. New York: Schocken, 1947-48.

———. *Der Weg des Menschen nach der chassidischen Lehre*. Gütersloh: Güterloher Verlagshaus, 2014.

Cargas, Harry James. *Harry James Cargas in Conversation with Elie Wiesel*. New York: Paulist Press, 1976.

———. "An Interview with Elie Wiesel." *Holocaust and Genocide Studies* 1, no. 1 (1986): 5-10.

———, ed. *Responses to Elie Wiesel*. New York: Persea Books, 1978.

Celan, Paul. *Die Gedichte. Kommentierte Gesamtausgabe in einem Band.* Edited with comments by Barbara Wiedemann. Frankfurt am Main: Suhrkamp Taschenbuch, 2012.

Chicago, Judy, with photographs by Donald Woodman. *The Holocaust Project: From Darkness into Light*. New York: Penguin Paperbacks, 1993.

Conermann, Stephan, and Jim Rheingans, eds. *Narrative Pattern and Genre in Hagiographic Life Writing: Comparative Perspectives from Asia to Europe.* Narratio Aliena? Studien des Bonner Zentrums für Transkulturelle Narratologie 7. Berlin: EB-Verlag, 2014.

Dalferth, Ingolf U., Karl Kardinal Lehmann, and Navid Kermani. *Das Böse. Drei Annäherungen.* Freiburg i. B.: Herder, 2011.

Dan, Joseph. *Kabbalah: A Very Short Introduction.* New York: Oxford University Press, 2007.

———. "Hasidic Tales." In *Encyclopedia of Jewish Folklore and Traditions*, edited by Raphael Patai and Haya Bar-Itzhak, vol. 1, 232-33. Armonk, NY: Sharpe, 2013.

Dauber, Jeremy. *The Worlds of Sholem Aleichem*. New York: Nextbook, 2013.

Davidowicz, Klaus S. *Gershom Scholem und Martin Buber. Die Geschichte eines Missverständnisses*. Neukirchener theologische Dissertationen und Habilitationen 5. Neukirchen-Vluyn: Neukirchener, 1995.

Davis, Colin. *Elie Wiesel's Secretive Texts*. Gainesville: University of Florida Press, 1994.

Dicker, Herman. *Piety and Perseverance: Jews from the Carpathian Mountains*. With a foreword by Elie Wiesel. New York: Sepher-Herman Press, 1981.

Dietrich, Walter, and Christian Link. *Die Dunklen Seiten Gottes. Willkür und Gewalt*. 2nd edition. Neukirchen-Vluyn: Neukirchener Verlag, 1997.

Diner, Dan, ed. *Zivilisationsbruch. Denken nach Auschwitz.* Frankfurt am Main: Fischer, 1988.

Dinur, Benzion. "The Origins of Hasidism and Its Social and Messianic Foundations." In *Essential Papers on Hasidism. Origins to Present*, edited by Gershon David Hundert, 86-208. New York: New York University Press, 1991.

Dössekker, Bruno. *Bruchstücke. Aus einer Kindheit 1939-1948.* Frankfurt: Jüdischer Verlag, 1995.

Dosse, François. *Geschichte des Strukturalismus*. Unabridged ed. 2 vols. Frankfurt am Main: Fischer-Taschenbuch-Verlag, 1999.

Downing, Frederick L. *Elie Wiesel: A Religious Biography*. Macon, GA: Mercer University Press, 2008.

Dubnow, Simon. *Geschichte des Chassidismus. In zwei Bänden.* Translated by A. Steinberg. Berlin: Jüdischer Verlag, 1931. Reprint, Jerusalem: Jewish Publishing House, 1969.

Dynner, Glenn, ed. *Holy Dissent: Jewish and Christian Mystics in Eastern Europe*. Detroit: Wayne State University Press, 2011.

———. *Men of Silk: The Hasidic Conquest of Polish Jewry, 1754-1830.* Vol. 1. Facsimile. Ann Arbor, MI.: UMI, 2002.

Eaglestone, Robert. *Holocaust and the Postmodern*. Oxford: Oxford University Press, 2004.

Eagleton, Terry. *Literary Theory: An Introduction*. Minneapolis, MN: University of Minnesota Press, 1983.

Eaton, Henry. *The Origins and Onset of the Romanian Holocaust*. Detroit: Wayne State University Press, 2013.

Elior, Rachel. *The Mystical Origins of Hasidism*. Oxford: The Littman Library of Jewish Civilization, 2006.

Ellis, Marc H. *Encountering the Jewish Future: With Elie Wiesel, Martin Buber, Abraham Joshua Heschel, Hannah Arendt, Emmanuel Levinas*. Minneapolis: Fortress Press, 2011.

Estraikh, Gennady, Jordan Finkin, Kerstin Hoge, and Mikhail Krutikov, eds. *Translating Sholem Aleichem: History, Politics and Art*. London: Legenda, 2012.

———. and Mikhail Krutikov. *The Shtetl: Image and Reality; Papers of the Second Mendel Friedman International Conference on Yiddish*. Oxford: European Humanities Research Centre, 2000.

Etkes, Immanuel. *The Besht: Magician, Mystic, and Leader*. Translated by Saadya Sternberg. Waltham, MA: Brandeis University Press, 2005.

Ettinger, Schmuel. *Geschichte des jüdischen Volkes*. Vol. 3, *Vom 17. Jahrhundert bis zur Gegenwart. Die Neuzeit.* Edited by Haim Hillel Ben-Sasson. Translated by Christian Spiel. Munich: C. H. Beck, 1980.

———. "The Hassidic Movement—Reality and Ideals." In *Essential Papers on Hasidism: Origins to Present*, edited by Gershon David Hundert, 226-43. New York: New York University Press, 1991.

Even-Chen, Alexander. "Abraham Joshua Heschel's Pre- and Post-Holocaust Approach to Hasidism." *Modern Judaism* 34, no. 2 (May 2014): 139-166.

Eylon, Dina Ripsman. *Reincarnation in Jewish Mysticism and Gnosticism.* Jewish Studies, vol. 25. Lewiston, NY: Edwin Mellen Press, 2003

.

Ezrahi, Sidra DeKoven. *By Words Alone: The Holocaust in Literature*. Chicago: University of Chicago Press, 1980.

Fackenheim, Emil L. "Midrashic Existence after the Holocaust: Reflections Occasioned by the Work of Elie Wiesel." In *Confronting the Holocaust: The Impact of Elie Wiesel*, edited by Alvin H. Rosenfeld and Irving Greenberg, 99-116. Bloomington, IN: Indiana University Press, 1978.

Feinberg, Anat. "Das Unbeschreibliche beschreiben: Literarische Annäherungen an den Holocaust." In *Kultur allein ist nicht genug. Das Werk von Elie Wiesel—Herausforderung für Religion und Gesellschaft,* edited by Reinhold Boschki and Dagmar Mensink, with Britta Frede, 47-57. Religion – Geschichte – Gesellschaft. Fundamentaltheologische Studien Band 10. Münster: LIT Verlag, 1998.

Felman, Shoshana, and Dori Laub, *Testimony: Crises of Witnessing in Literature, Psychoanalysis, and History*. New York: Routledge, 1992.

Felstiner, John. *Paul Celan: Poet, Survivor, Jew*. New Haven, CT: Yale University Press, 1995.

Feuchert, Sascha, ed. *Holocaust-Literatur. Auschwitz.* Arbeitstexte für den Unterricht. Für die Sekondarstufe 1. Stuttgart: P. Reclam jun, 2000.

Fiero, Petra S. *Schreiben gegen Schweigen. Grenzerfahrungen in Jean Amérys autobiographischem Werk.* Haskala Band 16. Hildesheim: Georg Olms Verlag, 1997.

Fine, Ellen S. "Fathers and Sons." In *Readings on Night,* edited by Wendy Mass, 98-107. The Greenhaven Press Literary Companion to World Literature. San Diego: Greenhaven Press, 2000.

———. *Legacy of Night: The Literary Universe of Elie Wiesel.* Albany, NY: State University of New York Press, 1982.

Flanzbaum, Hilene, ed. *The Americanization of the Holocaust.* Baltimore, MD: Johns Hopkins University Press, 1999.

———. "The Imaginary Jew and the American Poet." In *The Americanization of the Holocaust*, 18-32.

———. "Introduction." In *The Americanization of the Holocaust*, 1-17.

Fober, Magdalena, *Identität und Wissen in ausgewählten Werken Elie Wiesels und William Styrons. (Wissens-)Grenzen des Selbst.* Frankfurt: Peter Lang Edition, 2017.

Foucault, Michel. *Archeology of Knowledge and the Discourse on Language.* Translated by A. M. Sheridan Smith. New York: Pantheon Books, 1972.

Fowler, Bridget. *Pierre Bourdieu and Cultural Theory: Critical Investigations.* London: Sage, 1997.

Frank, Anne. *Diary of a Young Girl.* Translated by B. M. Mooyaart-Doubleday. Garden City, NY: Doubleday, 1952.

———. *Gesamtausgabe. Tagebücher – Geschichten und Ereignisse aus dem Hinterhaus – Erzählungen – Briefe – Fotos und Dokumente.* Edited by Anne Frank Fonds, Basel. Translated by Mirjam Pressler. Frankfurt: S. Fischer Verlag, 2013.

Franklin, Ruth. *A Thousand Darknesses: Lies and Truth in Holocaust Fiction.* Oxford: Oxford University Press, 2011.

Frei, Norbert. *Vergangenheitspolitik. Die Anfänge der Bundesrepublik und die NS-Vergangenheit*. Munich: C. H. Beck, 1996.

Friedman, Maurice. *Abraham Joshua Heschel and Elie Wiesel: You Are My Witnesses*. New York: Farrar, Straus, Giroux, 1987.

Fröhlich, Gerhard, and Boike Rehbein, eds. *Bourdieu Handbuch. Leben–Werk–Wirkung*. Stuttgart: J.B. Metzler Verlag, 2009.

Frunză, Sandu. "Elie Wiesel and Nostalgia for a Lost Paradise." *Transylvanian Review* XVIII, no. 2 (Summer 2009), 101-105.

———. "Ethics, Religion and Memory in Elie Wiesel's *Night*." *Journal for the Study of Religions and Ideologies* 9, no. 26 (Summer 2010): 94-113.

Gehring, Doris. *Die Holocaust Autobiographien als Speicher der Erinnerung im Wandel der Erinnerungskultur. Eine Analyse des Erinnerungsdiskurses anhand autobiographischer Texte von Thomas Geve, Elie Wiesel, Inge Deutschkron, Ruth Klüger, Binjamin Wilkomirski und als Vergleichsfall Wolfgang Koeppen mit der Bearbeitung von Jakob Littners: 'Mein Weg durch die Nacht.'* Master's thesis. University of Bern, December 2010.

Gesenius, William. *Hebrew and English Lexicon of the Old Testament with an Appendix Containing the Biblical Aramaic.* Translated by Edward Robinson. Oxford: Clarendon Press, 1906. Reprint. Oxford University Press, 1951.

Geve, Thomas. *Guns & Barbed Wire: A Child Survives the Holocaust*. Chicago: Academy Chicago Publishers, 1987.

———. *Youth in Chains*. Jerusalem: Rubin Mass, 1958.

Giersch, Paula, Florian Krobb, and Franziska Schössler, eds. *Galizien im Diskurs. Inklusion, Exklusion, Repräsentation.* Inklusion/Exklusion. Studien zu Fremdheit und Armut von der Antike bis zur Gegenwart. Band 17. Frankfurt am Main: Peter Lang Internationaler Verlag der Wissenschaften, 2012.

Görg, Manfred, and Michael Langer, eds. *Als Gott weinte. Theologie nach Auschwitz*. Regensburg: Verlag Friedrich Pustet, 1997.

Gorsky, Jonathan. "Elie Wiesel, Hasidism and the Hiddenness of God." *New Blackfriars* 85, no. 996 (March 2004): 133-43.

Graver, Lawrence. *An Obsession with Anne Frank: Meyer Levin and the Diary*. Berkeley: University of California Press, 1995.

Green, Arthur. "Wiesel in the Context of Neo-Hasidim." In *Elie Wiesel: Jewish, Literary, and Moral Perspectives,* edited by Steven T. Katz and Alan Rosen, 51-58. Bloomington: Indiana University Press, 2013.

Greenberg, Gershon. "The Hasidic Spark and the Holocaust." In *Elie Wiesel: Jewish, Literary, and Moral Perspectives*, edited by Steven T. Katz and Alan Rosen, 83-99. Bloomington: Indiana University Press, 2013.

Greenberg, Irving. "Dialectical Living and Thinking: Wiesel as Storyteller and Interpreter of the Shoah." In *Elie Wiesel: Jewish, Literary and Moral Perspectives*, edited by Steven T. Katz and Alan Rosen, 173-189. Bloomington: Indiana University Press, 2013.

Greenspan, Henry. "Imagining Survivors: Testimony and the Rise of Holocaust Consciousness." In *The Americanization of the Holocaust,* edited by Hilene Flanzbaum, 45-67. Baltimore, MD: Johns Hopkins University Press, 1999.

Grözinger, Karl Erich. *Jüdisches Denken. Theologie – Philosophie – Mystik*. Vol. 2. *Von der mittelalterlichen Kabbala zum Chassidismus*. Frankfurt: Campus Verlag, 2005.

Gutthy, Agnieszka, ed. *Exile and the Narrative/Poetic Imagination*. Newcastle upon Tyne: Cambridge Scholars Publishing, 2010.

Habermas, Jürgen. *Philosophisch-politische Profile*. Expanded edition. Frankfurt: Suhrkamp, 1987.

Halbwachs, Maurice. *On Collective Memory*. Edited, translated, and with an introduction by Lewis A. Coser. Chicago: University of Chicago Press, 1992.

———. *La mémoire collective*. Paris: Presses universitaires de France, 1950.

Halperin, Irving. "Loss of Innocence." In *Elie Wiesel: Readings on Night*, edited by Wendy Mass, 30-35. The Greenhaven Press Literary Companion Series. San Diego: Greenhaven Press, 2000.

Hamaoui, Lea. "Historical Horror and the Shape of *Night*." In *Elie Wiesel: Between Memory and Hope*, edited by Carol Rittner, 120-29. New York: New York University Press, 1990.

Haumann, Heiko. *Geschichte der Ostjuden*. Munich: Deutscher Taschenbuch Verlag, 1990.

Hawkins, Joyce M., and Robert Allen, eds. *The Oxford Encyclopedic English Dictionary*. Oxford: Clarendon Press, 1991.

Heschel, Abraham Joshua. *Die Erde ist des Herrn. Die innere Welt des Juden in Osteuropa*. Translated by Ruth Olmesdahl and illustrated by Otto Axer. Neukirchen-Vluyn: Neukirchener Verlag, 1985.

———. *God in Search of Man: A Philosophy of Judaism*. New York: Farrar, Straus and Giroux, 1983.

Heinsohn, Gunnar. *Lexikon der Völkermorde*. Reinbek bei Hamburg: Rowohlt Verlag, 1998.

Herlitz, Georg, and Bruno Kirschner, eds. *Jüdisches Lexikon. Ein enzyklopädisches Handbuch des jüdischen Wissens*. Vol. 1. Berlin: Jüdischer Verlag, 1927.

Die Heilige Schrift des Alten und Neuen Testaments. Die in Zürich kirchlich eingeführte Übersetzung aufs neue nach dem Grundtext berichtigt. Im Auftrag der zürcherischen Kirchensynode herausgegeben vom Kirchenrat des Kantons Zürich. Zurich: Reutimann & Co. 1934.

Hilburg, Erwin K. J. *Der Chassidismus*. Germania Judaica 7:2/3. Cologne: Germania Judaica, 1968.

Hoffman, Eva. *Shtetl: The Life and Death of a Small Town and the World of Polish Jews*. London: Secker and Warburg, 1998.

The Holy Bible Containing the Old and New Testaments with the Apocryphal/Deuterocanonical Books: New Revised Standard Version. Nashville, TN: Thomas Nelson Publishers, 1989.

Horowitz, Rosemary. "Creative Ambiguity in Wiesel's Storytelling." In *Elie Wiesel and the Art of Storytelling*, edited by Rosemary Horowitz, 38-56. Jefferson, NC: McFarland and Company, 2006.

———, ed. *Elie Wiesel and the Art of Storytelling*. Jefferson, NC: McFarland and Company, 2006.

———. "Introduction," in *Elie Wiesel and the Art of Storytelling*, edited by Rosemary Horowitz, 3-14. Jefferson, NC: McFarland and Company, 2006.

How, Alan. *Critical Theory.* Basingstoke: Palgrave MacMillan, 2003.

Hundert, Gershon David, ed. *Essential Papers on Hasidism: Origins to Present*. New York: New York University Press, 1991.

Hutner, Yitzchok. "Bürde der Erwählung." In *Wolkensäule und Feuerschein. Jüdische Theologie des Holocaust*, edited by Michael Brocke and Herbert Jochum, and translated by Gaetano Hassdenteufel and Michael Brocke, 27-42. Munich: Kaiser Taschenbücher, 1993.

Idel, Moshe. *Hasidism: Between Ecstasy and Magic*. Albany, NY: State University of New York Press, 1995.

Jaiser, Constanze. "Die Zeugnisliteratur von Überlebenden der deutschen Konzentrationslager seit 1945." In *Die Shoah in der deutschsprachigen Literatur*, edited by Norbert Otto Eke and Hartmut Steinecke, 107-34. Berlin: Erich Schmidt Verlag, 2006.

James, William. *The Varieties of Religious Experience*. Cambridge, MA: Harvard University Press, 1985.

———. "The Will to Believe." In *The Will to Believe and Other Essays in Popular Philosophy*. Vol. 6, *The Works of William James*, edited by Frederick H. Burkhardt, Fredson Bowers, and Ignas K. Skrupskelis, 13-33. Cambridge, MA: Harvard University Press, 1979.

Jonas, Hans. *Der Gottesbegriff nach Auschwitz. Eine jüdische Stimme*. Frankfurt: Suhrkamp Taschenbuch Verlag, 1987.

Jurt, Joseph. "Die Theorie des literarischen Feldes von Pierre Bourdieu." *LiTheS, Zeitschrift für Literatur- und Theatersoziologie* (Universität Graz), no. 1 (December 2008): 5-14.

Kahn, Lily. *A Grammar of the Eastern European Hasidic Hebrew Tale*. Studies in Semitic Languages and Linguistics. Vol. 77. Leiden: Brill, 2015.

Kahn, Lothar. *Mirrors of the Jewish Mind: A Gallery of Portraits of European Jewish Writers of Our Time.* New York: Thomas Yoseloff, 1968.

Kaplan, Dana Evan, ed. *The Cambridge Companion to American Judaism*. Cambridge: Cambridge University Press, 2005.

Katz, Steven T., and Alan Rosen, eds. *Elie Wiesel: Jewish, Literary, and Moral Perspectives.* Bloomington: Indiana University Press, 2013.

______. "Reflections on Wiesel's Hasidic Tales" in *Elie Wiesel: Jewish, Literary, and Moral Perspectives*, edited by Steven T. Katz and Alan Rosen, 59-68. Bloomington: Indiana University Press, 2013.

———, ed. *The Shtetl: New Evaluations*. New York: New York University Press, 2007.

———, Shlomo Biderman, and Gershon Greenberg, eds. *Wrestling with God: Jewish Theological Responses During and After the Holocaust*. Oxford: Oxford University Press, 2007.

———, and Alan Rosen, eds. *Obliged by Memory: Literature, Religion, Ethics: A Collection of Essays Honoring Elie Wiesel's Seventieth Birthday.* Syracuse, NY: Syracuse University Press, 2006.

Kiedaisch, Petra, ed. *Lyrik nach Auschwitz? Adorno und die Dichter*. Stuttgart: Reclam, 1995.

Klaghofer-Treitler, Wolfgang. *Die Fragen der Toten. Elias Canetti, Jean Améry, Elie Wiesel*. Mainz: Matthias Grünewald Verlag, 2004.

Klarer, Mario. *Einführung in die Grundlagen der Literaturwissenschaft. Theorien, Gattungen, Arbeitstechniken.* Darmstadt: Wissenschaftliche Buchgesellschaft, 2011.

Kleine, Marc. *Ob es überhaupt noch möglich ist. Literatur nach Auschwitz in Adornos ästhetischer Theorie*. Bielefeld: Aisthesis, 2012.

Klier, John Doyle. "What Exactly is a Shtetl?" In *The Shtetl: Image and Reality; Papers of the Second Mendel Friedman International Conference on Yiddish*, edited by Gennady Estraikh and Mikhail Krutikov, 23-35. Oxford: Legenda, European Humanities Research Centre, 2000.

Korte, Hermann. "'Es ist in aller Trauer der tiefste Hang zur Sprachlosigkeit.' Der Holocaust in der Lyrik nach 1945." In *Literatur und Holocaust*, Heft 144, edited by Heinz Ludwig Arnold, 25-47. Munich: Edition Text & Kritik, 1999.

Körtner, Ulrich H. J. *Wie lange noch, wie lange? Über das Böse, Leid und Tod.* Neukirchen-Vluyn: Neukirchener Verlag, 1998.

Kramer, Sven. *Die Folter in der Literatur. Ihre Darstellung in der deutschsprachigen Erzählprosa von 1740 bis "nach Auschwitz."* Munich: Wilhelm Fink Verlag, 2004.

Kremer, S. Lillian. *Witness Through the Imagination: Jewish-American Holocaust Literature: Ozick, Elman, Cohen, Potok, Singer, Epstein, Bellow, Steiner, Wallant, Malamud.* Detroit: Wayne State University Press, 1989.

Lamping, Dieter, ed. *Dein aschenes Haar Sulamith. Dichtung über den Holocaust*. Munich: Piper 1992.

Lane, Jeremy F., *Pierre Bourdieu: A Critical Introduction.* London: Pluto Press, 2000.

Langer, Jiri Mordechai. *Die Neun Tore. Geheimnisse der Chassidim*. Edited by Andreas B. Kilchner. Translated by Kristina Kallert. Wuppertal: Arco Verlag, 2013

.

Langer, Lawrence L. *The Holocaust and the Literary Imagination*. New Haven: Yale University Press, 1975.

———. *Holocaust Testimonies: The Ruins of Memory*. New Haven: Yale University Press, 1991.

———. "Whose Testimony? The Confusion of Fiction with Fact." In *Elie Wiesel: Jewish, Literary, and Moral Perspectives*, edited by Steven T. Katz and Alan Rosen, 201-210. Bloomington: Indiana University Press, 2013.

Langer, Phil C. *Schreiben gegen die Erinnerung? Autobiographien von Überlebenden der Shoah.* Hamburg: Krämer, 2002.

Lanzmann, Claude. "The Twisted Truth of Schindler's List." *London Evening Standard,* February 10, 1994.

Laub, Dori, "Bearing Witness, or the Vicissitudes of Listening." In *Testimony: Crises of Witnessing in Literature, Psychoanalysis, and History*, by Shoshana Felman and Dori Laub, 57-74. New York: Routledge, 1992.

———. "An Event Without a Witness." In *Testimony: Crises of Witnessing in Literature, Psychoanalysis, and History*, by Shoshana Felman and Dori Laub, 75-92. New York: Routledge, 1992.

Lenzen, Verena. *Jüdisches Leben und Sterben im Namen Gottes. Studien über die Heiligung des göttlichen Namens (Kiddusch HaSchem)*. Munich: Piper, 1995.

———. "Reden ist schwer, Schweigen unmöglich." (Elie Wiesel) "Sprache und Schweigen im Schatten der Schoah," in *Kultur allein ist nicht genug. Das Werk von Elie Wiesel— Herausforderung für Religion und Gesellschaft,* edited by Reinhold Boschki and Dagmar Mensink, with Britta Frede, 58-71. Religion – Geschichte – Gesellschaft. Fundamentaltheologische Studien Band 10. Münster: LIT Verlag, 1998.

Levi, Primo. *If This is a Man* and *The Truce*. Translated by Stuart Woolf. London: Abacus, 1987.

———. *The Drowned and the Saved*. Translated by Raymond Rosenthal. New York: Summit Books, 1988.

Levinas, Emmanuel. *Humanism of the Other*. Translated by Nidra Poller. Chicago: University of Illinois Press, 2003.

Littell, Franklin H., and Hubert G. Locke eds. *The German Struggle and the Holocaust*. Detroit: Wayne State University Press, 1974.

Lyman, Rick. "Elie Wiesel's Only Son Steps Up to His Father's Legacy." *New York Times*, May 12, 2017.

Maciejko, Pawel, ed. *Sabbatian Heresy*: *Writings on Mysticism, Messianism, and the Origins of Jewish Modernity*. Waltham, MA: Brandeis University Press, 2017.

Magilow, Daniel H., and Lisa Silverman. *Holocaust Representations in History: An Introduction*. London: Bloomsbury Academic, 2015.

Mahler, Raphael, *Hasidism and the Jewish Enlightenment: Their Confrontation in Galicia and Poland in the First Half of the Nineteenth-Century*. Translated by Aaron Klein, Jenny Machlowitz-Klein, and Eugene Orenstein. Philadelphia: The Jewish Publication Society of America, 1985.

Martin, Elaine. *Nelly Sachs: The Poetics of Silence and the Limits of Representation*. Berlin: de Gruyter, 2011.

Marrus, Michael R. *Lessons of the Holocaust*. Toronto: University of Toronto Press, 2016.

Mass, Wendy, ed. *Readings on Night*. The Greenhaven Press Literary Companion to World Literature. San Diego: Greenhaven Press, 2000.

Maybaum, Ignaz. "Der dritte *Churban*." In *Wolkensäule und Feuerschein. Jüdische Theologie des Holocaust*, edited by Michael Brocke and Herbert Jochu, and translated by Gaetano Hassdenteufel and Michael Brocke, 9-19. Munich: Kaiser Taschenbücher, 1993.

McAfee Brown, Robert. *Elie Wiesel: Messenger to All Humanity*. Notre Dame, IN: University of Notre Dame Press, 1983.

Mead, George Herbert. *Mind, Self, and Society: From the Standpoint of a Social Behaviorist*. Edited by Charles W. Morris. 9th impression. Chicago: Chicago University Press, 1952.

Mensink, Dagmar. "Erinnerung ist das Gegenteil von Gleichgültigkeit." In *Das Gegenteil von Gleichgültigkeit ist Erinnerung. Versuche zu Elie Wiesel*, edited by Dagmar Mensink and Reinhold Boschki, 148-71. Mainz: Matthias Grünewald Verlag, 1995.

———. "Zur Einführung: Elie Wiesel lesen." In *Kultur allein ist nicht genug. Das Werk von Elie Wiesel—Herausforderung für Religion und Gesellschaft,* edited by Reinhold Boschki and Dagmar Mensink, in cooperation with Britta Frede, 13-21. Religion – Geschichte – Gesellschaft. Fundamentaltheologische Studien Band 10. Münster: LIT Verlag, 1998.

———, and Reinhold Boschki, eds. *Das Gegenteil von Gleichgültigkeit ist Erinnerung. Versuche zu Elie Wiesel*. Mainz: Matthias Grünewald Verlag, 1995.

Mintz, Jerome R. *Legends of the Hasidim: An Introduction to Hasidic Culture and Oral Tradition in the New World*. Chicago: University of Chicago Press, 1968.

Miron, Dan. *The Image of the Shtetl and Other Studies of Modern Jewish Literary Imagination*. Syracuse, NY: Syracuse University Press, 2000.

Morgan, Michael L. *Beyond Auschwitz: Post-Holocaust Thought in America*. New York: Oxford University Press, 2001.

Moses, Stéphane. "Eingedenken und Jetztzeit. Geschichtliches Bewusstsein im Spätwerk Walter Benjamins." In *Memoria—vergessen und erinnern*, edited by Anselm Haverkamp and Renate Lachmann, with Reinhart Herzog, 385-405. Munich: Wilhelm Fink, 1993.

MrYeshivaGuy, "Elie Wiesel on Rabbi Nachman of Breslov." Welcoming remarks. Posted on the internet on January 9, 2017. https://youtu.be/YJ7nWgz7bLw. No further information provided.

Müller, Jan-Werner, ed. *Memory and Power in Post-War Europe: Studies in the Presence of the Past*. Cambridge: Cambridge University Press, 2002.

Münz, Christoph. *Der Welt ein Gedächtnis geben. Geschichtstheologisches Denken im Judentum nach Auschwitz*. Gütersloh: Ch. Kaiser, 1995.

Nathans, Benjamin, and Gabriella Safran, eds. *Culture Front: Representing Jews in Eastern Europe*. Philadelphia: University of Pennsylvania Press, 2008.

Nath, Kirsten. "The Function of Madness in Elie Wiesel's Works." Seminar paper, University of Hamburg. Ebook: GRIN Verlag, 2013.

Neher, André. *L'Exile de la parole. Du silence biblique au silence d'Auschwitz*. Paris: Editions du Seuil, 1970.

———. *The Exile of the Word: From the Silence of the Bible to the Silence of Auschwitz*. Translated by David Maisel. Philadelphia: The Jewish Publication Society of America, 1981.

Nigal, Gedalyah. *The Hasidic Tale*. Translated by Edward Levin. Oxford: The Littman Library of Jewish Civilization, 2008.

———. *Magic, Mysticism, and Hasidism: The Supernatural in Jewish Thought*. Translated by Edward Levin. Northvale, NJ: Jason Aronson, 1994.

Ofer, Dalia, Francoise S. Ouzan, and Judy Tydor Baumel-Schwarz, eds. *Holocaust Survivors: Resettlement, Memories, Identities.* New York: Berghahn Books, 2012.

Ogren, Brian. *Renaissance and Rebirth: Reincarnation in Early Modern Italian Kabbalah.* Studies in Jewish History and Culture. Vol. 24. Leiden: Brill, 2009.

Ong, Walter J. *Orality and Literature: The Technologizing of the Word*. London: Methuen, 1982.

Oppenheim, Michael. *Encounters of Consequence: Jewish Philosophy in the Twentieth-Century and Beyond*. Brighton: Academic Studies Press, 2009.

Ozick, Cynthia. "Afterword." In *Celebrating Elie Wiesel: Stories, Essays, Reflections*, edited by Alan Rosen, 335-37. Notre Dame, IN: University of Notre Dame Press, 1998.

Patai, Raphael, founding ed. and Haya Bar-Itzhak, ed. *Encyclopedia of Jewish Folklore and Traditions*. 2 vols. Armonk, NY: Sharpe, 2013.

Patterson, David. "Life and Afterlife: Judaism's Contribution to the Jewish-Christian Muslim Trialogue." In *Trialogue and Terror: Judaism, Christianity, and Islam after 9/11*, edited by Alan L. Berger, 37-50. Eugene, OR: Cascade Books, 2012.

———. "The *Maggid* of Sighet: Jewish Contexts for Wiesel's Storytelling." In *Elie Wiesel and the Art of Storytelling*, edited by Rosemary Horowitz, 102-122. Jefferson, NC: McFarland and Company, 2006.

Pethes, Nicolas. *Kulturwissenschaftliche Gedächtnistheorien. Zur Einführung*. Hamburg: Junius Verlag, 2013.

Petrovsky-Shtern, Yohanan. *The Golden Age Shtetl: A New History of Jewish Life in East Europe*. Princeton: Princeton University Press, 2014.

Polen, Nehemia. "Yearning for Sacred Place: Wiesel's Hasidic Tales and Postwar Hasidism." In *Elie Wiesel: Jewish, Literary, and Moral Perspectives*, edited by Steven T. Katz and Alan Rosen, 69-82. Bloomington: Indiana University Press, 2013.

Pourshirazi, Katja. *Martin Bubers literarisches Werk zum Chassidismus. Eine textlinguistische Analyse*. Frankfurt: Lang, 2008.

Rabinowicz, Harry M. *Hasidism: The Movement and its Masters*. Northvale, NJ: Jason Aronson, 1988.

Radstone, Susannah. "Trauma Theory: Contexts, Politics, Ethics." *Paragraph* 30, no. 1 (2007): 9-29.

Reichel, Peter. *Erfundene Erinnerung. Weltkrieg und Judenmord in Film und Theater*. Frankfurt: Fischer Taschenbuch Verlag, 2007.

Reiter, Andrea. "*Auf dass sie entsteigen der Dunkelheit." Die literarische Bewältigung von KZ-Erfahrung.* Wien: Löcker Verlag, 1995.

The Revised English Bible with the Apocrypha. Oxford and Cambridge: Oxford University Press and Cambridge University Press, 1989.

Ricoeur, Paul. *History and Truth*. Translated by Charles A. Kelbley. New edition. Evanston, IL: Northwestern University Press, 2007.

Rippl, Gabriele, Philipp Schweighauser, Tiina Kirss, Margit Sutrop, and Therese Steffen, eds. *Haunted Narratives: Life Writing in an Age of Trauma*. Toronto: University of Toronto Press, 2013.

Rittner, Carol, ed. *Elie Wiesel: Between Memory and Hope*. New York: New York University Press, 1990.

Robbins, Derek, ed. *Pierre Bourdieu*. Vol. 2. London: SAGE Publications, 2000.

Rosen, Alan, ed. *Celebrating Elie Wiesel: Stories, Essays, Reflection*s. Notre Dame, IN: University of Notre Dame Press, 1998.

———, ed. *Literature of the Holocaust*. Cambridge: Cambridge University Press, 2013.

Rosenfeld, Alvin H. "The Americanization of the Holocaust." *Commentary* 99, no. 6 (June 1995): 35-40.

———. *A Double Dying: Reflections on Holocaust Literature*. Bloomington: Indiana University Press, 1980.

———. *The End of the Holocaust*. Bloomington: Indiana University Press, 2011.

———. "The Problematics of Holocaust Literature." In Alvin H. Rosenfeld and Irving Greenberg, eds. *Confronting the Holocaust: The Impact of Elie Wiesel*, 1-30. Bloomington, IN: Indiana University Press, 1978.

———, and Irving Greenberg. *Confronting the Holocaust: The Impact of Elie Wiesel*. Bloomington, IN: Indiana University Press, 1978.

Rosensaft, Menachem Z., ed. *God, Faith & Identity from the Ashes: Reflections of Children and Grandchildren of Holocaust Survivors*. With a Prologue by Elie Wiesel. Woodstock, VT: Jewish Lights Publishing, 2015.

Roskies, David G. "Yiddish Storytelling and the Politics of Rescue." In *Jewish Literature and History: An Interdisciplinary Conversation*, edited by Eliyana R. Adler and Sheila E. Jelen, 15-32. Bethesda, MD: University Press of Maryland, 2008.

Roth, John K. *A Consuming Fire: Encounters with Elie Wiesel and the Holocaust*. With a prologue by Elie Wiesel. Eugene OR: Wipf and Stock: 2016.

———."Von 'Nacht' bis 'Abenddämmerung in der Ferne.' Ein Philosoph liest das Romanwerk." In *Das Gegenteil von Gleichgültigkeit ist Erinnerung. Versuche zu Elie Wiesel*, edited by Dagmar Mensink and Reinhold Boschki, 80-103. Matthias Grünewald Verlag: Mainz, 1995.

Roth, Joseph. *Juden auf der Wanderschaft.* Munich: Deutscher Taschenbuchverlag, 2006.

Rousset, David. *L'univers concentrationnaire.* Paris: Édition du Pavois, 1946.

Rubenstein, Richard L. *After Auschwitz: History, Theology, and Contemporary Judaism*. Indianapolis, IN: Bobbs Merrill, 1966.

Rürup, Reinhard. *Der lange Schatten des Nationalsozialismus. Geschichte, Geschichtspolitik und Erinnerungskultur*. Göttingen: Wallstein Verlag, 2014.

Safran, Bezalel, ed. *Hasidism: Continuity or Innovation?* Cambridge, MA: Harvard University Press, 1988.

Schindel, Robert. "Schweigend ins Gespräch vertieft. Anmerkungen zu Geschichte und Gegenwart des jüdischnichtjüdischen Verhältnisses in den Täterländern." In *Literatur und Holocaust*, Heft 144, edited by Heinz Ludwig Arnold, 3-8. Munich: Edition Text & Kritik, 1999.

Scholem, Gershom. *Major Trends in European Mysticism*. With a new foreword by Robert Alter. New York: Schocken Books, 1995.

———. *Judaica 1*. Frankfurt am Main: Suhrkamp, 1963.

Schuster, Ekkehard, and Reinhold Boschert-Kimmig. *Trotzdem Hoffen. Mit Johann Baptist Metz and Elie Wiesel im Gespräch*. Mainz: Matthias Grünewald Verlag, 1993.

Schweighauser, Philipp, "Trauma and Utopia: Benjamin, Adorno, and Elie Wiesel's *Night*," in *Haunted Narratives: Life Writing in an Age of Trauma*. Edited by Gabriele Rippl, Tiina Kirss, Margit Sutrop, and Therese Steffen, 45-82. Toronto: University of Toronto Press, 2013.

Schwencke, Olaf, ed. *Erinnerung als Gegenwart. Elie Wiesel in Loccum*. Feiburg: Herder, 1987.

Schwingel, Markus. *Pierre Bourdieu. Zur Einführung*. Hamburg: Junius Verlag, 2009.

Segev, Tom. *Die siebte Million. Der Holocaust und Israels Politik der Erinnerung.* Translated by Jürgen Peter Krause and Maja Ueberle-Pfaff. Reinbek b. Hamburg: Rowohlt, 1995.

Semprun, Jorge, and Elie Wiesel. *Schweigen ist Unmöglich*. Translated by Wolfram Bayer. Frankfurt: Edition Suhrkamp, 2012.

Seymour, David. "Adorno and Horkheimer: Enlightenment and Antisemitism." *Journal of Jewish Studies* 51, no. 2 (Autumn 2000): 297-312.

Shandler, Jeffery. "Aliens in the Wasteland: American Encounters with the Holocaust on 1960s Science Fiction Television." In *The Americanization of the Holocaust*, edited by Hilene Flanzbaum, 33-44. Baltimore, MD: Johns Hopkins University Press, 1999.

———. "The Shtetl Subjunctive: Yaffa Eliach's Living History Museum." In *Culture Front: Representing Jews in Eastern Europe*, edited by Benjamin Nathans and Gabriella Safran, 288-306. Philadelphia: University of Pennsylvania Press, 2008.

———. *Shtetl: A Vernacular Intellectual History*. New Brunswick, NJ: Rutgers University Press, 2014.

Shreter, Sheldon. "Selected Facts on the Jews in Sighet, Maramuresh, Transylvania." Accessed January 23, 2018. http://www.bigmeathammer.com/aushwitz1b.htm.

Sibelman, Simon P., *Silence in the Novels of Elie Wiesel*. New York: St. Martin's Press, 1995.

Silber, John. "From Thebes to Auschwitz: Moral Responsibility in Sophocles and Wiesel." In *Celebrating Elie Wiesel: Stories, Essays, Reflections*, edited by Alan Rosen, 173-202. Notre Dame, IN: University of Notre Dame Press, 1998.

SRF Kultur. Sternstunde Philosophie, „George Steiner: Die Schule des Lesens." Interview, aired on August 19, 2012. Posted on the internet on January 3, 2014. Video, 56:31. https://youtu.be/ ZByK3cXCAv4.

Steiner, George. *In Bluebeard's Castle: Some Notes Towards the Re-definition of Culture.* New Haven, CT: Yale University Press, 1971.

———. *Language and Silence: Essays on Language, Literature, and the Inhuman.* New York: Atheneum, 1967.

———. *Language and Silence: Essays 1958-1966.* 2nd ed. London: Faber and Faber, 1985. Reprint. London: Faber and Faber, 1990.

———. *Sprache und Schweigen. Essays über Sprache, Literatur und das Unmenschliche.* Translated by Axel Kaun. Berlin: Suhrkamp Taschenbuch, 2014.

Stern, Ellen Norman. *Wo Engel sich versteckten. Das Leben des Elie Wiesel.* Translated by Sibylle A. Niemoeller-von Sell. Freiburg i. B.: Herder, 1986.

Sternlicht, Sanford. *Student Companion to Elie Wiesel.* Student Companions to Classic Writers. Westport, CT: Greenwood Press, 2003.

Stöhr, Martin, ed. *Erinnern und nicht vergessen. Zugänge zum Holocaust.* In collaboration with Ulrike Berger, Petra Heldt, and Helmut Just. Munich: Chr. Kaiser, 1979.

Strümpel, Jan. "Im Sog der Erinnerungskultur. Holocaust und Literatur—'Normalität' und ihre Grenzen." In *Literatur und Holocaust*, Heft 144, edited by Heinz Ludwig Arnold, 9-17. Munich: Edition Text & Kritik, 1999.

Tal, Kali. *Worlds of Hurt: Reading Literature of Trauma.* Cambridge: Cambridge University Press, 1996.

Talabardon, Susanne. *Chassidismus.* Jüdische Studien Band 2. Tübingen: Mohr Siebeck, 2016.

———. "Judaism: Cross-Reading Hasidic Legends." In *Narrative Pattern and Genre in Hagiographic Life Writing: Comparative Perspectives from Asia to Europe*, edited by Stephan Conermann and Jim Rheingans, 281-303. Narratio Aliena? Studien des Bonner Zentrums für transkulturelle Narratologie 7. Berlin: EB-Verlag, 2014.

Thoma, Clemens. *Rabbi Nachman. Meister der Spiritualität.* Freiburg i. B.: Herder, 2002.

Trodd, Zoe. "Mosaics and Mirrors: Wiesel, American Autobiographies, and the Shaping of the Storied Subject." In *Elie Wiesel and the Art of Storytelling*, edited by Rosemary Horowitz, 15-37. Jefferson, NC: McFarland and Company, 2006.

Ueberschär, Gerd R., ed. *Handbuch zum Widerstand gegen Nationalsozialismus und Faschismus in Europa 1933/39 bis 1945.* In collaboration with Peter Steinkamp. Berlin: De Gruyter, 2011.

United States Holocaust Museum. "Sighet." Holocaust Encyclopedia. Accessed January 23, 2018. https://encyclopedia.ushmm.org/content/en/article/sighet.

Vanderwerken, David L. "Night is the Anti- 'Coming-of-Age' Story." In *Readings on Night*, edited by Wendy Mass, 123-28. The Greenhaven Press Literary Companion to World Literature. San Diego: Greenhaven Press, 2000.

Veidlinger, Jeffrey. *In the Shadow of the Shtetl: Small-Town Jewish Life in Soviet Ukraine*. Bloomington: Indiana University Press, 2013.

Vetlesen, Arne Johan. *Evil and Human Agency: Understanding Collective Evildoing.* Cambridge: Cambridge University Press, 2005.

Wagner, Gottfried, and Abraham J. Peck. *Unsere Stunde Null. Deutsche und Juden nach 1945. Familiengeschichte, Holocaust und Neubeginn. Historische Memoiren.* Vienna: Böhlau Verlag, 2006.

Walker, Graham B, Jr. *Elie Wiesel: A Challenge to Theology*. Jefferson, NC: McFarland and Company, 1988.

Weiler, Sylvia. *Jean Amérys Ethik der Erinnerung. Der Körper als Medium in die Welt nach Auschwitz*. Göttingen: Wallstein Verlag, 2012.

Weiss, Joseph. *Studies in East European Jewish Mysticism and Hasidism*. Edited by David Goldstein, and with a new introduction by Joseph Dan. London: The Littman Library of Jewish Civilization, 1997.

White, Hayden. *Metahistory: The Historical Imagination in Nineteenth Century Europe*. 40th anniv. ed. Baltimore, MD: Johns Hopkins University Press, 2014.

Wiseman, Hadas, and Jacques P. Barber. *Echoes of the Trauma: Relational Themes and Emotions in Children of Holocaust Survivors*. New York: Cambridge University Press, 2008.

Wistrich, Robert S., ed. *Holocaust Denial: The Politics of Perfidy*. Berlin: De Gruyter, 2012.

Wiggershaus, Rolf. *Theodor W. Adorno*. Munich: C. H. Beck, 1987.

Wittgenstein, Ludwig. *Tractatus Logico-Philosophicus*. Translated by C. K. Ogden, with an introduction by Bertrand Russell. Mineola, NY: Dover Publications, 1998.

Young, James Edward. *Texture of Memory: Holocaust Memorials and Meaning*. New Haven, CT: Yale University Press, 1993.

———. *Writing and Rewriting the Holocaust: Narrative and the Consequences of Interpretation*. Bloomington: Indiana University Press, 1988.

Yowa, Serge. *Eine Poetik des Widerstands. Exil, Sprache und Identitätsproblematik bei Fred Wander und Ruth Klüger. Beitrag zur neueren kulturwissenschaftlichen und fachübergreifenden Shoah-Autobiografieforschung*. Deutsch-Afrikanische Studien zur Literatur- und Kulturwissenschaft Band 3. Würzburg: Verlag Königshausen und Neumann, 2014.

Zborowski, Mark, and Elizabeth Herzog. *Life is With People: The Jewish Little-Town of Eastern Europe.* New York: International Universities Press, 1952.

Zimmermann, Rolf. *Philosophie nach Auschwitz. Eine Neubestimmung von Moral in Politik und Gesellschaft*. Reinbek bei Hamburg: Rowohlt, 2005.

Zollmann, Dan. *Shtetl*. Bruxelles: Marque Belge, 2016.

Zweig, Arnold. With 250 drawings by Hermann Struck. *Das Ostjüdische Antlitz*. Wiesbaden: Fourier Verlag, 1988.

Forum Christen und Juden

hrsg. von Prof. Dr. Erhard Blum (Tübingen) (bis 2017), Prof. Dr. Reinhold Boschi (Bonn), Prof. Dr. Hanspeter Heinz (Augsburg) PD Dr. Uri Kaufmann (Essen), Dr. Julia Münch-Wirtz (Tübingen) und Prof. Dr. Elisabeth Naurath (Augsburg)

Christoph Münz; Rudolf W. Sirsch (Hg.)
Über Grenzen hinweg zu neuer Gemeinschaft
Bilanz und Perspektiven des christlich-jüdischen Gesprächs
Bd. 23, 2021, 386 S., 34,90 €, br., ISBN 978-3-643-15083-7

Frauke Placke
Zur Geschichte des Evangelisch-Lutherischen Zentralvereins für Begegnung von Christen und Juden e.V.
Personen, Profile und Programme von der Nachkriegszeit bis zur Jahrtausendwende
Bd. 21, 2021, 276 S., 39,90 €, br., ISBN 978-3-643-14859-9

Arie Folger; Jehoschua Ahrens (Hg.)
Rabbiner im Gespräch mit dem Vatikan
Jüdisch-katholische Beziehungen nach Nostra Aetate, Korrespondenzen mit Benedikt XVI und Öffnung der Archive
Bd. 20, 2021, 224 S., 29,90 €, br., ISBN 978-3-643-14692-2

Jehoschua Ahrens
Gemeinsam gegen Antisemitismus – Die Konferenz von Seelisberg (1947) revisited
Die Entstehung des institutionellen jüdisch-christlichen Dialogs in der Schweiz und in Kontinentaleuropa
Bd. 19, 2020, 328 S., 49,90 €, gb., ISBN 978-3-643-14609-0

Martin Steiner
Zwischen Kirche und Synagoge
Messianische Juden in Jerusalem
Bd. 18, 2019, 170 S., 29,90 €, br., ISBN 978-3-643-50909-3

Hans Hermann Henrix
Israel trägt die Kirche
Zur Theologie der Beziehung von Kirche und Judentum
Bd. 17, 2019, 270 S., 34,90 €, br., ISBN 978-3-643-14248-1

Gottfried Mehnert
Jüdische Wissenschaft im Dialog mit evangelischer Theologie
Auseinandersetzung mit Adolf von Harnack; Marburger Rabbiner Prüfungen; Marburger Verein zur Abwehr des Antisemitismus
Bd. 16, 2017, 172 S., 29,90 €, br., ISBN 978-3-643-13670-1

Christian M. Rutishauser
Christlichen Glauben denken
Im Dialog mit der jüdischen Tradition
Bd. 15, 2016, 288 S., 39,90 €, br., ISBN 978-3-643-80223-1

Carina Pitschmann
Antisemitismus theologischer Wissenschaft im 19. Jahrhundert
Zur Konstruktion des Judentums in „Das Christenthum und die christliche Kirche der drei ersten Jahrhunderte“ von Ferdinand Christian Baur
Bd. 14, 2016, 220 S., 34,90 €, br., ISBN 978-3-643-13328-1

LIT Verlag Berlin – Münster – Wien – Zürich – London
Auslieferung Deutschland / Österreich / Schweiz: siehe Impressumsseite